The Complete Clavis Steganographia of Johannes Trithemius

An English Translation and Comparative Commentary

Demonic, Goetic and Necromantic Origins Series

Original Latin Text Written by Johannes Trithemius
Translation and Commentary by Anthony Uyl$_{MTS}$

CANDLE IN THE DARK
PUBLISHING

Candle in the Dark Publishing
Ingersoll, Ontario, Canada, 2025

The Complete Clavis Steganographia of Johannes Trithemius

An English Translation and Comparative Commentary

Demonic, Goetic and Necromantic Origins Series

Original Latin Text Written by Johannes Trithemius

Translation and Commentary by Anthony Uyl$_{MTS}$

This version of the book contains some corrected material and spelling. The corrected material concerns the statements I made about the Kngihts Templars in the footnote on pages 135–136. I came across better reserach that showed some of what I had said about the Knights Templar was incorrect. This information has been corrected.

This version is a black and white version with the coloured text, backgrounds and pictures removed.

ISBN: 978-1-77356-566-8

Contact Us Online:
Email: devotedpub@hotmail.com
Authors' X (Formerly Twitter): @AnthonyDevPub
Authors' Instagram: @uylanthony

Table of Contents

The only thing necessary for the triumph of evil is that good men do nothing.

- Edmund Burke (disputed)

Acknowledgements

The journey of bringing this book to life in the reading, research, writing, translating and other steps of getting this book to this point was not an easy path to tread. Having to walk into the realms of the occult and the ancient world knowledge that I needed to in order to make the truth of what the cultural background was to the texts of the Bible that we hold so dear was difficult. Once I dared to make that journey, I needed some good people behind me that were capable of carrying the burden with me in the best ways that these individuals could.

Whether that support was in allowing me to rant about the ridiculous theological beliefs that I was uncovering within so many church traditions, or the heretical notions pushed by so many church leaders as truly biblical, even to the all out occultic and necromantic beliefs that many in church leaderships are pushing as valid tests of the Christian faith, all of the following people have had a hand in encouraging, editing and making suggestions that made this book what it is.

As a result, in no particular order, I would like to thank: Paul, Christy, Chris, Jessica, Lizzie and Seth. Without your help and support this project would have taken longer and not had the outcome that it has become.

Thank you.

Most of all, I would like to thank the Lord and Saviour of my life, Jesus Christ, to whom I am forever grateful that he chose me, along with many others, to pursue the path of biblical truth in a time when so many more people than anyone can imagine are deciding to reject the words of our Lord and Saviour for the temptations of their own necromantic desires. With that, I also know that if Christ had not chosen me since before the world was spoken into existence ex nihilo, I would have followed these necromantic paths that this book is exposing. I will be eternally grateful for being saved from the bondage of that kind of occultic torment.

– Anthony Uyl MTS

Clavis Steganographia Introduction

Johannas Trithemius's medieval and renaissance text the *Clavius Steganographia* is a book that has been both mysterious and controversial since it was first written from 1499–1510. The book was originally published in Latin with instructions from the author to never translate the text into any other language. While the book has had certain parts of it translated into English over the last century, until the 21st century the entirety of this text has never been translated into English in full. While other publishers have pushed to get theirs out "first" in order to claim the title of "publishing it first", the hidden reality is that the text has been translated several times into different languages but never published for the public. Some of the translations of this text that have been published for the public have falsely claimed that the original text consists of four books. The original text only consists of three books with an explanatory text of how to decode it afterwards.

What always needs to be remembered is that when reading this book, it does indeed seem like an occult book. The book speaks about how to summon different "angels" to accomplish specific tasks for the magician. This gnosis/knowledge is not new up until the publication of this text back the 1500's. Previous occult texts such as those from Merkavah Mysticism's *Hekhalot Literature* and several different kabbalistic texts have shown the esoteric knowledge (knowledge only known by a specific few) about calling on angels for many centuries before the publication of the *Clavis Steganographia.*

With that in mind, and the slaughter of the hermetic magicians working during the time of the Inquisition, it is not absurd to suggest that the real purpose of this book was *not* for occult purposes. The knowledge concerning the summoning of spirits was known and available at the time of publication in the 16th century. While the possession of such knowledge would have caused the Inquisition to persecute someone, it left an available way for Trithemius to send encoded messages to persons that he believed needed them. Hiding the encoded message within what appeared to be an occult text would have turned most interested people away. The threat of the Inquisition would have made people that would read the *Clavis Steganographia* to immediately want nothing to do with the book because of the fear of torture and death.

Going over the considerations of the true intentions of the *Clavis Steganographia* is not the purpose of this translation. In order to fully understand the secret messages, the book really does need to stay in its original Latin. However, the purpose of this translation is to show the way the occult has used this text and the way that those occult uses have influenced Christian ecclesiological practices and theological beliefs. Some may think that it is *absurd* to suggest that an occult book would have that much of an effect on Christian belief structures, but the reason that thinking exists is because almost all modern day theologians have *forgotten* what terms like necromancy, spiritism or medium even mean from texts like Deuteronomy 18:11 which state that "a charmer or a medium or a necromancer or one who inquires of the dead" (ESV) are to be avoided and even put to death. While the *Baker Encyclopedia of the Bible* defines necromancy as the "[p]ractice of communicating with the dead",[1] as can be seen by the quoted text of Deuteronomy 18:11, the practices of necromancy and inquiring of the dead were identified as *separate* but *similar* offences. A better but still not all that accurate definition comes from the *Holman Illustrated Bible Dictionary* that necromancy is about "[c]onjuring the spirits of the dead to predict or influence future events." (italics mine)[2] The purpose of this introduction is to show what *necromancy* really was, and still is, from a *biblical* understanding.

A Short Definition of Goetia

While I will follow the biblical exegesis of necromancy with a connection from the ancient world through the Middle Ages, and to some of the practices within the present-day evangelical church, I need to define a term that most Christians are most likely unfamiliar with, that being the term of *goetia*.

The word *goetia* comes from the Greek word γοητεία (goēteia) which means "witchcraft, jugglery".[3] The word γοητεία contrasts with the other Greek word for magic, φαρμακεία (pharmakeia) which is understood to mean "the use of any kind of drugs, potions, or spells".[4] While most western Christians will not be familiar with the difference between the two, Margaret Belanger, an active occult goeticist defines goetia and says that "[d]uring the Renaissance, the Goetic arts were often associated with black magick [*sic*], in contrast to theurgy [what we know as pharmakeia], which represented basically white magick [*sic*]."[5] Jake Stratton-Kent who "has been called the most notorious necromancer in England",[6] defined goetia to be

> magical tones [that] can guide the deceased to the underworld, and raise the dead. This is the root of the long connection of goetia with necromancy, which has come to be termed black magic. Authors from Cornelius Agrippa to Mathers and Waite use the term goetic of most of the grimoires, particularly the darker ones. The recent fame of the Goetia of Solomon has obscured the long association of the term with supposed black magic generally. From Agrippa the negative associations of the word goetia go back beyond the medieval period into Classical antiquity. Therefore, it might appear feasible that goetia is a very old word for black magic. However, in Greek use magic was a term derived from a Persian root, whereas goetia originates within the Greek language. In the history of Western magic, not only did goetia come first, it possessed a character that distinguished it from many later forms.[7]

Although novels like J. R. R. Tolkien's *The Hobbit* and *The Lord of the Rings* would

1. Walter A. Elwell and Barry J. Beitzel, "Necromancer, Necromancy," in *Baker Encyclopedia of the Bible* (Grand Rapids, Michigan: Baker Book House, 1988), p. 1535.

2. Chad Brand et al., editors., "Necromancy," in *Holman Illustrated Bible Dictionary* (Nashville, Tennessee: Holman Bible Publishers, 2003), p. 1181.

3. Henry George Liddell et al., *A Greek-English Lexicon* (Oxford: Clarendon Press, 1996), p. 356.

4. Liddell, *Lexicon*, p. 1917. Note that the misuse of pharmakeia that was used during the Covid-19 pandemic. The kind of pharmakeia that was used in biblical times was very different than the pharmaceutical drugs we use today. The pharmakeia that was described in the Bible is more accurately described in "Appendix I. Translation of the *Hygromanteia of Solomon*" (italics original) in Pablo A. Torigano, *Solomon the Esoteric King*: *From King to Magus, Development of a Tradition* (Leiden, Netherlands: Brill, 2002), pp. 231–253.

5. Michelle Belanger, *Dictionary of Demons*: *Names of the Damned* (Woodbury, Minnesota: Llewellyn Publications, 2017), p. 140.

6. Unknown Author, "Jake Stratton-Kent," *Scarlet Imprint Publishing*, Last viewed August 15, 2024, https://scarletimprint.com/jake-stratton-kent.

7. Jake Stratton-Kent. *Geosophia volume I* (London, United Kingdon: Scarlet Imprint, 2010), p. ii.

make us think that "raising the dead" means bringing zombies and ghosts up from the dead, "raising the dead" from an occult, and even biblical definition, means to "raise spirits up for the purposes of communication" and nothing more.

A quick rebuke would be to say that "well, this is talking about the dead, not demons, and especially not *angels*", what we must understand is the magical/esoteric context that the Bible was written in. When referring to Greek culture Michal S. Heiser accurately states that in "classical Greek literature, which preceded the time of the New Testament, the term daimōn describes any divine being without regard to its nature (good or evil). A daimōn can be a god or goddesss, some lesser divine power, or the spirit of the departed human dead."[8] Seeing that understanding, which was not only used by the Greeks but *many* cultures from the Old Testament era into the present day, it is very *easy* to see that *goetia* and *necromancy* do in fact refer to the communication with *any* spirit *other* than the biblical God. This definition includes speaking to or even *praying for angel protection* since there is no biblical evidence that such a thing is permissible (this will be shown in the exegesis). The reference to Deuteronomy 18:11 above shows that the definition given for necromancy given here by Stratton-Kent does hold up. Deuteronomy 18:11 in condemning spiritism and mediumship does *in fact condemn communicating with angels, demons, dead saints and Mary as well.* The defense that the "saints" and "Mary" are "alive in heaven" (from Luke 20:38) does not work because the reality is the last part of that verse that states that "all live to him", is not a statement of salvation but a statement that all souls dead and living are always "alive" before God whether they are in heaven or hell.

Please note that the Greek/pagan definition by Heiser of what a demon/daimon is indicating that these were all beings of the same spiritual "substance", the Bible never affirms that the dead and angels/demons are of the same spiritual "substance". While Heiser uses the above description to justify his beliefs that *1 Enoch* is correct in identifying demons as the dead souls of the Nephilim killed in the flood that make them different than angels, by using that theory to defend Heiser's faulty belief about the dead Nephilim becoming demons, the definition in fact contradicts Heiser's intended use of it. The reason it is a contradiction is because demons, being neither evil nor good but neutral, in Greek thought could also be what Christians would call "angels". Therefore, the dead, demons and "angels" would all be beings of the same spiritual "substance". Since Heiser tries to claim that demons are a different spiritual being of a different "substance" than angels, Heiser's use of the above definition to defend his thinking is in fact a complete contradiction.

Understanding the Religious Context

Understanding the Bible within the proper context has always been a problem across Christendom. While certain sects within different Christian groups can be called worse at contextual arguments than others, the reality is that many churches are still making contextual errors in order to support their arguments. I learned once that the Bible can be used to prove literally *anything* once you take it out of context.

However, most people think that context means either the texts immediately around the verse, or just the chapter, or the chapter before or after, even others make the mistake of thinking context is just what is under the subheading added by modern day interpreters. One of the most famous of these is Revelation 3:14–22 which is the section about the

8. Michael S. Heiser, *The Unseen Realm: Recovering the Supernatural Worldview of the Bible, First Edition* (Bellingham, Washington: Lexham Press, 2015), p. 325.

letter to the church to Laodicea. The problem is that the context of that letter starts from the *beginning* of Revelation in chapter one when Jesus is describing the lampstands. The context then stretches through all the letters until it gets to Laodicea. The context goes even further to the end of Revelation. Revelation is a book that the textual context is the *entirety* of the book.

That being said, there are two other contexts that are often passed by in biblical hermeneutics, even by well meaning individuals. These two contexts are the historical and cultural context. The historical context is easy to understand. With the historical context, we need to understand the time of history the book was written in. Once we understand the Bible in the time that it was written, meaning each individual book, the text will start to make more sense in seeing what it says for us today. The most modern-day error that was made was the use of pharmakeia to say that taking the Covid-19 vaccine would result in a condemnation of sorcery by God. That is simply importing our world into the ancient world where it would *not* have been understood in that way.

The other context, cultural, is one that we must look at who the book was written to in the culture they were living in. This is often very difficult, but for the purposes of many texts that people use to defend questionable and even dangerous beliefs, people simply do not want to even consider what the context of the world was around them, especially when it comes to religious contexts around them. I will show the importance of this in a few examples including Gideon's use of the fleece in Judges 6:36–40 and also Paul's warnings against false tongues in 1 Corinthians 14. In the case of Gideon, yes Yahweh used Gideon's failure there to convince Gideon to do as he was commanded, but Yahweh in other situations, specifically with the use of Nebuchadnezzar and Cyrus who were not holy or good men but in fact incredibly evil, used evil or dark situations to show his judgment on the world and even his own people, or with Cyrus to set Israel free from exile. I explain how Nebuchadnezzar and Cyrus were evil men later in this *Introduction*.

While the Greco-Roman context of the New Testament has been firmly established and the effects of Hellenization on the Bible have been proven multiple times over, the surprising context about Greek religious culture is that it also stretches back into the time of Moses and the Israelites. Readers of that statement may find that surprising. What many do not know is that the Greek civilization was established *after* the fall of the Minoan civilization in Crete. There have been Minoan ruins found in the Greek peninsula and it has also been shown that the Greek city states were founded by Minoan settlers. The Greek pantheon even emerged from Minoan religious beliefs. Likewise, there have been studies to see if the Philistines were also founded by early Greek or even Minoan settlers. The Philistines being on the coast of the Mediterranean were most likely a sea-faring nation. With the water god Dagon being their primary deity, it is not a surprising thing to be true that the Philistines were sailors. Even on the small chance that they were not, the Minoans were proven to be highly seafaring, as is evident by the Greek city-state settlements, and would have had contact with the Philistine peoples. The Minoan sailors also had contact with the early Assyrians as there are spell bowls that mention that the Assyrian Lamaštu/Lilith was associated as being the Greek goddess Aphrodite which shows that the Minoans did have contact with the Assyrian peoples as well even as far from the coast that the city of Nineveh was.[9]

The religious beliefs of the Minoans are shown in what are known as the *Greek Magical Papyri* (or *Papyri Graecae Magicae* [*PGM*]). These texts found in Egypt show

9. Shaul Shaked, James Nathan Ford, and Siam Bhayro, *Aramaic Bowl Spells* (Leiden, Netherlands: Brill, 2013), pp. 139–140.

that the Greek gods, which as we commonly know lived on Mount Olympus, at one time were chthonic meaning "from the underworld" or what we would know as Hades, or possibly Hell (meaning the Greek Hell not the biblical one). The chthonic nature of all the Greek gods shows that these texts were originally from before the Greek epics such as Homer's *Iliad* and *Odyssey*, or Apollonius of Rhodes' *Argonautica*. Because we know the *PGM* texts had their roots from before those great poetic epics, the necromantic beliefs that emerged out of the *PGM* can be seen much more easily. With that in mind, it should not be surprising that Homer lived during the time of many of our Old Testament heroes. When exactly Homer wrote the *Iliad* and the *Odyssey* is hard to determine with absolute accuracy, however, the epic does come after the fall of the Minoan civilization and the original writing of the *PGM*. Even though the *PGM* texts we have now have obvious updates, such as texts from the Old Testament have inspired scribal updates, the original necromantic and goetic beliefs can still be found lingering within both Homer's and Apollonius's epics. Sections of the texts from Homer's *Odyssey* will be observed within the appropriate sections below.

Other considerations about the use of Daniel 10, with the "prince of Persia" and Psalm 91 as evidence that calling on angels is permitted will be considered and shown to be faulty. The text in Daniel is clearly prophetic in nature. Psalm 91 is pointing to a future fulfillment by Christ and not the church. Once the base arguments have all been made that are given above, other considerations will be shown such as the belief with Gideon that we should "put out a fleece" to determine God's will, the belief that "angel tongues" are real tongues that need to be practiced, that children are more likely to be able to see demons, the occurrence of what is known as the *witching/bewitching hour*, and lastly a conclusion showing that goetia was used in the ancient world as what we would know today as a "get-quick-rich" scheme in the same way that goetia is being used by so many churches today.

Readers who are new to goetic, demonology, spiritual warfare and occult studies from within the Christian community will find it difficult to believe that the Minoan civilization would have had that much of an effect on the development of the Old and New Testaments. That disbelief comes when we refuse to realize that we need to understand that historical and cultural context to help us understand what was *really* going on in the geographical area of the stories given to us. Once we understand what is happening in the story that the context explains, we start to see the glory of the truth of God and how he is truly trying to free us from the power of sin and goetic occultism by the power of the death and resurrection of the second person of the Trinity, Jesus Christ.

The Bible on Goetia/Necromancy

Before getting into the ancient world practices on goetia, we need to deal with what the Bible has to say on the issue. While many will think that the issue is quite clear, the reality is that it is not. As I said above, many in churches and those preaching behind pulpits are perfectly okay believing that necromancy/goetia is only a condemnation against communication with the dead. As the above explanation showed about what necromancers were really trying to communicate with via necromancy, that being demons, angels, the dead and gods, we can see that the misunderstanding about goetia has existed in the church for a very long time.

This is not to say that all of those in the church throughout history believed the faulty view of goetia to be true. For instance, John Calvin was quite informed on the matter and properly stated that

> the people are forbidden to consult a spirit of Python; for thus may we properly render the Hebrew אוב, *ob*, as St. Luke, a faithful and competent interpreter, has done, when he relates that a spirit of Python was cast out of the damsel at the command of Paul, (Acts 16:16;) and sometimes the Scripture calls these by the name of אובות, *oboth*, who allure evil spirits to give replies, of which deception a remarkable example is given in sacred history, (1 Sam. 28:7,) in the case of the witch (*Pythonissa*) who shewed Saul Samuel, although dead. The Greeks have translated the word Python, because the delusions of Apollo Pythius were particularly famous. The seventh class (Ang., wizards) is ידעני, *yadgnoni*, which may correctly be translated gnostics, or knowers; for I make no doubt that they adopted this honourable name for purposes of deceit, which is by no means an uncommon practice with impostors. (italics original)[10]

This commentary was given on Deuteronomy 18:11. The Hebrew word אוב (ob) that Calvin was commenting on is the word the ESV has translated as "medium". Since this verse is quoted above it will not be done again here. On dealing with the word אוב, Eugene H. Merrill says that the "'medium' (*šōʾēl ʾôb*, 'asker of the pit') was a necromancer, one who sought to communicate with the dead and thereby gain secret information." (italics original)[11] I am not going to get into the significance of the "pit" here, however we do need to realize that the "pit" in early Judaic personal eschatology (theology dealing with death/the afterlife), the realm of the dead, or שאול (Sheol), has often been understood as the underworld, or a "pit". The NIV is famous for translating שאול as "the grave" or "the pit" throughout the Old Testament. Ralph W. Klien has a bit of a different view. Klien associates "the term אוב to an extrabiblical word (ab), denoting a ritual hole in the ground and hence the spirits who issued from this hole or those people who operated such holes or pits." (italics original)[12] Klien continues that "the Hebrew word אוב is often plural and multiple pits do not seem to be indicated. In addition the original second phoneme [meaning the extra biblical literature] in Hittite and Assyrian is p instead of *b*." (italics original)[13] While Klien *may* have a point about אוב referencing a "pit" in a direct sense, the indication is still that the אוב is still attempting to communicate in some way with the realm of the dead, or in early Jewish understanding, שאול.

The significance of the underworld from a pagan perspective was touched on briefly above in the definition of what *chthonic* meant with the *PGM.* Since the "gods" were all at one time chthonic, and therefore in the "underworld", "pit" or "שאול", it is by no means difficult to understand that this condemnation *against* necromancy/goetia was to rebuke the communication with *any* spirit, whether that spirit was a demon, angel, the dead, another god, or even with the Catholic Church today with saints in heaven and also Mary.

Note some interesting and misunderstood facts about Sheol. First, what must be noted is that like surrounding historical contexts, the understanding of שאול was shared with other cultures that "the underworld [w]as the abode of the dead [that] [was] known from ancient Israel, as well as from the surrounding cultures."[14] What is interesting as well,

10. John Calvin and Charles William Bingham, *Commentaries on the Four Last Books of Moses Arranged in the Form of a Harmony, volume 1* (Bellingham, Washington: Logos Bible Software, 2010), p. 428.

11. Eugene H. Merrill, *Deuteronomy, volume 4, The New American Commentary* (Nashville, Tennessee: Broadman & Holman Publishers, 1994), p. 271.

12. Ralph W. Klein, *1 Samuel, volume 10, Word Biblical Commentary* (Dallas, Texas: Word, Incorporated, 1983), p. 270.

13. Klein, *1 Samuel*, p. 270.

14. H. M. Barstad, "Sheol," in *Dictionary of Deities and Demons in the Bible*, editors Karel van der

with what has been mentioned above, שאול is "similar to representations of underworld deities elsewhere, these biblical portrayals have been felt to reflect not only the underworld itself, but also the personified chthonic power behind death, a demon or deity Sheol."[15] This would make it sound like שאול is some kind of equivalent to the Christian "hell", but that is not the reality here. In proper theological considerations, שאול is really just a neutral place where *all* dead go. Some speculation has been suggested that there is a "paradise" side of שאול as well as a "hades" side of שאול, but beyond speculation, there is no biblical proof as to what שאול looks like. And Jesus himself did not want to give any specific details of what the afterlife looked like. The purpose behind Jesus' denial to give any information about the afterlife was to not have people looking forward to death, instead focusing on the life the people were living at that moment. While arguments have persisted that שאול is a place for the ungodly to be held under judgment,[16] it is undeniable that both Psalm 89 and Ecclesiastes 9 speak of שאול as a place for *all* people to go to after death.

In showing what words like אוב meant within their original context it was revealed that interpreters and commentators show that these chthonic spirits were thought to be able to foretell the future. Calvin, above, even admitted that God himself may have allowed the demonic to be able to do this in some small way in the attempt to allow these spirits to deceive other people. It is not unconceivable to believe this *because* some things that are prophesied among many other false prophecies do in fact come true. However, this does *not* verify these prophets as God sent prophets. When one prophecy turns out to be false God has told us that then the prophet is, in his whole being, a false prophet that is to be put to death under old covenant laws (Deuteronomy 13:1–5). In dealing with the goetic and chthonic prophecies, we have below a text from 2 Esdras that is now recognized as an apocryphal book. However, this book was included in the 1611 King James Version and was not taken out until 1885. The 1611 KJV did recognize these books as non-canonical, but there was still a danger including them in the "official" Bible at that time. By the time the year 1885 came along, the roots of many of the current false, and occult, forms of Christianity were *already* finding their roots in North America, such as the charismatic, Prosperity, Word-of-Faith (WOF) and New Apostolic Reformation. (NAR) With that in mind, note the following passage from one of those *formerly* included books.

> Then I answered and said, *How, and when shall these things come to pass? wherefore are our years few and evil?* And he answered me, saying, Do not thou hasten above the most Highest: for thy haste is in vain to be above him, for thou hast much exceeded. Did not the souls also of the righteous ask question of these things in their chambers, saying, How long shall I hope on this fashion? when cometh the fruit of the floor of our reward? And unto these things Uriel the archangel gave them answer, and said, Even when the number of seeds is filled in you: for he hath weighed the world in the balance. By measure hath he measured the times, and by number hath he numbered the times; and he doth not move nor stir them, until the said measure be fulfilled. Then answered I and said, O Lord that bearest rule, even we all are full of impiety. And for our sakes peradventure it is that the floors of the righteous are not filled, because of the sins of them that dwell upon the earth. So he answered me, and said, Go thy way to a woman with child, and ask of her when she hath fulfilled her nine months, if her womb may keep the birth any longer within her. Then said I, No, Lord, that can she not. And

Toorn, Bob Becking, and Pieter W. van der Horst (Leiden, Netherlands: Brill, 1999), p. 768.

15. H. M. Barstad, "Sheol," p. 768.

16. Philip S. Johnston, *Shades of Sheol*: *Death and the Afterlife in the Old Testament* (Downers Grove, Illinois: Intervarsity Press, 2002), pp. 79–83.

> he said unto me, *In the grave the chambers of souls are like the womb of a woman*: For like as a woman that travaileth maketh haste to escape the necessity of the travail: *even so do these places haste to deliver those things that are committed unto them*. From the beginning, look, what thou desirest to see, it shall be shewed thee. (italics mine, 2 Esdras 4:33–43 1900 KJV)

This text does show that ancient peoples believed there were secrets that were given to the dead and that the dead did desire to give up those secrets in the same way as a woman that was pregnant needed to give birth. While the book of 2 Esdras was *not* even accepted as scripture by Jerome when the Latin Vulgate was fully translated in 405 AD, this book *did* become part of scripture by *later* Bible translators. The fact that 2 Esdras was put into the officially King James sanctioned Bible has more background information that is beyond the scope of this study, however the necromancy promoted within this book, was accepted for a over two-and-a-half centuries. This error is one of the reasons why goetia has become such a problem in the current day church. This is also one of the reasons why many of the false prophets claim to have had a vision of "God" or an "angel" that has given them these false prophetic powers. These false prophetic powers are all based in goetia that the *inspired* word of God, not including apocryphal books, condemned in every way.

The Book of Isaiah Condemning Goetia/ Necromancy

Continuing with what the biblical literature has to say concerning goetia, we can now turn to two passages in the prophetic book of Isaiah. The first of these is Isaiah 8.

> Bind up the testimony; seal the teaching among my disciples. I will wait for the Lord, who is hiding his face from the house of Jacob, and I will hope in him. Behold, I and the children whom the Lord has given me are signs and portents in Israel from the Lord of hosts, who dwells on Mount Zion. And when they say to you, "Inquire of the *mediums* and the *necromancers* who chirp and mutter," should not a people inquire of their God? *Should they inquire of the dead on behalf of the living*? To the teaching and to the testimony! If they will not speak according to this word, it is because they have no dawn. They will pass through the land, greatly distressed and hungry. And when they are hungry, they will be enraged and will speak contemptuously against their king and their God, and turn their faces upward. *And they will look to the earth, but behold, distress and darkness, the gloom of anguish. And they will be thrust into thick darkness*. (italics mine, Isaiah 8:16–22 ESV)

First, note that in this passage of Isaiah, the way Yahweh says this in the Hebrew is in a very mocking, sarcastic, tone. What that will mean is that Yahweh is mocking the nations of Israel and Judah for relying on goetia to find answers or plead with the chthonic gods. While some may take this passage out of context to say that "it is only speaking of the *dead*", we do need to remember the cultural and religious context here. Even though Yahweh is mocking Israel and Judah for consulting the dead, the dead in the minds of the pagan leaders of both Israel and Judah did include the chthonic spirits of the dead, the demonic/angelic, and other gods. The fact that the word אוב is once again used here, we can reasonably conclude that Yahweh was including a mocking towards the two nations for consulting other chthonic spirits along with the dead. J. Alec Motyer confirms this mocking by Yahweh in noting that the "verbs mock the antics of the mediums and expose the absurdity of turning from the plain word of the Lord to mumbo-jumbo."[17]

17. J. Alec Motyer, *Isaiah: An Introduction and Commentary, volume 20, Tyndale Old Testament Commentaries* (Downers Grove, Illinois: InterVarsity Press, 1999), p. 98.

Second, with Isaiah condemning the nations of Israel and Judah for their goetic practices Yahweh wanted Isaiah to tell the people on his behalf that it did "not make much sense to go to the dead to find out about the living. The spirit of a dead person does not become a divine being with supernatural knowledge about the future."[18] Again, you can see that this completely denies the claims of all theological defenses of the saints, Mary, and even the Nephilim becoming demons after they died. Although not divine, the fact that any of the former were given demonic, even nearly divine souls/spirits shows that the Bible calls this complete nonsense. Because of that Moyer once again shows that when "leaving their bodies behind, the dead can be only shadows of what they were (Isa. 14:10); the dead Samuel knows no more after death than he proclaimed when alive (1 Sam. 28:16ff.)."[19]

From this passage alone, it shows that the practice of goetia is pointless and worthy of condemnation from God. Remember that goetia/necromancy does include the communicating with *any* spirit other than Yahweh/God himself. This condemnation from God will include saints, Mary and yes, even angels. Communicating with the saints and Mary has been a practice within the Roman Catholic Church for many centuries. Also, the petitioning to God to send angels, which *seems* biblical, is in fact not what it appears and is never approved of in biblical literature.

The next section of Isaiah that is notable when speaking about goetia is that of Isaiah 19 where we are given a prophecy against the nation of Egypt.

> An oracle concerning Egypt.
> Behold, the Lord is riding on a swift cloud and comes to Egypt;
> and the idols of Egypt will tremble at his presence,
> and the heart of the Egyptians will melt within them.
> And I will stir up Egyptians against Egyptians,
> and they will fight, each against another
> and each against his neighbor,
> city against city, kingdom against kingdom;
> and the spirit of the Egyptians within them will be emptied out,
> and I will confound their counsel;
> and *they will inquire of the idols and the sorcerers*,
> and *the mediums and the necromancers*;
> and I will give over the Egyptians
> into the hand of a hard master,
> and a fierce king will rule over them,
> declares the Lord God of hosts.
>
> And the waters of the sea will be dried up,
> and the river will be dry and parched,
> and its canals will become foul,
> and the branches of Egypt's Nile will diminish and dry up,
> reeds and rushes will rot away.
> There will be bare places by the Nile,
> on the brink of the Nile,
> and all that is sown by the Nile will be parched,
> will be driven away, and will be no more.
> The fishermen will mourn and lament,
> all who cast a hook in the Nile;

18. Gary V. Smith, *Isaiah 1–39*, editor E. Ray Clendenen, The New American Commentary (Nashville, Tennessee: B & H Publishing Group, 2007), p. 231.

19. Motyer, *Isaiah*, p. 98.

and they will languish
who spread nets on the water.
The workers in combed flax will be in despair,
and the weavers of white cotton.
Those who are the pillars of the land will be crushed,
and all who work for pay will be grieved.

The princes of Zoan are utterly foolish;
the wisest counselors of Pharaoh give stupid counsel.
How can you say to Pharaoh,
"I am a son of the wise,
a son of ancient kings"?
Where then are your wise men?
Let them tell you
that they might know what the LORD of hosts has purposed against Egypt.
The princes of Zoan have become fools,
and the princes of Memphis are deluded;
those who are the cornerstones of her tribes
have made Egypt stagger.
The LORD has mingled within her a spirit of confusion,
and they will make Egypt stagger in all its deeds,
as a drunken man staggers in his vomit.
And there will be nothing for Egypt
that head or tail, palm branch or reed, may do. (italics mine; Isaiah 19:1–15 ESV)

Not much needs to be said here to understand the condemnation that comes from a failure to trust in God. While Egypt was a pagan nation outside of the Mosaic covenant, there is still some condemnation pointed at them for not trusting in Yahweh as they, and all nations, should be. Motyer once again states that

> ineffectiveness (3ab) are symptoms, not maladies. Those who flocked to the cults at least saw that a spiritual solution was needed even though their solution was in fact another symptom of the real problem. Faced with all this disintegration, why not try force where appeal has failed (4)? If people will not do what they ought to do, they will do what they are made to do! But this also is a symptom, not the malady: the malady (1) is that they are not right with God.[20]

It is interesting that Motyer does in fact show what the real problem is when people, even Christians, resort to goetia when praying for angels to protect them, asking the saints or Mary to intercede for them, or even in situations of grave soaking. The reason that Christians, or anyone even those that deny the Christian faith, are relying on goetic magic to get the answers they desire is because it is a symptom of not *truly* trusting God like they are supposed to be. Like my previous book *The Emergence of the Neo-Satanist Church* showed, people that are practicing much of this plea for angels, grave soaking, even asking saints and Mary to intercede for them, are attempting to shed any reliance on God and to rely on themselves which will now mean that they are their own deified gods. Just as the temptation from the serpent to Adam and Eve said in Genesis 3:5, "you will be like God." Goetia in all its ways is an attempt to be able to command the chthonic spirits that only God has the authority over. Yet, many Christians want to assume that God-like power because they have stopped relying on God and instead are relying on themselves, their own god.

20. Motyer, *Isaiah*, pp. 156–157.

A Consideration of Exodus 33

While the previous observations show what was considered a violation of God's commands in the Mosaic Covenant (Deuteronomy) and also the prophetic era, an example would be helpful of when God gave Israel a spirit/angel to watch over them rather than himself. If such an example exists, then it must be observed. While some might point to the obvious story of the territorial spirit in Daniel 10 the context of the passage speaks to a different reality than is often considered. I will take a look at this in time, as well as the fallacious use of Psalm 91, for now we need to turn to the account of Exodus 33 which falls after the sin of Israel with the creation and worship of the golden calf at Sinai.

The passage referred to is

> The Lord said to Moses, "Depart; go up from here, you and the people whom you have brought up out of the land of Egypt, to the land of which I swore to Abraham, Isaac, and Jacob, saying, 'To your offspring I will give it.' I will send an angel before you, and I will drive out the Canaanites, the Amorites, the Hittites, the Perizzites, the Hivites, and the Jebusites. Go up to a land flowing with milk and honey; but I will not go up among you, lest I consume you on the way, for you are a stiff-necked people." When the people heard this disastrous word, they mourned, and no one put on his ornaments. For the Lord had said to Moses, "Say to the people of Israel, 'You are a stiff-necked people; if for a single moment I should go up among you, I would consume you. So now take off your ornaments, that I may know what to do with you.'" Therefore the people of Israel stripped themselves of their ornaments, from Mount Horeb onward. (Exodus 33:1–6 ESV)

What is interesting to note is that as a *judgement* from Yahweh, the people of Israel could now only expect an angel, and not the presence of Yahweh *himself* to go with them. As is obvious in the next few verses the people of Israel mourned that their God would not go with them. Douglas K. Stuart correctly comments that the

> people had shown by their idolatry that they craved a direct and obvious divine presence to lead them in their journeys. Indeed, the golden young bull was to their way of thinking a means of capturing the presence of some gods (gods that represented a distorted understanding of Yahweh), and the people rejoiced finally to be able to see the gods who had been—they thought—helping them on the exodus so far (32:4). Now as part of their punishment for that folly they would have to live with less then they had before. Instead of a God who directly communed with Moses and whose presence could be seen on the mountain, they would have to live with a much more elusive representation of God's presence, an angel, and therefore they realized that *they had been demoted from people who dealt with Yahweh directly through Moses to people who now would have an angel added to the chain of command.* (italics mine)[21]

Stuart continues that the

> [w]ithholding of divine presence is a *severe covenant punishment.* To be denied access to the presence of God (usually meaning to be expelled from the covenant community and therefore to be unable to worship and sacrifice, which means to be unable to have one's sins forgiven) constituted a sort of ultimate penalty for heterodox practice. An example of such a severe penalty is found in Lev 22:3: "Say to them: 'For the generations to come, if any of your descendants is ceremonially unclean and yet comes near the sacred offerings that the Israelites consecrate to the Lord, that person must be cut off from my presence. I am the Lord'"). Often the prohibition of Yahweh's presence is simply predicted directly by God; no Israelite court would be needed to impose such a penalty. (italics mine)[22]

---

21. Douglas K. Stuart, *Exodus, volume 2, The New American Commentary* (Nashville, Tennessee: Broadman & Holman Publishers, 2006), p. 691.

22. Stuart, *Exodus*, p. 692.

Note what Stuart is saying here about this punishment. Israel failed to rely on Yahweh because they were trying to receive what they were sinfully desiring from the chthonic golden calf (see Exodus 32). Since Israel decided to rely on a *chthonic* alternate version of Yahweh (see the contextual argument above, also, Aaron after creating the calf comments that "[t]omorrow shall be a feast to Yahweh" [verse 5b] meaning the golden calf was a chthonic idol of Yahweh), Yahweh put Israel under judgment which meant that Yahweh's presence would be removed from Israel and they were forced to now rely on an angel instead which the people of Israel *knew* was *not a good thing*. The mourning that Israel did was in an even more severe way than they would mourn someone who had *died*.

In his commentary on the same passage, John I. Durham says that

> the nature of the guidance this messenger is to give is immediately qualified by the stark announcement of the punishment Yahweh will mete out to Israel for their sin with the calf. It is not to be a plague, and it is not to be death by some other means. Indeed, it is to be the most appropriate response possible to Israel's compromise of their relationship with him, and *a punishment worse than death*. [...] Israel must leave Sinai, the place where they have known Yahweh's Presence, and they must journey forth in a way to have been graced by his Presence to a place to have been filled with his Presence *with no hope of his Presence ever again* [...]. (italics mine)[23]

The reliance on spirits *other than God* is of the most critical insult to and rejection of Yahweh. This rejection *will not be tolerated.*

Moses himself noticed just how terrible this judgment was in the following verses

> Moses said to the LORD, "See, you say to me, 'Bring up this people,' but you have not let me know whom you will send with me. Yet you have said, 'I know you by name, and you have also found favor in my sight.' Now therefore, if I have found favor in your sight, please show me now your ways, that I may know you in order to find favor in your sight. Consider too that this nation is your people." And he said, "My presence will go with you, and I will give you rest." And he said to him, "*If your presence will not go with me, do not bring us up from here. For how shall it be known that I have found favor in your sight, I and your people? Is it not in your going with us, so that we are distinct, I and your people, from every other people on the face of the earth*?" (italics mine, Exodus 33:12–16 ESV)

Moses correctly saw that if Yahweh himself was not going to go with the people of Israel, then there was no way for them to correctly be called the people of God. If even Yahweh had rejected his people and denied them his presence, instead sending an angel, then the nation of Israel would in fact be totally rejected by God and forced to rely on a much lesser spirit in their coming battles with the Canaanite nations. In a lengthy explanation, Durham once again explains that

> "Thus will I dispel your anxiety" is the confirmation of Moses' intent in his plea. Nothing else, indeed, will give Moses rest from the fear gripping him, as his relief-laden reply further indicates: if Yahweh's Presence is not to go, Moses does not want either Israel or himself (MT "us"; LXX's "me" is an alteration of the text probably based on a misunderstanding of it) brought up from Sinai. The reason for this is quite clear: without Yahweh's Presence, Israel and Moses are not just certain to fail the destiny set before them; they cannot even begin it, because they will have lost their identity as "a special treasure," Yahweh's "own kingdom of priests and holy people" (19:5–6; see above).
>
> All this is made doubly clear by Moses' summary confession of what Yahweh's Presence

23. John I. Durham, *Exodus, volume 3, Word Biblical Commentary* (Dallas, Texas: Word, Incorporated, 1987), p. 437.

> means to Israel, the final part of his plea, and the statement of the reason for Israel's abject grief and for his own urgent anxiety. Only Yahweh's Presence with Israel and with Moses will give credence to the assertion that Moses, and Israel along with him (and because of him), have found favor with Yahweh. Only Yahweh's Presence with Moses and Israel separates them from all other people throughout the world. It is the lesson Moses learned on Sinai at the time of his call: he alone was not equal to the task of challenging Pharaoh, but he was not to be alone. It is the lesson Israel learned, by the mighty acts in Egypt, by the deliverance at the sea, by the guidance and provision in the wilderness, and above all by the theophany and the revelation at Sinai: what they had seen, what they had been given, what they had the chance of becoming, all were the direct result of the Presence in their midst of Yahweh.
>
> Incredibly enough, the people had somehow not realized this until they were under the prospect of Yahweh's Absence; then it became all too terribly clear, and they were overwhelmed by bitter grief. Moses had known it all along, and so his reaction was the quickest and most passionate, and his need to reverse the terrible prospect of Absence was the most urgent. The matter had come down finally to whether Israel as a special people would continue to exist or not, and Moses' own fate is bound up with his people's fate. His plea for them is not merely the reflex of a sense of responsibility. Moses' own real existence is caught up in Israel's real existence.
>
> Whatever historical memory may or may not be preserved in this marvelous narrative is really beside the point. Its theological insight is universal, equally applicable to divine-human relationship and ministry in any age. No people, no matter how religious they are and for whatever reasons, can be a people of God without the Presence of God. Moses has posed the ultimate either/or: Yahweh's decision to withdraw his presence from Israel is the decision of Israel's fate. Without Yahweh's presence, in the dark and chaotic umbra of his Absence, Israel will cease to exist.[24]

Due to Israel's reliance on a *chthonic* spirit in Exodus 32, Yahweh's removal of his presence was of a punishment so severe that even *death* would have been more merciful. Moses recognized that without Yahweh's immediate presence among them, even if an angel was with them, the nation of Israel as *Yahweh*'s people would *cease* to exist. If Yahweh was not with the people of Israel, then the nation of Israel was not his people anymore at all.

Some readers may question the above assertions. The rebuke from those kinds of readers will most like be: "but we are not relying on the angel itself, but on *God* to send the angel." This is a theologically flawed statement. The reason this statement is flawed is because these people are calling on an angel instead of God. What can an angel do that God cannot? Why do these people want an angel present instead of asking God to do exactly what he has promised to in always being with *his* people? The previous two questions reveal that those who are calling on God to send them angels for whatever purpose have in reality stopped relying on God, much in the same way the Israelites did in Exodus 32 by calling on a chthonic golden bull.

The reality from the above exegesis that those that call on the chthonic to do what they believe Yahweh cannot reveals further that Yahweh is indeed *not* with those people or with the church that encourages that activity. This is also evident by those churches that believe that the Holy Spirit cannot be present until he is invited into the presence of the gathered church. Again, the realization of Moses that by not having the spirit of Yahweh with them at *all times* is a punishment that will result in their actual removal from God's covenant by no longer being Yahweh's people. If people believe that the Holy Spirit cannot be among them, or is even waiting to be invited in, then the reality by their own admission is that Yahweh, by his Holy Spirit, is not with them. If the third

24. Durham, *Exodus*, pp. 447–448.

person of the Triune-Yahweh, the Holy Spirit, is not with that church or people, then they *are not of the covenant people of God saved by Christ*. Christ promised the Holy Spirit to always be with those that believe in him. If a church or a group of people believe that the Holy Spirit is *not with them until his is invited in* these people are then admitting to their state of apostacy. Praying for angels to protect or help a church or its people is also the same admission of apostacy due to the condemnation of goetia/necromancy.

Other Issues Related to Not Relying on God

A related issue is the belief that Jesus did all his miracles as a man to show that we can do them as well. This belief about Jesus only doing his miracles as a man comes from the following verse: "But if it is by the Spirit of God that I cast out demons, then the kingdom of God has come upon you." (Matthew 12:28 ESV) In order to come to this incorrect belief, the same story in Luke must be denied as true. In that story Jesus states that, "if it is by the finger of God that I cast out demons, then the kingdom of God has come upon you." (Luke 11:20 ESV) Since churches do affirm that Jesus was indeed the second person of the Trinity, making Jesus in fact Yahweh, then Jesus did, according to Luke, perform all of his own miracles. It was by his own finger of deity that he performed his miracles but not just Jesus but all *three* persons of the Trinity. This was how Jesus was able to prove his divinity to the people of Israel in that day.

The author of Hebrews states that "It was declared at first by the Lord, and it was attested to us by those who heard, while God also bore witness by signs and wonders and various miracles and by gifts of the Holy Spirit distributed according to his will." (Hebrews 2:3–4 ESV) While some might split or inappropriately join the miracles and gifts to say that since the Holy Spirit gives us the spiritual gifts, the Holy Spirit also gave Jesus his miracles, is a fallacious way of reading the text. The author of Hebrews is indeed stating that all three persons of the Trinity were once again involved in everything Jesus did, including the miracles. Jesus did in fact perform his miracles *along with* the Holy Spirit and the Father.

It should not take much explaining from the use of goetia to show how a church or people have stopped relying on God so that they can believe that Jesus did his miracles *only* as a man to show we can do them ourselves. Sadly, when people argue that Jesus did his miracles only as a man, they are admitting their *lack of reliance* on Jesus, since they can do what Jesus did, without Jesus. These churches and people have taken Christ for the salvific purposes, but now that they are *done* with Christ, they will take his power, stop relying on him altogether, and now do things for themselves. In their minds, there is no longer any *need* for Jesus once we have attained his salvation and mediation. This should be a shocking statement. Whenever someone whether a minister, church, or leader of some other kind admits to that falsehood about Jesus only doing miracles as a man, they are *admitting* that they *no longer need Christ*, which means their reliance on Christ is gone and therefore, as Exodus 33 shows, Yahweh is no longer with that person, that church, or that people at all. It is an admission worse than *death* that many people are praising and worshipping *themselves* for because as the serpent said to Adam and Eve in Genesis 3:5, "you will be like God". If you are like God, you do not need him. This is the same lie that caused the fall in Eden that many false churches are now admitting to in the open and saying it is a good thing. This is not a good thing, as Exodus 33 shows, it is a sign of the *worst kind of judgment. It is a judgment worse than death.*

A rebuke can come from Mark 6:1–5 where Jesus did not do any miracles in Nazareth due to their lack of faith. The lack of faith was in Jesus as Yahweh and not due to the miracles. The people of Nazareth looked at Jesus as just a miracle worker. The churches that teach that Jesus did all his miracles as a man, are arguing the same Jesus. Churches that teach this Jesus while rebuking the Prosperity, WOF and NAR movements for their "miracles" are hypcrites. Jesus' miracles were evidence of his deity. If Jesus did the miracles as a man, then he was nothing more than a miracle worker and the people of Nazareth were correct and Jesus was wrong in not doing miracles due to their "unbelief."

In a book written by Darren Whitehead and Chris Tomlin, the extremely popular Christian musician whose songs many churches use during their Sunday services, the two men are quoted as saying that "[m]usic is more powerful than we even understand. It can soften our hearts, soothe our troubled souls. *It opens a door to the spiritual world. It paves the road for the Spirit's coming.*" (italics mine)[25] Given the arguments shown above, it should not be difficult for the reader to see that both Whitehead and Tomlin believing that their music has the power to open doors (or "portals") to the spiritual realm that will make it possible for the Holy Spirit to come is complete apostacy. Again, for both Whitehead and Tomlin to be confessing this, it is evident that as Moses so correctly pointed out above, if Yahweh, by the Holy Spirit, is not with them *at all times*, then these two men are *not* of the people of God and are *not included in the salvific covenant* given to us by Jesus at his resurrection. Since Whitehead and Tomlin have made it *clear* that the Holy Spirit *relies on them* and not them on the Holy Spirit, both Whitehead and Tomlin have both admitted to the fact that they can "be like God" and it therefore changes the focus of both of these men's music. The focus of Whitehead and Tomlin's music is in fact *themselves* or *yourself* when you sing it and what they can get from God because they *do not in fact rely on God, Jesus, and/or the Holy Spirit at all.*

People will argue about the fact that a "spiritual world/realm" does indeed exist, but when properly exegeting scripture within its proper context, there is no evidence of any separate space-time dimensions, universes, realities, worlds or "realms". The vision Jacob had in Genesis 28:10–22 does not give us proof that a separate spiritual "realm/world" exists. Jacob in that story *recognized that place* as the place where God dwelled. The ladder that Jacob saw in the context of Jewish cosmology spoke of God's throne being above the earthly cosmos, or "third heaven" what we would call "outer space", but God's throne did not, and does not, exist in a separate space-time reality, or "spiritual world". The belief in such a separate spiritual realm comes from ancient pagan goetic practice. Even *if* such a reality exists, the Holy Spirit would not need *anyone's assistance* in opening doorways/portals in order to *cross over* to this side. Since this is not the place for that discussion, I will instead reference you to *Magic, Witchcraft and the Otherworld* by Susan Greenwood[26] for more information.

The Failure to Kneel Before Our King

Before moving on to show what the common passages of the Bible that are used to attempt to prove that praying for angel protection and assistance is biblical, I want to instead get to the heart of the matter of where one of causes of all this failure to rely on the Triune-Godhead is coming from.

In Matthew 28:18 Jesus says, "All authority in heaven and on earth has been given to me." (ESV) Many end-times obsessed Christians believe that Jesus' authority is in the heavenly/spiritual only and not on earth. Jesus' statement here, evidenced in the Greek,

25. Chris Tomlin, and Darren Whitehead, *Holy Roar*: *7 Words That Will Change The Way You Worship* (Nashville, Tennessee: Thomas Nelson, 2017), p. 46, Kindle Edition.

26. Susan Greenwood, *Magic, Witchcraft and the Otherworld* (New York, New York: Berg, 2000).

does show that Jesus' authority is over *all creation including the physical earth.* The "proof" that is often given that Jesus is not currently ruling is all the evil and chaos in the world at the current moment. This belief that all this chaos shows that Satan is really ruling this world is misguided. The church is *not a rebellion against worldly authorities*. Due to the romanticized view of rebellions from franchises such as *Star Wars* or even the War of Independence fought by George Washington, rebellions are in *most cases* not for lawful or even justified reasons. While we believe *now* that Washington was justified in his rebellion, he was still waging a war against the rightful ruler of the future United States of America, that being the British Monarchy. Of course, history shows us that Washington's rebellion was justified, but when looking at the reports of rebellion in other parts of the world, especially ones happening today in 3rd world African and Asian countries, the rebels are always brutal, sadistic warlords who are there to terrorize and enslave the locals for their own selfish purposes. This is the type of rebellion that *Satan* is waging against the true king of the world, Jesus. Despite how many people believe that Satan is "winning" right now, history has shown that Satan's victories are short-lived. In the end Christ brings the church forward in a much mightier and stronger way than ever before.

Due to this belief that there is no kingly authority of Jesus here on this earth, it has led many churches to fall into the same errors as the book of Judges. The book of Judges closes with a haunting statement: "In those days there was no king in Israel. Everyone did what was right in his own eyes." (Judges 21:25 ESV) Seeing the evidence above that more churches and so-called Christians have rejected relying on God to instead rely on themselves and the chthonic spirits of the hell, we as Christians need to take this warning seriously. Because so many churches, and Christians that are part of these churches, are teaching that Jesus is *not ruling in the here and now* on this earth, as a result they have started to instead reject that rightful authority given to Jesus in Matthew 28:18. In rejecting Jesus' kingship, they have effectively usurped Jesus' throne to put *themselves* on that throne so that these people can rely on themselves to do what they believe in their hearts Jesus *cannot*. While many of them will deny that they believe Jesus cannot do in this world what needs to be done, the fact that these same churches are claiming Jesus did his miracles as only a man so that we can do them too, as well as believing that there is no king here, these false teachers have really all claimed themselves to be what Christ is not, that being the one who will save this world and provide for all that we need. The message is effectively this from these teachers: "Do not rely on a king that is not even here, instead rely on yourselves and especially *me*."

Looking at Daniel 10:1–14

The proof text that many will give in defense about being able to call on angel protection from Daniel 10:1–14 is a highly controversial piece of scripture in the way that it has been interpreted and used within the history of the Christian church. The passage I am referring to is quoted as follows:

> In the third year of Cyrus king of Persia a word was revealed to Daniel, who was named Belteshazzar. And the word was true, and it was a great conflict. And he understood the word and had understanding of the vision. In those days I, Daniel, was mourning for three weeks. I ate no delicacies, no meat or wine entered my mouth, nor did I anoint myself at all, for the full three weeks. On the twenty-fourth day of the first month, as I was standing on the bank of the great river (that is, the Tigris) I lifted up my eyes and looked, and behold, a man clothed in linen, with a belt of fine gold from Uphaz around his waist. His body was like beryl, his

> face like the appearance of lightning, his eyes like flaming torches, his arms and legs like the gleam of burnished bronze, and the sound of his words like the sound of a multitude. And I, Daniel, alone saw the vision, for the men who were with me did not see the vision, but a great trembling fell upon them, and they fled to hide themselves. So I was left alone and saw this great vision, and no strength was left in me. My radiant appearance was fearfully changed, and I retained no strength. Then I heard the sound of his words, and as I heard the sound of his words, I fell on my face in deep sleep with my face to the ground. And behold, a hand touched me and set me trembling on my hands and knees. And he said to me, "O Daniel, man greatly loved, understand the words that I speak to you, and stand upright, for now I have been sent to you." And when he had spoken this word to me, I stood up trembling. Then he said to me, "Fear not, Daniel, for from the first day that you set your heart to understand and humbled yourself before your God, your words have been heard, and I have come because of your words. The prince of the kingdom of Persia withstood me twenty-one days, but Michael, one of the chief princes, came to help me, for I was left there with the kings of Persia, and came to make you understand what is to happen to your people in the latter days. For the vision is for days yet to come." (Daniel 10:1–14 ESV)

What is interesting to note is that this event happens in the third year of the Persian king Cyrus, the same Cyrus that freed the people of Israel to return to Jerusalem to rebuild the temple. (2 Chronicles 36:22–23; note that the exiled Israelites were freed in the *first* year) With the reference to the angel "prince" in verse 14 above, René Péter-Contesse and John Ellington note that "[e]ach nation was thought to have its own angel who served as its protector."[27] Commenting also on this verse, Stephen R. Miller says that within

> this passage several important facts are evident concerning angels: (1) angels are real; (2) there are good and evil angels; (3) angels can influence the affairs of human beings. Particularly this passage teaches that angels inspire human governments and their leaders. [...] Daniel's experience should not be interpreted to signify that God is weak or that demonic forces have power to thwart the will of God.[28]

Since we can properly recognize that this angel prince was what we would also know as a demon, this shows that Cyrus was *not* a good or "Godly" king *despite* the fact that Yahweh used Cyrus to free the people of Judah to go back home. Cyrus did not just free the Jewish people from exile, but multiple nations were allowed to return to their homeland to rebuild the temples to their gods. By doing this Cyrus was hoping to gain favour from all of these nations' gods and not just the God of Israel, Yahweh.

What should be noted is that these verses have been used to justify the praying for angel assistance as well as the praying *against* territorial spirits. However, keeping the theme of the book of Daniel in mind, it is not difficult to see that this is an incorrect use of this passage.

The reason that is an incorrect use is because the theme of Daniel from beginning to end is the prophetic future of Israel in the immediate, and the hope of the coming Messiah in the future. Even with the dreams of Nebuchadnezzar, with Nebuchadnezzar's judgment that he should feed on grass as a punishment for placing himself *above* Yahweh, then the instances past Nebuchadnezzar's reign with the writing of the hand on the wall, and of Daniel's time in the lions den, all had an implied prophetic force to show that Yahweh will in fact protect his people and deliver them from the cruelty that was being poured out on them. This deliverance would happen at the appropriate time.

27. René Péter-Contesse and John Ellington, *A Handbook on the Book of Daniel, UBS Handbook Series* (New York, New York: United Bible Societies, 1994), p. 270.

28. Stephen R. Miller, *Daniel, volume 18, The New American Commentary* (Nashville, Tennessee: Broadman & Holman Publishers, 1994), pp. 285–286.

Going back to Daniel 9, Daniel offers a prayer up to God in the days of Darius about the freeing of the city of Jerusalem from Persian oppression. Note the prayer below:

> O Lord, the great and awesome God, who keeps covenant and steadfast love with those who love him and keep his commandments, we have sinned and done wrong and acted wickedly and rebelled, turning aside from your commandments and rules. We have not listened to your servants the prophets, who spoke in your name to our kings, our princes, and our fathers, and to all the people of the land. To you, O Lord, belongs righteousness, but to us open shame, as at this day, to the men of Judah, to the inhabitants of Jerusalem, and to all Israel, those who are near and those who are far away, in all the lands to which you have driven them, because of the treachery that they have committed against you. To us, O LORD, belongs open shame, to our kings, to our princes, and to our fathers, because we have sinned against you. To the Lord our God belong mercy and forgiveness, for we have rebelled against him and have not obeyed the voice of the LORD our God by walking in his laws, which he set before us by his servants the prophets. All Israel has transgressed your law and turned aside, refusing to obey your voice. And the curse and oath that are written in the Law of Moses the servant of God have been poured out upon us, because we have sinned against him. He has confirmed his words, which he spoke against us and against our rulers who ruled us, by bringing upon us a great calamity. For under the whole heaven there has not been done anything like what has been done against Jerusalem. As it is written in the Law of Moses, all this calamity has come upon us; yet we have not entreated the favor of the LORD our God, turning from our iniquities and gaining insight by your truth. Therefore the LORD has kept ready the calamity and has brought it upon us, for the LORD our God is righteous in all the works that he has done, and we have not obeyed his voice. And now, O Lord our God, who brought your people out of the land of Egypt with a mighty hand, and have made a name for yourself, as at this day, we have sinned, we have done wickedly. O Lord, according to all your righteous acts, let your anger and your wrath turn away from your city Jerusalem, your holy hill, because for our sins, and for the iniquities of our fathers, Jerusalem and your people have become a byword among all who are around us. Now therefore, O our God, listen to the prayer of your servant and to his pleas for mercy, and for your own sake, O Lord, make your face to shine upon your sanctuary, which is desolate. O my God, incline your ear and hear. Open your eyes and see our desolations, and the city that is called by your name. For we do not present our pleas before you because of our righteousness, but because of your great mercy. O Lord, hear; O Lord, forgive. O Lord, pay attention and act. Delay not, for your own sake, O my God, because your city and your people are called by your name. (Daniel 9:4–19 ESV).

Note what is missing in this prayer: that being the request for an angel to deliver Jerusalem. Daniel, during the reign of *Darius*, requested that *Yahweh* deliver Jerusalem and *not an angel.* As was seen in Exodus 33, to have an angel come and deliver Jerusalem, it would be have been worse than death and would have meant it would be *better* for the two Jewish nations to *remain* in exile.

Gabriel does bring an interesting answer in the following verses about the seventy weeks. While many have twisted this statement to make it about a future eschatology, the reality is that from the first Babylonian exile of Judah in 605 BC, until the final release of all Israelite exiles in 586 BC, that does add up to seventy years because 586 BC would have been the year that the 70th week, or year, fell on.

With the arrival of Cyrus, and the prophecies of Isaiah in hand, Daniel was most likely expecting the two Israelite nations to be released very soon, however while Daniel was fasting and pleading before God, Gabriel comes to tell Daniel about how he was held up by the "prince of Persia". This indicates two things. The first is that "prince of Persia" not only refers to a ruling demonic being but that it is also

literally "with prince of the kings of Persia," but RSV takes this as having the same meaning as the initial clause in this verse. It is true that in Daniel "kings" and "kingdoms" are frequently interchanged (compare 7:17; 8:21 and comments). Some versions (NJB, for example) follow a different text that says "with the kings of Persia." This, in fact, is the reading recommended by HOTTP/CTAT. It is, however, interesting to note that the proposed interpretation of CTAT allows for an explanatory note indicating that the "king" in fact represents the empire, as in 7:17 and 8:21. (italics mine)[29]

This gives us a clearer picture that there "are also times when God fully intends to respond affirmatively to a request but in his wisdom delays because he knows that the proper time has not yet come."[30] This gives us the obvious *prophetic* element of this statement by Gabriel. The prophetic element is that the king and nation of Persia have been allowed to hold up the deliverance of the Israelite nations until the *proper time*. When that time comes the archangel Michael will come to deliver the city of Jerusalem and thus deliver the two nations of Israel. This future prophetic deliverance is shown at the end of the original Tanakh ending of Daniel.

> *At that time shall arise Michael*, the great prince who has charge of your people. And there shall be a time of trouble, such as never has been since there was a nation till that time. *But at that time your people shall be delivered*, everyone whose name shall be found written in the book. And many of those who sleep in the dust of the earth shall awake, some to everlasting life, and some to shame and everlasting contempt. And those who are wise shall shine like the brightness of the sky above; and those who turn many to righteousness, like the stars forever and ever. (italics mine; Daniel 12:1–3 ESV)

Again, the italics that I added for emphasis show that the prophecy given in Daniel 10 by Gabriel about the prince of Persia holding up his delivering of the message, is a foretelling of the coming of Michael to deliver the two nations of Israel.

Critics will once again note that 2 Chronicles 36:22 says that Cyrus released the Israelite nations in his first year of rule, but that this message was delivered by Gabriel in Cyrus's third year of kingship. So, we need to observe what is happening here.

To understand what is going on in Daniel 10–12 we need to go back to Daniel 7. Daniel 7 is the famous passage of scripture that details the four great beasts that conquer and rule the Mediterranean area. After Alexander the Great died, four of Alexander's commanders divided up his empire into four other kingdoms. These kingdoms were the Seleucids, the Ptolemies, Antigonus and the Attalids. Each of these four areas commanded particular areas of Alexander's conquered territories. The one of biblical note is that of the Seleucids which ruled the area of Judea. Daniel then in 7:7–8 notes the existence of ten horns, one of these horns is louder and more arrogant than the rest.

It is easy to see that the four beasts are representing the four coming Greek kingdoms *after* Alexander. The ten horns represent ten Seleucid kings from the years of 312 BC until 161/160 BC. Note that the text of Daniel does not mention *which* horn is the one speaking "great things". It is interesting to note therefore that Antiochus IV Epiphanes, the Seleucid king to whom the Maccabean revolt was started in opposition to, would have been the "ninth" horn. The Maccabean revolt lasted from 167–160 BC which would have been the end of the ten horns who were the causes of the atrocities prophesied by Daniel through Daniel chapters 7–9.

Even though Judas Maccabeus, the Jewish leader that started the revolt was killed in 160 BC, which ended the revolt with the Seleucid empire in control of Judea, the larger

29. Péter-Contesse, *Daniel*, pp. 270–271.
30. Miller, *Daniel*, p. 286.

family of the Maccabees did manage to sever the Judean area from Seleucid rule in 134 BC. This resulted in the Jewish Hasmonean dynasty, which although of the tribe of Levi, were *not* the rightful priestly line of Aaron to oversee the temple cult detailed in the Mosaic Law. This is one of the prophetic elements that led to Christ coming as a priest in the order of Melchizedek to start a new priestly order with himself as the high priest. This would have also led to both John the Baptizer and Jesus referring to the Pharisees and Sadducees as a "brood of vipers" which I will explain in the exegesis of Psalm 91 below.

Going back to the prophetic part of Daniel 10 with the prince of Persia, Gabriel and Michael going into Daniel 12, the nations of Israel were in fact able to deliver Jerusalem from the rule of Gentile kings that brutally oppressed them. Since Michael is identified as "Israel's prince/angel" then it is not surprising that just as Michael came to deliver Gabriel from the nation and demonic prince of Persia, a figurative "Michael" would also come to free Israel from the Seleucid empire that was descended from the Greek empire of Alexander that was currently held back by the Persian nation. While Persia was never able to conquer Greece, Greece did remain an area free of Persian control until Alexander the Great waged war against the Persian Empire. This shows that Persia would give way to the "four beasts" that were to come from the Greek Empire that would lead to the deliverance of Jerusalem by the Maccabean family. This figurative "Michael" would deliver Jerusalem in this way, but not from the Persian Empire, but the Seleucid kingdom.

With all of that explained, Daniel never once asked for Yahweh to send an angel to do all of this, yet Yahweh decided to send Michael to free the nation of Israel and the holy city of Jerusalem at the *proper time* and not when Daniel was asking or hoping for. An angel possibly being sent to deliver Jerusalem would have been appropriate here as both nations of Israel had been officially divorced from the covenant. (Jeremiah 3:8–11) Being divorced from the covenant, Israel had no ability to rely on Yahweh's Deuteronomy covenant promises. Yet, Daniel still did rely on Yahweh as is proper for a non-covenant nation, even like the nation of Egypt should have in Isaiah 19. As a result, the prophetic nature of Daniel 10:12–14 with the prince of Persia, Gabriel and Michael had absolutely *nothing* to do with asking for angels to assist us when we want them to. The perversion of the text to defend requesting angel assistance is goetic in origin and has *nothing to do with proper exegesis*. That faulty goetic perversion of Daniel 10:12–14 is therefore a rejection of reliance on Yahweh in an attempt to self-deify.

Looking Carefully and Properly at Psalm 91

Most theologians and scholars are not aware of the controversy around Psalm 91. This Psalm has been another one of the key texts used in the defense of praying for angel protection. The reason that this Psalm is used for angel protection purposes is because of Satan's use of verses 11–12 "For he will command his angels concerning you to guard you in all your ways. On their hands they will bear you up, lest you strike your foot against a stone." (Psalm 91:11–12 ESV) in the second temptation of Christ quoted in Matthew 4:6 "He will command his angels concerning you, […] On their hands they will bear you up, lest you strike your foot against a stone." (ESV) and also Luke 4:10–11, "'He will command his angels concerning you, to guard you,' and 'On their hands they will bear you up, lest you strike your foot against a stone.'" (ESV) While some critics of the exegesis I will show below will think that these verses confirm the fact that we can pray for angel protection, the reality is that within a proper hermeneutic, that faulty exegesis is not possible.

When dealing with the Old Testament being used in the New Testament, G. K. Beale makes some very interesting observations that we *must* keep in mind when interpreting any part of the New Testament where the Old Testament is being used. The first of these observations is that, "NT writers may interpret historical portions of the OT to have a forward-looking sense in the light of the whole OT canonical context."[31] Understand that what is being shown here is that when Satan was quoting Psalm 91:11–12, both Satan and Jesus *knew* that Satan was calling on Jesus to prove that Psalm 91 was a true prophetic Psalm *about Jesus*. Second, in showing how Matthew used Hosea 11:1 in Matthew 2:15, Beale says that "Matthew's use of Hosea 11:1 may also be called "typological" in that he understood, in the light of the entire chapter 11 of Hosea, that the first exodus in Hosea 11:1 initiated a historical process of sin and judgment, to be culminated in another final exodus (11:10–11)."[32] Again, this helps us as readers understand that Satan was intending the *entirety* of Psalm 91 when tempting Jesus. I will deal with how Psalm 91 predicts Christ below. One last point that Beale makes about the use of the Old Testament in the New Testament is that we must "gather an overview of the outline of the entire NT book in which the OT reference occurs."[33] When we realize that both Matthew and Luke were part of the synoptic gospels, that Matthew was trying to show to Jewish people that Jesus was indeed the Son of David that was to come as Yahweh promised David in 2 Samuel 7:1–17, and that Luke's audience was a gentile governor who was wanting to learn more about Jesus, it is not difficult to see that the emphasis on the entirety of Psalm 91 was evident in Matthew 4:6 and Luke 4:10–11. The entirety of Psalm 91 was another text that *proved* that Jesus was exactly whom he claimed to be.

Below I will provide a table of the various parts of Psalm 91 and the reference verses to the fulfillment in Christ. After the table, I will provide the explanation.

Verses of Psalm 91	Christ's Fulfillment
1–2	Matthew 26:61, 27:40; Mark 14:58, 15:29; John 2:19–22
3–6	Luke 10:19; Acts 28:3–6*
7–8	John 18:6
9–10	Matthew 3:16–17; Mark 1:9–11; Luke 3:21–22; John 1: 32–34
11–12	Matthew 26:52–54
13	Matthew 3:7, 12:34, 23:33; 1 Peter 5:8
14–16	John 7:30; 8:20

* Note that I have excluded the text of the longer ending of Mark 16 due to the controversy over the views of critical and majority text.

Now, I will continue by quoting the verse(s) of Psalm 91 in question, then I will explain each of the fulfillment verses previously given in the adjacent column.

> He who dwells in the shelter of the Most High will abide in the shadow of the Almighty. I will say to the LORD, "My refuge and my fortress, my God, in whom I trust." (Psalm 91:1–2 ESV)

While most people will assume that there is more of a pragmatic interpretation to these two verses in the life of Christian believers, within the context of ancient Israel, the

31. G. K. Beale, H*andbook on the New Testament Use of the Old Testament: Exegesis and Interpretation* (Grand Rapids, Michigan: Baker Academic, 2012), p. 15.

32. Beale, *Old Testament*, p. 62.

33. Beale, *Old Testament*, p. 43.

dwelling place of the Most High was always considered to be the temple in Jerusalem. While it is true that Yahweh has always had an omnipresent reality to his existence, considering the spiritual beliefs within the ancient world, it was believed that the god of any nation resided in the official temple devoted to him or her in the city of choice. In this case, that city was Jerusalem and the temple in which Yahweh dwelled was the only temple that should have existed in Israel.

It is interesting to note that the "idea of 'refuge' (מחסה) in the psalm seems to be that of a secure, protective area guaranteed by Yahweh himself with his presence."[34] Since the only place in Israel that was guaranteed to have his presence there was the temple itself, it is not hard to conclude that the writer of this psalm was indicating that the "refuge" and "fortress" that he was seeking shelter in was the temple in Jerusalem. This shelter is possible to be temple since the Psalm is *not* attributed to David.

I will next list the fulfillment verses below in the order in which they appear in our English Bibles, but I will deal with the text from John 2:19–22 first.

> and said, "This man said, 'I am able to destroy the temple of God, and to rebuild it in three days.'" (Matthew 26:61 ESV)

> and saying, "You who would destroy the temple and rebuild it in three days, save yourself! If you are the Son of God, come down from the cross." (Matthew 27:40 ESV)

> We heard him say, "I will destroy this temple that is made with hands, and in three days I will build another, not made with hands." (Mark 14:58 ESV)

> Jesus answered them, "Destroy this temple, and in three days I will raise it up." The Jews then said, "It has taken forty-six years to build this temple, and will you raise it up in three days?" But he was speaking about the temple of his body. When therefore he was raised from the dead, his disciples remembered that he had said this, and they believed the Scripture and the word that Jesus had spoken. (John 2:19–22 ESV)

The immediate rebuke that will come with the John 2 text is that Jesus was talking about his body and not the literal temple. However, if you read through the prediction about the second temple at the end of Ezekiel, it is not hard to determine that the temple being described there would overtake the temple mount and most likely the ancient city of Jerusalem itself. The reality of the temple that Ezekiel was predicting, the true second temple, was that it would be a temple that even the city of Jerusalem could *not* contain. Since the Jewish authorities could not contain the gospel from going into the Gentile world and even into Rome itself, the critique that Jesus was not the literal temple that was predicted to come simply does not work.

Jesus does however affirm himself as the temple in this statement. Many commentators attempt to deny this, but again, when you look at what Ezekiel was saying about the second temple, the only way that the prediction could have been fulfilled was by Christ himself. Gerald L. Borchert interestingly states that the

> recollection or remembrance (emnēsthēsan) of the disciples is thus from the victory side of the tomb. Accordingly, the way John wrote the stories of Jesus presupposes that the disciples were convinced he was alive. Moreover, it was also their firm conviction that he was the fulfillment of Scripture. Therefore, the way the believer looks at the Old Testament is forever determined by the fact that Jesus the Christ (20:31) lives.[35]

---

34. Marvin E. Tate, *Psalms 51–100, volume 20, Word Biblical Commentary* (Dallas, Texas: Word, Incorporated, 1998), p. 453.

35. Gerald L. Borchert, *John 1–11, volume 25A, The New American Commentary* (Nashville, Tennessee:

Looking at what Borchert says it is not hard to see that if Jesus is the fulfillment of Scripture, of which the temple was a *key* part of it, we need to be aware of how any of us as current believers look at the Old Testament is determined at *how we view Jesus*. If Jesus is the fulfillment of the Old Testament, then Jesus *is the true temple* as Ezekiel had figuratively described.

Considering this issue, R. T. France states that

> John 2:19 does indeed record Jesus as speaking of the restoration of "this temple" in three days with reference, John says, to his own body (John 2:21), and since that prediction is set in the context of Jesus' demonstration against the temple régime it is not surprising that it was taken literally; but it attributes the destruction not to Jesus but to "you."[36]

France's commentary on the whole points to Jesus as not being the true second temple but rather using this saying as a metaphor for his own death, but the text and the redemptive arch of scripture does not seem to support that conclusion. The statement by France above points more directly to the fact that Jesus was the actual second temple, despite France's later conclusions that Jesus was not.

R. Allan Cole within his commentary on the Mark passage supports the idea of Jesus being the true temple by saying that

> From John, we see that this saying, understood by the disciples only after the resurrection, was a reference to the dissolution and raising up again, three days later, of the Lord's body; and from this springs the whole 'New Temple' concept. This metaphor was apparently freely used in Christian catechesis within the early church, of which space will not allow a full discussion here (e.g. Eph. 2:21).[37]

While Cole also says in his commentary that the Pharisees did not take Jesus' claim literally in reference to the Herodian temple in Jerusalem, it was still a statement of the "New Temple" which was Christ and that the church is brought into this temple by his death and resurrection (see Romans 6:3–4). James A. Brooks supports this conclusion by saying that the "Jews understood the reference to be to the Jerusalem temple (v. 20), but John indicated that the reference was to the body of Jesus (v. 21). [...] Still further the early church came to look upon the individual Christian (1 Cor 6:19; cf. Rev 3:12) and the whole church (1 Cor 3:16; 2 Cor 6:16; Eph 2:20–22) as the new temple."[38] While France above will have disagreed with the conclusion, he does also say that "the new congregation of God's people focused not on a building but on Jesus himself."[39] The new congregation is centred around the true new second temple, Jesus.

Critics will take all of the above and state something along the lines of, "well, if Jesus is the second temple, and Paul in 1 Corinthians 6:19–20 calls us the temple of the Holy Spirit, then Psalm 91 still applies to us." Looking at 1 Corinthians 6:19–20 we can see that this simply does not apply. The text says "do you not know that your body is a temple of the Holy Spirit within you, whom you have from God? You are not your own, for you were bought with a price. So glorify God in your body." (1 Corinthians 6:19–20 ESV)

Broadman & Holman Publishers, 1996), p. 166.

36. R. T. France, *The Gospel of Matthew*, *The New International Commentary on the New Testament* (Grand Rapids, Michigan: Wm. B. Eerdmans Publication Co., 2007), p. 1023.

37. R. Alan Cole, *Mark*: *An Introduction and Commentary*, *volume 2*, *Tyndale New Testament Commentaries* (Downers Grove, Illinois: InterVarsity Press, 1989), p. 311.

38. James A. Brooks, *Mark*, *volume 23*, *The New American Commentary* (Nashville, Tennessee: Broadman & Holman Publishers, 1991), p. 242.

39. France, *Matthew*, p. 384.

The second sentence which stretches from the end of verse19 and starts verse 20 shows that we "are not [our] own" and that we "were bought with a price". This shows that the temple of our body belongs to Christ. Being part of the body of Christ, the text of Psalm 91 still applies to Jesus and not us. The text of Romans 6:3–4 which states that we were baptized into the death of Christ also shows that Psalm 91 does not apply to us but still to Christ. It is *Christ's* death we are baptized into and not our own.

Recognizing the truth of the opening lines of Psalm 91, the next section should be read in the same way. Psalm 91:3–6 is as follows:

> For he will deliver you from the snare of the fowler and from the deadly pestilence. He will cover you with his pinions, and under his wings you will find refuge; his faithfulness is a shield and buckler. You will not fear the terror of the night, nor the arrow that flies by day, nor the pestilence that stalks in darkness, nor the destruction that wastes at noonday. (Psalm 91:3–6 ESV)

It is not difficult to say that there are times in the gospels where incidents from these verses *could* apply to Jesus but there is nothing that *directly* applies to Jesus. Considering the fact that the church is baptized into Jesus' death making it possible for some of these instances to apply to the church, we need to recognize that these promises are happening *through* Jesus. It is important to see here that all "who trust in their own perceptions will be defeated by fear, but the Lord is sufficient to defend them from the full range of their threats."[40] Considering the number of charlatans throughout history that have attempted to prove they had some kind of divine status in playing with poisonous snakes during church services, or even attempting to drink and/or consume dangerous poisons and foods, it is not hard to see that if Jesus is the one giving these gifts, then they can easily be withdrawn because these are promises given to *Jesus* and not us.

To show the reality of this: consider the report of the seventy-two in Luke 10 when they returned to Jesus after he sent them out into the wider countryside to teach the Jews of that day of the fact their Messiah had come.

> The seventy-two returned with joy, saying, "Lord, even the demons are subject to us in your name!" And he said to them, "I saw Satan fall like lightning from heaven. Behold, I have given you authority to tread on serpents and scorpions, and over all the power of the enemy, and nothing shall hurt you. Nevertheless, do not rejoice in this, that the spirits are subject to you, but rejoice that your names are written in heaven." (Luke 10:17–20 ESV)

We can also observe here a similar instance with Paul after he was told by Jesus that he was going to stand before Caesar to teach the Roman Emperor at that time (who was Nero) about the gospel of Jesus Christ. Acts 28:3–6 states that

> When Paul had gathered a bundle of sticks and put them on the fire, a viper came out because of the heat and fastened on his hand. When the native people saw the creature hanging from his hand, they said to one another, "No doubt this man is a murderer. Though he has escaped from the sea, Justice has not allowed him to live." He, however, shook off the creature into the fire and suffered no harm. They were waiting for him to swell up or suddenly fall down dead. But when they had waited a long time and saw no misfortune come to him, they changed their minds and said that he was a god. (Acts 28:3–6 ESV)

Going back to the text from Luke 10:17–20 it is accurately said by Leon Morris that it

---

40. Daniel J. Estes, *Psalms 73–150*, editor E. Ray. Clendenen, *volume 13*, *New American Commentary* (Nashville, Tennessee: B&H Publishing Group, 2019), p. 186.

> is not certain whether the words are to be taken literally or figuratively. It is probably the latter, for there is no record of a Christian preacher treading on literal snakes or scorpions without taking harm (though once Paul escaped when a viper fastened on his arm, Acts 28:3–5). More, they had authority *over all the power of the enemy*. Satan himself could not prevail against them. Their security is emphasized with *nothing shall hurt you*. All this makes a dazzling picture for such humble people. But Jesus goes on to teach that they must get their priorities right. Their real ground for rejoicing is not their victory over *the spirits*. The people from whom they had expelled demons would in due course pass away, as would even this earth, the scene of their triumph. Much more important is it that their names *are written* (perfect tense pointing to what is permanent) *in heaven* (cf. Exod. 32:32; Dan. 12:1; Heb. 12:23; Rev. 3:5, etc.). Jesus turns their attention to realities that will last. (italics original)[41]

Note what Morris is saying here: it should not matter what you are able to do while doing what Christ has set before you when your *priorities are right*. In other words, the idea that many of those in charismatic, Prosperity, Word-of-Faith (WOF) and New Apostolic Reformation (NAR) churches are pushing that they are validated because of the signs they are performing are *not setting their priorities correctly*. In other words, these leaders are focusing on their "special powers" to be able to prove their "divine status" rather than allowing the gospel to speak for itself. This is the point Jesus is trying to make, and that Morris points out in saying "there is no record of a Christian preacher treading on literal snakes or scorpions without taking harm". While there is some promise in this Psalm to the Christian, the fact that it applies directly to Christ and to the authority given to *Jesus* and not immediately to us *unless* Christ desires. That it is Christ's authority is the point of what is being said in Luke 10. The seventy-two came back boasting of what they were able to do while *forgetting* the point that it was because their God had come among them. The seventy-two had completely missed what the message was.

We also need to emphasize the point that Jesus was saying that the real enemy here was Satan and not literal snakes and scorpions. Note what Joel B. Green says that within Luke 10:19–20

> however, a key interpretive move is introduced. This is the explicit identification of Satan as the real "enemy" that is to be overcome. Rome is not the adversary, only one of its partners, joined by many others; in the current scene Satan's minions are referred to as "snakes and scorpions" and, more generally, by all that would "harm" these messengers—that is, reject the good news manifest in Jesus', and their, redemptive activity. When it is recognized that Luke identifies "the enemy" as the cosmic power of evil resident and active behind all forms of opposition to God and God's people.[42]

While the instance with Paul in Acts 28 shows that there is some pragmatic real-world reality to this power given to the seventy-two and Paul, the ability to tread on snakes and scorpions is much bigger in context. Since Jesus was the one that was given the promise to tread on snakes in Genesis 3:15, it was a promise that he was able to pass on to us as he deemed necessary when the priorities of the Christian are correct and not when the priorities become mixed as they did in Mark 9:28–29. See the following text from Mark 9:28–29: "And when he had entered the house, his disciples asked him privately, 'Why could we not cast it out?' And he said to them, 'This kind cannot be driven out by anything but prayer.'" (Mark 9:28–29 ESV) In the same synoptic story in Matthew Jesus tells the rea-

41. Leon Morris, *Luke: An Introduction and Commentary, volume 3, Tyndale New Testament Commentaries* (Downers Grove, Illinois: InterVarsity Press, 1988), p. 204.

42. Joel B. Green, *The Gospel of Luke, The New International Commentary on the New Testament* (Grand Rapids, Michigan: Wm. B. Eerdmans Publishing Co., 1997), pp. 419–420.

son that the disciples could not cast the demon out. Jesus told the disciples that it was "Because of your little faith." (Matthew 17:20 ESV) In other words, the disciples could not cast out demons because they were not trusting in Jesus. As a result, the promises of Psalm 91, that have come to reality in Jesus, will not be applicable to us as the people of God if we assume our *own* authority in this situation. Psalm 91 here is about Jesus, and not us. Once we get our faith priorities correct, then the demonic will not be able to stand against the *spread of the gospel*.

In dealing with the incident in Acts 28, as this introduction is attempting to show about the cultural and religious context of the ancient world in dealing with goetia and necromancy, the cultural context of the island of Malta and the Roman empire should be present here. John B. Polhill correctly shows what

> is clear from the text is the perception of the natives. They obviously saw the creature as venomous and expected Paul to die. Since they were native to the island and should have known their own species, their reaction probably is the best clue about how the narrative is to be taken. For them the serpent's bite was a sure sign that Paul was a fugitive from the gods and that divine retribution had finally caught up with him (v. 4). In this they were reflecting a common ancient concept. The Romans, for instance, told the story of a fugitive who escaped a shipwreck but was killed by a snake that bit him as he lay recovering on the beach; and Jewish tradition told of the murderer who got his just deserts from the fangs of a viper.61 But this was not the case with Paul. He simply shook the snake into the fire and suffered no ill effects from its bite (v. 5). Justice was not catching up with Paul. Quite the contrary—providence was *preserving* him. (italics original)[43]

Seeing this context, the full picture that the end of the book of Acts is trying to show makes sense. While the passed down promises of Psalm 91 *may* be in effect here, the reality is that Paul was being shown as *innocent* to the people of the Malta who would have assumed Paul's guilt simply by being a prisoner and *especially* by being bitten by a serpent. When Paul was proven to be unharmed by the snake, it was evidence of Paul's innocence. Unfortunately the people of Malta also took this show of innocence incorrectly and instead saw Paul as one of the pagan Greco divine men[44] and also a "god".

Moving on to Psalm 91:7–8 we get the following:

> A thousand may fall at your side, ten thousand at your right hand, but it will not come near you. You will only look with your eyes and see the recompense of the wicked. (Psalm 91:7–8 ESV)

Again, some critics will attempt to point out that this never happened with Jesus. The gospel evidence says otherwise. See the following from John 18:

> Then Jesus, knowing all that would happen to him, came forward and said to them, "Whom do you seek?" They answered him, "Jesus of Nazareth." Jesus said to them, "I am he." Judas, who betrayed him, was standing with them. When Jesus said to them, "I am he," they drew back and fell to the ground. (John 18:4–6 ESV)

This is one of the times that the English of John's gospel does not do readers much good. That is not to say that the translation here is wrong, it simply means that the Greek trans-

43. John B. Polhill, *Acts, volume 26, The New American Commentary* (Nashville, Tennessee: Broadman & Holman Publishers, 1992), p. 532.

44. The issue of the θεῖος ἀνήρ (theios aner) or "divine man" is quite complicated and there is no room for it here. In order to understand this concept better please see: Carl H. Holladay, *Theios Aner in Hellenistic Judaism: A Critique of the Use of This Category in New Testament Christology* (Missoula, Montana: Scholars Press, 1977).

lated in this way is not the most helpful. When Jesus is translated as saying "I am he" the actual Greek words that are used are 'Εγώ εἰμι (egō eimi). The significance of these two Greek words for "I am" is underplayed here in our English. In the Greek Septuagint (LXX), or what we call the "Old Testament", with Exodus 3 we have an interesting and notable use of the Greek. Here is the English text, followed by the text of the LXX:

> God said to Moses, "*I AM* WHO I AM." And he said, "Say this to the people of Israel: 'I AM has sent me to you.'" (italics mine, Exodus 3:14 ESV)

> καὶ εἶπεν ὁ θεὸς πρὸς Μωυσῆν λέγων *Ἐγώ εἰμι* ὁ ὤν· καὶ εἶπεν Οὕτως ἐρεῖς τοῖς υἱοῖς Ἰσραήλ Ὁ ὢν ἀπέσταλκέν με πρὸς ὑμᾶς. (italics mine)[45]

Note how Jesus spoke the same *divine name* that Yahweh had given Moses in Exodus 3. When Jesus spoke the divine name of יהוה (Yahweh; it would have been said in either Hebrew or Aramaic when Jesus spoke it, and in Hebrew and Aramaic יהוה is said and pronounced the same) all of the *men that came to arrest Jesus* were knocked *backwards* to the ground. This also speaks *against* the "slain in the spirit" phenomenon as it was the *enemies* of Jesus that were knocked backwards and *not* the true followers of Jesus.

Seeing all of the above, Psalm 91:7–8 was fulfilled by *Jesus* and *only* Jesus. Just as the rest of Psalm 91 up to this point had been.

The statements made in Psalm 91:9–10 are not all that theologically different from verses 1–2, but with the way the text is written, the text allows for us to look at another part of the gospels for this part of the Psalm's fulfillment in Christ.

> Because you have made the LORD your dwelling place—the Most High, who is my refuge— no evil shall be allowed to befall you, no plague come near your tent. (Psalm 91:9–10 ESV)

In this case, I will quote all of the relevant gospel scripture and bring them all together at the same time since all of these reference the same moment in Jesus' ministry: his baptism.

> And when Jesus was baptized, immediately he went up from the water, and behold, the heavens were opened to him, and he saw the Spirit of God descending like a dove and coming to rest on him; and behold, a voice from heaven said, "This is my beloved Son, with whom I am well pleased." (Matthew 3:16–17 ESV)

> In those days Jesus came from Nazareth of Galilee and was baptized by John in the Jordan. And when he came up out of the water, immediately he saw the heavens being torn open and the Spirit descending on him like a dove. And a voice came from heaven, "You are my beloved Son; with you I am well pleased." (Mark 1:9–11 ESV)

> Now when all the people were baptized, and when Jesus also had been baptized and was praying, the heavens were opened, and the Holy Spirit descended on him in bodily form, like a dove; and a voice came from heaven, "You are my beloved Son; with you I am well pleased." (Luke 3:21–22 ESV)

> And John bore witness: "I saw the Spirit descend from heaven like a dove, and it remained on him. I myself did not know him, but he who sent me to baptize with water said to me, 'He on whom you see the Spirit descend and remain, this is he who baptizes with the Holy Spirit.' And I have seen and have borne witness that this is the Son of God." (John 1:32–34 ESV)

The first thing to note here is that this is one of the few stories that is recorded in all four

45. Henry Barclay Swete, *The Old Testament in Greek: According to the Septuagint* (Cambridge, UK: Cambridge University Press, 1909), Ex 3:14.

of the gospels. The fact that this story is in all four gospels should make all of us recognize that there is something significant about this account.

When considering the fact about Jesus being the true second temple in the observations about Psalm 91:1–2, look at this specific prophecy about the second temple (Jesus) that was made by Ezekiel.

> As the glory of the LORD entered the temple by the gate facing east, the Spirit lifted me up and brought me into the inner court; and behold, the glory of the LORD filled the temple. (Ezekiel 43:4–5 ESV)

Going to Haggai, the temple built after the exile was not nearly as impressive as Solomon's which contrasts with Haggai 2:9. See what Haggai says:

> The latter glory of this house shall be greater than the former, says the LORD of hosts. And in this place I will give peace, declares the LORD of hosts. (Haggai 2:9 ESV)

The only glorious temple that was greater than Solomon's was that of Jesus himself. With the arrival of the Spirit to the second temple that would be part of the second temple becoming greater than the first in its glory, we can once again look at the baptism of Jesus and the arrival of the Holy Spirit in the form of a dove. This was the visible notice to the post-exilic Jews that the Spirit of Yahweh, had returned to the temple, the true second temple, Jesus.

It is notable that Jesus' Triumphal Entry into Jerusalem is also a sign of Yahweh's return to the temple, but it is more of a *symbolic* return so that the people of Jerusalem would celebrate not only the return of Yahweh to the temple, but the arrival of the promised Davidic heir to his rightful throne.

While other theologians have said that the Spirit descending on Jesus is an indication of Isaiah 61,[46] there is more in Isaiah 61 that once again shows that the Spirit is inhabiting the second temple that is Jesus. Look at Isaiah 61:4–6

> They shall build up the ancient ruins; they shall raise up the former devastations; they shall repair the ruined cities, the devastations of many generations. Strangers shall stand and tend your flocks; foreigners shall be your plowmen and vinedressers; but you shall be called the priests of the LORD; they shall speak of you as the ministers of our God; you shall eat the wealth of the nations, and in their glory you shall boast. (Isaiah 61:4–6 ESV)

Referencing the building of the ancient ruins, and the making of those that follow Christ as the priests, it again shows that the Spirit descending on Christ is an indication of Christ as the true second temple and the Spirit's return to that temple at that moment. Looking back at Psalm 91:9 where the writer says that the LORD is now his "dwelling place" and that "no evil shall befall you" which no evil was allowed to "befall" Christ until it was his proper time, it is not difficult to see Christ was the fulfillment of Psalm 91.

The next part of Psalm 91 is the most controversial in this discussion. The part of Psalm 91 that needs to be considered here is verses 11–12 which are as follows:

> For he will command his angels concerning you to guard you in all your ways. On their hands they will bear you up, lest you strike your foot against a stone. (Psalm 91:11–12 ESV)

Noting Satan's second temptation to Christ where Satan was quoting Psalm 91, I will show the text below.

46. Robert H. Stein, *Luke, volume 24, The New American Commentary* (Nashville, Tennessee: Broadman & Holman Publishers, 1992), pp. 139–140.

> If you are the Son of God, throw yourself down, for it is written, "He will command his angels concerning you," and "On their hands they will bear you up, lest you strike your foot against a stone." (Matthew 4:6 ESV)

And also, Luke's account

> If you are the Son of God, throw yourself down from here, for it is written, "He will command his angels concerning you, to guard you," and "On their hands they will bear you up, lest you strike your foot against a stone." (Luke 4:9–11 ESV)

Understanding why Satan was quoting this text from Psalm 91 as a temptation for Jesus at that moment to prove that he was the Messiah, it is not hard to say that many Jews would have believed that Jesus was whom he claimed to be if he was seen plummeting to the temple grounds and was suddenly gently settled in the temple courtyard by angels. That however, like with the first and third temptation, would have upset the plans of the triune-Godhead and it would not have resulted in the greater glory of Christ dying on the cross and his resurrection. All of this is shown clearly in Matthew's account of Jesus' arrest. Look at what Matthew tells us:

> Then Jesus said to him, "Put your sword back into its place. For all who take the sword will perish by the sword. Do you think that I cannot appeal to my Father, and he will at once send me more than twelve legions of angels? But how then should the Scriptures be fulfilled, that it must be so?" (Matthew 26:52–54 ESV)

While Jesus could have called on twelve legions of angels to set him gently on the temple grounds and also to save him from being arrested, neither of them would have seen the scriptures fulfilled. This again shows that Psalm 91 is pointing to Christ. R. T. France once again makes a notable observation supporting the above evidence.

> Jesus is not a helpless victim, needing any human help available. He is being arrested because he chooses; if he wanted help he could call on far more than a few swords. [...] His refusal to thwart his enemies' plans either by evasion (see on v. 36) or by supernatural power derives from his repeatedly voiced conviction that his mission must be one of rejection and suffering (see on 16:21; 17:22–23; 20:17–19, 28). *Behind these earlier predictions it has not been hard to discern the scriptures as the source of Jesus' conviction; now that source is made explicit. And for Jesus there is no other option but that the scriptures be fulfilled. That issue had been settled in Gethsemane.* (italics mine)[47]

Like Psalm 91:11–12, verse 13 is also a very controversial verse in today's churches. Verse 13 is as follows:

> You will tread on the lion and the adder; the young lion and the serpent you will trample underfoot. (Psalm 91:13 ESV)

This prophecy is clearly pointing to its fulfillment in Christ given to us in Genesis 3:15

> I will put enmity between you and the woman, and between your offspring and her offspring; he shall bruise your head, and you shall bruise his heel. (Genesis 3:15 ESV)

Realize here that it is the "seed" that the prophecy being given is truly about. The question then arises: who are the seed? The Bible does in fact tell us.

> But when he saw many of the Pharisees and Sadducees coming to his baptism, he said to them, "You brood of vipers! Who warned you to flee from the wrath to come?" (Matthew

47. France, *Matthew*, pp. 380–381.

3:7 ESV)

You brood of vipers! How can you speak good, when you are evil? For out of the abundance of the heart the mouth speaks. (Matthew 12:34 ESV)

You serpents, you brood of vipers, how are you to escape being sentenced to hell? (Matthew 23:33 ESV)

In all the references here the word "brood" is the Greek word γέννημα (gennēma). What γέννημα means is noted by two different Greek lexicons as referring to the same meaning. The lexicon by Henry George Liddel et al. states that γέννημα means "that which is produced or born, child."[48] Similarly the Louw-Nida lexicon states that

γέννημαa, τος n: (derivative of γεννάωb 'to give birth,' 23.52) that which has been produced or born of a living creature—'offspring, brood, child.' γεννήματα ἐχιδνῶν 'brood of vipers' Mt 3:7. In some languages it may be possible to translate this phrase in Mt 3:7 more or less literally, for example, 'the offspring of vipers,' in which 'vipers' means poisonous snakes, but in other languages this would be impossible, and one must therefore use 'little snakes.'[49]

In the verses from Matthew that were referenced, both John the Baptizer and Jesus were referring to the Jewish leaders as the *seed of the serpent*. This is something that many in churches have not noticed. Some errant exegetes have tried to claim that the Genesis 3:15 reference to the serpent's seed somehow indicates that Satan had intercourse with Eve and that was how Cain was conceived.[50] As the above shows, that theory about the seed of the serpent is an exegetical fallacy. Jesus names who the seed of the serpent was, and it was the Pharisees, Sadducees and scribes of his day.

Some might refer back to Romans 16 to say that the reference is to Satan himself. While Satan is included in the act of Christ's "trampling" there is more happening in the context of Romans 16 that many choose to skip over. The entirety of the text is as follows:

I appeal to you, brothers, to *watch out for those who cause divisions and create obstacles contrary to the doctrine that you have been taught*; *avoid them. For such persons do not serve our Lord Christ*, but their own appetites, and by smooth talk and flattery they deceive the hearts of the naive. For your obedience is known to all, so that I rejoice over you, but I want you to be wise as to what is good and innocent as to what is evil. The God of peace will soon crush Satan under your feet. The grace of our Lord Jesus Christ be with you. (italics mine; Romans 16:17–20 ESV)

Note an interesting identification of whom the false teachers of verse 17 may have been.

It is not necessary to believe that they were all of one kind. Some may have been legalists (Judaizers), others antinomians or perhaps ascetics, or advocates of a combination of two or more disruptive isms.[51]

48. Liddell, *Greek*, p. 344.

49. Johannes P. Louw and Eugene Albert Nida, *Greek-English Lexicon of the New Testament: Based on Semantic Domains* (New York, New York: United Bible Societies, 1996), p. 256.

50. See Zen Garcia, *Lucifer – Father of Cain* (Atlanta, Georgia: Sacred Word Publishing, 2011). Reading Garcia's material and even looking at his publishing website, it is evident that not only he, but all those associated with him are highly involved in hermetic occultism. While Garcia claims to be a Christian, the plethora of Gnostic and Hermetic content on his website in his books speaks contrary to that claim. Unfortunately, I have seen many people on various social media platforms (Facebook, Instagram, X [formerly Twitter]) that are involved in the Prosperity, WOF, and NAR movements that have bought into his claims.

51. William Hendriksen and Simon J. Kistemaker, *Exposition of Paul's Epistle to the Romans, volume 12–13, New Testament Commentary* (Grand Rapids, Michigan: Baker Book House, 1953–2001), p. 510.

Is there more support that Paul's reference here was to Judaizers, or even possibly Jews? In fact, there is. The entire book of Hebrews was written to Christians in Rome under threat of persecution from Roman authorities. The easiest way to avoid being killed by the Roman government was to flee back to the Jewish synagogues where they would show they were not real believers. These false Christians at the time would have thought they were Christians but were proving they were not. F. F. Bruce makes an interesting observation about this in his commentary on Hebrews.

> If Jewish Christians relapsed into Judaism, it is implied, this would not involve a renunciation of "the living God"; relapsing into Judaism would at least mean that they continued to worship the God of Israel. [...] From our author's point of view deliberate disobedience to the living God was practical apostasy against him, whether those guilty of it were Jewish or Gentile by birth.[52]

Realize what Bruce is saying: while it may appear like the Jews fleeing back to the synagogues in Rome would not *seem* like apostacy, it really was. The author of Hebrews is attempting to discourage Roman Jews and the Gentiles in the Christian church with them, not to succumb to the pressures of persecution and to continue on in the faith. This makes the statement by Paul in Romans 16:17–20 more clear. Under the persecution of Rome that was causing Jews and the Judaizers to flee in apostacy to the Jewish synagogues in Rome, Paul was making it clear that "soon" (whenever in the near future that might have been) God would crush these enemies that were causing people to flee back to Judaism. While this crushing would be under the feet of the Christians, it was still *Christ* doing the crushing and not the *believers themselves*. This once again refers back to Jesus telling the disciples not to focus on the great things they could do with *Christ's* authority, but simply do as they were commanded by Christ. Similarly, Paul is telling the Christians in Rome to remain faithful and with that show of faith, Christ would be the one to crush Satan and not the church itself.

With all of this in mind, when we look at the Psalm 91:13 reference to the "lion", it is not hard to see that Peter was likewise speaking of Christ being able to overcome Satan and for not letting Satan be able to "devour" us as 1 Peter 5:8 tells us: "Be sober-minded; be watchful. Your adversary the devil prowls around like a roaring lion, seeking someone to devour." (1 Peter 5:8 ESV)

Now I move on to the last few verses of Psalm 91.

> Because he holds fast to me in love, I will deliver him; I will protect him, because he knows my name. When he calls to me, I will answer him; I will be with him in trouble; I will rescue him and honor him. With long life I will satisfy him and show him my salvation. (Psalm 91:14–16 ESV)

There are two verses in the gospel of John that show Psalm 91:14–16 being fulfilled in Christ.

> So they were seeking to arrest him, but no one laid a hand on him, because his hour had not yet come. (John 7:30 ESV)

> These words he spoke in the treasury, as he taught in the temple; but no one arrested him,

There are still movements of Judaizers that are "Gentiles" who are pushing that Christians must obey the Mosaic Law dietary laws in order to be saved under the covenant of grace. These are the same false teachers Paul was speaking out against in Romans 16:17.

52. F. F. Bruce, *The Epistle to the Hebrews, Rev. ed., The New International Commentary on the New Testament* (Grand Rapids, Michigan: Wm. B. Eerdmans Publishing Co., 1990), p. 5.

because his hour had not yet come. (John 8:20 ESV)

We can note the importance of these verses in seeing what Colin G. Kruse says that the

> 'hour' is an important concept in this Gospel. In the early part of the Gospel, things move towards the 'hour', which is the hour of Jesus' passion, death and subsequent exaltation (see commentary on 2:4). No machinations of Jesus' opponents could bring his ministry to a premature end; he would not surrender himself to their hands until his 'hour' had come.[53]

Kruse also notes with John 8:20 that the "hour towards which everything was moving was the hour of Jesus' glorification, which took place through his death, resurrection and exaltation. This 'hour' was determined by God, not by Jesus' opponents."[54]

J. Ramsey Michaels in a similar way says about John 7:30 that the arrest "failed because God determined that it would fail: that is, because Jesus' 'hour had not yet come'"[55] Michaels comments on John 8:20 that there is a difference with John 7:30 in that "the difference here is that they did not try and fail, but that no one even *tried* to arrest Jesus. The Pharisees are now as baffled and helpless on meeting Jesus in person as the officers they sent to arrest him were a chapter earlier [John 7]" (italics original)[56] We see here that the Pharisees and Sadducees were attempting to arrest and bring harm to Jesus, but they could not until the triune-Yahweh had determined what was the proper time. This protection, while it was pulled back for the purposes of fulfilling the Mosaic covenant (the Old Testament), was once again fulfilled in Christ. And through this, the "long life" that Christ's resurrection would result in was also given to all those that belonged to him. This long life is not *ours*, but this long life is Christ's that has been given to us in eternity as he has determined and desired.

While all of this may be a bit to take in for those that are new to the topic and discussion about Psalm 91, in seeing that entirety of Psalm 91 is fulfilled and pointing to Christ, many other present-day beliefs about how we can pray Psalm 91 over ourselves and our homes to expel the demonic simply fail. Considering the purposes of this book and this introduction, the goetic/necromantic nature of the beliefs that Psalm 91 can be used in exorcisms of people and homes need to be shown and it will be shown now.

To start a translation will be given for the Dead Sea Scroll 11Q11 that is otherwise known as *Songs to Disperse Demons*. The reason this scroll is being fully translated (tranlation mine), without the tiny fragments which do not add anything sensible to the text, is because of the use of Psalm 91 at the end of the scroll in Column 6.

> Column 1
> [...] crying [...] oath [...] Yahweh [...] dragon [...] agree the earth [...] causing to swear [...] you in [...] more to and fro [...] in the demon [...] he dwells [...]
>
> Column 2
> [...] there [...] in retribution he called the spirits and the demons [...] these are the demons and the chief persecutors who go straight to the depths [...] in regard to the great destruction [...] with him giving exorcisms by your name on which we lean, we call upon Israel the strong by Yahweh, God of gods who made the heavens and the earth and all that is in them, the Lord which he separated between the light and the darkness [...]

53. Colin G. Kruse, *John: An Introduction and Commentary*, editor Eckhard J. Schnabel, *Second edition, volume 4, Tyndale New Testament Commentaries* (London: Inter-Varsity Press, 2017), p. 215.

54. Kruse, *John*, p. 234.

55. J. Ramsey Michaels, *The Gospel of John: The New International Commentary on the New Testament* (Grand Rapids, Michigan: William B. Eerdmans Publishing Company, 2010), p. 453.

56. Michaels, *John*, p. 485.

Column 3
[...] The abyss, the land and the land who made the signs and those who are afflicted in the land of Yahweh is the Lord who made is all in his power, satisfying all his needs and all the holy seed who were placed before him and testified to the heavens and the earth and all in them which he will do in them. Every human is a sinner and every human has wicked blood and God knows that which is wasting away and which of the [...] is not. They will be seen before Yahweh who will kill the soul [...] Yahweh and they will fear the great plague to come and one thousand of you servants will be persecuted by Yahweh great and [...]

Column 4
Great swearing of the great [...] the mighty in all of the heavens and the earth [...]

May the Lord be so great that he will smite you and the horn of his nose [will send] upon you a strong angel to do all his words that will do no mercy on you. Upon all of which these they [the angel] will bring down to the depths of the Sheol which is below the water and darkness [tohu wabohu?]. And in the very great depths of the earth they will not escape for eternity the curse of Abaddon where they will have the wrath and anger of Yahweh in total darkness. These testimonies of humiliation [will be part] of your portion

Column 5
For the possessed ones volunteering to Raphael to be restored. Amen, Amen, Selah [peace].

To David, [against ...] call on the name of Yahweh at all times towards the heavens because he will come to you at night and you command him, "Who are you demon?" make the ones born from man depart from the son of the holy ones. Your face is worthless and your horns are horns of nightmares and not light and are also unjust. The Prince of the host of Yahweh will bring all of you down to Sheol below. The Prince will shut the bronze doors and will not let the light pass through or the sun that shines. And the righteous will say to the evil to come, "his demon [not to] do harm to him [or divert] truth from righteousness to [...]

Column 6
[...] to the world. All the sons of Bel, Yael, Amen, Selah: for David dwells [secretly] in the upper shadow of my heart [Psalm 91:1] I will say to Yahweh who protects and is the fortress of my God who absolutely secures him [Psalm 91:2] Because he will deliver you from the snare of the fowler, and from the plague of desires. [Psalm 91:3] Under his wings you shall dwell in grace, and upon you shall be in peace and prosperity, his truth shall your shield and bulwark. [Psalm 91:4] Don't be afraid of the fear of the night, or of an arrow that will fly by day. [Psalm 91:5] nor destruction that will come at noon, nor plague that comes in the darkness. [Psalm 91:6] A thousand shall fall at your side, and a myriad shall fall at your right hand, but it will not touch you. [Psalm 91:7] If you look only with your eyes you will see the retribution of the wicked. [Psalm 91:8] You called [name?] your refuge, [Psalm 91:9] he will not see evil and he will not let plague touch your house. [Psalm 91:10] For will command his angels to watch you and keep you in all your paths. [Psalm 91:11] On their palms they will lift you up should you injure your foot on a stone. [Psalm 91:12] On the snake you will tread, on the lion you will trample and also the dragon. [Psalm 91:13] Because you desire Yahweh, I will protect him and deliver him. [Psalm 91:14] I will show him salvation. Selah. [Psalm 91:16b] Amen, Amen, Selah. [...]

Most of this will read rather strangely for those in biblical studies. Much of it will "sound" biblical but will also seem *strange* from a biblical standpoint. One thing to take note of is that in Column 5, the first use of the English word "call" in this translation is the word לחש (lāhāsh) which is indicating a magical use of an incantation and/or summoning.[57] What the use of לחש shows is the goetic nature of 11Q11 and the fallacious goetic use of Psalm 91 in the post-exilic period. Edward M. Cook in his translation of 11Q11 shows that Psalm 91 was also "a psalm that continued to be used throughout the centuries in

57. Francis Brown, Samuel Rolles Driver, and Charles Augustus Briggs, *Enhanced Brown-Driver-Briggs Hebrew and English Lexicon* (Oxford: Clarendon Press, 1977), p. 538.

magical exorcisms in both Judaism and Christianity."[58] This gives the evidence that the goetic use of Psalm 91 was present even before the time that Jesus came to earth, and it was used *improperly* and was part of the *traditions* that were *rebuked* by Christ. The translation of Psalm 91 in 11Q11 seems a bit different but this can be easily explained by translation preferences. There will be some notable differences in the way the text reads, however it is still in its textual meaning Psalm 91.

To show that Psalm 91 had been used for goetic purposes since the post-exilic time when 11Q11 was written, the following from an 18th century goetic text called The Sixth and Seventh Books of Moses that were originally written in German state the following about Psalm 91:

> Psalm 91.—The holy name of this Psalm is El, which means Strong God. After speaking this Psalm, and the preceding one, *over a person tormented by an evil spirit*, or one afflicted by an incurable disease, in the name of Eel Schaddei, then pray humbly: Let it be thy holy pleasure, oh my God! *to take from N., son of R., the evil spirit by which he is tormented*, for the sake of thy great, mighty and holy name El Schaddei. Wilt thou presently send him health and let him be perfectly restored. Hear his prayer as thou once did that of thy servant Moses when he prayed this Psalm. Let his prayer penetrate to thee as once the holy incense arose to thee on high. Amen. Selah!
>
> The two letters of the name Eel are contained in the words Jeschuti, verse 16, and Orech, verse 16.
>
> Again *write this Psalm in connection with the last verse of the previous Psalm upon clean parchment, and conceal it behind the door of your house, and you will be secure from all evil accidents*. Kabalists ascribe to this Psalm when taken in connection with the above verse, the most wonderful virtue, when it is used in accordance with the nature of existing circumstances, and *when it is combined with other scriptural passages, holy names of angels*, characters and prayers, it is said, for example:
>
> Prayer through which all distress, danger and suffering may be turned aside. If any one should be in danger of his life, or become distressed, be it what it may, such as being attacked by an incurable disease, pestilence, fire or water, overwhelmed by enemies or murderers, in battles, sieges, robberies, close imprisonment, etc., let him confess his sins first of all, and then speak the Vihi Noamprayer (the name by which the 91st Psalm with the aforesaid verse is usually known), ninety-nine times, according to the number of the two holiest names of God, Jehovah Adonei. Each time when he comes to the fourteenth verse, "Because he hath set his love upon me," etc., he shall keep in mind the holy name, and then pray devoutly each time: "Thou art the most holy, king over all that is revealed and hidden, exalted above all that is high, sanctify and glorify thy adorable name in this thy world, so that all the nations of the earth may know that thine is the glory and the power, and that thou hast secured me from all distress, but especially out of the painful emergency (here the object of the prayer must be distinctly stated), which has overtaken me N., son of R. And I herewith promise and vow that I will now and ever after this, as long as I shall live upon the earth, and until I return to the dust from which I was taken." (Here the vow must be verbally-stated,—stating what we will do, perform or give in the service of our Creator. The vow may consist in fasting, giving alms, or in the daily reading of several chapters of the Holy Scriptures, Psalms, of the Sohar or of the Talmud, releasing of captives, nursing the sick and burying the dead.) "Praised be Jehovah, my Rock and my Salvation. Thou wilt be my representative and intercessor, and wilt help me, for thou helpest thy poor, feeble and humble creature, and in time of need releasest from fear and danger, and dealest mercifully with thy people; merciful and forgiving, thou hearest the prayer of every one. Praised art thou, Jehovah, thou who hearest prayer." (The last words should be repeated seven times at each ending of the prayer.)
>
> And now, whoever will punctually observe the foregoing instructions three days in succession, in full trust in the mighty help of God, he may rest assured of the assistance

58. Michael O. Wise, Martin G. Abegg Jr., and Edward M. Cook, *The Dead Sea Scrolls: A New Translation* (New York, New York: HarperOne, 2005), p. 590.

which he desires.

Kabalists, and especially the celebrated Rabbi Isaac Loria have assured us that in a time of pestilence or general emergency, the Vihi Noamprayer should be prayed seven times daily, connecting with it in the mind the figure of the golden candlestick, when it is composed of the forty-one holy and important words and names of this Psalm, with which we should especially consider the holy names in their order. The following are the

Vean, Aim, Mii, Tmol Im,
Aki, Aab, Bich, Veal, Retak, Betu,
Lakad, Mili, Schin, Aki,
Iba, Wich, Ika, Aan, Beni,
Ktaz, Ilu, Mehoh, Imi, Becha,]
Lir, Uma, Ima, Miz, Mehi,
Ibak, Rul, Leta, Afcham, Pesch,
Acchu, Kuck, Vetat, Raasch, Jaub, Ana.
(See Fig. A.)

Fig. A.

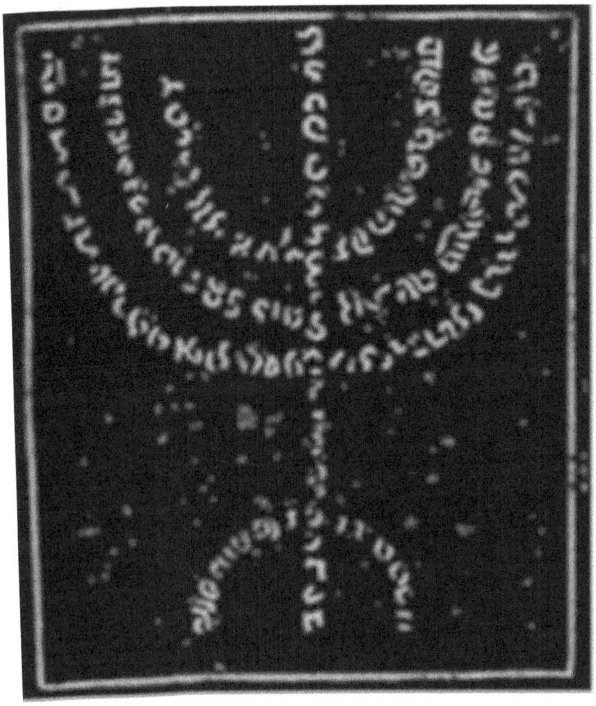

After this should be spoken verses 21–28, chapter xii. of Exodus, and with them keeping in mind the names contained in the 23d and 28th verses, in the following order: Awal, Jahel, Ito, Huj Husch, Aha, Imo, Vil.

As also Vohu, Uha, Bam, Bili, Zel, Holo, Vcsop, and finally the holy mame: Nischaszlas.

And now, he who observes all these things to the very letter, and who can keep in his memory all the letters, points or vowels, he shall be safe from all danger, and shall be as strong as steel, so that no firearms can harm him. The certainty of this is shown by the Kabalists, because the letter Seijid is not to be found in the entire Psalm, and since the word Seijin or Kie Seijin embraces within its meaning all deadly weapons, this conclusion is entirely correct. (italics mine)[59]

59. L. W. de Laurence, *Sixth and Seventh Books of Moses: The Mystery of All Mysteries* (Chicago, Illinois: de Laurence, Scott & Co., 1910), pp. 162–164.

Reading through the above from *The Sixth and Seventh Books of Moses* it is not hard to see how a kabbalistic-based text such as this that is devoted to goetia is all deceivingly making it look like a "Christian" practice. This deception is inherently why so many Christians today are believing that the goetia that has overtaken so many churches is perfectly biblical. The incorrectly exegeted and read Bible passages given above by so many people have given way to the above text from *The Sixth and Seventh Books of Moses* to become incorporated into church practice as a legitimate show of "faith". The problem is that by using Psalm 91, specifically here, in this manner many Christians are getting involved in the type of goetia and אוב forbidden by texts like Deuteronomy 18:11–12. Remember that in verse 12 that it was for these practices that Yahweh threw the Canaanites out of the land. God warned about such people in saying:

> Beware lest there be among you a man or woman or clan or tribe whose heart is turning away today from the LORD our God to go and serve the gods of those nations. Beware lest there be among you a root bearing poisonous and bitter fruit. (Deuteronomy 29:18 ESV)

Yet, many people in churches are doing these exact things forbidden by God and calling it "holy".

This faulty use of Psalm 91 does not end there. Many defend the use of Psalm 91 for exorcisms in their homes with other fallaciously exegeted biblical texts. Two other texts are from Exodus that are incorrectly used in the defense of Psalm 91.

> Go and select lambs for yourselves according to your clans, and kill the Passover lamb. Take a bunch of hyssop and dip it in the blood that is in the basin, and touch the lintel and the two doorposts with the blood that is in the basin. None of you shall go out of the door of his house until the morning. For the LORD will pass through to strike the Egyptians, and when he sees the blood on the lintel and on the two doorposts, the LORD will pass over the door and will not allow the destroyer to enter your houses to strike you. [...] At midnight the LORD struck down all the firstborn in the land of Egypt, from the firstborn of Pharaoh who sat on his throne to the firstborn of the captive who was in the dungeon, and all the firstborn of the livestock. (Exodus 12:21–23, 29 ESV)

> Then you shall take the anointing oil and anoint the tabernacle and all that is in it, and consecrate it and all its furniture, so that it may become holy. (Exodus 40:9 ESV)

Doing a straight reading the connection may not be clear. Different people within the charismatic, Prosperity, WOF and NAR movements will claim that the blood from Exodus 12 is equivalent to the oil used in Exodus 40. Somehow these same individuals will then attribute the tabernacle to being their physical homes and therefore pulling these texts out of context these fallacious exegetes somehow apply these texts to themselves. The reason these people use these texts in this way is because the desire to believe that the *demonic* will pass over their homes if it is made *holy* is something so magically enchanting that they need this rather than faith in God. Again, in relying on oil rather than God, these people are admitting that God is absent of the situation.

There is something unfortunately even worse. The fact that these false exegetes claim that the destroyer was demonic.

> The "destroyer" could be none other than the Angel of the Lord, revealed as the angel that causes death in such contexts as 2 Sam 24:16 and Isa 37:36. This angel directly represents God and is thus "the Angel Yahweh"—Yahweh manifesting himself in angelic form. God *personally* spared those who showed their trust in him by keeping the Passover regulations. He restrained the angel that would otherwise manifest his personal judgment against his

enemies.[60]

Keeping context in mind, Yahweh is the one that sent and *caused* all the plagues as part of his judgment on Egypt and the Egyptian chthonic gods. To send a demon to condemn their own spiritual beings in the context of the tenth plague would be contradictory. See Jesus' words in Mark 3:23–26:

> How can Satan cast out Satan? If a kingdom is divided against itself, that kingdom cannot stand. And if a house is divided against itself, that house will not be able to stand. And if Satan has risen up against himself and is divided, he cannot stand, but is coming to an end. (Mark 3:23–26 ESV)

The ten plagues of Exodus were not just on the Egyptians, but the goetic Egyptian gods as well. What we must take note of is that the "god" that was being judged in the tenth plague was in fact Pharoah himself. Egyptian Pharoah's were seen as the physical embodiment of the Egyptian god Horus. Therefore, that it was God's judgment against the Egyptian gods via *all* the plagues is made evident from Exodus 12:12, "on all the gods of Egypt I will execute judgments." (Exodus 12:12 ESV) With Yahweh executing these judgments, especially the last tenth plague, these fallacious exegetes are really arguing to anoint their homes so that Yahweh will pass over the house or be *exorcised* out of the home. The *destroyer* was not demonic. The *destroyer* was *Yahweh* himself.

Another fallacious assumption I have seen made on different social media platforms into this text is that the *destroyer* is the angel, Azrael. Please be aware that it is extremely dangerous to be asserting angel and demon names as real when they are *not* mentioned in the Bible. The name Azrael comes from Islam. Note the following:

> Azrael. Also pronounced "Izrael," this name is given to the Angel of Death in Muslim sources. Along with Gabriel, Michael, and Israfil, he is one of the four archangels. The Quran states that the Angel of Death will take every person and return them to God (Q 32:11), and Q 31:34 reports that only God knows where each person will be taken by death. Several of the stories of the prophets describe encounters between prophets and the Angel of Death.[61]

Some have attempted to say that Azrael is another form of the kabbalistic angel, Azriel. However, since this is a kabbalistic name for an angel, and not a biblical one, both names of Azriel and Azrael *must* be rejected since they are goetic in origin. Another counter argument is that the angel Ezrael from *The Apocalypse of Peter*, an apocryphal New Testament text, is another form of Azrael. "Ezrael the angel of wrath shall bring men and women, [...] the half of their bodies burning, and cast them into a place of darkness, even the hell of men."[62] But what this text says about Ezrael and what is said about Azrael being the angel of death before God are clearly not the same "angel". Coming from a non-biblical text, Ezrael can only be considered a goetic name and *not* the name of a real angel. Since all these names are goetic in nature, none are appropriate for use in Christian theology or church practice.

Answering the objection from the text of Exodus 40 in that the person's home that got anointed by oil is somehow "holy" and therefore will be avoided by demons is just as easy. Jesus, God himself on earth, was approached by the demonic and the demonic even

60. Stuart, *Exodus*, p. 289.

61. Scott B. Noegel and Brannon M. Wheeler, *The A to Z of prophets in Islam and Judaism* (Plymouth, United Kingdom: The Scarecrow Press, Inc., 2010), p. 47.

62. Montague Rhodes James, *The Apocryphal New Testament: being the Apocryphal Gospels, Acts, Epistles, and Apocalypses* (Oxford, England: Clarendon Press, 1924), p. 515.

spoke to him proclaiming who Jesus was (God) without any hesitation. The demonic could approach the person of Jesus with his entire godhood intact in human flesh. Jesus was the most holy human and material being to have ever walked the earth and the demonic had no problem approaching him at all. The idea that a home is made "holy" by anointing it with oil which makes it unapproachable to the demonic is biblically absurd.

Observing all of the above it is not difficult to see that the goetic way that Psalm 91 has been used in churches today is completely flawed. The reason that Psalm 91 has been adopted in this way is because of the removal of reliance on Christ as the fulfillment of Psalm 91 and the placement of ourselves in Christ's place. Like the Egyptians of Isaiah 19 and the Israelites of Exodus 32, relying on anyone other than Christ/Yahweh and replacing him with goetic spirits and/or ourselves was worse than a death sentence that would ultimately bring God's judgment.

The Reality Behind Gideon's Fleece In Judges 6:36–40

Next, I will move on to other texts that are commonly used by Christians in defense of practices that are goetic in nature. The first is Judges 6:36–40

> Then Gideon said to God, "If you will save Israel by my hand, as you have said, behold, I am laying a fleece of wool on the threshing floor. If there is dew on the fleece alone, and it is dry on all the ground, then I shall know that you will save Israel by my hand, as you have said." And it was so. When he rose early next morning and squeezed the fleece, he wrung enough dew from the fleece to fill a bowl with water. Then Gideon said to God, "Let not your anger burn against me; let me speak just once more. Please let me test just once more with the fleece. Please let it be dry on the fleece only, and on all the ground let there be dew." And God did so that night; and it was dry on the fleece only, and on all the ground there was dew. (Judges 6:36–40 ESV)

The first error that people make when using this text as a defense for asking God for a sign is that this event happens at an unknown amount of time *after* the angel of Lord spoke to Gideon face-to-face in chapter 6:11–24. Between the time that the angel of the Lord had appeared to Gideon until Gideon tested Yahweh with the fleece was the tearing down of the family's altar to Baal. The testing of the fleece happened *after* the appearance of Yahweh before Gideon which sets this event at a separate and later time than the visit under the tree and the offering at the altar.

Taking note of the reality of Gideon's heart in this situation we see that contrary

> to popular interpretation, this text has nothing to do with discovering or determining the will of God. The divine will is perfectly clear in his mind (v. 16). Gideon's problem is that with his limited experience with God he cannot believe that God always fulfills his word. The request for signs is not a sign of faith but of unbelief. Despite being clear about the will of God, being empowered by the Spirit of God, and being confirmed as a divinely chosen leader by the overwhelming response of his countrymen to his own summons to battle, he uses every means available to try to get out of the mission to which he has been called. The narrator apparently recognizes the incongruity of the situation by deliberately referring to God by the generic designation Elohim rather than his personal covenant name Yahweh. Apparently Gideon has difficulty distinguishing between Yahweh, the God of the Israelites, and God in a general sense. The remarkable fact is that God responds to his tests. He is more anxious to deliver Israel than to quibble with this man's *semipagan notions of deity*. (italics mine)[63]

63. Daniel Isaac Block, *Judges, Ruth, volume 6, The New American Commentary* (Nashville, Tennessee: Broadman & Holman Publishers, 1999), pp. 272–273.

Understanding that Gideon has a "semi-pagan" notion of deity helps to explain why in Deuteronomy Yahweh commands that you

> shall not put the LORD your God to the test, as you tested him at Massah. You shall diligently keep the commandments of the LORD your God, and his testimonies and his statutes, which he has commanded you. And you shall do what is right and good in the sight of the LORD, that it may go well with you, and that you may go in and take possession of the good land that the LORD swore to give to your fathers by thrusting out all your enemies from before you, as the LORD has promised. (Deuteronomy 6:16–19 ESV)

While this text is famous for being quoted in the second temptation of Jesus, Gideon is also showing that it was not soon after the crossing of the Jordan River that the nation of Israel as a whole began to fail the covenant agreements in Deuteronomy. Understanding how Judges is considered the second book of Deuteronomistic History[64] that shows the descent of Israel until the rise of King David is critical. After making the connection to the Deuteronomistic History, the order of the book of Judges shows its importance. If you go to the last Judges story of Samson, you will note that Samson, of the tribe of Dan, takes place in the southern end of the settled land. Dan by this time in the story had settled in the northern area of Israel because they were unable to force the Philistines out of the land that the tribe of Dan had been allotted in the book of Joshua. The reason Samson's story is at the end of the book is because the book is noting that the apostacy in Israel was getting worse. Even though the worst of the judges was probably more likely one of the earlier judges, the overall moral degeneracy of the nation was increasing. The way that the book of Judges is laid out shows that "with time the apostasy of the nation intensified."[65] With the story of Gideon falling in the exact middle of the Judges chronicle, it shows a drastic change in the moral state of the nation as a whole.

So, what is the significance of the fleece when it comes to goetia? In his book *Greek and Roman Necromancy* Daniel Ogden translates a few Greek texts to show the significance of the fleece in their necromantic rituals. In the only translation of Ogden's I will give here, Ogden states that "they sacrifice a ram, spread out the fleece, and go to sleep waiting for the revelation in a dream."[66]

> Souls of the dead will come forth.
> Then indeed I urged my companions and called them to action.
> "Sheep, indeed, lying slain in the pitiless bronze."
> "Having *flayed their skin*, to offer prayers to the gods,"
> "To the mighty Hades and to the praised Persephone." (italics and translation mine)[67]

This quote is from Homer's *The Odyssey* book 10 lines 530–534. Note the italicized words "flayed their skin", the word there is δείραντας (deirantas) which comes from the word δέρω (derō) which is translated as "skin, flay, of animals, […] to have one's skin flayed off".[68] The same word is used in the following text again indicated by the italicized words.

64. Block, *Judges*, p. 64.

65. Block, *Judges*, p. 39.

66. Daniel Ogden, *Greek and Roman Necromancy* (Princeton, New Jersey: Princeton University Press, 2001), p. 86.

67. Homer, *The Odyssey*, 10.530–534. Greek text pulled from: Homer, "The Odyssey with an English Translation by A.T. Murray, PH.D. in Two Volumes" (Cambridge, MA., Harvard University Press; London, William Heinemann, Ltd., 1919).

68. Liddell, *Greek*, p. 380.

"I turned around, and having taken the apples, I cut them up."
Into the pit, the dark blood flows; and they gathered.
Souls beneath Erebus of the dead who have perished.
"Nymphs and young men, and the very patient old men."
"Virgin and tender, they possess a new-born spirit."
Many, struck by bronze-tipped spears,
"Men of war, equipped with battle gear."
"Those who were many, coming from different places, were hovering around the pit."
With a divine cry; but a pale fear seized me.
Then I urged my companions and commanded them.
"The sheep, which were indeed lying slaughtered with cruel bronze,"
"Having *flayed their skin*, to offer prayers to the gods."
"To the mighty Hades and to revered Persephone."
But he, drawing a sharp sword from beside his thigh...
I was, nor did I allow the lifeless heads of the dead.
"Let us go closer to the blood, before we inquire of Tiresias."
"The first soul that came was that of Elpenor, a companion."
"For I have not yet been buried beneath the broad earth."
For we left our bodies in the hall of Circe.
Unwept and unburied, since another pain was pressing.
I wept upon seeing him and felt compassion in my heart. (italics and translation mine)[69]

While critique may come that this is just an epic poem telling a mythological story, in the world of ancient Greece, these tales were more than just myths but were stories about the gods and the supernatural realities around them. As the text from the translated text from Ogden shows, even the idea of using a piece of "flayed skin" or a "fleece" from sheep are used in goetic rituals to draw/conjure up the dead and even the gods like Hades and Persephone.

But the king, troubled by the oracles of Faunus,
fateful; when he was born, he went to the groves under the trees
consults Albunea, the most sacred of the forests
the fountain sounds and breathes out fiercely darkly.
Hence the nations of Italy, and all the region of Oenotria
in their doubts they ask for answers; give it to the priest
When he took Caesar's sheep under the silence of the night
He lay down in layers of skins and went to sleep.
In many ways he sees strange flying images
And he hears the various voices of the gods and enjoys them
Avernis is brought to the Acheron by the colloquium and at the bottom.
Here and then the father himself asked for Latin answers
a hundred woollens he made in the manner of a bident
and the rest of these lay behind the layers
to the *fleece*: suddenly from a deep place a voice was heard in the forest:
"Do not seek to associate with the Latins the woman born of wedlock,
O my descendants, prepare your chambers or believe:
Foreigners will come to the race who are of our blood
let their name be borne in the stars, and their descendants from their lineage
all under the feet, through which the Sun both recedes
he looks at the ocean, and the kings will see."
These were the answers of Father Faunus, and the admonitions of silence (italics and translation mine)[70]

69. Homer, *The Odyssey*, 11.35–55.

70. Virgil, Aeneid, 7.81–101. Latin text from: P. Vergilius (Virgil) Maro, "Bucolics, Aeneid, and Georgics Of Vergil," ed. J. B. Greenough (Ginn & Co., 1900).

The word "fleece" that is italicized is the Latin word "velleribus" that comes from the word "vellus" meaning: "*wool shorn off, a fleece* [...] *A sheepskin, pelt, woolly*"[71] which again shows the fact that the Roman era (that was also pushing Hellenization), along with the Minoan empire that preceded the Greek empire, used the fleece of sheep for goetic/necromantic purposes in divining the will of, and to get a glimpse of the future from, the chthonic deities, demons, dead and other possible spirits.

Once we understand the Minoan religious context that existed at the time of the book of Judges, as well as the goetic practices that were common in the Ancient Near East and that Daniel Isaac Block identified that what Gideon was doing was thinking of Yahweh in a semi-pagan way (see above), it helps us to understand that what Gideon was doing with the fleece was goetic and *anti*-biblical in every way. The argument that we can "put out a fleece" as Gideon did is a request to justify goetia in our Christian walks, a practice that many Christians ignorantly support because relying on God and having faith in Yahweh's will for us is something many people do not want to accept.

The question that will inevitably come up is the mention of Gideon's faith in Hebrews 11. While the end of Gideon's story ends in apostacy, the rebuke always comes that Gideon was mentioned in Hebrews 11, therefore everything Gideon did before his apostacy was justified. However, Raymond Brown explains that in

> those days, instead of obeying God's voice, or honouring a devoted leader, everyone did 'what was right in his own eyes'. *It was a period of backsliding and apostasy*. The devout minority recalled the stories of God's power in days gone by to bring the people renewed confidence in the God who could deliver them. Yet for the Judges as well as for David after them, faith was not stereotyped. *God works as he pleases and uses whom he will.*
>
> All six men were vastly different in human personality, social circumstances and spiritual opportunity, yet in various ways God used them. He did not press them into an identical mould or demand the same response from each of them. [...] *He delights in choosing those who seem most unsuitable and using those who seem most rebellious.*[72]

Looking at this explanation it is not hard to argue that Gideon, while showing his failures very close to the start of his narrative, was still used by Yahweh anyway, because like Nebuchadnezzar and Cyrus, both of whom were extremely evil men, Gideon was used by Yahweh for Yahweh's purposes. This shows that Yahweh can still be glorified in the way he uses wicked/evil men to bring about his will/plan. Since Solomon's repentance was never directly shown in either books of Kings or Chronicles but was attested to by his writing of Ecclesiastes later in his life, Gideon may have repented sometime before he died in his apostacy. In the end we will never know if Gideon repented, but the text of Hebrews 11 is not always meaning saving faith, but it was a faith that allowed these men to trust that Yahweh knew what he was doing in that moment, even if someone like Gideon later apostacized.

Explaining the Goetic Controversy Around 1 Corinthians 14 and "Angel Tongues"

The question about spiritual gifts has been a hotly debated topic since the late 19th century when Pentecostalism and the first roots of the Word-of-Faith movements started with

71. Charlton T. Lewis, *An Elementary Latin Dictionary* (Medford, Massachusetts: American Book Company, 1890).

72. Raymond Brown, *The Message of Hebrews: Christ above All, The Bible Speaks Today* (Downers Grove, Illinois: InterVarsity Press, 1988), p. 221.

the emergence of Aimee Semple McPherson. Although her "tongues" proved to be false, and the Chinese characters she claimed to be able to write without knowing the Chinese language or alphabet have proven to be random scribbles and not Chinese in any way, many people still claim that what she claimed were "spiritual gifts" were in fact real. McPherson's motives have been shown to be financial in origin since she was married a couple times after her "gifts" manifestations and her marriages were initially to poorer men. However, McPherson's fame later drew more wealthy men to her in her third and fourth marriages. Considering the charismatic, Prosperity, WOF, and NAR's hard stance on marriage, it is strange that they would find so much validation in a woman that proved to be an adulteress by WOF and charismatic standards. This shows that marriage standards by these groups often prove to be hypocritical. These hypocritical standards are also shown in the case of Carl Lentz who committed adultery while pastoring the Hillsong campus in New York City. In 2023, Lentz was hired by Mike Todd as a "strategist" which is still a form of a ministry position Lentz is not qualified to fulfill.

While this is all character based in origin the reality is that McPherson was proven to be a con-woman. Yet, regardless of the verifiable evidence about McPherson, many people still use her as an example and continue to push her false manifestations of tongues even further. Many of her supporters have pushed the tongues issue still further to include what are called "angel tongues" which are languages of a supernatural origin which no one is able to understand.

The question is: are these tongues, in their proper context, biblical? Here is the text that is often used as evidence for the verification of "angel tongues".

> Pursue love, and earnestly desire the spiritual gifts, especially that you may prophesy. For one who speaks in a tongue speaks not to men but to God; for no one understands him, but he utters mysteries in the Spirit. On the other hand, the one who prophesies speaks to people for their upbuilding and encouragement and consolation. The one who speaks in a tongue builds up himself, but the one who prophesies builds up the church. Now I want you all to speak in tongues, but even more to prophesy. The one who prophesies is greater than the one who speaks in tongues, unless someone interprets, so that the church may be built up.
>
> Now, brothers, if I come to you speaking in tongues, how will I benefit you unless I bring you some revelation or knowledge or prophecy or teaching? If even lifeless instruments, such as the flute or the harp, do not give distinct notes, how will anyone know what is played? And if the bugle gives an indistinct sound, who will get ready for battle? So with yourselves, if with your tongue you utter speech that is not intelligible, how will anyone know what is said? For you will be speaking into the air. There are doubtless many different languages in the world, and none is without meaning, but if I do not know the meaning of the language, I will be a foreigner to the speaker and the speaker a foreigner to me. So with yourselves, since you are eager for manifestations of the Spirit, strive to excel in building up the church.
>
> Therefore, one who speaks in a tongue should pray that he may interpret. For if I pray in a tongue, my spirit prays but my mind is unfruitful. What am I to do? I will pray with my spirit, but I will pray with my mind also; I will sing praise with my spirit, but I will sing with my mind also. Otherwise, if you give thanks with your spirit, how can anyone in the position of an outsider say "Amen" to your thanksgiving when he does not know what you are saying? For you may be giving thanks well enough, but the other person is not being built up. I thank God that I speak in tongues more than all of you. Nevertheless, in church I would rather speak five words with my mind in order to instruct others, than ten thousand words in a tongue.
>
> Brothers, do not be children in your thinking. Be infants in evil, but in your thinking be mature. In the Law it is written, "By people of strange tongues and by the lips of foreigners will I speak to this people, and even then they will not listen to me, says the Lord." Thus tongues are a sign not for believers but for unbelievers, while prophecy is a sign not for unbelievers but for believers. If, therefore, the whole church comes together and all speak in

tongues, and outsiders or unbelievers enter, will they not say that you are out of your minds? But if all prophesy, and an unbeliever or outsider enters, he is convicted by all, he is called to account by all, the secrets of his heart are disclosed, and so, falling on his face, he will worship God and declare that God is really among you.

What then, brothers? When you come together, each one has a hymn, a lesson, a revelation, a tongue, or an interpretation. Let all things be done for building up. If any speak in a tongue, let there be only two or at most three, and each in turn, and let someone interpret. But if there is no one to interpret, let each of them keep silent in church and speak to himself and to God. Let two or three prophets speak, and let the others weigh what is said. If a revelation is made to another sitting there, let the first be silent. For you can all prophesy one by one, so that all may learn and all be encouraged, and the spirits of prophets are subject to prophets. For God is not a God of confusion but of peace. (1 Corinthians 14:2–25 ESV)

First off, note that in verse one that Paul elevates *prophecy* over *tongues*. Many supporters of tongues however elevate *tongues* over *prophesy*. Next, Paul mentions that someone who speaks in tongues speaks to God and not to people by uttering mysteries in the Spirit. Following that sentence, Paul mentions the superiority of prophecy in that the church community is built up while the person speaks in tongues builds up himself. The word that Paul uses for *himself* is the Greek word ἑαυτοῦ (eautou) which is said in an accusative way. This should be notable in the way Paul says this. Unlike English where more words would be needed to note the strong emphasis on a person or action, Greek is more elegant in using one word to emphasize what would take an entire set of sentences in English. The accusative here is not in a "negative" way as we understand "accusing" but it is more of a singling out and a speaking directly to rather than in a "by the way" sort of speech.

Understanding how much Paul is singling out the "himself" here, we can note the presence of community versus individual tension from the beginning of the Bible until the end. From Genesis 2:18, Yahweh states that it is not *good* for Adam (people) to be *alone*. This should be an indicator that God has always meant for people, whether they believe in God or not, to be in a community. This is evident all over the world as people left in isolation often start to exhibit strong anti-social behaviours that can even become dangerous to society or even the person themselves.

Also, we need to note that Paul refers to the *entire* church as the bride of Christ, and not just each individual believer. (2 Corinthians 11:2–3, Ephesians 5:25–33) This shows that the church is always in a community and not living a one-on-one life between themselves and God. Even the other references to spiritual gifts in Romans 12, 1 Corinthians 12, Ephesians 4, and 1 Peter 4 are always referring to the spiritual gifts as a gift to the community and not just the individual believer. The text in 1 Corinthians 14:4 about building up himself with tongues is an odd divergence from the other texts. Using proper hermeneutics, we must take note of this divergence between both Paul and Peter about how the gift of tongues *only* builds up the individual believer. Since this is the only time in the context of spiritual gifts that self-edification is mentioned, we must note that *building yourself up is* not *a good thing*. I have seen people again on social media (X, formerly Twitter) try to claim that reading the Bible is for self-edification to support speaking in "angel tongues" as a form of self-edification that is good and biblical. Again, as this introduction is showing, all that does is place *yourself* at the centre of the Bible and *removes* Christ from the central theme of the entire Bible. Since there is always a conflict between community, which is good and individualism, which is seen as bad, we must conclude that edification of self via tongues, is an evil act and not justified by this text in 1 Corinthians 14.

Interestingly Mark Taylor says that the

> broader argument suggests that Paul is not commending the use of tongues as a means of self-edification, which would not only counter the recurring emphasis on "others"; it would contradict the purpose of spiritual gifts, which are given for the common good (12:7). Paul is not expressing contempt for tongues in 14:4 but rather stating a fact concerning uninterpreted tongues as he does in 14:2. It is the reality that no one but God understands uninterpreted tongues and that no one is edified except the speaker that meets with Paul's disapproval. Paul's argument allows that tongues may be expressed in prayer and praise to God in corporate worship, but he also insists that intelligibility is essential to edification when so expressed (14:13–17), which raises doubts about incomprehensible private tongues as a means of self-edification. If intelligibility is essential to edification corporately (14:6–19), why would unintelligibility be acceptable privately if Paul is conceding that the one who speaks in tongues edifies himself in a positive sense? In other words, if uninterpreted tongues cannot edify the church, then how can tongues edify the individual privately apart from comprehension? Or to state the question in reverse, if unintelligible tongues can edify the individual why not also the whole church? The notion of incomprehensible tongues as private, edifying prayer runs counter to Paul's argument as a whole and to the corporate purpose and function of spiritual gifts.[73]

Likewise, Leon Morris says

> Paul does not deny that 'tongues' have a value for edification. But (unless interpreted) they profit only the person who exercises the gift, whereas *he who prophesies* builds up the whole church. There can be no doubting which of the two acts is done in love. (italics original)[74]

Putting both Taylor and Morris's comments on verse 4 together, it shows that self-edification is both *selfish* and *unloving*. Also, what can be noted is that people that claim to be speaking in "tongues" in private are claiming that because they are "in the spirit" when doing this that they somehow believe their prayers will have some more "force", "power" or "faith" to make them happen. Since the false use of tongues is being used in this way, it is in fact pointing to a goetic and occult use of this practice.

The community versus individual tension is shown even more in further verses from 1 Corinthians 14; in verse 5 "unless someone interprets, so the church may be built up," or verse 6, "if I come to you speaking in tongues, how will I benefit you unless I bring you some revelation of knowledge or prophecy or teaching?" continuing in verse 9, "[s]o with yourselves, if with your tongue you utter speech that is not intelligible, how will anyone know what is said?" What is even more condemning are verses 22, and 23, "[t]hus tongues are a sign not for believers but for unbelievers. If, therefore, the whole church comes together and all speak in tongues, and outsiders or unbelievers enter, will they not say that you are out of your minds?" (ESV) Even the manifestation of tongues in Acts 2 states that "we hear them telling in our own tongues the mighty works of God." (Acts 2:11 ESV) If outsiders do *not understand* what is being said, it is a sign of confusion and madness and *not a true sign of the presence of the Holy Spirit*. This is again shown in Paul's statement in verses 10–11, "There are doubtless many different languages in the world, and *none is without meaning*, but if I do not know the meaning of the language, I will be a foreigner to the speaker and the speaker a foreigner to me." (italics mine; 1 Corinthians 14:10–11 ESV) Paul is directly saying that *true* tongues are languag-

73. Mark Taylor, *1 Corinthians*, editor E. Ray Clendenen, *volume 28, The New American Commentary* (Nashville, Tennessee: B&H Publishing Group, 2014), pp. 323–324.

74. Leon Morris, *1 Corinthians: An Introduction and Commentary, volume 7, Tyndale New Testament Commentaries* (Downers Grove, Illinois: InterVarsity Press, 1985), p. 184.

es that are known in the world. There is no evidence in this text that the reference to "angels" and their tongues in 1 Corinthians 13:1 that the angels speak any kind of unknown "heavenly" language different from ones known on earth. Keeping this text in context then, with 1 Corinthians 14 following chapter 13, tongues must be understood as *known earthly* languages and does not give credit to the belief that "angels" have their own language. Legitimate tongues within the context of this section of 1 Corinthians are languages that can be understood by people not only in the church, but also by unbelievers outside the church. Tongues were never meant for a select few inside the church walls that would take them as a special sign to that single congregation alone. Neither were tongues ever meant to be used in individual prayer without anyone else present.

Considering the topic of this introduction being one of goetia/necromancy, the question will come of what these "angel tongues" have to do with goetia? Several sources inform us of the relevance of the issue. In referring to a kabbalistic exorcism technique, in his book *Between Worlds: Dybbuks, Exorcists, and Early Modern Judaism*, J. H. Chajes states that the exorcism in question

> is more or less understood by the kabbalistic exorcist and, given its effectiveness, by the spirit it addresses. It is not, however, an ordinary human language and could not be fathomed by most victims or onlookers. And most of this kabbalistic "demon language" would have been whispered into the ear of the victim rather than intoned aloud.[75]

The *PGM* mentioned above also reference several incantations with incomprehensible words. Of multiple examples here is one:

> This is the spell spoken [seven times seven] to Helios as an adjuration of the assistant: "ORI PI … AMOUNTE AINTHYPH PICHAROUR RAIAL KARPHIOUTH YMOU ROTHIRBAN OCHANAU MOUNAICHANAPTA/ZŌ ZŌN TAZŌTAZŌ PTAZŌ MAUIAS SOUŌRI SOUŌ ŌOUS SARAPTOUMI SARACHTHI A … RICHAMCHŌ BIRATHAU ŌPHAU PHAUŌ DAUA AUANTŌ ZOUZŌ ARROUZŌ ZOTOUAR THŌMNAŌRI AYŌI PTAUCHARĒBI AŌUOSŌBIAU PTABAIN AAAAAAA AEĒIOYŌYŌOIĒEA CHACHACH CHACHACH CHARCHARACHACH AMOUN Ō ĒI / IAEŌBAPHR GNEMOUNOTHILARIKRIPHIAEYEAIPHIRKIRALITHON OMENERPHABŌEAI CHATHACH PHNESCHĒR PHICHRŌ PHNYRŌ PHŌCHŌCHOCH IARBATHA GRAMME PHIBAŌCHNĒMEŌ." This is the spell spoken seven times seven to Helios.[76]

That entire quoted text of all capitalized words is all non-sensical and is not any kind of known language. Commenting on the use of texts like these, Hans Deiter Betz states that this "type of magician no longer understood the old languages, although he used remnants of them in transcription."[77] Considering the quote from Chajes and Betz, these were never *old languages* but were always languages steeped in goetia. Likewise, the "angel tongues" that many in certain church movements attempt to fallaciously defend are goetic in nature and are in no way biblical. More so, with the knowledge that goetia and the *PGM* in particular were being used during the time that Paul was writing to the Corinthian church, ironically in Greece, sounding like the goetic's outside the church walls that were actively deceiving people was not a good practice. The church was to do better which required the languages to be *known* languages that could be interpreted at the

75. J. H. Chajes, *Between Worlds: Dybbuks, Exorcists, and Early Modern Judaism* (Philadelphia, Pennsylvania: University of Pennsylvania Press, 2003), p. 77.

76. E. N. O'Neil, "PGM I, 42–195", in *The Greek Magical Papyri in Translation Including the Demotic Spells* editor Hans Deiter Betz (Chicago, Illinois: The University of Chicago Press, 1986), p. 6.

77. Hans Deiter Betz, *The Greek Magical Papyri in Translation Including the Demotic Spells* (Chicago, Illinois: The University of Chicago Press, 1986), p. xlvi.

moment they were given.

Again, on social media platforms, some have criticized these facts because when that person read a text like this, because *they* could not make it out, it meant it was nonsense. The truth is however, that if that person could not make out what someone was saying "in tongues" during a church service, and this person then tries to say that these "tongues" are "legitimate", the person is showing themselves to be a hypocrite.[78]

Showing the Belief That Children Can See Demons Is Not Biblical

The next goetic belief that many in churches believe is factual is that children are able to see demons while adults are not as likely to. From the book *Pentecostalism and Witchcraft*

> [w]e cannot hide anymore! Where will you hide now? There is no place to hide. If you do anything not good, if you think badly about another man, steal or have *posen*, the children will tell you right away now. Because they can see it. (italics original)[79]

With *posen* indicating witchcraft and the demonic associated with witchcraft, the belief that children somehow are able to see things like evil spirits/demons is an idea that needs justification. Unfortunately, there are no biblical texts to prove that children are able to see spirits more naturally than adults. The reality is that adults saw angels much more, but there was never any visible sight of a manifested demon outside of possession in the entire Bible by anyone other than Jesus. (Luke 10:18)

The *PGM* again show us the goetic nature of the belief that children are able to see the demonic: "Oracle of Sarapis, [by means of] a boy, by means of a lamp, saucer and bench: 'I call upon you, Zeus, Helios, Mithra, Sarapis, unconquered one.'"[80] Again "Divination by means of a boy: After you have laid [him] on the ground, speak, and a dark-colored boy will appear to him."[81] Ogden agrees with this observation. "It becomes clear from these [*PGM*] in particular that the observation of the bowl [for divination] was often performed by a boy-medium, probably under hypnosis."[82] Likewise, later in the Early Tudor period of England, Frank Klaassen and Sharon Hubbs Wright state that with "Wilkinson [a known necromancer] claims to have been involved in the world of clerical necromancy from his childhood, when he was used as a child-scryer"[83] The connection of children being able to see the demonic/spiritual more easily than adults is drawn from goetia/necromancy and not from the Bible. The most notable child-scryer and diviner of our current day and age is Margaret MacDonald from 1861 when she claimed to have

78. In all of the cases of these mentions of social media accusations, the handles and names of all of these accounts have proven to be from anonymous, ghost or shadow accounts (accounts that do not show their real face or name for the sake of coming after other people). Therefore, there is no need to reference the statement since no one knows who these people are anyway.

79. Tom Bratrud, "Chapter 9 Spiritual War: Anointing Ahamb Island" in *Pentecostalism and Witchcraft: Spiritual Warfare in Africa and Melanesia*, editors Knut Rio, Michelle MacCarthy, and Ruy Blanes (Ingersoll, Ontario: Devoted Publishing, 2023), p. 225.

80. W. C. Grese, "PGM V. 1–53", in *The Greek Magical Papyri in Translation Including the Demotic Spells* editor Hans Deiter Betz (Chicago, Illinois: The University of Chicago Press, 1986), p. 101.

81. W. C. Grese, "PGM VII. 348–58", in *The Greek Magical Papyri in Translation Including the Demotic Spells* editor Hans Deiter Betz (Chicago, Illinois: The University of Chicago Press, 1986), p. 127.

82. Ogden, *Necromancy*, p. xxvii.

83. Frank Klaassen, Sharon Hubbs Wright, *The Magic of Rogues: Necromancers in Early Tudor England* (University Park, Pennsylvania: The Pennsylvania State University Press, 2021), p. 12.

seen visions of the "rapture".

The Truth About 3 am and "Angel Visitations" At That Time

The last piece of goetic beliefs in the church that I will show here is the errant belief that God has a special interest in making visible manifestations of himself or of angels at three o'clock in the morning. Note what one of the most well-known NAR teachers has to say about an occurrence he had at three o'clock in the morning.

> The evening before was glorious. We were having meetings with a good friend and prophet, Dick Joyce. The year was 1995. At the end of the meeting, I prayed for a friend who was having difficulty experiencing God's presence. I told him that I felt God was going to surprise him with an encounter that could come in the middle of the day, or even at *3 a.m.* When the power fell on me that night, I looked at the clock. It was *3 a.m.*, exactly. I knew I had been set up.
>
> For months I had been asking God to give me more of Him. I wasn't sure of the correct way to pray, nor did I understand the doctrine behind my request. All I knew was I was hungry for God. It had been my constant cry day and night.
>
> This divine moment was glorious, but not pleasant. At first I was embarrassed, even though I was the only one who knew I was in that condition. As I lay there, I had a mental picture of me standing before my congregation, preaching the Word as I loved to do. But I saw myself with my arms and legs flailing about as though I had serious physical problems. The scene changed—I was walking down the main street of our town, in front of my favorite restaurant, again arms and legs moving about without control.
>
> I didn't know of anyone who would believe that this was from God. I recalled Jacob and his encounter with the angel of the Lord. He limped for the rest of His life. And then there was Mary, the mother of Jesus. She had an experience with God that not even her fiancée believed, although a visit from an angel helped to change his mind. As a result she bore the Christ-child...and then bore a stigma for the remainder of her days as the mother of the illegitimate child. It was becoming clear; the favor of God sometimes looks different from the perspective of earth than from Heaven. My request for more of God carried a price.[84]

This seems like a very strange experience. While many are looking for existential moments to affirm their beliefs, the reality is that there is a much more sinister goetic belief at work here.

People that were involved in the occult often come out knowing about a time of night known as either "the witching hour" or "the bewitching hour". This time of night is believed to be a time when the "veil" between the physical world and the spirit world is at its weakest making it possible to have spirits cross from one world to the next and also make any ritual spells more powerful.

> The association of witches with midnight is rooted in folk beliefs that supernatural phenomena are most prevalent at certain times of the day and year. Much like seasonal events, such as the solstices and equinoxes, midnight was deemed to evoke magic, allowing for unpredictable and possibly malevolent happenings. It is said that during the witching hour the boundary between the living and the dead becomes blurred and the living are more sensitive to the spirits of the dead. Witches, sorcerers, and fairies were among the spirits and figures believed to have stronger powers during these times and to carry out their mischief or dark practices at night.[85]

---

84. Bill Johnson and Heidi Baker, *Hosting the Presence: Unveiling Heaven's Agenda* (Shippensburg, Pennsylvania: Destiny Image, 2012), Logos Edition.

85. René Ostberg, "witching hour", *Britannica*, last accessed October 6, 2024, https://www.britannica.

This all sounds strange that the night is wrongfully believed to have more "spiritual" power. When it comes to the time of the witching hour, Ostberg continues that some

> beliefs set the witching hour's boundaries between 12:00 am and 3:00 am or between 3:00 am and 4:00 am. Biblical references to the death of Jesus were calculated as having occurred at 3:00 pm. Accepting this calculation, the inversion or opposite of this time was then considered the "devil's hour."[86]

It is interesting to note that three in the morning is considered to be the "devil's hour". This belief is not directly tied to the goetic Minoan and Greek civilization. When we realize that the child of kabbalism, hermeticism, was a form of witchcraft that was adopted by Helena Blavatsky's *Theosophical Society*, we can then discover that Blavatsky took the Hindu pantheism and merged it with hermeticism. This merging brought in a lot of Far East Asian beliefs into the western form of occultism and into magical and goetic culture.

In an interview with a blood lab worker, Janet Carsten in her book *Blood Work: Life and Laboratories in Panang* shows us that "Sometimes still get feeling in this lab. In bewitching hour—3:00 a.m. or something. Some people more sensitive. In old lab heard similar stories. Here in new lab haven't heard any yet."[87] The rough English here is because the person being interviewed, "Sharon", is native to Malaysia and is trying to communicate in English. The chapter that this is quoted in is "Chapter 4: Ghosts, Food, and Relatedness" which proves the belief about three in the morning being a goetic time of day was brought over from nations like Malaysia and other Far East Asian regions. That more Far East Asian occult systems held to this belief is shown by Ōta Gyūichi.

> The Hour of the Ox, from one to three in the morning, is the witching hour, when one versed in the proper maledictory ritual might communicate with the demonic powers in order to cast a fatal curse on an object of hate or jealousy. That ritual is called *ushi no toki mairi*, ox-hour devotions; often, as here, the name of the hour alone is used to refer to the hoodoo. (italics original)[88]

This tale comes from ancient Japan showing that the idea of the "witching hour" as we believe it today comes from goetic beliefs in Japan, Malaysia and more countries of that area of the world. What all of this shows is that Johnson, along with many other Christians, have stopped relying on the Christ of the Bible by also giving into goetic beliefs about nighttime and more specifically about three in the morning. While this may seem like a weird conclusion to come to, we need to realize that the Bible never supports the idea that angels or Jesus are more likely to appear at three o'clock in the morning. Believing that this time of night has some special spiritual reality is relying on goetic beliefs and not the true word, Christ.

Some ex-occultists will correctly comment that the "witching hour" during their time in the occult was between 2:00 am and 4:00 am. The problem here was finding verifiable academic literature on the subject to confirm that time frame. Since the point of this section is to show what 3:00 am is within the realm of the occult, the fact that many in the occult refer to the "witching hour" as between 2:00 am and 4:00 am is effectively

com/topic/witching-hour.

86. Ostberg, "witching".

87. Janet Carsten, *Blood Work: Life and Laboratories in Penang* (Durham, North Carolina: Duke University Press, 2019), p. 190.

88. [Footnote 9] Ōta Gyūichi, *The Chronicle of Lord Nobunaga*, edited and translated by J.S.A Elisonas and J.P. Lamers (Leiden, Netherlands: Brill, 2011), p. 359.

irrelevant.

The Cold Hard Facts Of Gold

If this is all true, then why is this teaching and practice so common in many churches? Betz again gives us a picture into the ancient world about the goetia that was common back then.

> The answer appears to be that, in general, *people are not interested in whether or not magicians' promises come true. People want to believe, so they simply ignore their suspicions that magic may all be deception and fraud.* The enormous role deception plays in human life and society is well known to us. In many crucial areas and in many critical situations of life, deception is the only method that really works. As the Roman aphorism sum it up, "Mundus vult decipi, ergo decipiatur" ("*The world wishes to be deceived, and so it may be deceived*"). To an immeasurable extent, *people's lives carry on by what they decide they want to believe rather than by what they should believe or even know, by what appears to be real rather than by what is really real, by props and by fads, and by gobbledygook of this kind today and that kind tomorrow.*
>
> Magicians are those who have long ago explored these dimensions of the human mind. Kather than decrying the facts, they have exploited them. Magicians have known all along that people's religious need and expectations provide the greatest opportunity for the most effective of all deceptions. But instead of turning against religion, as the skeptics among the Greek and Roman philosophers did, the magicians made use of it. After all, magic is nothing but the art of making people believe that something is being done about those things in life about which we all know that we ourselves can do nothing.
>
> Magic is the art that makes people who practice it feel better rather than worse, that provides the illusion of security to the insecure, the feeling of help to the helpless, and the comfort of hope to the hopeless.
>
> Of course, it is all deception. But who can endure naked reality, especially when there is a way to avoid it? This is why magic has worked and continues to work, no matter what the evidence may be. Those whose lives depend on deception and delusion and those who provide them have formed a truly indissoluble symbiosis. Magic makes an unmanageable life manageable for those who believe in it, and a profession *profitable* for those who practice the art. (italics mine)[89]

Seeing the above, people are so desperate that they will believe in anything that makes them feel better. Even if what is being taught is proven to be erroneous biblically, the reality is that the person who believes all this has both denied Jesus' kingship over the earth in the here and now and also placed themselves in the place of Christ as their own god and king. In doing so, these people have chosen what is preferrable rather than what the Bible commands. The charismatic, Prosperity, WOF, and NAR churches, as the last sentence of the Betz quote above shows, are profiting financially from this openness to desperate false hope.

Betz, a page before the above quote states what it is that people that are either practicing goetia or hiring a necromancer to perform magic for them are hoping for: "Apart from this fascination with the control of death and the underworld powers, there is an equally important fascination with the universe."[90] Again this shows that the serpents temptation in Genesis 3:5 that "you will be like God" is one of the reasons so many people are being willing deceived. These people are wanting this false truth because in the end, they are wanting to control the universe and become a god among many gods, or their own supreme god. The same lie has been pushed since the Garden of Eden

89. Betz, *Greek*, p. xlviii.
90. Betz, *Greek*, p. xlvii.

because it is such a successful lie. It is this lie of godhood that many charismatic, and all Prosperity, WOF and NAR churches are pushing every day, but they have twisted it to make it seem biblical. The whole act of "claiming" and "declaring" is no different than the goetic beliefs about controlling the chthonic realms and also the universe at large. By believing that they can "declare" or "claim" things into existence simply by "saying it aloud" these people that are *wanting to be deceived* are attempting to use goetia to alter the universe in *their own* favour.

This belief about using goetia for financial gain was still active in Tudor England as well. Going back to Klasssen's book, he states that, necromancers "provided a range of services, including identifying or locating thieves, finding lost or stolen property, curing illnesses, and *treasure hunting*." (italics mine)[91] In talking about Henry V's act against witchcraft in 1542, we need to realize that the act was

> never actually used against any magicians, the amount of attention it gives to *treasure hunters* reflects the broader relationship of magic and authority in the period. Prior to the witch trials in the 1560s, treasure hunting magic appeared more often in legal cases than any other form of magic except the identification of thieves. (italics mine)[92]

The use of goetic/necromantic magic for the purposes of "treasure hunting" and having a "profitable" practice is well attested in the pages of history. The fact that charismatic, Prosperity, WOF, and NAR churches have used the same tactic for the purposes of financial gain is not hard to see because of the open deception and the willingness of their followers to believe such falsehood. This willingness to believe such falsehood lies in the hopes that these churches are able to show the willingly deceived the process of gaining their own divinity. What is also interesting, going back to the quote with footnote 83 on p. 76 (this volume), the words "clerical necromancy" were used. When looking through different occult texts, and also the Roman Catholic acts of calling on dead saints and Mary, the fact that the very clerics that should have been protecting the church, this includes pastors who should have bee protecting their churches, have brought goetic practices into their churches for the purposes of bringing in the financial benefits associated with goetia. This clerical necromancy was present at the time that Martin Luther nailed his 95 theses to the door of the Schlosskirche church in Wittenburg, Germany. The "indulgences" that were being paid to supposedly move deceased loved ones from purgatory to heaven was nothing more than a goetic money making effort. Luther never mentioned the goetia that was involved here in his writings, but Luther still knew that something was wrong about it biblically. The same is still happening today in Roman churches with many other acts like rosaries and "hail Mary's". These acts that the papacy have their deceived faithful perform are nothing more than a goetic effort to elevate yourself from the pit, שאול, to heaven.

The Bible does have support for the wealth that magic, which in the times that the Bible was written was goetic in nature, could generate.

> Also many of those who were now believers came, confessing and divulging their practices. And a number of those who had practiced magic arts brought their books together and burned them in the sight of all. And they counted the value of them and found it came to fifty thousand pieces of silver. (Acts 19:18–19 ESV)

First, we should note that many people have attempted to claim that the reason these

91. Klaassen, *Magic*, p. 5.
92. Klaassen, *Magic*, p. 9.

ex-magicians burned their books was because the books would draw demonic spirits to them. There is absolutely no indication in this text, or others that are falsely pulled out of context, that inanimate objects are capable of drawing demonic spirits to a home. See the text below from the *PGM.*

> "I summon you, Headless One, who created earth and heaven, who created night and day, I you who created light and darkness; you are Osoronnophris whom none has ever seen; you arc Iabas; you arc Iapos; you have distinguished the just and the unjust; you have made female and male; I you have revealed seed and fruits; you have made men love each other and hate each other.
>
> [...]
>
> Preparation for the foregoing ritual: Write the formula on a new sheet of papyru, and after extending it from one / of your temples to the other, read the 6 names, while you face north saying,
>
> "Subject to me all daimons, I so that every daimon, whether heavenly or aerial or earthly or subterranean or terrestrial or aquatic, might be obedient to me and every enchantment and scourge which is from God." / And all daimons will be obedient to you.[93]

Note in this *PGM* ritual that the goeticist is "summoning" the "Headless One" for the purpose of ironically saving another person from another daimon/demon. However, note that the ritual is written down on a piece of papyrus and it is by that writing and reciting that the daimons/demons are able to come to the goeticist. This is where the idea that "occult" items or "un-Christian" items can draw demonic powers into someone's home comes from. This idea is diretly from goetia/the occult. There are many other *PGM* spells/rituals which state the same reality, but they are too numerous to mention here. People that will admit that this biblical text does not speak about the belief that keeping these items in your home will draw the demonic to the residence have still defended the belief saying that either people they know or even themselves, have "experienced" this "fact". Unfortunately, existentialism of this sort is what the goetic world wants you to believe. So, relying on existential evidence for something the Bible does not support, but texts like those in the *PGM* above do, is again wanting to believe something that is plainly false because in some way, it makes them not want to rely on Christ's ability to protect the home from inanimate objects and therefore needing to take measures for themselves. This belief about inanimate objects is the exact same belief that many believe that anointing their homes will make it too holy for the demonic to enter into. Inanimate objects do not cause sin. God is the only one who can decide if a demonic presence is due for punishment or even for testing (see Saul in 1 Samuel 17:15 and Job in Job 1–2).[94] In both these cases it is Yahweh that sent the demonic spirit, and not the items in the homes of the people afflicted with the demonic. In every case in the Bible of a demon oppressing a member of the covenant community (Israel pre-Christ, the Church after Christ) it is always Yahweh/God that sends the spirit and not an inanimate object, or even the person's sin in that moment.

Going back to the Acts 19:18–19 text there are some notable things to be aware of.

> The Ephesian abandonment of magic was not without some personal sacrifice. Their magical books must have been much like the papyrus collections that have been unearthed and are now on display in museums in Paris, Berlin, Rome, and London. All ancient books were

93. D. E. Aune, "PGM V. 96–172", in *The Greek Magical Papyri in Translation Including the Demotic Spells* editor Hans Deiter Betz (Chicago, Illinois: The University of Chicago Press, 1986), p. 103.

94. Also see my book: Anthony Uyl, *Biblical Demonology: Their Origins and Unwilling Role in Sanctification* (Ingersoll, Ontario, Canada: Devoted Publishing, 2022).

> expensive, but magical collections brought a considerable premium. Luke estimated the value of those burned in Ephesus at 50,000 pieces of silver. If the piece of silver concerned is the drachma, the most common Greek silver coin, that would come to about $35,000 in current silver value. Translated into terms of living standards, however, the sum was greater still, since the drachma was an average day's wage.[95]

John B. Polhill notes here the financial value of the texts themselves if the new Christians had simply sold them. Even if these new Christians had kept them, with what Betz had shown about how easy it was to profit from the texts, with these Ephesian Christians now plunging themselves into poverty in the first century world, the temptation to once again take up the goetic arts for a living would have been too tempting. To avoid the temptation, the new Christians burned their magic books. Earlier Polhill notes that "[m]agic was part of Ephesian culture".[96] To abandon such a lucrative career to be plunged into financial despair was a true sign that these new Ephesian Christians understood the gospel. This new understanding showed "the futility of pagan attempts to master evil spirits [that] led many of Paul's Ephesian converts to realize that the pagan magic to which they were still attached was both useless and sinful."[97] Just as in the ancient world, where goetia was a get-rich-quick career, the charismatic, Prosperity, WOF, and NAR movements have used goetia for the exact same purposes. The problem is that this "justified" use of goetia by the charismatic, Prosperity, WOF, and NAR movements is still just as "useless and sinful."

Conclusion

All of this information and study is undoubtedly heavy for many. For many years people in churches have been taught that goetia/necromancy is a part of the normal Christian life. All of that teaching, as the argument above shows, is all based on a willing misunderstanding of the religious context of the entire timespan that the Bible was written during and also a complete and again willing misunderstanding of what אוֹב (ob, necromancy) even is within the Bible itself. The final argument, shown by Betz shows why this unwilling understanding has existed for so long, people simply do not want to believe it. People want to believe what *they* want to believe, and it does not matter what the Bible, when properly exegeted, has to say about the issue. All of this shows that goetia is first about an interest in controlling the realms of Sheol/Underworld and the entire universe. This interest in goetia for use in Christian churches all goes back to the temptation of the serpent in Genesis 3:5, "you will be like God." Second, this desire to control the universe is not just about being a "god", but also the financial pillaging of those wanting to be deceived.

Starting out, the entire religious context of the entire time that the Bible was written during was shown. The reality is that the Minoan empire, which pre-dated the Greek empire, gave us the earliest *PGM* rituals that show the chthonic nature of their gods which helps us to understand how Yahweh's condemnation of אוֹב (ob, necromancy) includes any spirit whether angel, saint, Mary, demon or false god. Further biblical evidence from Isaiah 8 and Isaiah 19 that goetia is an outright admission of the refusal to rely on God is telling for us today.

The above has also shown the arguments supporting the practice of praying for angel

95. Polhill, *Acts*, pp. 405–406.

96. Polhill, *Acts*, p. 405.

97. I. Howard Marshall, *Acts: An Introduction and Commentary, volume 5, Tyndale New Testament Commentaries* (Downers Grove, Illinois: InterVarsity Press, 1980), p. 330.

protection are based on completely misunderstood and out of context parts of the Bible. In response I showed what those defenses are and the passages of the Bible they are drawn from and that in the end they all fail. The final part of this argument showed that asking for angels to protect us is a rejection of God and Christ in our lives because people are choosing to rely on a goetic spirit rather than God himself. As was shown, even ancient Israel in Exodus 33 would not accept an angel going with them and would not move forward until Yahweh himself came with them from Sinai. If Israel had moved on from Sinai, the people understood it was under a condemnation worse than death. That condemnation was that their God had abandoned them.

Further examples from many of the errant theological teachings about Jesus only doing his miracles as a man, as well as the charismatic, Prosperity, WOF, and NAR musicians Darren Whitehead and Chris Tomlin who have openly admitted to the reality that the Holy Spirit is not with them were given. This admittance is because they both believe that their music is what *allows* the Holy Spirit to come. The goetic meaning behind this belief is now made clear.

Afterwards, the text of Psalm 91 was fully exegeted to show that in every way it points to a fulfillment in Christ and is not a text for use in praying for angel protection, or for exorcising demons out of a persons' home with anointing oil. The occult connections from the Second Temple period within the Dead Sea Scrolls along with medieval and late Renaissance/Enlightenment texts also show that the goetic use of Psalm 91 was being carried forward into our current day.

Next, the use of Gideon and churches teaching it is appropriate to "put out a fleece" to ask God's will is rooted in ancient Minoan and Greco goetia. This belief is shown as errant once we understand the true heart of Gideon by keeping the text in context and also keeping the religious context in mind as well. Suggestions were also offered for why Gideon is mentioned in Hebrews 11 which range from that Gideon's repentance is not recorded, to the possibility that Hebrews 11 is not always an immediate indicator of salvific faith but a faith that God will do what he said he is going to do.

The topic of tongues is highly controversial in today's church, so I deal with this issue by relying on biblical evidence to see if there are such a thing as "angel tongues". Since the context of 1 Corinthians 14 shows that "angel tongues" are tongues that are *always known earthly languages* and not some mysterious language that is spoken in the spiritual "realm", it was next appropriate to show that the belief in angel/demon tongues is drawn from the *PGM* and also kabbalistic beliefs.

Next, I dealt with the belief that children can somehow see demons when adults cannot. The texts quoted show that there is no biblical support for that belief and that the belief that children are able to see demonic spirits is drawn from the *PGM* and likely other goetic texts.

Then, the false belief that angels and "Jesus" will come to believers at three o'clock in the morning was shown to be goetic in nature. There is no biblical evidence for that belief, and the evidence shows that this belief in that special time of night comes from the Far East Asian nations of Japan, Malaysia and more. In these nations the "witching/bewitching" hour is at its height at three o'clock in the morning and according to the occult it is when the veil between the spirit and physical worlds is weakest.

As a finalizing thought, I show that the use of goetia throughout history has always been a way to get-rich-quick. Even though many people knew it was all deceptive, the people wanted to believe in goetic intervention for the purposes of giving them what they believed they wanted, which is a false hope in something other than Christ. That false hope today inevitably results in people relying on the goetic/demonic rather than Christ.

Is there a biblical way forward from all this? First, we need to stop relying on existential feelings and affirmations to validate what *we want to believe*. If the biblical text, when properly exegeted via context, textual and historical (including cultural and religious), along with the use of the original languages, does not support these beliefs, simply accepting the beliefs as perfectly fine is not the biblical standard. The reason it is not the biblical standard is because we as faithful students of God's word should be asking where these beliefs come from. Instead of giving in to our feelings when we want to believe something, so who cares what the Bible says, we need to find out where these errant teachings are from.

Second, we need to start asking the questions about where these teachings are coming from when faulty theology, even heretical theology, and especially the sinful accumulation of money (having money is not inherently sinful) become forefront in a church's existence. Even when the congregants of such churches start to obsess over money and income of their spouses or potential spouses, we need to start asking questions about the validity of the church that person attends and also the validity of that person's faith in relying not on Christ but on beliefs that are goetic in nature.

Lastly, refuse to have anything to do with these movements. In Matthew 7 Jesus says to

> [b]eware of false prophets, who come to you in sheep's clothing but inwardly are ravenous wolves. You will recognize them by their fruits. Are grapes gathered from thornbushes, or figs from thistles? So, every healthy tree bears good fruit, but the diseased tree bears bad fruit. A healthy tree cannot bear bad fruit, nor can a diseased tree bear good fruit. Every tree that does not bear good fruit is cut down and thrown into the fire. Thus you will recognize them by their fruits. (Matthew 7:15–20 ESV)

Since the charismatic, Prosperity, WOF and NAR churches all have proven several times to have prophesied falsely, as the practice of goetia has proven to be used for false prophecy as well, the commands of Christ here are clear. The goetic beliefs which are revealed in this entire introduction shows that the "fruits" of these churches, even the ones that we deem "okay" are in fact "diseased". There can never be a truly "healthy" piece of fruit from a "diseased" tree, especially a tree/church diseased by goetic magic.

If we ever want to get the goetia out of our churches that has taken over it in a quick and theologically violent way, we need to do as Christ commands and cut the diseased tree down. The only way to do that is to have nothing to do with their "fruit" whether it is music, teaching material, along with numerous other materials, and relying on Christ's word alone in all things.

Considering all that has been shown here, read the following verses I will end with from Isaiah 28:15 and 18 and ask yourself a final question: is this all really worth it?

> Because you have said, "We have made a covenant with death, and with Sheol we have an agreement, when the overwhelming whip passes through it will not come to us, for we have made lies our refuge, and in falsehood we have taken shelter" [...] Then your covenant with death will be annulled, and your agreement with Sheol will not stand; when the overwhelming scourge passes through, you will be beaten down by it. (Isaiah 28:15, 18 ESV)

Notes on Commentary Text

So that there is no confusion on how the notations in the commentary chapters are indicated, I will explain how I intend them to be read before getting into the actual text. The indicators for where the text that is in italics is within the previous chapter is indicated in enclosed square brackets "[...]". The numbers in those brackets are explained in the table below.

Note Indicator	Meaning
p. #	the page of this volume the text is found on.
; then either an E, or #	"E" indicates that the italicized text is in a paragraph that began on the page before. The "#" indicates which new paragraph on that page the text is in. Each new indented, block or quoted block text at 9.5 pt font will count as a new paragraph number.
; then R#	R refers to any section that has "Red" on one side of that section. This can either be "Red" or "R.". "#" refers to which section or paragraph if there is more than one with "Red" or "R."
; then T#	"T" refers to any tables that are given in the text. The number refers to which table if there is more than one per page.

Note on references to *The Key of Solomon*

While current scholarship believes that a goetic text called *The Key of Solomon* was written in the 13th century, no such text has survived. The text that we know as the *Lemegeton* or *The Lesser Key of Solomon* was a text that was written and/or compiled as early as the 16th century which does place it after the writing of the *Steganographia.* When I state in my commentary towards the *Lemegeton* being written after Trithemius's *Steganographia*, the later writing/compiling of that text is the fact that is being used here.

Book I

This is: the art of revealing the will of one's soul to the absent through secret writing; to the author of the most reverend and enormous man, John Trithemius Abbot of Spanheim, and the most perfect master of natural magic.

To this work is prefixed his notes, or a true introduction prepared by the author himself; hitherto indeed much desired by many but seen by very few; but now it has been made public in favour of the secretive philosophical students.

With the privilege and consent of the Superiors. Darmbstadii, Ex Officina Typographica Balthasar Aulæandri, Sumptibus vero Ioannis Berneri, Bibliop. Franco in the year 1621.

Reader

You must be advised, Candid Reader, of the letters R. & C. (in this work sometimes by numbers, sometimes by characters, sometimes by words either written on the page, or added in the margin) that you should be marked by the rubric, or red color, and this by the ink, or black color. Moreover, you will observe this: that the titles of each individual chapter are to be painted and decorated in the same way. The importance of this matter is that you ask for the prefixed work is the key. Goodbye.

The Book Begins

The First Steganography of John Trithemius Abbot of Spanheim, of the Order of St. Benedict, Diocese of Mainz, To the Serenest Prince, Lord Philip, Count Palatine, Rhine, Duke of Bavaria, Prince Elector of the Sacred Empire, etc.

It is the opinion of the most learned that the most ancient sages, whom we call *philosophers* in the Greek language, if they had discovered any secret things either of nature or of art, to prevent that they should come to the knowledge of ordinary men, concealed them in various ways and shapes. Moses, the most famous leader of the Israelite nation, in the description of the creation of Heaven and Earth, covered the most extreme of the mysteries in simple words, the more educated of the Jews confirm this for us. Jerome, the divine and the most educated among us, states the fact that so many mysteries are hidden in the Apocalypse of John, as are many words of the wise men of the Greeks, who are not considered insignificant among themselves. They handed down a series of narratives with the approval of the educated philosophers. I cannot perfectly imitate these, who are the most diligent lovers of wisdom, and because of their slowness of mind, yet I do not fail to admire them, and to read them as diligently as I can. Because I consider them to have been devised by the greatest of ancient men with their own zeal, rubbing myself with a kind of violence, in order to just get angry, so, I greatly urge to try and imitate those who considered these things before me. Nor, as I think, did the opinion deceive me in a complete way; for I have learned many things which I had not known before, through the continuous study of reading. By my thoughts I have unlocked access to the more secret and totally mysterious things of these philosophers and sages. For even if I am not of such great learning or work ethic, as if I had grasped that method of concealing the mysteries of the ancient sages, I dare to confess from every side that some of the many and various methods, not altogether (it seems to me) to be despised, are to be kept, by which the most secret intention of my mind to another I can intimate this art to the most educated, as widely as I wish, securely and without illusion, suspicion, or detection by anyone through open messages or letters. And for the new invention of this most secret art, at the instance of the Most Serene Prince, Dom. To Philip, Count Palatine of the Rhine, Duke of Bavaria, and Prince Elector of the Holy Roman Empire, always invincible, the wisest of all the philosophers of Mecoena, whom I have seen no one more worthy, to whom this great secret should be revealed, I commended in writing, and not without the greatest labours I brought the volume into the subject. But that this great secret should not reach the ears of ordinary, uninformed or ignorant people, I considered it not the least of my duties, namely, that since mysteries teach the uninformed to understand, to conceal mysteries, that none should be of the number of the uninitiated, none but those that study the most, who owns the secret of this knowledge can by virtue perfectly and fully understand all our intentions, except by reception from a teacher, which the Hebrews call Kabbalah, the mysteries placed in charge of the most hidden secrets. Nor would the Republic, if the knowledge of this most secret art be disseminated to the unscrupulous and the heretic, be more harmful than it would be to the good. For indeed, like those who are determined to study things of goodness and virtue, men everywhere who approve of this, these men turn to good and common prosperity. Therefore, the evil and the heretic not only from evil, but truth and from good, even in the most holy institutions, find opportunities for themselves, in other words to become worse. Similar to this our most secret and otherwise useless Republic. And it can happen with the most honest approval as good and holy men that he presents himself as an instrument for the good, so that the wicked and the impious may render service to the wicked. For as a good man and lover of honesty, the secret of his will, for private or common good, to another who knows this art, when and as often as he wills, securely, secretly, and without any suspicion of any mortal, completely, copiously, and completely through openness to all, whether open or closed letters (that is, no one, no matter how educated or curious he may be, can suspect anything of the secret of the sender, nor, even if suspected, be able to detect the secret) at all times, and make known and express at any distance of places. Therefore, every perverse or person intending harm, if they are an expert in the art, by which he will reveal to me the secret of his will alone for a year with so many mysteries by Kabbalistic power, that no one, no matter how much they study or are educated, without this art, of which I am about to speak, will be able to be penetrated by the spirits. Henceforth he would write educated and uneducated, man and woman, young and old, good and bad, those withholding from sex and those involved in perverse sexual practices, in Latin or in any other language known to him, in all cultures of the world Latin, Greek or barbarian/pagan in their languages being free from all suspicion. It is one thing for the ignorant to exhibit art in the open, and another for those who know in secret. Neither would the faith received by the holy Christian religious ceremony, published by this knowledge among those who will go to Hell, remain secure between even a married couple. Even if the wife, though the speaker of the Latin speech is ignorant, through the nonsexual, honourable, and most holy words of any language or idiom already sufficiently learned; the evil and disrespectful mind of someone that also has the intentions like a adulterous lover or a fornicator, such a man using letters and praising them, as the best, may understand very widely, and through his desire in the same way as widely and in as large amounts as he wished, he could most definitely send away this secret in the same or other languages in a beautiful and very well-decorated book. I think that this science is in itself the best, and for the nation this secret is quite useful; yet if this mystery should come to the knowledge of the right people, (which God forbid) the whole nation and the order could not be disturbed in the least by how successful that book is over time. The faith of the public would be endangered, all documents, instruments, conscriptions, and finally the conversations of men would be turned into the worst of all suspicions. No one of secret languages any longer. This man would believe as much as he pleased in the holy and honest ones, without weakness, but he would seldom use the credit of the written documents. For no matter how honest and modest the words may have been, it would always be thought that there was deceit, fraud, and deception in that writing; and men would become suspicious of everything, and no less suspicious of their friends than of their enemies. And no one, even if they lived a thousand years, could be such a learned expert and so experienced in this knowledge with his teacher, that there should not be left an infinite number of ways, secretly, most secretly, and most securely in this very art of writing, and according to the will of any one experienced enough for all things to be worked upon the evil man he and his teacher had just caught. For as the spirits of good and evil were created by the supreme God for our service and progress (through whose intelligence all the secrets of this art are revealed) are to us without number infinite and completely incomprehensible; so neither is this secret writing of ours, as *Steganography* mysteries, to no mortal, no matter how educated or having knowledge of a few select people, let us call the content of this secret writing prefect in all manners, ways, differences, qualities, and operations, will this writing forever be unable to become fully understood. For this science is a chaos of infinite height, which no one can fully comprehend because however much you may know and all the experience you may have been in this art, you have always understood less than that which you do not know. For this profound and most secret art has the property that it makes the pupil incomparably easy to the master, so to speak, better educated. However, only if he is favourably chosen by his inner nature to proceed and is also willing to study the things which he has perceived in the Kabbalistic tradition. And should any reader of this work, during the process, often encounter the names, offices, orders, differences, properties, prayers, and any other operations of the spirits, by whose understandings these secrets of this science are all closed and opened that he is a Necromancer and a Magician, or that he had made a formal agreement with a demon, or by any other superstition, or that he believed or thought that he wanted, I have found it necessary and expedient to preserve my reputation and name from so much damage, injury, guilt, and stain by a solemn protest in this prologue, by proving without question the truth of this writing. I say, therefore, in the presence of Almighty God, whom nothing can completely conceal, and in the presence of Jesus Christ, his only-begotten son, who is about to judge the living and the dead, I say in truth, swear and protest: everything and every detail that I have said in this work, or I am going to say, or otherwise; the properties, manners, forms, operations, traditions, receptions, formations, consents, institutions, changes, alterations, and all that pertain to its speculation, discovery, achievement, operation, and practice, either in part or in whole, of this science or art, and everything that is contained in this volume of ours is based on true Catholic and natural principles, and everything and every thing is done with God, with a good conscience without injury to the Christian faith, with the integrity of Ecclesiastical tradition, without superstition of any kind, without idolatry, without any explicit agreement with evil spirits or implicitly, without fumigation, adoration, veneration, worship, sacrifice, offering to demons, and without all guilt or sin, both venial and mortal, and everything and every thing is done with truth, rectitude, syncretism, and purity. That the knowledge of this assent, and its practical application to good, should not be unbecoming of a wise man, a good Christian – indeed, a faithful Christian. For I too am a Christian, and willingly attached to monastic conversation. I desire to live and converse in no other way than is truly fitting for a Christian and a monk professed under the rule of God the Father Benedict himself. I accepted the Catholic faith according to the tradition of the St. Roman Church at the cradle, baptized in the name of the Father, and of the Son, and of the Holy Spirit, which I hold with it and the universal Christian Church, I believe, and how long I shall live, with the help of God, I will always serve you firmly, with a heart, I will keep it by word and work, and never deviate from it in any way. I intend to take the opportunity, far be it from me, not to either learn or teach anything that is contrary to the Christian faith and purity, injurious to the saints, or in any way opposed to the regular purpose. I fear God, and I have sworn to his worship, from whom neither the living nor (I trust) the dead will be separated.

It is not without a purpose that I place this protest before our whole work. Because I know that there are more to come. Those who, being unable to understand what we have written, have resorted to wrongdoing, that our good and holy studies will be conceded to evil arts or superstitious purposes. To these, when they are to come, and to all those who are to read these syntheses of ours, we earnestly ask, that if they have understood this secret tradition of ours, they will forever keep it secret, and not pour out such wonderful mysteries into the public. But if they do not understand (which we know will happen to many), let them learn before they criticize. Enimuero shows himself to be a rash judge, who, before acknowledging the truth of the case, pronounces a verdict on it. Learn this art first, and afterwards judge. For if you are unable to understand this work, you do not condemn this writing (for it is good) but only your dull talents. For I know and am certain that no one in his right mind can criticize this work of ours unless he happens to be completely ignorant of it. But those to whom it is more familiar to reject wisdom than to have learned it, I neither desire nor wish to penetrate these mystiques of ours.

Commentary: The Book Begins

[p. 93; E] *It is the opinion of the most learned that the most ancient sages, whom we call philosophers in the Greek language, if they had discovered any secret things either of nature or of art, to prevent that they should come to the knowledge of ordinary men, concealed them in various ways and shapes. ...* Looking at this opening statement by Trithemius, it would be helpful to understand the definition of *esotericism* that highlights the issues that this book is attempting to reveal. Karl Hoheisel gives us a very good definition of what *esotericism* is.

> In antiquity the word "esoteric" was used for knowledge that was imparted only to an inner circle of fully initiated students, while "exoteric" denoted that which in principle was accessible to everybody. In a broader sense the esoteric soon became anything that is entrusted only to a select group on the basis of certain qualities. In contrast to secret societies, whose very existence is meant to be secret, such a circle is a nonsecret order or group that guards a secret. We find such circles in all cultures in the cultic field, as well as philosophical and, increasingly, political fields.
>
> Whereas in modern usage the adjective "esoteric" may be used for anything that is not accessible to the public at large, in practice the derived noun "esotericism" has come to be equated with occultism, a new term for magic without the connotation of dealings with the devil. In the widest sense esotericism presupposes that alongside objective things that we try to explain rationally and scientifically there are hidden forces at work in us and the world that transcend normal sensory experience and causal analytic thinking. Since the religions, especially the higher and universal religions, postulate reciprocal dealings between us and the supersensory, they must be grouped to some extent under esotericism [...]
>
> Often the search for truth beyond dogma leads to the forming of special societies directed in many cases against exoteric groups, though even in the West esotericism involves more than sects or heresies. Distinctions in the exoteric that esotericism opposes means that esotericism is ultimately not homogeneous; it might embrace, for example, in Western esotericism and in the official Eastern confessions, transmigration of souls, divine immediacy, or the divine likeness of the soul. The only typical thing is the striving by way of secret relations to overcome existing institutional structures and to set up an invisible fellowship of believers. The justification and danger of esotericism lie in this transcending of everyday reality and experience in the religious field. Only a fine line separates the desired vanquishing of rigidity and the undesired relapse into uncritical fantasizing.[1]

In defining *Gnosticism*, Erwin Fahlbusch and Geoffrey William Bromiley make the connection between modern esotericism and the heresy of Gnosticism that existed in the first centuries AD.

> Their themes are cosmogony, anthropogenesis, soteriology, and eschatology. These four basic themes are only seldom present as a whole in a myth (e.g., Ap. John; Orig. World, NHC 2.5). Yet in various settings one may find partial Gnostic statements about God, humanity, the cosmos, or redemption.

---

1. Karl Hoheisel, "Esotericism," in *The Encyclopedia of Christianity* (Leiden, Netherlands: Brill, 1999–2003), pp. 132–133.

> [...]
>
> Gnosis was an esoteric religion of redemption and revelation [...] whose members grouped themselves around particular teachers and gathered in conventicles.[2]

Looking at the above definition of *esotericism* and *Gnosticism* it is not difficult to see how many groups in the current world and in the current church can be defined as both *esoteric* and *gnostic*. Those that would argue for secret doctrines of the Bible that only the "true" flock will know, such as the special selection of the national Jews even past the fulfillment of the Old Testament law, would fit into this category since those that are not of their conviction are seen as unbiblical Christ deniers. In the same way, Trithemius makes the same statements to justify the teaching of the secret messages given in this overall text. While in the *Introduction* of this book I state that Trithemius did not intend this book for occult purposes, the fact that many *esotericists* in history have based their beliefs on the teachings of Trithemius means that many current *esoteric* forms of Christianity, like those in Prosperity, WOF and NAR groups do fit under the *esoteric*/*gnostic* label in the same way Trithemius's claims do.

I quoted from Jake Stratton-Kent who was a well-known, now deceased, necromancer from the United Kingdom in my *Introduction* (p. 13) to help us understand what goetia is. Stratton-Kent also connects esotericism and goetia together by stating the following about goetic beliefs:

> Trithemius, a major influence on both Dee and Agrippa, is also the source for a popular magical alphabet. In his work Polygraphia (1518) he attributed this script to a magician called Honorius, a Theban, which seemingly connects it with Liber Juratus. He gives as his source Peter of Abano (1250 to 1316), which if correct would push the origins of the alphabet back into the medieval period. Agrippa also mentions Peter of Abano in connection with this alphabet, but may as easily be drawing on Trithemius as his own reading.[3]

Connecting these all together by understanding Trithemius's opening sentences in this goetic work helps us to understand the fallacy of so many of the goetic beliefs being used in churches today. Trithemius, who greatly influenced some of the most famous occultists such as John Dee and Henry Cornelius Agrippa, opened the way for goetia and occultism to be accepted into church practice.

[p. 93; E] *Jerome, the divine and the most educated among us, states the fact that so many mysteries are hidden in the Apocalypse of John, as are many words of the wise men of the Greeks, who are not considered insignificant among themselves. They handed down a series of narratives with the approval of the educated philosophers.* [...] *Nor, as I think, did the opinion deceive me in a complete way; for I have learned many things which I had not known before, through the continuous study of reading. By my thoughts I have unlocked access to the more secret and totally mysterious things of these philosophers and sages*. ... First, we need to understand that studying ancient writings is not *inherently* bad or sinful. However, there are some current day writers and scholars that are attempting to take ancient or even first/second century texts and attempting to redefine biblical doctrine using fallacious texts. The most infamous example of this is the use the 1 (*Ethiopic Apocalypse of*) *Enoch* to redefine the nature of the demonic and even the work and person of Christ by creating alternate gospels.[4]

2. Erwin Fahlbusch and Geoffrey William Bromiley, "Gnosis," in *The Encyclopedia of Christianity* (Leiden, Netherlands: Brill, 1999–2003), p. 418.

3. Jake Stratton-Kent. Geosophia-I (Kindle Locations 713–717). Kindle Edition.

4. For more information, please refer to: Michael S. Heiser, *Reversing Hermon*: *Enoch, The Watchers*

I referred to Zen Garcia in the *Introduction* (p. 52, Footnote 50), but I want to show that Gracia likewise uses this goetic ideology to redefine biblical doctrine. Garcia states that the

> Most High God declares in the Scriptures that at the end of days, the Spirit of truth would be poured out upon all flesh and that those things which had been lost, forgotten, hidden, and forbidden to the masses would at that time be brought once more to light so that all that had been made known and treasured previously with regard to the sanctity of the Scriptures would be restored to those seeking them.[5]

Garcia's defence that these fallacious texts are legitimate texts that we need to understand in these "end of days" is obvious in his statement that the Bible is to be reinterpreted in light of these fallacious and even heretical texts. The most popular eschatology movement in current evangelicalism have likewise used fallacious texts to create a new form of eschatology, much like those involved in esotericism and goetia are *obsessed* with doing. Like Garcia, these same movements have *joined* with the Prosperity, WOF and NAR groups in using fallacious texts and redefining the Bible so suit their own selfish desires and purposes. Trithemius is one of the most influential men in history to make that interpretive method as a standard to be followed. Since Trithemius was a devout and renown Roman Catholic, Trithemius's beliefs on this matter, along with the Roman Catholic defence of extra-biblical *tradition* that often *contradicts* the biblical narrative, are still influencing evangelicals and those that hold to the Protestant branch of Christendom.

[p. 93–94; E] *But that this great secret should not reach the ears of ordinary, uninformed or ignorant people, I considered it not the least of my duties, namely, that since mysteries teach the uninformed to understand, to conceal mysteries, that none should be of the number of the uninitiated, none but those that study the most, who owns the secret of this knowledge can by virtue perfectly and fully understand all our intentions, except by reception from a teacher, which the Hebrews call Kabbalah, the mysteries placed in charge of the most hidden secrets. …* After seeing the above descriptions about esotericism, gnosticism and the use of fallacious texts to fallaciously "better understand" the Bible, it should not be all that surprising to see Trithemius connect this all in a positive way to the teachings of the *Kabbalah* as well. The *Kabbalah*'s primary defense in what it teaches is that the kabbalistic texts are a secret teaching that can only be understood by those that have special education of an esoteric and/or magical nature. Instead of arguing for a Bible that is easy to understand and that the message is *plainly* clear in a direct reading of it, current day interpreters, scholars and laypeople are instead using an esoteric method, like the *Kabbalah* and as Trithemius taught, that esoteric knowledge is important to understanding "truth". Unfortunately, this knowledge is only for those that deserve it in some special method of study or teaching.

[p. 94; E] *And it can happen with the most honest approval as good and holy men that he presents himself as an instrument for the good, so that the wicked and the impious may render service to the wicked. …* This is extremely common in Prosperity, WOF and NAR movements as the "preachers" and "teachers" present themselves as "good and holy men that presents himself as an instrument for the good" so that they may as "the wicked and impious may render service to the wicked". So many people in charge of those move-

& *The Forgotten Mission of Jesus Christ* (Bellingham, Washington: Lexham Press, 2017), p. 55, 72, 73.

5. Zen Garcia, *The Collected Works of Enoch The Prophet* (Atlanta, Georgia: Sacred Word Publishing, 2017), p. 4.

ments being involved in goetia for the purposes of deceiving people for wealth are in fact *wicked* and *impious*. Those that are wanting to be deceived (as p. 80 in my *Introduction* shows) from a biblical perspective are just as evil.

> But false prophets also arose among the people, just as there will be false teachers among you, who will secretly bring in destructive heresies, even denying the Master who bought them, bringing upon themselves swift destruction. And many will follow their sensuality, and because of them the way of truth will be blasphemed. And in their greed they will exploit you with false words. Their condemnation from long ago is not idle, and their destruction is not asleep. […] For it would have been better for them never to have known the way of righteousness than after knowing it to turn back from the holy commandment delivered to them. What the true proverb says has happened to them: "The dog returns to its own vomit, and the sow, after washing herself, returns to wallow in the mire." (2 Peter 2:1–3, 21–22 ESV)

Peter in 2 Peter speaks plainly that those that follow false prophets and false teachings willingly will follow those false teachers and prophets into their own destruction (Hell). By justifying their teachings with the goetia presented in Trithemius's text, they have turned this condemnation around into a *good* thing rather than as something that all Christians should be warned about concerning these false prophets and false teachers.

In arguing that those that are the "true Christians" are able to show legitimacy of their "faith" by the goetic practices that these Prosperity, WOF and NAR leaders are teaching, these esoteric and goetic teachings are a "secret" knowledge that only those under the tutelage of these false and goetic teachers will understand.

[p. 94; E] T*herefore, every perverse or person intending harm, if they are an expert in the art, by which he will reveal to me the secret of his will alone for a year with so many mysteries by Kabbalistic power, that no one, no matter how much they study or are educated, without this art, of which I am about to speak, will be able to be penetrated by the spirits.* … Trithemius here is stating that if someone is not of the right "heart" that these goetic techniques will fail. Again, Prosperity, WOF and NAR teachers are teaching the same ideology that those who are not showing their "faith" via goetia are perverse and are holding these false churches back as well.

In an article published by Elle Hardy, Hardy shows that Prosperity movements are calling for a war on the poor, which involves physical violence because the poor are holding these churches back from bringing "heaven to earth" in the form of health and wealth. Again, seeing the above claims from Trithemius, it is not hard to see that the Prosperity, WOF and NAR beliefs about a "war on the poor" are coming from goetic desires instead of truly biblical ones. Showing what Hardy is saying, it makes the matter much more of a frightening issue.

> Jason Mattera, son of Joseph Mattera, one of the most influential modern prophets of the New Apostolic Reformation—which emerged from the Pentecostal-Charismatic tradition that is sweeping all of evangelical Christianity before it—wrote a piece outlining a new direction for prosperity theology. In the article, titled "A Biblical View of Work and Welfare," Mattera junior opined that, while Christians should help to alleviate poverty, they are not "under any obligation to help indolent bums." Such people, he added "are not entitled to our generosity" (emphasis his). […] This is a worldview that seeks to wage not a war against poverty but a war against the poor instead—those who have, in his view, shown insufficient faith. […] Emerging from the New Thought movement espoused by Ralph Waldo Emerson and friends in the 1830s, ideas about "mind power" found an amped-up audience in America's new world primacy.[6]

6. Elle Hardy, "The Evangelicals Calling for War on Poor People," *The New Republic*, Accessed

Again, this "esoteric faith/knowledge" that these Prosperity, WOF and NAR adherents teach that shows "true faith" but is in reality a goetic form of false teaching, is being pulled directly from books such as this one by Trithemius. Yet, many of these Prosperity, WOF and NAR followers are refusing to see it because it is what these followers *want to believe.*

[p. 94; E] *Neither would the faith received by the holy Christian religious ceremony, published by this knowledge among those who will go to Hell.* Not much needs to be said here. ... Trithemius here is defending the use of goetia (to hide his true intentions) as a *Christian* practice. Since the text in this book says this, many are using it to defend goetic practices in the church even if Trithemius himself did not support goetia. Being a Roman Catholic, Trithemius did support goetic practice in the veneration of the saints and Mary, but the Prosperity, WOF and NAR movements have taken the direct goetic principles from this book as biblical truth when it is not.

[p. 95; E] *For as the spirits of good and evil were created by the supreme God for our service and progress (through whose intelligence all the secrets of this art are revealed) are to us without number infinite and completely incomprehensible.* ... This statement shows once more the belief that angels, even demons, saints and Mary, are believed to service a person. If the spirits are servicing you, then you are in fact a god, just as goetia wants you to believe.

Note the following from the Hekhalot Literature of Merkavah Mysticism which is the form of Jewish occultism that the Kabbalah was based on:

> I call you by the five chosen names that are among your names. [...] Upon them you are commanded and you are warned from the mouth of the Most High, that if you hear an adjuration by these names, do glory to His name and hasten and descend and do the will of the one who adjures you. And if you delay, behold (I) will thrust you into Rigyon of pursuing fire and I will set another in your place.[7]

This quote from the Hekhalot literature of the earliest form Judaic occultism again shows the belief of how calling on angels was coming from occult literature. By the Qumran and other occult texts shown in the *Introduction*, and also by the italicized quote of Trithemius for this comment, the goetic influence of this text that brought goetia into wider Protestant practice is evident.

[p. 95; E] *And should any reader of this work, during the process, often encounter the names, offices, orders, differences, properties, prayers, and any other operations of the spirits, by whose understandings these secrets of this science are all closed and opened that he is a Necromancer and a Magician, or that he had made a formal agreement with a demon, or by any other superstition, or that he believed or thought that he wanted, I have found it necessary and expedient to preserve my reputation and name from so much damage, injury, guilt, and stain by a solemn protest in this prologue, by proving without question the truth of this writing.* ... Trithemius here is defending the practices in this book that if anyone should call someone a necromancer (or goeticist) for practicing the ideology in this book, that this book proves the legitimacy of goetia. Even though the Bible is directly against any occult practices including necromancy/goetia as my *Intro-*

October 23, 2024, https://newrepublic.com/article/176117/prosperity-gospel-christian-war-poor.

7. James R. Davila, *Hekhalot Literature in Translation: Major Texts of Merkavah Mysticism* (Leiden, Netherlands: Brill, 2013), pp. 362–363.

duction shows.

[p. 96; E] *in the presence of Almighty God, whom nothing can completely conceal, and in the presence of Jesus Christ, his only-begotten son, who is about to judge the living and the dead, I say in truth, swear and protest: everything and every detail that I have said in this work, or I am going to say, or otherwise; the properties, manners, forms, operations, traditions, receptions, formations, consents, institutions, changes, alterations, and all that pertain to its speculation, discovery, achievement, operation, and practice, either in part or in whole, of this science or art, and everything that is contained in this volume of ours is based on true Catholic and natural principles, and everything and every thing is done with God, with a good conscience without injury to the Christian faith, with the integrity of Ecclesiastical tradition, without superstition of any kind, without idolatry, without any explicit agreement with evil spirits or implicitly, without fumigation, adoration, veneration, worship, sacrifice, offering to demons, and without all guilt or sin, both venial and mortal, and everything and every thing is done with truth, rectitude, syncretism, and purity. …* Notice here that Trithemius is appealing to "God" to defend the goetia of this book. Like the Israelites in Exodus 32 bowing to a goetic version of Yahweh, we have Trithemius appealing to a goetic version of God as well. Not only does Trithemius appeal to a *goetic* version of God, but to the *Ecclesiastical tradition* of Roman Catholicism. It should be notable that Trithemius does not once appeal to the pages of the Bible to defend the goetic occultism presented in the entirety of this book. The Bible outright condemns goetia, yet Trithemius is appealing to tradition to defend this occultism.

[p. 96; E] *That the knowledge of this assent, and its practical application to good, should not be unbecoming of a wise man, a good Christian – indeed, a faithful Christian. For I too am a Christian, and willingly attached to monastic conversation. I desire to live and converse in no other way than is truly fitting for a Christian. …* This statement should be taken notice of since many people will simply claim that the Prosperity, WOF and NAR teachers are preaching "Christ" therefore we should not just totally avoid them. Jesus plainly tells us to avoid these "churches" in Matthew 7:15–20. Just because someone claims to be a Christian, does not mean that the person necessarily is. Therefore, once we see what these "Christians" believe, we can then determine whether these false teachers truly are "Christians". Just because someone claims to be of a particular faith, like Christianity, *does not mean that the person is*. These teachers are in fact "wolves in sheep's clothing". (Matthew 7:15) That goetia like Prosperity, WOF and NAR false teachers are pushing is being taught as "fitting for a Christian" should make us immediately recognize these false teachers as false Christians.

[p. 96; E] *I intend to take the opportunity, far be it from me, not to either learn or teach anything that is contrary to the Christian faith and purity, injurious to the saints. While some Protestants here will assume that Trithemius is referring to the dead saints in heaven, this is a statement that refers to all Catholics and not just dead saints in heaven. …* Trithemius is appealing to the intention not to injure the saints. Trithemius here believes that if he were to withhold the goetia being taught in this book that he would be *injuring the saints*. Robert Norton in the 1861 book *The Restoration of Apostles and Prophets: In the Catholic Apostolic Church* states that:

> The various experience which I have had of the work of the Holy Ghost, and the work of Satan, hath convinced me that until the discernment of spirits shall be given as a distinct gift

> in the Church, there is no rule so certain as that which our Lord hath given, of trying them by their fruits. And taking this rule, I solemnly declare, that if the fruits of the Spirit be 'joy, peace, love, long suffering, gentleness, meekness, patience, temperance,' these fruits have been produced by the Spirit speaking in our church, whether you respect the persons in whom He speaketh, or those who have grace to recognise and confess it as the Holy Ghost. [...] Ah! let the gifts of the Spirit be manifested; the word of wisdom, with its branches; the word of knowledge, with its branches; faith, with its branches, healing and miracles; these are the knops. And let the beauty of the flowers be the rejoicing of the Church of God; love branching into joy and peace; long-suffering, into gentleness and goodness; faith into meekness and temperance. Faith, hope, and charity, — let them be manifested, O ye Church of God, and God shall bless you; and Jesus your High Priest shall ever walk about with the tongs and snuffers; the tongs (raising the wick), the voice of apostolic exhortation and encouragement; the snuffers, the utterance of prophetic rebuke, to cause the light to shine more brightly.[8]

Norton, along with charismatic, Prosperity, WOF and NAR followers defend the use of spiritual gifts that are plainly illegitimate, like the use of "tongues", since these followers believe it is true and it gives them "joy" which is a "fruit of the Spirit". That is all the fallacious evidence these individuals require that something is "good". The biblical facts again do not matter because these are experiences people *want to believe in* even if the Bible says that such things are evil, or even goetic, in nature. Trithemius is also defending the use of goetia so that it does not injure the people. Trithemius does not believe that the truth of God's word should bring repentance. Trimethius believes the Bible should not be used for what he would consider "injury" to the saints of which repentance in this context would be an "injury".

This same attitude is shared by many Protestant churches who use musical, teaching and preaching material from these churches. At the core of the reason why these fallacious leaders accept these materials into church liturgy is simply because these leaders like them and want to use them. Many will defend the use with a defence often coined as "The Doctrinal Smell Test"[9] Despite what Jesus says in Matthew 7:15–20, church leaders want to defy Christ by letting their hearts determine what is *theologically* "good" and "bad" much like the serpent convinced Adam and Eve to in Eden. Understanding that these songs are coming from goetic "churches" and that the main drive of goetia is to bring in money, it is not surprising that a false defence of "The Doctrinal Smell Test" will be used. The reality is that the church leaders like this music, with them teaching others to believe it is okay, and once they have convinced others that the music is okay, to pull the music and material from services would *injure* the church. But the injury to the *church* would not be to the congregation, but to the church's *finances*. That is all the issue comes down to. If someone were to doubt that claim, simply walk up to someone after a church service and ask them "how was the worship this morning?" In every case, the person will comment on the *music* first and rarely anything else. Any other parts of the "worship" will be brought up *after* the music if the other parts of the "worship" service are even brought up at all. Playing the music that is goetic in nature for the purposes of drawing wolves into the church for the sake of a bigger bank account is evident in every case.

[p. 97; E] *Learn this art first, and afterwards judge. For if you are unable to understand this work, you do not condemn this writing (for it is good) but only your dull talents. For*

8. From "Chapter II. The Outpouring of the Spirit in England". in *The Restoration of Apostles and Prophets: In the Catholic Apostolic Church* by Robert Norton Forthcoming by Devoted Publishing.
9. See my refutation of this defence in my book *The Emergence of the Neo-Satanist Church.*

I know and am certain that no one in his right mind can criticize this work of ours unless he happens to be completely ignorant of it. … The deception here should be evident. Much like the Prosperity, WOF and NAR churches preach that their "miracles" are evidence of the legitimacy of their teaching, Trithemius many centuries before was teaching the same idea regarding goetia. The idea of "do not diss it until you have tried it" is completely fallacious and was used by the occult before it was appropriated by the Prosperity, WOF and NAR teachers and their followers. Just because the magic and goetia they are teaching is "working" does not validate its legitimacy. Jesus did say that there would be people coming performing "false miracles" and that many would follow these false prophets and false teachers because of the deception of these "false miracles". (Matthew 24:24)

Chapter I

Citizen's key and operation is held by the principal spirits Pamersyel, Anoyr, Madriel through the ministry of Ebra, Sothean, Abrulges, Itrasbiel, Nadres, Ormenu, Itules, Rablion, and Hamorfiel. To these is made the commission of all with exorcism.

The content of the first chapter is a very difficult procedure and full of dangers, because of the pride and rebellion of these spirits, who do not obey anyone unless he is very experienced in this art. For the novices and those less skilled in this art not only do the spirits not obey, but even if the spirits are scolded too much, they will frequently injure the novice, and he will fall into various illusions. These spirits are much more malicious and unfaithful than all other aerial spirits, and they do not obey anyone unless compelled by the greatest religious practices. For as soon as the spirits have been sent out, when they shout their words, and to the person to whom they are sent, the spirits rush in without discipline, like an army fleeing without a leader from a battle. The spirits rush in madly, filling the air with their chaos, often revealing to all in the area the secrets of the novice who sent the spirits. Therefore, we advise that no one who works in this art appeals to them and does not even require their services because they are unfaithful and treacherous. However, there are many of these spirits whom we say in their full value can be found sufficiently benevolent, who even offer themselves ready for obedient service. But if anyone wishes at all to test the spirits' honesty, and to prove that what we have said is true, he must know how to observe this method. The person prepares a paper on which he is going to write the invocation of the divine name, in the name of the Father and the Son and the Holy Spirit. Then he writes on it however simple and open, a narrative he wishes, which all readers will understand, in Latin, in the native language or in any other language. But when he sits down to write, write towards the East so that the spirit will address him. Then he must say:

> Pamersiel oshurmy delmuson Thafloyn peano charustea melany, lyaminto colchan, paroys, madyn, moerlay, bulre atloor don melcour peloin, ibutsyl meon mysbreath alini driaco person. Crisolnay, lemon asosle mydar, icoriel pean thalmon, asophiel il notreon banyel ocrimos esteuor naelma besrona thulaomor fronian beldodrayn bon otalmesgo mero fas elnathyn bosramoth.

When he has said this and sees that the spirits are present to obey him, he can continue the work he has begun. But if the spirits have not yet appeared, repeat the words as often as possible, until they appear. When you have finished the letters, send them with a message to a friend who is well-versed in the art. Once the friend receives them, let that friend tell you about this secret.

> Lamarton anoyr bulon madriel traschon ebrasothea panthenon nabrulges Camery itrasbier rubanthy nadres Calmosi ormenulan, ytules demy rabion hamorphyn.

With these words the friend will soon understand your mind perfectly, the spirits already offering themselves quickly and crying out, so that most others present in the area may be able to perceive the secret of the sender. But observe that in all the letters which you send, written with this art, you affix your own seal, that the friend to whom you write may know by whom you have worked by which spirits. For if he himself were to work through others to understand, and you through others to send, the spirits would never obey him forever, but for an undue reason the spirits would injure him and not reveal your secret in any way. For all the spirits whom we worship in this art only keep the orders and offices entrusted to them, and in no way neglect others. Consider carefully all that we have said in this chapter, and you will be able to understand more easily what we are going to say in the following. And in order that we may prove what we have said by an example, let us put our intention in common language, which we will consequently notify to our friend in the manner we just mentioned.

Let This Be the Secret Intent of the Mind of some prince, whom he wishes to know of his absent vassal. **Red.**

Better be aware that we are willing to defeat those from Strasbourg by honest means and attack them with all our might the next Wednesday after Viti and Modesti. This is why our earnest desire is for you, as you are related to us with many vows and are bound to faithful service. You want to appear on the same day well prepared, according to your ability, every day after Wittemtage near Stauffenburg in the forest. Here they were literally so placed so that being modestly found there they would comply and not be left out. We want to show mercy towards you and keep this our plan with you in high secrecy, etc.

To Notify This Secret

Vasallo is written with a broader intention of the sender in this or another way. **Red.**

Almighty and everlasting God, who created all things out of nothing, have mercy on us through the most bitter passion of your only begotten Son dying on the cross, who was conceived of the Holy Spirit without male intercourse, born of the most pure Virgin Mary, and voluntarily gave himself up for us in death with his most holy blood, dying for our souls that he delivered by his death. Hear us the wretched, O most merciful Father, and through the shedding of the most sacred blood of the same Son of our sweet Lord Jesus Christ. Forgive us our sins and pour into our hearts your grace, as you are in everything and above all things. Being diligent with sincere fervor, let us always obey your commands with devotion, and continually advancing in mutual love, let us love nothing earthly, let us seek nothing transitory. For you are the Lord our God, who created us in your image and likeness from the beginning when we were not. And through your beloved Son, you redeemed us when we were perishing, who was dead for our sins and buried on the third day, you raised him from the dead, and his disciples rejoiced in him. Forty days you have shown those who are living much consolation. We believe that the very true God and man will come again to judge the living and the dead with you in your indescribable majesty without end at the end of the world to judge the living and the dead and will render to each one of us according to his works. Through him we beseech you, O Most Merciful Father, hear us and have mercy on us now and in that terrible hour in which we are to be judged by your own Son. Look upon us most merciful God. For we are frail and pitiable sinners, naked of good works, who offend your most holy majesty by sinning in many ways. But having come to your mercy in repentance of our sins, we groan with tears. Humbly we beseech you through Jesus Christ, your Son, that you turn away your holy wrath from us, and indulge us in compassion, forgiving our crimes, leading us to pleasantness. John Trithemius wrote this in the country of Coe.

A simple and open narrative of this kind, or any other you wish, which all may read and understand, which contains nothing secret, and which you are not afraid of coming into the sight of all, you shall write in the opening paragraph, which we have said by the secret prayer of the Spirits. Say this secret prayer with your face turned to the east, in which you write your secret intention which you wish to me to know, what is absent, express it before the spirits, challenging them to act faithfully, and they will immediately fly away. When the person to whom they are sent has received your letters, he, having recognized the sign of the east, turning his face towards the East, will utter the secret prayer which we have mentioned – Lamarton, Anoyr – and he will at once understand your secret intention, which you have committed to the Spirits for a certainty.

To Know the Spirit Places, names & signs, subject known. **Red.**

But since it is necessary for every worker in this knowledge to know the places and names of the principal Spirits and signs, or else he who dwells in the south through ignorance calls a spirit from the north, which would not only impede his intention, but might also injure the worker, I will consequently place for you in a circle the places in which the principal Spirits they dwell, with their names and signs.

Red.

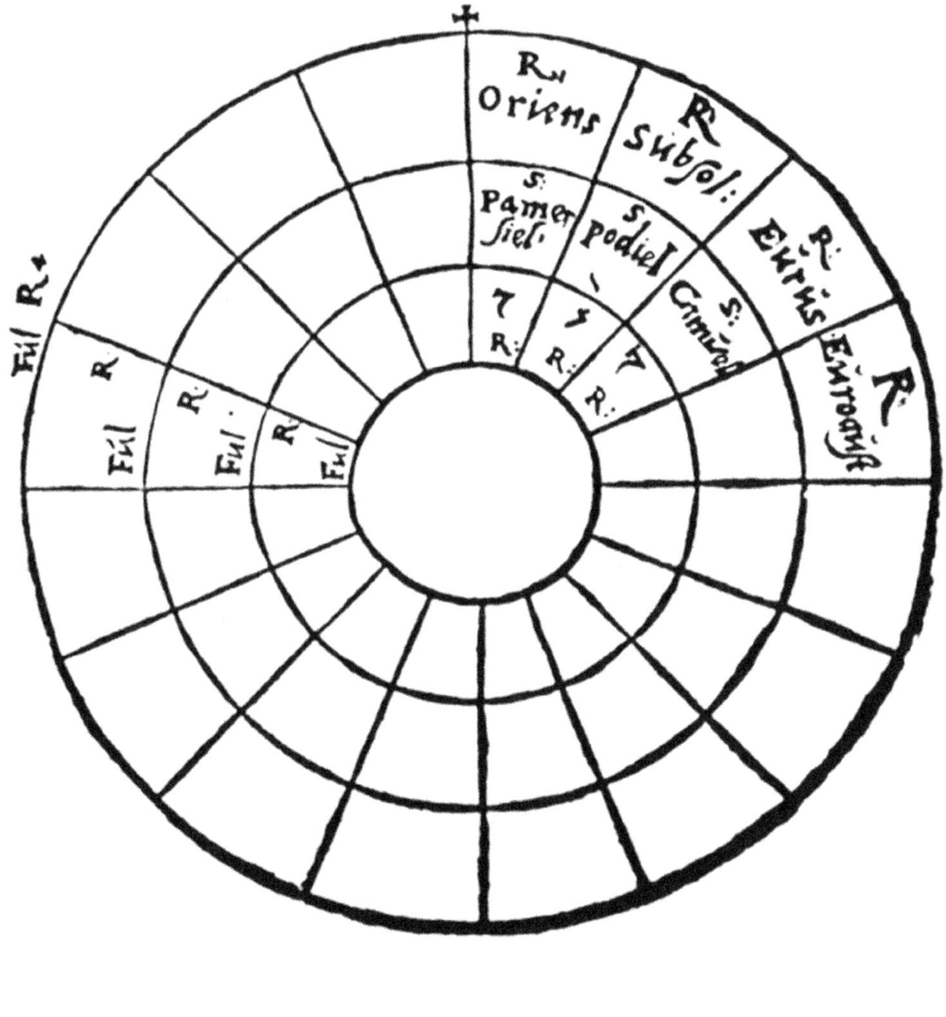

Behold, you already have the various plagues of the world, which it is necessary to know in the operation of this art in the present book first and foremost, and without the knowledge of which will have no effect in this art.

Again, it is necessary for you to know the first substitutes of each of the principal spirits, how many there are in number, to whom the secret mysteries are entrusted. That way you may know their orders, in what manner they are to be called, and how they are again sent to their offices, and how many illuminators they have in the day, and how many luminaries in during the night, and which friends and how many enemies they usually fear, and I will teach you about all these in the presentation board, which is called the board of direction.

Black.	Red.	B.[1]	R.	B.	R.	B.
Oriens.	Pamersiel.		1,000.	10,000.	100.	0.0.
Subsolanus.	Padiel.		10,000.	200,000.	10.	0.0.
Eurus.	Camuel.		10.	10.	10.	10.0
Euroauster.	Aseliel.		10.	20.	10.	0.10.
Auster.	Barmiel.		10.	20.	10.0.	10.0.
Austafricus	Gediel.		20.	20.	10.0.	10.0.
Africus.	Asyriel.		20.	20.	120.	10.
Fauonius.	Maseriel.		30.	30.	10.0.	0.10.
Occidens.	Malgaras.		30.	30.	0.30.	210.
Chorus.	Dorothiel.		40.	40.	0.40.	30.0.
Subcircius.	Vsiel.		40.	40.	0.30.	0.0.
Circius.	Cabariel.		50.	50.	80.0.	80.0.
Septentrio.	Raysiel.		50.	50.	80.0.	0.80.
Aquilo.	Symiel.		10.	1,000.	10.	100.
Boreas.	Armadiel.		1,000.	180.	810.	00.
Vulturnus.	Baruchas.		10.	180.	810.	00.

I would like you to understand here that the east is not where the sun rises every day, but the place where it was created from the beginning, which we call the equinoctial. For unless you observe this consideration very carefully, you will not be able to make progress in this art. But even now I will teach you the series of these tables, so that you may understand them all from one spirit. Let us therefore take Malgaras as an example, through which the operation of this art takes place in the ninth chapter of the present first book. He is of the West, his sign is such that he has under you thirty who are in charge of the day and have a great power to drive away the spirits of darkness. These spirits are subject to thirty other spirits who preside over the night and are always in darkness, and do not come to the light except through the command of their princes, to whom they are subject at all times. And these again have under them, as guardians and ministers subject to full right, sometimes thirty, sometimes twenty, sometimes ten, and sometimes all, together with all of them, go forth to the command of their princes, namely in such order according to the number of those who have been called by the command of the great Virtues from the second or third order. Many servants and guards should come with them to the spirit prince, who in this example is Malgaras. Again, under there are others like messen-

1. This column contained symbols for the varoius spirits. In this edition, these symbols have been removed. Any of these symbols that also show up in the rest of this book have also been removed.

gers and gatekeepers who are without a certain number and who often meet mixed with other spirits. However, we do not keep the names of all these spirits. But what is necessary for the worker to know, we will express in each chapter. And note that all these spirits are with their chief commander, each place of the world assigned to him, as is clear in the table.

Commentary: Chapter I

[p. 111; 1] *The content of the first chapter is a very difficult procedure and full of dangers, because of the pride and rebellion of these spirits, who do not obey anyone unless he is very experienced in this art. For the novices and those less skilled in this art not only do the spirits not obey, but even if the spirits are scolded too much, they will frequently injure the novice, and he will fall into various illusions. These spirits are much more malicious and unfaithful than all other aerial spirits, and they do not obey anyone unless compelled by the greatest religious practices. …* The opening sentences to Chapter I make some interesting statements when taken into consideration with other practices within the Prosperity, WOF and NAR movements. Referring back to the discussion of goetic tongues in the *Introduction* (pp. 69–75), see what John Eckhardt has to say about these goetic tongues.

> This is a manifestation of being filled with the Holy Spirit and is also a powerful weapon in spiritual warfare. Tongues provide rest and refreshing for the workers while engaging in spiritual warfare (Isa. 28:11–12). This is important due to the spiritual drain of the deliverance ministry. Speaking in tongues during deliverance sessions also irritates and weakens demon spirits. Jesus cast out demon spirits by the Holy Spirit. Through the Holy Spirit and tongues we too can drive out evil spirits. Praying in tongues also keeps us built up and edified that we may be strong in the Lord and the power of His might (1 Cor. 14:4; Jude 20; Eph. 6:10–12).[1]

Eckhardt uses a part of Isaiah 28 to back up his claim. However, the text around these two verses show that this is *not* what Isaiah 28:11–12 is talking about. See the larger text below:

> "To whom will he teach knowledge, and to whom will he explain the message? Those who are weaned from the milk, those taken from the breast? For it is precept upon precept, precept upon precept, line upon line, line upon line, here a little, there a little." For by people of strange lips and with a foreign tongue the LORD will speak to this people, to whom he has said, "This is rest; give rest to the weary; and this is repose"; yet they would not hear. And the word of the LORD will be to them precept upon precept, precept upon precept, line upon line, line upon line, here a little, there a little, that they may go, and fall backward, and be broken, and snared, and taken. (Isaiah 28:9–13 ESV)

Looking at what verses 9–13 say, it is clear that the "people of strange lips and with a foreign tongue" are Gentiles who will be the ones bringing the speech of Yahweh's judgment. What will bring rest to the weary is what is said in verses 9–11 that if the people will obey the word of Yahweh then this will rest will come. Isaiah reinforces that promise in verses 12–13. These "strange lips" and "foreign tongues" are not in fact a "good thing" but a sign of God's condemnation on the people.[2] These "strangle lips" have nothing to

1. John Eckhardt, *Deliverance and Spiritual Warfare Manual* (Lake Mary, Florida: Charisma House, 2014), p. 238.

2. Gary V. Smith, *Isaiah 1–39*, ed. E. Ray Clendenen, The New American Commentary (Nashville, Tennessee: B & H Publishing Group, 2007), pp. 482–483.

do with comforting people engaging in spiritual warfare *or* that these "foreign tongues" that Eckhardt is referring to "also irritates and weakens demon spirits." Again, Eckhardt is pulling this verse out of context to defend the goetic use of tongues as shown on pages 80–81 of the *Introduction* where I show that goetic tongues were used to cast "daimons" (demons) out of homes with a spell written on parchment.

Note in paragraph two of page 111 that these nonsense goetic tongues are being used to summon a spirit in the same way that was shown on page 74 of the *Introduction* as well. Since the *PGM* show that these goetic languages are used for both summoning and repelling daimons/demons, for Eckhardt to be using them as a "religious practice" to control and exorcise demonic spirits out of people, the source of that thinking is shown by Trithemius as goetic in the opening sentences of Chapter I.

Another "religious" practice that is thought to "subdue" or "control" demonic spirits is "worship music." The following text is from *Extravagant Worship: Holy, Holy, Holy Is the Lord God Almighty Who Was and Is, and Is to Come…* by Darlene Zschech and Brian Houston, who were the former worship pastor of Hillsong Church in Australia and former head pastor of the same church, respectively.

> When we, God's people, come into His presence with thanksgiving and praise, warfare is waged against our enemies, and our battles are won by the supernatural power of God. In the face of challenge and persecution, God's people are to unite and praise Him. The Enemy has no chance of winning against people who are consumed with praising God. There is no victory against those who rejoice in God's great glory.
>
> I used to joke with my worship team that the reason Jehoshaphat's enemy was defeated was because the singers and musicians were so bad—perhaps it was more like torture! Their enemies conceded quickly, saying, "Okay, you win, we give up; just stop the singing!" But even if the people were tone deaf and couldn't carry a musical note, the Lord would have eagerly received their praises. It wasn't the harmony that defeated their enemy; it was the presence of God's mighty power that warred on their behalf and won their battles.[3]

The text of 2 Chronicles:22–23 does say that when the army began to "sing and praise" that Yahweh set an ambush against the armies of Ammon, Moab and Mount Seir. However, this is one example of Yahweh's intervention in warfare for the people of Israel. Examples of other times that Yahweh intervened for his people in battle would be the separating of the Red [Reed] Sea (Exodus 14:26–31), Moses praying for the people fighting the Amalekites in Exodus 17:8–13), the battle of Jericho (Joshua 6), and also the saving of Jerusalem by an angel that slew 150,000 Assyrians (2 Kings 19:35, 2 Chronicles 32:21, Isaiah 36:36). There are many other examples that could be given. These are all examples of Yahweh's promise to Israel in Deuteronomy 3:21–22: "And I commanded Joshua at that time, 'Your eyes have seen all that the LORD your God has done to these two kings. So will the LORD do to all the kingdoms into which you are crossing. You shall not fear them, for it is the LORD your God who fights for you'" (Deuteronomy 3:21–22 ESV). The evidence used by Zschech to claim that music will *literally* wage war against "our enemies", is pulling a text out of context for goetic purposes. However, note the following from the *Orphic Argonautica* which is a well-known goetic version of the classic *Argonautica.*

> There, sitting, they sing a sweet song.
> Daughters, but they delight in the sound of mortals.

3. Darlene Zschech and Brian Houston, *Extravagant Worship: Holy, Holy, Holy Is the Lord God Almighty Who Was and Is, and Is to Come…* (Grand Rapids, Michigan: Bethany House, 2004), Logos Edition.

Then Minyae were filled with the sound of the song of the
Sirenes; nor were they about to sail past them
A voice full of curses, and the oars of his hands reached him.
Ancaeus directed his gaze towards the foreboding hill.
If I were not strumming the lyre with my palms
My mother mixed a delightful adornment of song.
And he sang with a clear voice through a sacred hymn,
Once they had harnessed the storm-footed horses for him.
Zeus, the High-Thunderer and Earth-Shaker;
But Cyan-haired, enraged, to father Zeus
struck the land of Lyctus with a golden spear
And he scattered them over the boundless sea,
To remain on the islands by the sea; they were all accounted for.
Sardis and Euboea, and then Cyprus, wind-swept
Indeed, then, as the fog was gathering, from the snow-covered cliff
The Sirens were amazed, and they ceased their song.
And she, on the one hand, cast away the lotus, and on the other hand, the turtle from her hands.
They groaned terribly, as the grievous fate approached.
Of the fatal destiny; from the edge of the cliff
They plunged into the depths of the sea, full of fish.
And they changed their bodies and their haughty form into stones.[4]

Notice how Orpheus in this version of the story uses music to cast down the supernatural sirens, or demons, to allow the argonauts to pass through the area. Not only does Orpheus use music to cast down the demons, but also to overcome and drown out the song for the Minyae ship crew so that these sailors would not be overcome by the goetic song of the sirens. My *Introduction* shows that these Greek tales were used to establish Greek goetia. This version of the *Argonautica* was composed sometime in the early AD era, but it does still establish the use of music for goetic purposes in the same way that charismatics, Prosperity, WOF, and NAR groups are convincing other Christians of the same use of goetic music as "biblical" when it is not.

Making the connection from goetia to ancient Greek mythology, Stratton-Kent makes the connection clear. In commenting on Orphic texts such as the *Orphic Argonautica*, Stratton-Kent makes a clear connection that these texts, whether fallacious or not in their authorship, were the basis for goetic practice and thought.

> In reality, Orphic rites reverted to chthonic forms even though seeking the Apollonian dignity of celestial religion, and the rites of the Magi – generally pre-Zoroastrian in origin – were as barbarous as the goetia Cumont supposed their rites were intended to replace. Myths were employed to describe this magic, to explain it, provide authors for its texts and founders for its schools. To reach back through the Orphic reforms to the more primitive levels necessarily involves examination of this mythic background.
>
> [...]
>
> The relationship of the Orphic reforms and of goetia with the Dionysian currents provides a creation myth for transforming modern magic. This creation is conceptually prior to the emergence of Goetia and its involvement with older religious traditions.[5]

And also

> More comprehensively significant in relation to the grimoires and to magical Holy Books in general are the Orphic books. The right place of these books in the history of culture has

4. *Orphic Argonautica*, lines 1260–1290, my translation.
5. Jake Stratton-Kent. *Geosophia-I* (Kindle Locations 373–377. 385–387). Kindle Edition.

> scarcely begun to be assessed. These books, which began to appear at least as early as the fifth century BCE, were of a revolutionary character. The received traditions of both local and state cults possessed poetry, but not holy books. Orphic texts were an entirely new literary form; the first occurrence of a religio-magical tradition founded entirely on mysterious texts rather than the time honoured, and often scarce understood, traditions of the collective.
>
> It is important to place this literature in the context of the cultural developments in Greek society. With the rise of the polis the conditions for the rise of the individual as differentiated from the collective had been created. The Orphic books represent an enormous revolution in human spirituality arising from this development. The conditions had been created for private religious associations and for individual interpretation to compete both with the state cults and with localised traditions, and indeed to supersede them in importance. The Orphic books are thus the first written expressions of a personal relationship with the divine and the world of spirit semi-independent of – and in competition with – received tradition. It cannot be sufficiently underlined that this literary expression of spiritual independence is the basis for the entire future development of the grimoires.[6]

While Stratton-Kent's statements about how early the *Orphic Argonautica* was written are factually incorrect, as a well-known necromancer, Stratton-Kent's observations about the importance of texts like the *Orphic Argonautica* and its emphasis on the use of goetic magic to apparently defeat demonic spirits is helpful.

This all relates to the Trithemius's opening sentences in Chapter I in showing how the use of "religious practices" as Trithemius argues, is being argued as a justified use of church "ritualism" in the same method of occultic practices in the *PGM* and elsewhere. These same "religious practices" such as goetic tongues and goetic music are being used to control demonic, or any goetic, spirits.[7]

[p. 111; 2, 4] There is no need to copy the text here as it is non-sensical like all goetic languages are. The use of goetic languages, as is used as an example here, is also being used by Prosperity, WOF, and NAR groups as "angel tongues" for "self-edification" and occult goetic purposes.

[p. 111; 3] *But if the spirits have not yet appeared, repeat the words as often as possible, until they appear. ...* Trithemius here is telling us to continuously "repeat the words" until the called on spirits do what the magician desires. Note the following below, again from Eckhardt: "Repeatedly remind these spirits that your authority is given to you by Jesus Christ, who is far above all rule and authority (Eph. 1:21). [...] Use the statement 'The Lord Jesus Christ rebukes you' repeatedly as a battering ram."[8]

There is no standard in scripture where a command to rebuke spirits is to be told repeatedly until the demon leaves. Paul did not repeat the command to leave to the spirit of divination in Acts 16:16–18. The spirit that approached Paul was told only once to leave and it did. Likewise in Jude 9, Moses did not assume his own authority, as that would be blasphemy, but asked the Lord once and only once for Satan to be rebuked. Since the form of the word "rebuke" here is an optative, it is a "rebuking" that is ultimately up to Jesus and not to Michael or any believer themselves. It is Jesus' authority involved

6. Jake Stratton-Kent. *Geosophia-I* (Kindle Locations 1077–1088). Kindle Edition.

7. Some people may not like the term "ritual" here but not all ritualism is necessarily a bad thing. For instance, speaking the Lord's Prayer as given to us in Matthew 6 as formulaic, would fit under a definition of a "ritual". Even the order of service that we expect every Sunday at our favourite church is still technically a "ritual" that we instead refer to as "liturgy" or as already mentioned, an "order of service". All these terms mean the same thing; however, some people will prefer one term over another even though in this case they are synonyms.

8. Eckhardt, *Deliverance*, pp. 69–70.

here and not ours. Eckhardt's argument follows that of Trithemius in attempting to claim our own authority that is apparently "given to you by Jesus Christ". This "authority" Eckhardt is falsely using for goetic purposes which means Eckhardt and all that follow these kinds of teachings do not have Christ's authority at all as the example of Exodus 33 shows in the *Introduction* (pp. 24–29) because of his and their use of goetia.

[p. 116; E] *However, we do not keep the names of all these spirits. But what is necessary for the worker to know, we will express in each chapter. ...* Note what Eckhardt once again has to say: "Address the spirit by name, and if that is not known, address it by function. You will learn either the name or the function of the demon through discernment of the Holy Spirit. or the demon will tell you its name. You can also ask it its name as Jesus did when He cast out demons (Luke 8:30)."[9]

First what must be noted about the incident with "Legion" was that "Legion" was *not the name of the "demon"*. "Legion" was a name/title given to the massive number of demons that inhabited the man. Jesus *never* asks for the names of any other demons in other demonic encounters in the gospels. As I pointed out about the use of "edify yourself" as a notable exception apart from the command to use spiritual gifts to edify the church in 1 Corinthians 14, this instance of Jesus asking for the name of the collective of demons has a significant point. Since the Gerasene's were a Gentile area outside of the originally promised area of Judea, this moment in Jesus' ministry was him showing that he had authority over the demonic powers that were in control of the world at that time and that the time of demonic rule had come to an end. Jesus never says that he is *not* there to judge them before the time. The time had in fact come and it was in that "now" that the demonic were required to leave their authority behind.

The Roman Ritual which is a lengthy set of documents around the proper liturgical rituals followed by the Roman Catholic Church similarly tell an exorcist to ask the name of a demon during an exorcism. "But necessary questions are, for example: about the number and name of the spirits inhabiting the patient."[10] We see here that the Roman Catholic *Roman Ritual* is likewise using a goetic process for their exorcisms. Since the Roman Catholic Church has been actively involved in goetia through their defences of veneration/worship of the saints and Mary, it should not be surprising that like with the *PGM* spells that call on spirits/demons/gods directly by name, so does the *Roman Ritual* and those that follow in the Prosperity, WOF and NAR movements that writers like Eckhardt are promoting.

9. Eckhardt, *Deliverance*, p. 69.

10. Philip T. Weller, *Roman Ritual II: Christian Burial, Exorcism, Reserved Blessings, etc.* (Jeffersonville, Indiana: Caritas Publishing, 2017), p. 173.

Chapter II: Padiel

Whose prince is called Padiel and Subsolanus, having under him 10,000 servants by day, 200,000 by night, and many other servants, whose number is uncertain. **Red.**

Since, as we said in the previous chapter, let it be known that Pamersiel with his identified spirits are unappeasable and unfaithful, and do not obey all those who wish to work in this art; even the most experienced in this art. We want in this present chapter to make the art safer, and to show the way of working in it by better spirits who are benevolent, ready, and cheerful to obey those who call. Who come without delay when called in due manner and time, and faithfully carry out what has been committed to them without any deception. Now the first chief of this operation, the emperor and president, is said to be Padiel, by the name of Subsolanus, with a circular residence, which is the first room after the east. He has under him ten thousand who preside over the day and all the daily operations of this art, who command and bring forth the spirits who hide in the darkness at night, who are in number two hundred thousand, all fleeing the light and day, besides one who is a messenger to the presiding spirit. They are all good and benevolent, and do not injure the worker unless he is malicious, or less skilled in the art. It is not necessary to train them all at once, but a few are sufficient, and sometimes one can satisfy the worker, whether the work is night or day. For since they are good-natured, quiet, and calm, they are more often solitary than in a chaotic crowd. Therefore, when you wish to work through them, and show the secret of your mind to anyone, however much absent, to make personal connections with them, or to do work with them, write on the paper previously prepared in the proper manner, as you know, whatever narration you want and in whatever language because the friend you are sending the message to is indifferent. When your friend is about to perceive your mind, not from paper, but from spirits, then by writing you must turn yourself to write the words, by which you say that this secret prayer is complete.

> Padiel aporsy mesarpon omeuas peludyn malpreaxo Condusen, vlearo thersephi bayl merphon, paroys gebuly mailthomyon ilthear tamarson acrimy lon peatha Casmy Chertiel, medony reabdo, lasonti iaciel mal arsi bulomeon abry pathulmon theoma pathormyn.

When you have finished these words, you will see two or at least one of the spirits very calmly present and ready to obey your will. And you can entrust your secret to him, and he will faithfully carry out what you ordered. Now when the letters have come to him to whom they are sent by messenger, if he is alone, he will receive them well. If he is with others, let him withdraw to a side if he can, or if he cannot, towards the basement. Let him say this secret prayer in silence.

> Padiel ariel vanerhon chio tarson phymarto merphon am prico ledabarym, elso phroy mesarpon ameorsy, paneryn atle pachum gel thearan vtrul vt solubito beslonty las gomadyn triamy metarnothy.

When these words have been properly spoken, the spirit sent forth will immediately appear, revealing to him perfectly, without anyone else perceiving, whatever you have committed to him, to be revealed without deception and without any danger. But no one who is malicious and wicked will be able to work easily in this art, but when someone is of a better and purer nature, the spirit obeys him so much more willingly and with greater cheerfulness. And when anyone knows this, the more he conceals it, the easier it will be to work. And note, that this Padiel with his spirits is appointed to announce secret directions for the correction of evildoers, imprisonment, and punishment, as we have shown in the subject example.

The Secret of Intention, Which is Not of letters but is entrusted to the spirits of the second mansion.[1] **Red.**

He was brought before the prince, on whom some crime of injury to majesty or any other is imposed. He wants to be punished by his official from whom he is far removed. He does not want to write the same to him, or else by manifest letters he should on any occasion be found guilty, and flee, or with the strength of all his friends resist, or plot against the prince or against the laws of the country. He writes this or any other narrative to his prefect, which is not to be read by all, but he commits the secret to the spirit, in the manner we have foretold, who will faithfully tell his secret to him to whom it is sent first in this art.

Sincere charity, I send you a prayer for the devotion of repentant sinners, quite beautifully composed, and short, which the whole benevolence of my mind did not wish to request of you alone, and it is as follows. Deliver us, Jesus Christ, the eternal saviour of all good things, and pardon the offenses of the guilty, and hear our groans, softening the storms of our vices, and renewing the oldness of conscience, by returning us to eternal paradise. Good Jesus, forgive us our urging sins, for we have greatly stumbled and often fallen away. We ask that the sweetest healer heal our infirmities. Be kind to those who ask you, Jesus, and hear us, your servants, who are appealing to you. We are a people surrounded by constant miseries and immersed in the greatest storms. Deliver us, victorious comforter of the afflicted since our life is constantly being buried in happiness, yet it is still corrupted. Have mercy on us Jesus, the most merciful saviour. Look at the humility of those who love you and do not allow banished people to sink in the mud and filth of their vices, in their love of the evil world. Up until now we have lain dormant and entangled with sinful weaknesses. We have shortened our salvation and have not remembered the future examination in the least. Most kindly Creator, be more merciful to your servants, and save the tearful ones who have been deceived by the most miserable acts of self-love in this world; you who despises no one. The unfailing joy and everlasting happiness of the saints. You are our hope, the glory of Christians, the light of angels, the rewarder of undefeated martyrs, the crown of virgins, the honour of widows. Good Jesus, hear us humble ones, crying out to you. Deliver us from the present exile, granting us grace, that we may live without end. Quicken us, we beg of you not to be exiles, your poor servants, whom you have redeemed, that we may obtain the true passion of justice. Save us almighty God, infinite majesty, unbounded mercy, eternal salvation of noble souls. Amen. The end of the prayer of John Trithemius Abbot.

Another Prayer, Whose Conspiracy

Padiel Melon, Parme, Camiel Busayr, Ilnoma, Venoga, Pamelochyn.

I also accept this prayer that is not unconsecrated. The lover of human salvation, the greatest creator of the universe, has shown us obedience to the commandments which we are all bound to obey out of love, and promised the reward to the obedient to inherit the tabernacle of eternal happiness. Let us look at the obedience of Christ, which we are careful to imitate, that we may deserve to enter the eternal happiness promised to us and with the angels to be associated

1. Uyl – The next two paragraphs are a "prayer" for another person that has done wrong.

with eternal dwellings. Let us make repentance while we can, spending our precious time productively. Let us take care that death does not give birth to the unlearned, which refuses to grant rest to anyone. Therefore, brothers, do not give up doing repentance. For death will come to you quickly, which none of you can escape for a long time. See therefore that your days pass and begin repentance when you have time. The hour is drawing near to depart from here. Oh most terrible death of terrible things, how quickly do you consume us evil people, and do you make our smallest population full of many injuries and cruel just to be cruel? Let us cry out to the poor Christ Jesus, our most faithful saviour, encouraging and reprimanding us, that we may scold shameful negligence, and diligently guard the paths of righteousness by good works. Dear Redeemer of humanity, hear us and grant us forgiveness for our sins. Oh father of mercy, be merciful to us in all our difficult sufferings. Heal, O Lord, our weak souls since we are yours. Prepare for us afflicted worms the rest of eternal beauty because we always look to you and praise you.

Amen. John Trithemius. I was born in Spanheim, Written in the year 1500.

Commentary: Chapter II

Translator and Commentator's Note: The chapters from this point on become very repetitive at times. There are a few exceptions but for the most part, those exceptions are either rare or happen in Trimethius's prayers. As a result, if there are some new additions to Trithemius's argumentation, the new additions will be commented on, but any details already commented on will be given the text that was quoted earlier in this commentary. Also, unless there is a note, the name of the "angel" in each section will not be commented on as the origins of many of the angel names in this overall book cannot be verified. The only name-based information that will be given is where the angel name can be found if there is nothing to say about who the angel, or demon, is.

[p. 125; R1] *Padiel* ... Apparently the name of a Merkavah and kabbalistic angel of childbirth in the *Sepher Raziel*. *Padiel* shares this role along with seventy total angels.[1] According to kabbalistic myth in the *Sepher Raziel*, *Padiel* was also the angel that appeared to Samson's parents.[2]

[p. 125; 1] *Since, as we said in the previous chapter, let it be known that Pamersiel with his identified spirits are unappeasable and unfaithful, and do not obey all those who wish to work in this art; even the most experienced in this art.* ... See pp. 117 and 121 with note. This is another circumstance where Trimethius would be arguing for "religious practice" to subdue these "unappeasable and unfaithful" spirits. The ritualism that is being suggested here is copied by many "deliverance" ministries like the ones Eckhardt argues in favour of in the same chapter.

[p. 125; 1] *Therefore, when you wish to work through them, and show the secret of your mind to anyone, however much absent, to make personal connections with them, or to do work with them, write on the paper previously prepared in the proper manner, as you know, whatever narration you want and in whatever language because the friend you are sending the message to is indifferent. When your friend is about to perceive your mind, not from paper, but from spirits, then by writing you must turn yourself to write the words, by which you say that this secret prayer is complete.* ... Walter Burkert in his book *Greek Religion* makes the following observation about Greek daimones (demons).

> For such is the nature of the *daimones*: they stand in the middle between gods and men, they are 'interpreters and ferrymen' who communicate the messages and gifts from men to the gods and from gods to men, prayers and sacrifices from one side, commands and recompenses from the other. (italics original)[3]

1. Rosemary Ellen Guiley Ph.D., *The Encyclopedia of Angels: Second Edition* (New York, New York: Checkmark Books, 2004), p. 83.

2. Gustav Davidson, *A Dictionary of Angels including the fallen angels* (New York, New York: The Free Press, 1971), p. 219.

3. Walter Burkert, *Greek Religion* (Malden, Massachusetts: Blackwell Publishing, 1985), p. 331–332.

This observation by Burkert is interesting when we take into consideration what people that adhere to charismatic, Prosperity, WOF and NAR teachings about calling on "angels" are using these "angels" for. Many of the individuals in these movements will argue for "angels" to protect themselves, to protect others, convict others, and many other activities that would classify them as Greek daimones and not angels. Burkert confirms this statement earlier in his book by saying that "[d]aimon is occult power, a force that drives man forward where no agent can be named. The individual feels as it were that the tide is with him."[4] While Trithemius would consider these daimones angels, when keeping mind the meaning of אוב from the Old Testament, what Trithemius is suggesting here along with the practices of those in the charismatic, Prosperity, WOF and NAR movements are all based in Minoan and Greek goetia as I showed in the *Introduction*.

[p. 125; 2, 4] non-sensical goetic "angel tongues".

[p. 127; 1] *The lover of human salvation, the greatest creator of the universe, has shown us obedience to the commandments which we are all bound to obey out of love, and promised the reward to the obedient to inherit the tabernacle of eternal happiness. Let us look at the obedience of Christ, which we are careful to imitate, that we may deserve to enter the eternal happiness promised to us and with the angels to be associated with eternal dwellings. …* The command about "obedience to the commandments which we are bound to obey out of love" must be remembered in the context of Trithemius's devotion to the Roman Catholic Church. With Trithemius being so devoted to Roman Catholicism, the commands that he is saying "we are all bound to obey out of love" are undoubtedly the *anti*-biblical traditions that were introduced by the different popes and bishops. Trithemius *also* attempts to argue that Christ was obedient to these *future* created traditions as well by commanding people to "look at the obedience of Christ, which we are careful to imitate." Christ was not loyal to any traditions, including the Pharisaic traditions of the post-exilic Jews. That the Roman Catholic Church would suggest that Christ was likewise obedient to their *future* created traditions completely goes against the rebukes that Jesus consistently gave *against tradition-based doctrine*.

4. Burkert, *Greek*, p. 180.

CHAPTER III: CAMUEL/CAMAEL

Whose prince CAMUEL, *having himself the presiding spirits of the operations of the day, ten. and likewise at night, ten. With the same number of lower servants, whose duty it is to send messengers to announce the arrival, the Ways and Iter.*

Red.

The first and highest of all the spirits of the third residence is called Camuel, who is very benevolent and ready to send his representatives to him who works in this knowledge according to the due form. He has few ministers indeed, but all good, willing, and faithful. That is to say, ten who are in charge of the day, and as many who are in charge of the night. The spirits are always sent in twos to the labourer from before in order, since those who preside over the day do not fear darkness, nor those who preside over the night, the light. Always, wherever necessity demands, in every task asked of by the worker, one is helped by the other. When they appear visible, then one sees they are in a beautiful dress of a mixed color, and another at times in a form of bright splendor and are accustomed to appearing that way. Often, however, they appear only with a perceptible effect, but they are not seen unless it pleases the operator. But this Camuel, together with his ministers and servants, has the authority and the power to announce to a friend who is not there the state, will, condition, way, journeys, arrival, and departure of the sender, whenever he who works in this art wills. Therefore, when you work according to your will, through the angels of this mansion, you must first of all know who the ten angels of Camuel are who preside over the day, and how many of them each have representatives. Likewise, about the night ones, which you should know perfectly, you will consider the present table.

Black.	Red.	B.	R.	R.	R.	R.	R.	R.	R.
Orpeniel	10.	Citgara	100e	Daniel	10.	Dobiel	100.	Azimo	10.
Camyel	100.	Pariel	10.	Omyel	10.	Nodar*	10.	Tediel	0.
Budiel	10.	Cariel	10.	Asiniel	100.	Phaniel	10.	Moriel	0.
Elcar	10.	Neriel	10.	Calym	100.	Meras	100.	Tugaros	0.

*Magic seemed to be read with mockery.

Here you have in this table the ten angels of Camuel who preside over the day, having replaced him in number, and as many who preside over the night with their own supporters. But the last ones, as you see, have no replacement, since, as you know, it means nothing at all in the actual number. Therefore, when you wish to work through these angels, prepare your writing as if you are about to die, and write any narrative in verse to Eutus, and in any language you choose, which need not be concealed. When completed, read the following secret prayer in silence.

> Camuel aperoys, melym meuomanial, casmoyn cralti busaco aeli lumar photyrion theor besamys, aneal Cabelonyr thiamo vesonthy.

Having completed this secret prayer in silence, make your request to the spirits that you know are present, and send them out, working all in silence and without disturbance. If possible, afterwards give the letters to whom you wish to convey the message. Open the letters to the spirits as you please, and let them go, for the spirits do not neglect their duty. Whether the message comes quickly or slowly, concerning which let there be no doubt for you that you are faithful. But it is necessary for you to know which spirit you wish to send from the aforesaid, in so far as in the conspiracy you express his name immediately after the principal one. This in all operations in which the names of the angels to be sent are placed in the chapter itself. But now let us put the likeness of what has been said to us upon those which pertain to the office of Camuel and the spirits of his subjects.

LET THIS BE THE MOST SECRET INTENTION OF MY MIND, which I would like to know is missing through the before mentioned spirits. **Red.**

Having been placed in Rome, I understand from the most secret counsel of the supreme pontiff, that he wished to transfer the Roman empire to the Franks. I desire to inform the princes of Germany. I cannot by messengers, whom I do not trust. I cannot by letters, for in all the cities of Italy they are stationed at the gates, who search the passersby with the utmost scrutiny. I am therefore writing a devotional prayer, which I am sending by an open message, together with other family letters closed to the same princes. I compel the spirits of the third house and command them to deliver the letters sent. When these spirits were called to the addressee, they did not fail to reveal to him my secret intention, which I did not dare to confirm in writing. They come, they go, they obey. We all die because we all contracted the hereditary guilt of the original sin. No one has lived who will not die in a very short time. We contracted the original offense in Adam and Eve. However, all men die by the death of the body because of the rashness of Mother Eve. But the death of the soul, by Jesus, the Victor of death, has made us all able to soar by freeing us. Oh, crucified Jesus Christ, look upon our humility, for we are wretched, unhappy, and afflicted with many tribulations. Therefore, we plead of the king of heaven most graciously, grant us repentance, and the forgiveness of all our sins because of your extraordinary humility, with which you redeemed us from the darkest darkness of hell, and the noxious passions. Oh, our most merciful Jesus, oh most sweet lover of innocence, what shall I repay you? You, holy and innocent, suffer for us. Where shall we flee when you come for judgment? You will come with power to pay everyone according to their conscience. All things shall be naked unto you. Nothing shall be hidden from you of which you have no knowledge. Therefore, while you are alive, repay your forgiveness, brothers, and prevent the trial of Almighty God by works of mercy.

Wipe away with tears the crimes and make lighter the labours of the poor, so that you will make God favourable to you. Because God is kind to those who call on him. Therefore, while there is time, seek his mercy. Always give thanks to him who redeemed you, Jesus Christ crucified for the salvation of men who fear the Lord.

THERE IS ANOTHER FORM OF THE SECRET MESSAGE that is committed to the spirits.

The secret remains stored in my mind, about my approach to my male or female friend in the near future. I do not dare to write this very thing, should it be made public, because this issue that is forbidden is difficult, nor to be demanded is this message, which is the same danger. I call the spirit, I commit the matter, it comes, it goes, it carries the secret most secretly, I am safe in the form of the letters that I send, it is done as it pleases the family, should the opportunity be missed.

Salute Mr. Arnoldus Bostius, the brother of the Entities, who composed many admirable volumes on various matters. For in our book which I sent you a while ago, among other things, which pre-notes about the ecclesiastical writers, you will find it written at the end, where mention is made of the living. This man, remarkable for your sincerity in religion and the beauty of the arts, I commend and praise as the dearest supporter, to the extent that you receive him with the familiarity with which you have been willing to receive all who are united to us in friendship. He will unlock for you many secrets of nature and will be able to entertain you with the sweetest conversation, if you so desire. I beg you to send me the code of my magical experiments which you have, as soon as possible. I will send you the volume of Synesis by the power of spirits as soon as you have sent my experiments. Take care of yourself as you are. And be sure to often write back to me. Dated at Spanheim on the sixth day of March. In the year of Sunday's Incarnation 1500, John Trith. Abb. — Now he, receiving the letters to whom you have sent the spirit, should do what he knows must be done in this art, and having recognized the circular sign, he turns to them and in silence utters this appeal.

> Camuel Busarcha, menaton enatiel, meran sayr abasremon, naculi pesarum nadru lasmõ enoti chamabet vsear lesponty abrulmy pen sayr thubarym, gonayr asmon friacha rynon otry hamerson, buccurmy pedauellon.

Having said these things, let him take the letters again in his hand, looking back at the verse you know. It must be noted that all these spirits are with their leader, and for that reason it is necessary for everyone who works through them to turn to him. Observe and understand what we have told you.

Commentary: Chapter III

[p. 131; R1] *Camuel*, [also, *Camael*] ... Believed by the occult to be the ruler of powers and dominions, a type of faulty angelic authority. Powers and dominions have been assumed to be angelic authorities by traditional and kabbalistic teaching. Again, we need to take notice of the context of the following verses that people appeal to in order to claim that there are different "hierarchies" of angels:

> according to the working of his great might that he worked in Christ when he raised him from the dead and seated him at his right hand in the heavenly places, far above all rule and authority and power and dominion, and above every name that is named, not only in this age but also in the one to come. And he put all things under his feet and gave him as head over all things to the church, which is his body, the fullness of him who fills all in all. (Ephesians 1:19–23 ESV)

> Then comes the end, when he delivers the kingdom to God the Father after destroying every rule and every authority and power. For he must reign until he has put all his enemies under his feet. The last enemy to be destroyed is death. (1 Corinthians 15:24–26 ESV)

In both passages we need to keep in mind Matthew 28:18 where Jesus makes it clear that all authority in "heaven" and "earth" is now his. With Matthew 28:18 in mind it is not hard to see that all of these different, "rulers", "authorities", "powers" and "dominions" have nothing to do with angels but are earthly powers. Satan had already been cast down and subdued when Jesus rose from the grave. The only peoples left to subdue were the rebellious human agents left on earth.

> Baptism, which corresponds to this, now saves you, not as a removal of dirt from the body but as an appeal to God for a good conscience, through the resurrection of Jesus Christ, 22 who has gone into heaven and is at the right hand of God, with angels, authorities, and powers having been subjected to him. (1 Peter 3:21–22 ESV)

Again, here the assumption is that "authorities" and "powers" are angelic in nature. However, since the other passages give evidence that these "authorities" and "powers" are human in nature, 1 Peter 3:21–22 is showing once again that Matthew 28:18 is here shown to being fulfilled at that time.

In Eliphas Levi's *The History of Magic*, Levi mentions of *Camuel* that, "Camul or Camael, [is] a name which personifies divine justice in the Kabalah."[1] Showing that

1. Eliphas Levi, *The History of Magic* (London, United Kingdom: William Rider & Son Limited, 1922), p. 229. Levi is also the one that brought the current faulty myth of the demon Baphomet to the western world in his books *The Doctrine and Ritual of Transcendental Magic*. Baphomet was nothing more than a slur of the western European name for Muhammed at the time, *Mahomet*. The truth behind the collapse of the Knights Templar was that they had converted to Islam. The plan was to prevent the Knights Templar seizing the French Empire, whose king was deeply in debt to the knightly order and turning the French Empire over to the current Muslim Imam. Since Muslim settlers had already come to southern Spain, the threat of the Knights Templar turning the French Empire over to the currently reigning Imam was very real. The apparent head that was worshipped in the Templar chapel was nothing more than unsubstantiated confessions given

Camuel is a kabbalistic name, and that Trithemius does refer to the validity of the *Kabbalah* in *The Book Begins* of this volume, reveals once more where the idea of calling on angels for protection or any other task by current day evangelicals is really coming from. *Camuel* was also believed to be one of the angels that appeared to "Jesus during his agony in the Garden of Gethsemane".[2]

[p. 131; 1] *who is very benevolent and ready to send his representatives to him who works in this knowledge according to the due form. ...* See p. 123; 1.

[p. 131; T1] While numbers were mentioned along with "angel" names in *Chapter I*, it is easier to comment on the numerology of this issue here. Many people in popular movements are determined to use numbers and abstract mathematical formulas to determine when events they believe were be prophesied will happen. A common one is the use of 2 Peter 3:8 that since Jesus was in the grave for three days and because the Bible says that "a thousand years is like a day" that means that Jesus will return in the "third millennium". The reference is also in Psalm 90:8, but the text in 2 Peter 3 also mentions the inverse that a day is also like a thousand years meaning that time is meaningless to God. God will fulfill his promises when he desires and not when we want or expect him to. John Hagee and John Bevere both refer to 2 Peter 3:8 in the fallacious ways mentioned above.[3] Both of these men have prophesied falsely, like goetics do, several times and yet their "ministries" are constantly supported. Both men are what would be known as "7th day dispensationalists" who would say that since the earth was founded in 4,000 BC, that Christ will return in the 3rd millennium AD because of both of them hacking apart 2 Peter 3:8 to suit their numerology arguments. The "7th day" ideology comes from another kabbalistic text known as the *Sepher haTemunah* which argues for six millennia of chaos filled with one millennium of peace and security (or as the occult knows it, the *Age of Aquarius*) before the cycle begins once again of six millennia of chaos followed by another millennium of peace and enlightenment.[4]

The connection between these years and the number of angels may not be immediately clear. The obsession over numbers, and the number of angels comes from goetic texts like 1 Enoch, 2 Enoch and several Merkavah Mysticism texts. This obsession with numbers and numerology is rampant in many dispensational circles where numbers are taken in a way that they simply should not be. The number "1,000" was often figurative such as in Psalm 50:10 mentioning "cattle on a thousand hills". This is not a literal one thousand hills, and likewise interpreting "one thousand years" as a literal "one thousand years"

---

by the Templars under torture. King Philip, the one who convinced the Pope to disband the Knights Templar, had many political and social enemies who were all accused of the same crimes by Philip and were also tortured into confessing the those same crimes. Despite what people believe about torture, the human mind only has so much tolerance until it will give the torturer any information they want in order to make the pain and torment stop. Many of the Knights Templar actually renounced their confessions after they were released. A document known as the *Chinon Parchment* was found in 2001 forgotten in the Vatican Libraries. This document, written in 1308, absolved the Knights Templars of their crimes of heresy which would allow them to go to heaven. The *Chinon Parchment* did not declare the Templars *not guilty* of other apparent crimes, but the Templars were effectively not responsible for the guilt of heresy that Philip imposed on them.

2. Gustav Davidson, *A Dictionary of Angels including the fallen angels* (New York, New York: The Free Press, 1971), p. 80.

3. See: John Hagee, *The Four Blood Moons*: *Something Is About To Change* (Brentwood, Tennessee: Worthy Publishing, 2013), p. 47, and John Bevere, *The Fear of the Lord*: *Discover the Key to Ultimately Knowing God* (Lake Mary, Florida: Charisma House, 2006), p. 127.

4. Gershom Scholem, *Origins of the Kabbalah* (Princeton, New Jersey: Princeton University Press, 2018), p. 463.

is fallacious. Much like the "40 years" that Israel was in the desert wandering before going into the land of Canaan. The number "40" was indicative of a standard lifetime in ancient Israelite society and was indicating that the nation of Israel was wandering "for a lifetime". There is no way to know for certain that Israel was wandering for a literal "40 years". In the same way, using numbers in this way as specific descriptors and to find out *esoteric prophetic* knowledge is no different than the goetic use of numbers of angels for use in goetia. Since dispensationalism is guilty of more false prophecies in the last two-hundred years than even the Prosperity, WOF and NAR movements, the connection between the use of numerology in goetic texts like this one, 1 Enoch, 2 Enoch, Merkavah Mysticism's Hekhalot Literature and the texts by Hagee and Bevere above is clear.

[p. 131; 3], [p. 133; 4] non-sensical goetic "angel tongues".

[p. 132; 1] *I understand from the most secret counsel of the supreme pontiff, that he wished to transfer the Roman empire to the Franks. I desire to inform the princes of Germany. …* From a historical standpoint, it must be understood that the French Empire was not officially part of the Holy Roman Empire which went from the borders of the French Empire to the borders of the former Byzantine Empire in the East. With the Turks conquering Constantinople, the capitol of the Byzantine Empire in 1453 46–47 years prior to this book being written, and the weakening of the Holy Roman Empire and French Empires due to the nine different Crusades, a real fear of invasion did exist. The First Crusade happened from 1096–1099 AD and the Ninth Crusade took place from 1271–1272 AD. While today we might think that two-hundred twenty-eight years would be enough to restore the attrition of soldiers lost through those nearly two-hundred years of warfare, the low birth rates and high infant mortality made it unlikely that during that time that the armies of the Holy Roman Empire, stationed in current day Austria, were strong enough to repel any Turkish invaders. The pope, according to Trithemius, was conspiring with the French king to surrender the Holy Roman Empire to the French Empire effectively committing an act of treason against the Holy Roman Emperor that at this time was living in current day Germany. Thankfully, as history shows, the Turks were never able to get far into European lands, but this was mostly due to the Holy Roman Empire needing other nations such as Wallachia and the infamous Vlad III, who is infamously known Vlad the Impaler or Dracula, to repel the Turkish invaders in the year of 1492. While there is no confirmed connection between Vlad III and the Holy Roman Emperor, the Holy Roman Empire did owe a big debt of gratitude to Vlad III. Since the threat of Turkish retaliation over the Crusades was something the papacy feared, the vengeance the Turkish armies would take against the Holy Roman Empire for the devastation and horrors the papacy encouraged their crusaders to commit would be something the papacy would not have wanted to answer for. The only way for the papacy to avoid the guilt of those kinds of grisly horrors was to surrender the Holy Roman Empire to the French Empire and consolidate both armies in Austria to repel any Turkish armies looking to conquer European lands. Vlad III was a sort of bloody anti-hero in the war against the Turks, but the papacy still had a lot to answer for in light of the Crusades.

Chapter IV: Aseliel/Asiel

Long live Prince Aseliel who has moved to Eastern Europe, having under him forty chiefs complimented with their servants, and they are in charge of those that pertain to emotions of love.

Red.

The great prince Aseliel holds the fourth mansion from the East in Euro-south with his spirits, ten of whom preside over the operations in this art by day, and twenty by night. It is the power and duty of all these to announce those things which pertain to the love of women. Now these have thirty spirits as principals under them, and as many others whom they send by order to their offices, when they have been duly called by the operator of the art. Again, below these there are others, of whom there is a great number. As for you, when you wish to work through the chief of this mansion in steganography, it is not necessary to bring in all the spirits subject to him, but one or two are sufficient for you, whether the operation be nocturnal or done during the day. I will therefore tell you the names of a few, with the number of those who follow them. Of which you will always bring one or two, whomever you want, and you do not need more, unless the use of the art is for several women. This is the table:

Mariel (R)	20	Cubiel (R)	20	Asphiel (R)	20	Melas (R)	20	Nom. rub.
Charas (R)	20	Aniel (R)	20	Curiel (R)	20	Sariel (R)	20	Num. nig.
Parniel	20 (R)	Asahel	20 (R)	Chamos	20 (R)	Othiel	20 (R)	Nom. nig.
Aratiel	20 (R)	Arean	20 (R)	Odiel	20 (R)	Bufar	20 (R)	Num. rub.

You now have sixteen chiefs from among the elders, who are under the great Asiel. Eight of these spirits are in charge of the day, and eight of whom are in charge of the night. Each of them has twenty subordinate servants, whom they send to their duties whenever necessary. All princes are good, and are good to the obedient, but not all of their servants, since they are sometimes proud and relentless, especially to those whom they trusted to be less perfect in this art. But these sixteen princes with their subjects are sufficient to inform you of everything, and there is no need for you either to know or to have these spirits instruct you more. And when you wish to work in steganography through Asiel, instead of the usual premises in the art, observe the place of his residence, which is in Euro-southern, and call one of the above-mentioned spirits for his time. For each spirit you will speak this secret prayer.

> Aseliel aproysy, melym, thulnear casmoyn, mauear burson, charny demorphaon, Theoma asmeryn diuiel, casponti vearly basamys, ernoti chaua lorson.

Completing the usual secret methods, join with others who are experienced in the art, and the result of your operation will be most certain. Let us make examples.

Let us imagine the mystery of your mind. You have a friend in who you are in love, and she herself is no less in love with you. However, you cannot approach or address her because of the attitude of her family towards you. You have at last found a plan by which you are able to take control of the situation, but it is necessary to agree to this plan first. You cannot do it by yourself, you do not dare to let the letters fall into the hands of others. You cannot decide to entrust the matter to messengers or elders, or else they will make you known later. This thing, therefore, artfully concealed for a time, which you trust cannot be made public. You call ministers who are invisible. You write letters that are suspected by no one. You send these letters to your friend even through the guards themselves, they praise the writing, they give it to your friend to read. She, recognizing the sign of the hidden messenger, listens to the advice, orders the agreement to the spirits. Then you come, and you will get these things.

The death of Jesus Christ revived humanity, whose innocently afflicted life freed us from all calamities. Therefore, let us honour his humility in us by resisting temptation. And resisting sinful acts, instead insisting on through good works that Christ Jesus saved our souls. Let us give eternal thanks to our redeemer because he brought us all back to safety. Jesus, whose name we praise with ferocity at all times, preoccupying his most holy face with our prayers. Let us live virtuously in the love of moral uprightness, shunning the confusion of worldly affairs, let us follow the rule of justice, resist evil lives most faithfully, wash away our negligence with tears and with the greatest care remembering the future judge, whose unimaginable horror is in no way inferior to the punishment of Hell. In the year of Sunday's birth 1500. Marÿ. When he has received letters of this kind, he to whom they are sent, an expert in the art, does what he knows to be done according to their institutions, and turns to the aspect of Euro-Austria, whose sign reads the resistance of the spirits, which is like this:

> Aseliel murnea casmodym bularcha vadusynaty belron diuiel arsephonti si pa normys orleuo cadon Venoti basramyn.

With these objections, he will continue the operation of the art, and listen to the secret of the sender.

Commentary: Chapter IV

[p. 133; R1] *Aseliel* [or, *Asiel*] ... According to the apocryphal book *2 Esdras*, *Asiel* is an angelic scribe that was to write some books. Some of these books were to be published while others were only for "the wise". The relevant text is below:

> But look thou prepare thee many box trees, and take with thee Sarea, Dabria, Selemia, Ecanus, and Asiel, these five which are ready to write swiftly; And come hither, and I shall light a candle of understanding in thine heart, which shall not be put out, till the things be performed which thou shalt begin to write. And when thou hast done, some things shalt thou publish, and some things shalt thou shew secretly to the wise: to morrow this hour shalt thou begin to write. (2 Esdras 14:24–26 1900 KJV)

Gustav Davidson claims that "*Asiel*" is also mentioned in the goetic text *The Testament of Solomon* as a demon that reveals thieves and hidden treasure. While this reference is believable considering the money-driven desires of goetic practice, but I could not find such a reference to a spirit/demon of that name in *The Testament of Solomon*.[1] *The Testament of Solomon* does mention a spirit that uncovers hidden treasure, but that spirit is not named as *Aseliel*/*Asiel*.

[p. 133; R1] *who has moved to Eastern Europe* ... The Bible is not the only text to support "territorial demons". The Bible is the only text to show that the authority of territorial demons has to come an end. As is shown in another goetic text known as *Grimorium Verum*: *The True Grimoire* the idea of "territorial ruler demons" that is fallaciously believed by NAR advocates such as the late C. Peter Wagner, is the origin of such teaching. There are more goetic texts that claim that demonic spirits, some of which are good, some are bad, rule areas of the world. The text of Daniel 10 does support that demons once ruled over certain areas of the world, but as the story of "Legion" explains in Mark 5 the authority of the territorial demons was torn down. The statement by Jesus in Matthew 28:18 that Jesus now has all authority on heaven and earth is also a clear statement that the demonic powers are no longer in authority over any country or territory at all. The *Grimorium Verum* however states that the "inferiors of Lucifer are in Europe".[2]

C. Peter Wagner argues that the "invasion of the territory of Diana and her defeat constitute the fifth and final episode of strategic-level spiritual warfare I believe we find in the New Testament."[3] However this is Wagner reading into the text that Paul was praying against a spiritual power of Ephesus. Wagner continues to defend this type of spiritual warfare in saying to do "strategic-level spiritual warfare (which some prefer to

1. Gustav Davidson, *A Dictionary of Angels including the fallen angels* (New York, New York: The Free Press, 1971), p. 57.

2. Author Unknown, *Grimorium Verum*: *The True Grimoire*, edited by Tarl Warwick (Vermont: Tarl Warwick, 2018), p. 11, Kindle Edition.

3. C. Peter Wagner, *Spiritual Warfare Strategy*: *Confronting Spiritual Powers* (Shippensburg, Pennsylvania: Destiny Image, 2011), p. 216.

call "cosmic-level" spiritual warfare) in which territorial principalities and powers are confronted."[4] However, the Bible *never* says to pray, or even to address the demonic, in this way. To do this Wagner argues to "do Marches for Jesus, prayerwalks, prophetic acts, and strategic-level spiritual warfare involving the kind of head-on confrontation with the principalities and powers."[5] Considering all that has already been said about territorial spirits and the reality of biblical goetia, Wagner's conclusions here are misguided and *anti*-biblical. There is never any command to do "prayerwalks" to effectively gain "divination" about what "spirits" are controlling an area and then to rebuke them. Like I said in my *Introduction*, because so many people have bought into goetic magic for the purposes of self-divination and to gain mastery over the universe, these are goetic practices these people want to believe are legitimate. The reason people *want* to believe this is because it allows them to assume their own godhood as a supposedly "Christian" truth even though it is not.

[p. 137; 3], [p. 138; 2] non-sensical goetic "angel tongues".

4. Wagner, *Spiritual Warfare*, p. 253.
5. Wagner, *Spiritual Warfare*, pp. 237–238.

Chapter V: Barmiel

Whose supreme prince, named Barmiel, dwells in the south, having under him ten princes who are in charge of the day, and twenty princes who are in charge of the night with their servants. They are above the secrets to be announced, which belong to the traditions of the camps.

Red.

The great prince of the five mansions in the south is called Barmiel. Having under his authority ten principal leaders who preside during the day with their subordinates and twenty principal leaders who preside over night operations with their servants. Therefore, they are more in number than the day because the operation of this residence takes place more often during the night than during the day. For their duty is to tell the secret traditions of the camps and towns, especially at nighttime. But when you wish to work in this art through Barmiel: call one of his princes, whomever you please. The prince will come to you at once with twenty servants, because it was customary for some of the princes of this mountain to never go alone or with a few, but many. However, you do not give your secret to the servants because they are proud and malicious, but entrust it to the prince, because he is good, calm, faithful, and very benevolent. But now I will name for you eight of the princes of the day, and likewise eight of the night princes, who are better and more ready to obey, and we do not need more.

Black.	Red.	R.	B.	B.	R.	R.	B.
Sochas	20.	Acterar	20.	Barbis	20.	Marciaz.	0.
Red.	Black.	B.	R.	R.	B.	B.	R.
Tigara	20.	Barbil	20.	Marquus.	20.	Baabal	0.
Black.	Red.	R.	B.	B.	R.	R.	B.
Chansi	20.	Carpiel	20.	Caniel	20.	Gabir	0.
Red.	Black.	B.	R.	R.	B.	B.	R.
Keriel	20.	Mansi	20.	Acreba	20.	Astib	0.

-->

You have sixteen spirits, twelve of whom each has twenty ministers, with whom they usually appear to the caller. The remaining four, whom have zero, which also means nothing is assumed, they have no lower servants. They always come alone, and are most faithful in their service, and energetic in all things. You will command them, who are willing to attack, to work through any one of them, with the assumption of those who are in the art are to be believed. Tell this mysterious prayer to the south.

> Barmiel buras melo charnotiel malapos veno maspian albryon, chasmia peluo morophon apluer charmya noty Mesron alraco caspiel hoalno chorben ouear ascrea cralnoty carephon elcfor bumely nesitan army tufaron.

After you have completed the commandment, trust this secret to the appearing spirit whom you have called, but send the letters by each one you will, and with whatever you will. But let us show an example.

Let Us Put the King's Secret, Which is Not to be Trusted to Anyone in Any Way.

A king is not able to obtain the city or the fortifications of any person or prince with the weapons he desires. He attacks the matter with skill. He bribes the guards with wages. The king trusts no one's advice, not even of letters, and if he is not caught, and does not succeed in his intention, they lose their wages with their lives. The prince turns himself to the mansion of Barmiel, summons a spirit with a message, and commits to the spirit a secret. He comes, carries the message, is captured in the night, but it is not known how. For these, if it pleases us, let us imagine the letters in no way at all fearing that the reader will understand.

> We shall attain happiness by living justly: only for the humble to be exalted, only for the temperate to condemn. If you seek happiness, hold on to eternal justice, and you will attain the highest glory. Be the most fervent zealot for the truth, and do not love falsehood, which corrupts honesty and dissolves temperance. Flee from the vanity of the world, for it is very short. Be a lover of justice and do not wrong anyone. Cultivate the virtues. Run away from life. Protect justice and freedom. Beware of all insolence. Always be humble. Love the Saviour of our souls, he who loves him will never die unhappily. Contempt the glory that is suddenly transitory. Love the eternally uncorrupted happiness of the saints. Carefully flee the snares of our ancient enemy, who will be overcome by the humility of never-ceasing devotion. Be on the watch that you are not overcome by the passion of the flesh. Manfully defend the paths of justice and remember to uphold righteousness with fearless perseverance. Always avoid empty glory like poison in order to behold the ever-abiding beauty of the Paradise of God. The joys of the age pass quickly, today happy, tomorrow robbed of everything and dies. Flee from the vicious zeal of bitterness. Flee from the swelling of pride, since you do not know that the guilt of both of you is subject to perpetual evils. Every proud person is hateful to God. Dying he is tormented in the intermission and will never be comforted. What, then, will they expect from the dead but lamentation? Therefore, woe to you who are exalted, worthy of eternal punishment reserved for eternal darkness and horrors. O vanity of the vanities of the world. Exterminator of the light of souls. Deceiver of the exile. Most pernicious unlocker of hell, John Trithemius Abbot Spanheim writes. 5th of March, 1500.

On receiving the letters, he immediately turned to the south, as soon as he could, on learning the sign of Barmiel. For no danger to the obedience of the spirit can arise from delay, even if much has been reconciled. For when they call, he is always more than willing to come, whether soon or late, even after many days. Here is his secret prayer, on the premises which this art demands to be carried out.

> Barmiel any casleon archoi bulesan eris, Casray molaer pessaro duys anale goerno mesrue greal cusere drelnoz, parle cufureti basriel aflymaraphe neas lo, carnos erneo, damerosenotis anycarpodyn.

When he says this mysterious prayer, as he must towards the south, he will hear and understand your mind which you committed not to the letter but to the spirit. If he turns to another quarter, he will never understand.

Commentary: Chapter V

[p. 143; R1] *Barmiel* ... There was no information from reliable sources that I could find about this name. *Barmiel* is neither an angel nor a demon name mentioned in the Bible and is therefore a goetic name that should not be considered as real by any Christian.

[p. 143; 1] *preside over night operations with their servants. Therefore, they are more in number than the day because the operation of this residence takes place more often during the night than during the day. For their duty is to tell the secret traditions of the camps and towns, especially at nighttime.* ... It is interesting what Trithemius says here along the information I showed about the "witching hour" on pages 76–79 of my *Introduction*. That this goetic "angel" is presiding over the operations of night where the duties of this spirit and this spirits' servants is to reveal "secret traditions" is evidence about the way the Prosperity, WOF and NAR movements are using these nighttime encounters. Encounters such as the ones that I showed Bill Johnson mentioned in the *Introduction* and that we should also see that Michal Ann and James Goll mention in their book *Angelic Encounters*: *Engaging Help from Heaven* where Michal says that:

> I sat up in bed, wide-awake. The room was thick with the manifest presence of God. The very atmosphere conveyed the sense of destiny. (When angels cross over from the eternal realm to the temporal one and bring with them the manifest presence of God, there can be different "flavors" to the way the presence feels. This time God's presence felt like destiny.) This sense of God's presence and this sense of destiny lasted for maybe twenty minutes, while I just sat there in the bed, not saying a word. Then, at the end of my bed, I saw an angel.
>
> I don't know how tall this angel was, because the angel wasn't in the appearance of a man. This angel looked more like a "typical" angel, if there is such a thing, covered with glowing, feathery, satiny, radiant white garments. Its wings were held to its sides, and they were enormous. I couldn't say a word. I didn't want to say a word. I was speechless because of the incredible radiant presence in the room and the fear of the Lord and the tangible sense of destiny. I don't know what kind of angel this was, but I know it was some kind of a covering angel or covering cherub, maybe even an archangel—some kind that has authority over other angels. I could tell that much by what happened next.
>
> The angel opened up its wings. I don't know how many wings it had, at least two. Then a hand like a man's hand proceeded out from under the wings. It reminded me of scriptural descriptions of the seraphim. In the angel's hand was a green measuring cup, an incredibly green measuring cup. I associate the color green as the color of the Levites, the priests, who are the ones who intercede. And green could also be interpreted to mean new life.
>
> In this cup was fresh oil. And then for the next twenty minutes, I watched this angel dispatch scores of other angels, hundreds, maybe even thousands of them. They were just taking off as fast as they could— swoosh! Swoosh! Swoosh! They were being released to go out over the whole world. These angels carried bottles of fresh oil, and they carried bottles of new wine. I was amazed.
>
> Over in the corner of the room, I saw a large bottle of oil perhaps eighteen inches tall. The bottle was labeled "Crisco." For a split second, I allowed my unspiritual thoughts to rise up and wonder, "Oh, why does the prophetic always have to be so parabolic?" Then

> immediately I understood the meaning. "Oh, of course! It's Crisco. Cris—Jesus Christ." The Greek word is Christos, which means "the Anointed One." "And the 'co'—the anointing is not being released for one person, but for a company." I understood it—fresh oil was being released through the messengers of Jesus Christ to the company of the body of Christ.
>
> As these angels were going out, swoosh, swoosh, all over the earth, I understood the word that had been spoken aloud at the first sound of the trumpet-shofar. The word I had heard was, "It's time to begin!" It was time to begin a new outpouring. It was time to cross a new threshold in church history. We had the Jesus movement thirty years before, and now it was time to begin something new.[1]

Then see what Michal has to say after the previous story:

> With the help of a discerning friend, I began to realize that the different aspects of that first night had meaning for the broader body of Christ. It was as if I had entered into a prophetic intercessory experience that had implications for the church as a whole. For instance, the intense pressure in my head and the incredible pushing on my back represented God's desire to push fear and unbelief out of His bride. That's why I felt as if my heart had stopped. It was as if Jesus came and said, "I want to rearrange your heart. My own heart cries out for an exclusive relationship with you." That's why I couldn't hold on to Jim in the night; the Lord wanted me to cling to Him alone. The Lord was saying, "I am jealous after you with true jealousy, and I will not be satisfied to have a relationship with you through your husband, your pastor, or anyone else."[2]

None of this sounds biblical in any kind of way. Even in the encounter with Isaiah in Isaiah 6, the prophet was not visited by an angel or by Yahweh, he was in the temple and had a viewing of Yahweh in his throne room. That Isaiah would have a glimpse of Yahweh's throne room is not absurd considering the importance of the Most Holy Place in the temple cultus. Isaiah was not *in* the Most Holy Place, but he was able to see Yahweh in his *throne room* as if Isaiah were looking into the Moly Holy Place. Isaiah was neither visited by an angel who worked on behalf of God's commissioning of Yahweh, nor was Isaiah "raptured" to heaven to receive his commissioning before Yahweh's throne as Merkavah Mysticism's *Hekhalot Literature* explains. Many false prophets in charismatic, Prosperity, WOF and NAR movements claim similar types of "commissioning". If *anyone* claims that they have received a commissioning for prophecy by an angel or by being "taken up" (raptured) into heaven, what these "prophets" are saying is a lie embedded in occultic ideology. What is even more telling about these "encounters" is that all these supernatural "experiences" all happen at night when goetic magic is believed to be more active and more "powerful". These "encounters" are also being used to give "secret traditions" where Michal, in the quoted text above, used a mishearing of a word to assume a meaning of a "commissioning" by using the meaning behind "the Anointed One" as a secret commissioning that was goetic in origin.

[p. 143; 1], [145; 1] non-sensical goetic "angel tongues".

[p. 144; 3] *Carefully flee the snares of our ancient enemy, who will be overcome by the humility of never-ceasing devotion. ...* Notice once again how Trithemius is defending that adhering to the ritual and liturgical practices of a church is what will "overcome" the enemy (Satan) instead of faith in Christ. This "devotion to ritual" is something heavily practiced by those in Prosperity, WOF and NAR movements as well as shown in the cri-

1. James W. Goll, *Angelic Encounters: Engaging Help from Heaven* (Lake Mary, Florida: Charisma House, 2013), Logos Edition.

2. Goll, *Angelic Encounters*, Logos Edition.

tique of John Eckhardt in *Commentary*: *Chapter I*.

Chapter VI: Gediel/Gdiel

Whose supreme prince was Gediel, having a residence in South Africa. He has under him twenty spirits during the day, and as many at night with their servants. These spirits have the duty of announcing the dangers that must be guarded against.

In the sixth house, which is in South Africa, presides the great prince Gediel, who has under his authority twenty other principal leaders by day, and as many by night, with many of their servants. The duty of these is to tell all that relates to the calling of a friend about: imminent future danger, and especially to the leaders for the defense of the country, camps, and cities; and to announce all things that are useful to friends. Also, to those whom we favour, for salvation, and not against any enemies and adversaries. For it is not necessary to assign twenty princes, but two are sufficient with their servants, whom you know by name. I will number some of them in sequence, that is to say, eight for the day and eight for the night.

Black.	Red.	B.	R.	B.	R.	B.	R.
Coliel		Sariel		Reciel		Aroan	
	20.		20.		20.		20.
Naras		Rantiel		Sadiel		Cirecas	
Red.	Black.	R.	B.	R.	B.	R.	B.
Sabas		Mashel		Agra		Aglas	
	20.		20.		20.		20.
Assaba		Bariel		Anael		Vriel	

First, before we proceed to work, you must know that at least two spirits are always to be called, with their twenty servants, without whom they never proceed, although not all of them always appear visible. But there is no need to worry about this. Only you will achieve what you intend through their invisible service. When then, through their service you wish to work something in steganography, turn yourself to the South; for all dwell there with their chief Gediel at all times. Then do what you know to be done according to order. This is the mysterious prayer:

> Gediel asiel modebar mopiel, casmoyn, rochamurenu proys nasaron atido casmear vearsy maludym velachain demosar otiel masdurym sodiuiel mesray seor amarlum, laueur pealo netus fabelron.

When these are completed, there will be two princes called to the candidate present, good, benevolent, and secure, whom you need not fear. Commit to them confidently whatever you will, and they will faithfully fulfill your command. This sign will be red.

Red. YOU HAVE IN YOUR MIND SUCH A SECRET, WHICH YOU DARE NOT COMMIT TO LETTER.

In return for the many favours of my prince, I received the secret plan of his adversaries to take the castle this night by ambush and tradition. I desire to persuade my prince this way, so I do not say so by letter. When the scrutiny of those who pass by the enemy is done on the road, I will call the spirit, I will commit the secret, and I will send letters only for whatever form I want, so that the prince knows who is to be called and from the number of spirits (for without the letters otherwise he would not know the spirit sent to me) he goes and announces for the prince who preoccupies the castle.

LET THE FORM OF LITERATURE BE THIS OR ANOTHER, WHICH, WHEN HE HAS READ, HE FORBIDS HIM TO GO. **Red.**

The highest nobility and supreme virtue of humanity is to love God purely, to seek his glory, and to adore him with uprightness of mind. For the humility of a pure heart will reign in heaven, and patience will be exalted. Only the naked mind of man, with the fear of God, will be set up for true nobility. Love God, despise the world. Flee from sin forever. Love religion, brotherly charity, the bond of peace, and the courage of those who speak correctly. Christ warns in the Gospel, that it is not necessary for us to be concerned about needless human concerns. Having (says the Holy Apostle) only what is necessary, let us be content. Let us therefore have the love of God and the zeal of justice. For they are truly solid riches, purity of mind, simplicity of heart, neglect of earthly honour, the cleansing of beauty, and the institution of the saints. Let us be intent on good works, or else vices overwhelm us. Let us live innocently in all righteousness, as if we were to die tomorrow. Let us love God with a pure heart, diligently obeying his commandments with humility, let us mourn for our sins at all times, imploring the most faithful Saviour to forgive us our sins. Instill in our hearts self-love and in humility give to others. Let us abandon the sexual desires of this world as well as vain and false honours, thinking diligently of our death. To live virtuously, to love the neighbor, to do wrong to no one, to fear God, to give alms, to feed the hungry, to defend the good, to rebuke the sins of the good, to persist in prayer, to despise the glory of the world, and to lean on lessons, are the treasures of Christians. For the worthless glory of the world will suddenly fall away, even false riches, which we shall leave behind, exhaling the pitch, our only happiness is justice. In our humility let the glory and the possession of riches remain with us at all times, the memory of death, the fear of judgment and the remembrance of our sins.

When these or any other letters contained no secret, my prince received, seeing the sign of Gediel, he knew where to turn, and who to call the Spirit.

SECRET PRAYER.

Gediel aprois camor ety moschoyn diuial palorsan, fermel, asparlon Crisphe Lamedon ediur cabosyn arsy thamerosyn.

With these words, it is necessary, by submitting and not by any other things that are necessary in art, by revealing the spirit, not the letter, of the secret of my mind, that he should know the secret, and preoccupy the enemy.

Commentary: Chapter VI

[p. 151; 1] *Gediel* [or, *Gdiel*] ... *Gediel* is believed to be another one of the "childbirth" angels as indicated in the *Book of the Angel Raziel*. Davidson also states that *Gediel* is used in astrological beliefs within the occult as an angel of the zodiac. According to another goetic text, *The Almadel of Solomon*, Gediel is a prince of a chorus of angels once again giving suggestion to goetic's use of music.[1]

[p. 151; 3], [p. 151; 2], non-sensical goetic "angel tongues".

[p. 152; 2] *love God purely, to seek his glory, ...* While the statements here will not seem problematic, that Trithemius snuck in the act that is a "supreme virtue" is to "seek [God's] glory" is problematic. In Isaiah 42:8 "I am the Lord; that is my name; my glory I give to no other, nor my praise to carved idols." (ESV) The indication here is that Yahweh will not share his glory with other gods or spiritual beings. Yet, the Prosperity, WOF, and NAR movements have usurped that verse to mean that they are able to gain God's very glory. Bobbie Houston, wife to the former Head Pastor of Hillsong Church in Sydney, Australia stated that, "God's glory in the coming days will attach itself to such spirited people and thus we will witness more and more as we venture the Church into her future."[2] We need to remember that even Moses in Exodus 33:20 was told by Yahweh that *no one* could see Yahweh's face and live. The fullness of God's glory cannot be seen or contained by *sinful* man. The reason Jesus' body could contain God's glory was because Jesus was *sinless*, but we must also remember the fact that Jesus is also *God*. To presume, like Bobbie Houston does, that we can bear Yahweh's glory in this manner is to assume our own divinity. If we had God's glory put on us in the way that Houston states, not only ourselves, but everyone in our *immediate* vicinity would instantly be struck dead.

[p. 152; 2] *Let us be intent on good works, ...* The deception in this statement may not be clear. While antinomianism, the belief that because we are saved by grace that we can do whatever we want and do not need to worry about the results of such sin, is an incorrect view of the biblical doctrine of "saved by grace alone". The other problem is that many take the following text in James too far:

> What good is it, my brothers, if someone says he has faith but does not have works? Can that faith save him? If a brother or sister is poorly clothed and lacking in daily food, and one of you says to them, "Go in peace, be warmed and filled," without giving them the things needed for the body, what good is that? So also faith by itself, if it does not have works, is dead. (James 2:14–17 ESV)

---

1. 1. Rosemary Ellen Guiley Ph.D., *The Encyclopedia of Angels: Second Edition* (New York, New York: Checkmark Books, 2004), p. 83; and Gustav Davidson, *A Dictionary of Angels including the fallen angels* (New York, New York: The Free Press, 1971), p. 123.

2. Bobbie Houston, *Heaven is in this House* (Castle Hill, New South Wales Australia: Leadership Ministries Inc., 2001), p. 134.

James here is stating pretty clearly that your works will show your faith. If you are not doing good works, you have no faith. However, just because you are doing good works, does not prove your faith either. The trueness of your faith is shown by what you do in this world. But some have gone so far as to say that unless you do good works "all the time", you have no faith. This is where the belief that if you sin, you will lose your salvation until you repent, has come from. That ability to "lose" salvation so easily makes the issue of saved by faith rather trivial and meaningless. If it were possible for us to "lose our faith" at all, especially that easily, then Christ's work on the cross was *not* complete as he stated it was. (John 19:30)

Trithemius's statement here is fallacious in the "determination to do good works". If someone is *intentionally* doing good works for the sake of proving his faith, that faith is non-existent. Good works should be a fruit of our faith and not something that makes us have to consciously do good works to prove our faith. If we have to make a conscious decision to do good, our faith is a lie. This does not mean that we will *always* do good, but the saved nature of a person will show in the fruit that they bear by what they do. Adhering to occultic/goetic doctrine, as many do like this book shows, is the evidence that Jesus says in Mark 7 that shows that their hearts are "unclean" or, unsaved.

Chapter VII: Asiriel/Asimiel

Asiriel, the fiftieth prince, is the supreme prince, whose abode is in Africa. He has under his authority twenty princes who preside over the day, and as many who preside over the night. Whose duty it also is to announce the counsels of the princes to their friends.

The prince and supreme ruler of the seventh mansion is called Asiriel. He has in that quarter of the world, which we call Africa, under him twenty princes who preside over the day, and as many who preside over the night, all of whom have many servants under them. If two leaders are called by the worker to the service of this art from those reporting twenty, then they always have servants serving them. The same happens with the night spirits. Therefore, if you call only one of the princes, especially the nighttime ones, it is proved that he has not ten but twenty servants. You will not call those spirits reporting, except at least two, since they are not accustomed to coming alone. You will be able to bring in one or two of the night spirits, as you please. If you call two, twenty. If you call one, ten. You will know that the servants in the secret will be added by custom. And should you know that those who are to be called alone, and those called with a partner; consider the table.

		Red.	Black.	R.	B.	R.	B.	R.
	Astor		Buniel		Arcisat		Cusiel	
B.		20.		20.		20.		20.
	Carga		Rabas		Adriel		Malqueel	
	Red.							
	20.——	20.——	20.——	20.——	20.——	20		
	Black.							
	20.——	20.——	20.——	20.——	20.——	20		

		Black.	Red.	B.	R.	B.	R.	B.
	Amiel		Maroth		Buder	10.	Fassua	10.
R.		20.		20.				
	Cusiel		Omiel		Aspiel	10.	Hamas	10.

These spirits, who are principal among the forty, have the duty of announcing the secret plans of the princes to their subjects and friends. You have eight of the daytime ones, and as many of the nighttime ones with their many servants, who are sufficient for everything, and there is no need to call the others. Pay careful attention, for when you call one or two princes from among those already named, express the same number of servants in the poem. For they are proud, and it is wonderfully pleasing to them that they are said to preside over many clients. When then, you wish to work through them in steganography, turn your face to Africa, and do what you know must be done with care. For nothing is completely due to the efforts of those who belong to this art.

Secret Prayer

Asiriel aphorsy Lamodyn to Carmephyn drubal asutroy Sody baruchõ, vsefer palormy thulnear asmerõ chornemadusyn coleny busarethõ duys marphelitubra nasaron venear fabelronty.

When these are completed, those called will stand there whom you will decide to stand there. Be it known that the princes generally appear in an airy dress, that is, but Sapherin, whose servants are in white. But tell your secret to the princes themselves because they are faithful. Before this, all the leaders have a custom among themselves, in other words, when the operator addresses them, then they send the servants away. After he has ceased to speak to the princes, the servants will appear again.

Let the prince's secret be such that he believes no one should be exposed. Red.

The council of the prince is great and most secret about difficult and important matters. He wants the prince to know that any other friend, because he has reason, but he fears to come with the greatest danger to himself and his people to the public. Therefore, he calls the spirit, which will not reveal the secret. He commits, he sends, he completes, he is secure.

Let the letters command you to be suspicious of nothing, and do not be afraid of the public in anything. Red.

Jesus Christ the unfailing Light, the eternal happiness of all the saints. Creator of the universe and ruler, have mercy on us. We who are weak, groaning, and weeping ask for your mercy. Give us the courage to overcome the temptations of the devil, that we may find rest after the present evils. Oh, most sweet Saviour of Jesus, forgive us the sins of those who pray. For most merciful Father, we are your humble creatures. Look upon us, your wretched, useless servants since we beg of you for the strength of your servanthood. Let us have the determination of your love, adorned with good works always in us. Give us the true operations of righteous works, the observance of justice, honour, and inseparable love. Make us truly humble and active despisers of worldly things because we are always strong with your love. Let us love nothing earthly, let us not value anything temporally amusing to us. Oh, teacher of humility, Jesus Christ, teach us to imitate your teaching. We are (unfortunately) covered with many sins, not exposed to good works. Save us, Jesus Christ, that we may not perish. Oh, supreme truth, give us life, the most refreshing refuge of souls. Be to us a tower of strength. For you are our reviver. You are the salvation of souls, the sweetest restorer of the mind. You are the indescribable joy of the angels, and the souls of the faithful rest most healthily. You are the happiness of the saints who love you. You are the inextinguishable light of the heavenly bodies. You, the motivator of the dead, look at our frailty. Jesus Christ, most sweetly, help us your frail servants, in so far as we walk along the path of truth without offense, obtain eternal rest. Oh, most merciful Lord Jesus, soften the labours of our exile. And when the end of this life begins to draw near, you are then to descend to come to our aid in mercy, since the adversary of your power rushes crushed before the face of all evils. Let the devil's allies, the princes of eternal death, our most vicious persecutors flee far away. We ask, through the power of your most noble death, sweetest Jesus: do not despise us useless servants on the day of our exit, whom you wanted to redeem with your blood. Praise our excesses, so that we may enter the joys of the heavenly country, with the angels waiting for us. Amen.

I wrote John Trithemius, Abbot, to them March 1500.

We therefore send the letters to him to whom the spirit was also to be sent. Because no principle or servants come from the spirits themselves, unless they are called, neither to the one who sends them, nor to him to whom they are to be sent. Let it be known, therefore, to whom it is sent, to which place of residence, and to whom the spirit must be called, that letters are sent sealed with the sign of the prince and written in such a way as to please the spirit, and he desires to be refreshed by their fuel. But we will speak of these in the last chapter.

This is a Spiritual Conviction for the Recipient.

> Asiriel onear Camot Laueuiel gamer sothin ianoz alnay bulumer palorson, irgiel lamedon, ludiel Caparosyn nauy asparlon nadiel bulephor ianos pesonty tresloty Camõ elyr, mearsu nosy thamerosyn.

Having said these things in the most secret way towards Africa, and adding other things which are required by art. The spirit will appear to him with his servants visible, no one else seeing him, and they will not hear him, and he will reveal the secret of the one who sent it into the ear.

Commentary: Chapter VII

[p. 157; 1] *Asiriel*, [or, *Asimiel*] ... A demon that is apparently in the service of *Camuel*.[1] The same *Camuel* as *Chapter III* of this book.

[p. 157; 2] *turn your face to Africa*, ... Going once again to the text of the *Grimorium Verum* we get the following information that "Beelzebub lives in Africa,"[2] With Asiriel being the supposed "supreme ruler" of Africa it shows that there is absolutely no consistent truth in the occult and within goetic literature. With there being no consistent truth, it makes goetia able to be whatever someone, including those in the charismatic, Prosperity, WOF and NAR movements make goetia anything they need it to be including if it is renamed as "Christian" and "biblical".

[p. 158; 1], [p. 159; 3] non-sensical goetic "angel tongues".

[p. 158; 2] *Sapherin*, ... Another angel that has no known origin.

[p. 159; 2] *Because no principle or servants come from the spirits themselves, unless they are called, neither to the one who sends them, nor to him to whom they are to be sent*, ... The statement here that spirits will not come "unless they are called" is also the same reason used for "asking the Holy Spirit to come" or the Holy Spirit will not be there. The goetic nature of that belief about the Holy Spirit is shown here.

---

1. Michelle Belanger, *The Dictionary of Demons: Names of the Damned* (Woodbury, Minnesota: Llewellyn Publications, 2017), p. 43.

2. Author, Unknown. *Grimorium Verum: The True Grimoire* (p. 11). UNKNOWN. Kindle Edition.

COMMENTARY: CHAPTER VII

Chapter VIII: Maseriel

Whose supreme prince is Maseriel that lives in that quarter which we call Faunium, having under him sixty chief commanders with many of their servants.

Red.

The eighth mansion is about the west, in that place, to which the wind is called Faunium, and there dwells a great prince, who is called Maseriel. Who with an infinite number of captains, princes, and stewards, of whom there are thirty princes appointed to this art who are also in charge of the daily operations, and as many who preside at night, with many attendants. All these spirits are appointed to announce and report the secrets of the human arts of philosophy, magic, necromancy, and all the wonderful and most secret operations which are known to very few men. And upon these subjects the spirits are quick and very faithful, and do not turn back unless they have accomplished all that had been committed to them. They are quiet and come without noise, as they are ordered by themselves, with many or with a few, or even without servants, at least visibly. They frighten no one, except he who is not trained in the art. Unless he has presumed to call them by the true principles of the art, which no one easily reaches without training. But in order that you may have at hand the voices for the operation of the spirit, you know that you do not need all of them, but some. And therefore, let twelve be sufficient for you for the actions that take place during the day, and as many for those that take place at night, with their attendants.

Red.	Black.	R.	B.	R.	B.	R.	B.
Mahuc	30.	*Zerael*	30.	*Azimel*	30.	*Alsuel*	30.
Red.	Black.	R.	B.	R.	B.	R.	B.
Rouiel	30.	*Athiel*	30.	*Chasor*	30.	*Aliel*	30.
Red.	Black.	R.	B.	R.	B.	R.	B.
Fariel	20.	*Vessur*	30.	*Potiel*	30.	*Espoel*	30.

Red.	Black.	R.	B.	R.	B.	R.	B.
Arach	30.	*Sarmiel*	30.	*Baros*	30.	*Rabiel*	30.
Maras	30.	*Amoyr*	30.	*Eliel*	30.	*Atriel*	30.
Noquiel	30.	*Badiel*	30.	*Paras*	30.	*Saluar*	30.

Of the three hundred chief spirits of Maseriel, you have twenty-four with seven hundred and twenty servants, the first twelve of whom are in charge of the operations of the day, and the remaining twelve of the night. When, therefore, you wish to work something in steganography through them, turn to Faunium, and having given the necessary premises which are required of the art, call one of the pre-named whom you wish, as it should be. He will come without delay.

Secret prayer:

Maseriel bulan lamodyn charnoty Carmephin iabrum caresathroyn asulroy beuesy Cadumyn turiel busan Seuear; almos lycadusel ernoty panier jethar care pheory bulan thorty paron Venio Fabelronthusy.

With the apparent spirit whom you have called, entrust him to carry your secret safely, without any hesitation at all, speaking quietly to him, if you were in the midst of others, as you know.

Red. *Let the secret of your mind be like this.*

You have secret knowledge in the occult sciences, philosophy, the magic of the stars, the kabbalah, arithmetic, or any other arts that you wish to know a friend near or far absent. But only send such things as it is safe to commit neither to letters nor to messengers. Take one or two of the before mentioned spirits and explain the secret. He will take up the burden and bear it for his friend, and he will take back to you what was entrusted to him.

Write any prayer you wish, or any letters containing nothing confidential. Red.

Almighty and eternal God, the most equitable rewarder of good things, who willed your Son to be a partaker of our race, for he redeemed the diabolical hostility of us miserable ones. Who, overflowing with kindness alone, received our form uncorrupted from the virginal flower of the virgin birth, insinuating to the holy archangel Gabriel, that the virgin conception of your most blessed spirit is a perpetual virgin may it continue, immaculate, more glorious than men, angels, and pre-eminent spirits. She gave birth to the almighty king, God and man, the most holy and reverent Virgin Mary, completely unaware of male consorts, giving birth without pain, without sorrow receiving the wandering God and man, and always standing immaculate, most pure, most innocent, superior to men in virtue of humility, full of charity, worthy of all praise, and to be venerated by all. The most blessed of the angels and always praised, the most resplendent empress, noble, famous, and truly splendid. Whom your Son in everything he has asked for, he accepts with the most generous graciousness, let him be reverently revered as his mother; the most excellent of all creatures. To whom he was not willing to deny anything to the person asking, but repentantly consents to your most holy will, conceding all things to the honour of him who will stand for us in the new day, helping us to venerate the soul of the glorious Virgin. God, the light of truth for us, we pray most devoutly, pour out grace and mercy, God, to all who call upon you and humbly ask for the forgiveness of their sins, and do not look down on us wretched, but sitting in your goodness, mercifully receive with the love of the nursing Virgin Mary, the God of all your elect. Amen. John Trithemius, Abbot. I wrote from Spanheim. Sunday Incarnation or Nativity, 1500, March 4th.

He who receives the letters to whom they are sent, knowing the sign of Maserial, turns himself to the Faunium, and after secretly presupposing what is required for the art, calls upon the very spirit that was sent, adding the secret prayer.

Secret prayer

Maseriel onear Camersin, Cohodor messary lyrno balnaon greal, lamedon odiel, pedarnoy nador ianozauy chamyrin.

When the secret prayer is completed, as it should be, the sent spirit will appear in the mist. And with the said mystical word he will speak the truth in the ear, and faithfully secretly trust to you all that had been committed to him. However, no one sitting around will feel anything. But continue steadfast and undaunted, as you should.

COMMENTARY: CHAPTER VIII

[p. 163; 1] *Maseriel* ... Rules in the west and is a supposed servant of *Caspiel*. *Maseriel* is apparently easy to control and a good-natured spirit.[1]

[p. 163; 1] *appointed to announce and report the secrets of the human arts of philosophy, magic, necromancy, and all the wonderful and most secret operations which are known to very few men* [...] *be sufficient for you for the actions that take place during the day, and as many for those that take place at night,* ... Considering the number of people in Prosperity, WOF and NAR movements that claim to receive their "commissions" from God at night either by an apparent "angel" visitation or being "raptured" to God's throne room, it should not be surprising that this ideology was taught once again here, as elsewhere in this book. The fact that Prosperity, WOF and NAR movements have adopted goetic beliefs to validate their false theology should not be a surprise at this point.

[164; 1], [165; 2] non-sensical goetic "angel tongues".

[164; 3] *You have secret knowledge in the occult sciences, philosophy, the magic of the stars, the kabbalah, arithmetic, or any other arts that you wish to know a friend near or far absent.* ... The relation to this phrase within the Prosperity, WOF and NAR movements is that they will teach that only those with the "faith" that they approve of will be able to understand and also perform their same goetic miracles. The goetic origins of that defense is once again made clear from this statement.

[164; 4, 5] *the most holy and reverent Virgin Mary* [...] *giving birth without pain, without sorrow receiving the wandering God and man, and always standing immaculate, most pure, most innocent, superior to men in virtue of humility, full of charity, worthy of all praise, and to be venerated by all. The most blessed of the angels and always praised, the most resplendent empress,* [...] *Whom your Son in everything he has asked for, he accepts with the most generous graciousness, let him be reverently revered as his mother; the most excellent of all creatures. To whom he was not willing to deny anything to the person asking, but repentantly consents to your most holy will, conceding all things to the honour of him who will stand for us in the new day, helping us to venerate the soul of the glorious Virgin,* ... Calling Mary "reverent" and claiming she gave birth "without pain" is absurd. There is no evidence outside of Roman Catholic tradition that such a thing ever happened. From a biblical standpoint, the fact that Mary had to ride a donkey to Bethlehem because she was so far along in the pregnancy also goes to show that Mary's pregnancy with Christ was not without its burdens on her as a sinful woman. There is also absolutely no evidence that Mary was eternally a virgin since the Bible is

1. Michelle Belanger, *The Dictionary of Demons*: *Names of the Damned* (Woodbury, Minnesota: Llewellyn Publications, 2017), p. 204. Rosemary Ellen Guiley Ph.D., *The Encyclopedia of Demons & Demonology* (New York, New York: Checkmark Books, 2009), p. 169.

clear that Joseph had sexual relations with Mary after she gave birth to Jesus. (Matthew 1:25) Also, Mary had other sons as is evident in Mark 3:30 with the use of ἀδελφόι [adelphos] or, "brothers". Claiming that Mary was also "most pure" and "most innocent" is also shown as faulty in the story of Mark 3 since in verse 21, Jesus' family says that, "He is out of his mind." These family members, as verses 30–31 show, also included Mary which makes clear that even Mary at this point did not believe that Jesus was whom he claimed to be. This may be shocking to all of us considering what Gabriel told her, however, Mary's doubt about Jesus' divinity is evident here. The phrase, "but repentantly consents to your most holy will, conceding all things to the honour of him who will stand for us in the new day, helping us to venerate the soul of the glorious Virgin," should be the most appalling statement for all of us. Trithemius here is showing the Roman Catholic belief that Jesus, Yahweh himself, is submitted to Mary a human being that was born in sin and that even doubted his deity while on earth. The way that the Roman Catholic Church uses tradition to introduce goetic ideas from the *PGM* to the point that a human being can be elevated with greater authority, and therefore divinity, than Yahweh (Jesus and the other two members of the triune-Godhead) is heretical idolatry of the greatest kind. This same thinking is taught by what are known as *theistic-Satanists* who take Anton LaVey's Satanism, who taught there are no supernatural beings but you yourself, and claim that there are some kind of "spirits" that exist that will help guide them to becoming a god, or a god greater than the demons. Michael Ford, a well-known, Satanist/Luciferian says that Satanists/Luciferians "do not worship Satan, nor do we bow before anything else. There are many types of Luciferians; some are Theistic: believing deeply in the spirit of the Adversary yet view this Spirit as a guide."[2] While it is unfair to say that the Roman Catholic Church in the 1500's was teaching LaVeyan Satanism, since LaVey was not born at that time, that the idea of self-deifying yourself as a "god" that could be a higher "god" than even Yahweh is evident in Trithemius's text.

2. Michael W. Ford, *The Bible of the Adversary: 10th Anniversary Edition* (Houston, Texas: Succubus Productions, 2017), p. 22, Kindle Edition.

CHAPTER IX: MALGARAS/MAIGARAS

Red. *Whose chief is called, Malgaras, who dwells in the west, having thirty leaders under him for the activities of the day, and as many for the night. Whose duty it is to announce the family secrets of their friends.*

Ninth, the inhabitant of the mansion, which is to the west of the equinox, is Malgaras, the greatest prince of the west, who has under him thirty leaders who are in charge of the day, and thirty others who are in charge of the night with their servants. It is the duty of all these to convey the secrets and mysteries of the family of friends to friends. They are good leaders and most ready to obey those who call, especially during the day, since they are more used to being among men. For night spirits, though they are good, yet do not gladly converse with men, but shun and detest the light most of all, desiring to hide in darkness, and for this reason they frequently appear to be called by mysterious prayers like bats. Of all these we shall place their twenty-four names in the table, of which twelve are sufficient for the day, and as many for the night.

Red.	B.	R.	B.	R.	B.	R.	B.	R.	B.
Carmiel	*30.*	*Agor*	*30.*	*Cabiel*	*30.*	*Misiel*	*20.*	*Aroiz*	*10.*
Black.	R.	B.	R.	B.	R.	B.	R.		
Meliel	*30.*	*Casiel*	*30.*	*Vdiel*	*30.*	*Barfas*	*20.*		
Red.	B.	R.	B.	R.	B.				
Borass	*30.*	*Rabiel*	*20.*	*Oriel*	*30.*	B.	30.20. 30.30.10.		

Red.	B.	R.	B.	R.	B.				
Aroc	*30.*	*Libiel*	*30.*	*Caron*	*30.*				
Black.	R.	B.	R.	B.	R.	B.	R.		
Dobiel	*30.*	*Robac*	*30.*	*Zamor*	*30.*	*Aspor*	*20.*		
Red.	B.	R.	B.	R.	B.	R.	B.	R.	B.
Cubi	*30.*	*Aspiel*	*30.*	*Amiel*	*30.*	*Delias*	*20.*	*Basiel*	*10.*

You have now twelve of the princes of Malgaras for the day's activities, and as many for the night's, with their six hundred and forty servants. And it is known that Aroyz and Basile are always alone. Whether you decide to have three or two or one, be careful not to make a mistake in their names. As the table instructs you, do so without change, or else you might fall into danger.

SONG OF THE SECRECY Red.

Malgaras ador chameso bulueriny mareso bodyr Cadumir auiel casmyo tedy pleoryn viordi eare viorba, chameron vesy thuriel vlnauy, beuesy meuo chasmironty naor ernyso, chony barmo caleuodyn barso thubra sol.

You must be a strong and unflinching man for the secret prayer. The visible ones whom you have called will appear to you at once. But if they do not come at once when called by night, however, do not interrupt your work, but rebuke them with repeated secret prayers until they obey. For they are a little lazy, and they do not lightly come among men, as we have said.

Let it be a secret of the mind, which neither man nor letters like to commit. **Red.**

In those things which apply to family matters, money, deposits, loans, credit, or to any business of human conversation, you have a secret, which you desire a friend to know who is far away, or he would undergo a public examination at risk or loss. For this reason, neither letters or men are to be trusted. So be safe, and no one's conscience will be aroused. You turn to the west, you call the leader, you commit the secret, he goes, and faithfully carries out everything. If anything has been committed to you, it matters.

WRITE WHATEVER LETTERS YOU WILL, FEARING NO ONE'S SIGHT.

Safety and grace, my dearest and most single of friends, the bearer of the present, the most beneficent and glorious of our friends, born from Ruremund, whom you wish to receive humanely, I beseech you to explain his necessity. He who has always been united to me in my old relationship for my strength, I would judge it most sweet to relieve him and accumulate benefits. And I would that I could spend comfort in his painful struggles. But when I am exhausted by great losses (for it is clearer to you in the light), I cannot satisfy my zeal, as I would wish. But you, who are abounding in temporal necessities, show yourself happy to your friend, and human, whom you have been very accustomed to show yourself to the needs of your patron friends. So, I beg you to lend him two hundred florins[1] under a certain term, because he is set up in the greatest need, as he will teach you. I am confident that he will restore everything completely when the time appointed for him comes. If you do, I will never die of gratitude, and I will stand by you in greater things. Come, let us prove your honest love for us. I want you to know that what you have done for him has been done, and that you have required of him no less (believe firmly) and that at the end of the term he will fully restore the omens. For he was willing to keep his promises unfailingly, to show himself constant to all men. Anyway, I would like to write something when you are happy to hear new reports. He nourished the dog (by the Greek term it will be rightly called) with such learning, learning and the memory of all things, that it seems to some to have put off a beast, and to have put on a man. He understands Greek and Latin words, he knows how to ask forgiveness for his crimes. Whatever I command, he does, with his nodding gestures, he spreads the secrets of men. You would see him filled with so much discipline of manners, that you would honour him more learned than many. Commanding to open the window, he opens it, transcending nature, and cunningly he stores the forbidden food. The burden imposed on him; he loves to be presented as a zealous defender of mine. John Trith. The abbot of San Martin in Spanheim wrote March 3, in the year 1500.

1. A currency of the Republic of Florence since the 7th century. Germany also had a version of the Rheingulden (a Germany currency value) that was also called the "florin."

Having received these, or any others to whom they are sent, the friend understands that they are the sign of the prince of the west. Where as usual, he turns to the west, calls the spirit, contesting the invisible spirit sent, that he may be visible, and tell no one.

Song of the Spirit

Malgaras boar chameron asoty mesary throes Zameda sogreal paredon adre Caphoron onatyr tirno beosy. Chameron phorsy mellon tedrumarsy dumaso duise Casmiel elthurny peson alproys fabelronty Sturno panalmo nador.

When the song is complete, the spirit himself will be present, called in his own way, revealing to you what he received in the commands. Faithfully with whom you will be able to argue with your friend whatever you wish him to know as a secret.

Commentary: Chapter IX

[p. 167; 1] *Malgaras* [or, *Maigaras*] ... A demon that is said to serve under another demon named *Amenadiel*. *Malgaras* is believed to be courteous and kind[1] and to rule somewhere in the "west".[2]

[p. 167; 1] *but shun and detest the light most of all, desiring to hide in darkness*, ... Due to the belief in the "witching hour" that I showed in my *Introduction*, (pp. 76–79; this volume) many people believe that demons are most active, or only active, at night. This belief that demons are more active at night has no basis in biblical truth. Demons are always as active whether it is day or night. While the belief about the "witching hour" being between 1 am and 3 am comes from the Oriental East, the Greeks did believe in a "witching hour" that came around the time we know as "midnight." The Greeks believed, like the Oriental East, that after midnight the "veil" between the material and spiritual worlds was weakest and that magic would be more powerful during that time. This "witching hour" belief mixed with the false goetic idea that demons will not be as active, or active at all, during daylight hours is completely faulty. Many Christians believe that the hours of night are when the demonic are most active which is part of an overall lie that the demonic want ignorant people to believe.

[p. 169; 1], [p. 170; 2] non-sensical goetic "angel tongues".

[p. 169; 2] *You must be a strong and unflinching man for the secret prayer.* [...] *rebuke them with repeated secret prayers until they obey*, ... There is a false belief that we must be confident and not show any fear when confronting the demonic. While the Bible does say that we should not be filled with a "spirit of fear", the reality is that encountering the demonic can be a very frightening experience. Having courage, and faith, is about being willing to stand in the face of your fear and believe that God will do exactly what he has promised he will, as my exegesis of Hebrews 11, on p. 68 (this volume) shows. The command to continuously "rebuke" the spirits with your own authority is again falling into the goetic errors made by individuals such as John Eckhardt like I explained on p. 117.

1. Michelle Belanger, *The Dictionary of Demons: Names of the Damned* (Woodbury, Minnesota: Llewellyn Publications, 2017), p. 198.
2. Rosemary Ellen Guiley Ph.D., *The Encyclopedia of Demons & Demonology* (New York, New York: Checkmark Books, 2009), p. 166.

CHAPTER X: DOROTHIEL/DOROCHIEL

Of which he is called the supreme prince Dorothiel inhabiting that region, which is called Chorus in the wind, and he has many leaders and servants under him.

The tenth mansion is called Chorus in the wind, in which dwells the great prince Dorothiel, who has under his power and authority forty leaders who are in charge of the operations of the day, and as many who are in charge of the nighttime affairs. These spirits have almost unlimited servants. The duty of these is to announce all the secret things that pertain to spiritual affairs, and to ecclesiastical gifts, benefits, prelatures, dignities, and the like. But in the operation of steganography, it is not necessary for the leaders of Dorothiel to put forward the names of all in the middle, but a few from each order are sufficient. We will explain the names of the rest in their own place with the others. And consider the table of these.

Red.
Mugael 0.
Choriel 0.
Artinc 0.
Efiel 0.

B.	B.	R.	B.	B.	R.	B.	B.	R.	B.	B..	R.
Mugael	*40.*		*Gudiel*	*400.*		*Nachiel*	*40.*		*Phutiel*		*400.*
Choriel	*40.*		*Asphor*	*400.*		*Ofisiel*	*40.*		*Cayros*		*400.*
Artinc	*40.*		*Emuel*	*400.*		*Bulis*	*40.*		*Narsyel*		*400.*
Efiel	*40.*		*Souiel*	*400.*		*Moniel*	*40.*		*Moziel*		*400.*
Maniel	*40.*		*Cabron*	*400.*		*Pafiel*	*40.*		*Aroziel*		*400.*
Suriel	*40.*		*Diuiel*	*400.*		*Gariel*	*40.*		*Cusync*		*400.*
Carsiel	*40.*		*Abriel*	*400.*		*Soriel*	*40.*		*Vraniel*		*400.*
Fubiel	*40.*		*Danael*	*400.*		*Darbori*	*40.*		*Pelusar*		*400.*
Carba	*40.*		*Lomar*	*400.*		*Paniel*	*40.*		*Abael*		*400.*
Merach	*40.*		*Cesael*	*400.*		*Curfas*	*40.*		*Meroth*		*400.*
Althor	*40.*		*Busiel*	*400.*		*Aliel*	*40.*		*Cadriel*		*400.*
Omael	*40.*		*Larfos*	*400.*		*Maziel*	*40.*		*Lobiel*		*400.*

Behold, of the princes of Dorothiel, you have twenty-four chiefs of every order, day and night, with a number of ten thousand, one hundred and sixty servants. And note, that the operation through these is much different from the rest, as we shall say generously of the masters. For according to the twelve hours of the day and of the night, it is necessary to work in that mansion, and four princes are always in charge at two hours, both in the day and in the night, so that it is not lawful for you to bring in another, except from the order which the hour concerns. For example, if the operation is in the first or second hour of the day, call whomever you wish, from the first four who are in charge of the day. If in the third or fourth, from the second four you know that a leader is to be called. And so, it must be done in consequence throughout all the orders and twenty-four hours both in the day and in the night. But when you wish to work in steganography by the spirit of Dorothiel himself, having given the usual generals in the art mentioned above, write whatever letters you wish. Then, turning yourself to that part of the world which we commonly call the Chorus, call one or more of the four who are in charge at the hour in which you are working.

> Dorothiel cusi feor madylon busar pamersy chear ianothym baony Camersy vlymeor peatha adial cadumyr renear thubra Cohagier maslon Lodierno sabelrusyn.

With these words you will see the spirit appearing, whom you have called, ready and cheerful to obey, to whom you entrust your secret safely and faithfully. Look at the previous table.

Key.

Let us assume that whatever secret of the mind is committed to the letter.

It is a task for you, in any spiritual matter, to the prince, very difficult and secret, which you do not think to be believed by any mortal, not even by letters. He does everything side-by-side.

YOU WILL GIVE WHATEVER LETTERS YOU WILL, IN WHICH YOU WILL NOT BE AFRAID OF ANYTHING.

I mean that Your Most Illustrious Grace, the beneficent Conrad Hummel, died last night on the altar of St. John the Evangelist. But let your Grace not let even one of the unskilled or unworthy, of whom I think a large number will (as is usually the case), be found waiting at the said altar. May they seem to receive some benefit, worthy as much as your grace deems fit to bestow upon the exhibitor of those present, the aforesaid repulsion, the aforesaid altar. I have known him to be worthy of the best favours, for indeed he was adorned with the beauty of manners, learned in knowledge and letters, modest, temperate, and with love of religion. And he will be not ungrateful for the favours presented to him but always remember him. Dated from Spanheim, the day before. Idus March, in the year of our Lord 1500, John. Trithemius.

When the prince, or any other of mine, has received these letters, or any other, to whom they are sent, an expert in the art. Having recognized Dorothiel's sign, he turns to the Chorus (where the spirit himself dwells with his guides and servants), doing everything and every thing that the art itself requires. Then, in a low voice, he called out silently as he knew.

> Dorothiel onear chameron vlyfeor madusyn peony oriel nayr druse mouayr pamerson etro dumeson, dauor caho. Casmiel hayrno, fablerunthon.

Having completed this poem, if the spirit delays in coming, read it again and the third time, and without any doubt it will appear visible and will reveal what was told to the spirits ear.

Commentary: Chapter X

[p. 175; 1] *Dorothiel* [or, *Dorochiel*] ... Another demonic spirit submitted to the demon *Amenadiel.*[1] In order to work with *Dorothiel*'s servants one is supposed to be mindful of the hours of the day and night. *Dorothiel*'s servants are believed by the occult to be good-natured and agreeable.[2]

[p. 175; R1] The image used on the right side of the page is interesting considering the use of sigils and icons in certain branches of Christendom, specifically the Eastern Orthodox branch of Christendom, and also the use of such symbols in goetic texts in books such as this one.

Commenting on different talismans and in choosing which symbols to inscribe these talismans with, an occult author explains that "a talisman works in a positive way, attracting the forces necessary to create whatever effect its owner desires. An amulet, on the other hand, has the more 'negative' function of neutralizing certain causes before they produce an unwelcome effect."[3] If you recall my explanation on Psalm 91 and the way some charismatic, Prosperity, WOF and NAR adherents will use anointing oil to mark their houses and pray Psalm 91 over it (see pp. 61–63, this volume), the connection from that faulty practice to the occult use of "amulets" is no different. What is shocking as well from the book quoted above by David Conway is that the very first talisman/amulet example he shows is one that has the word "ADONAI" and also the Hebrew for Yahweh, יהוה, which shows that even Christian symbols and items can be used for occultic purposes.[4]

Bob Larson is a false teacher that has been taking advantage of "spiritual warfare" and goetic teaching to fool many. The Larson family, including his children, have each hosted a couple network television series that was documenting first Bob Larson, then the next network series, Larson's children, going around and "casting demons" out of people. Remember how goetic magic is used for the purposes of gaining monetary rewards. There is no reason to put this kind of false "deliverance" on network television all over the world. The desire for money however drove both Bob Larson and his children to do exactly that and make a mockery of "spiritual warfare". The financial support that came in from donors wanting to support the Larson family was substantial.

Looking at the statement from David Conway above, we need to look at what Larson has to say in his book *Jezebel: Defeating Your #1 Spiritual Enemy.* Keeping in mind what Conway has to say about amulets, Larson is using a *Bible* in the same way. Larson

---

1. Michelle Belanger, *The Dictionary of Demons: Names of the Damned* (Woodbury, Minnesota: Llewellyn Publications, 2017), p. 112.

2. Rosemary Ellen Guiley Ph.D., *The Encyclopedia of Demons & Demonology* (New York, New York: Checkmark Books, 2009), p. 69.

3. David Conway, *Magic: An Occult Primer* (Newport, Rhode Island: The Witches Almanac LTD, 2017), p. 211.

4. Conway, *Magic*, p. 214.

says that with "my ever-present Cross of Deliverance in one hand and a Bible in the other, I spoke with a demanding tone. […] I pressed my Bible on Ellen's head as a symbolic gesture indicating that I was submitting Jezebel to God's authority."[5] Not only does Larson use a *Bible* in this way but Larson also states in later part of the same book that "I pressed my Cross of Deliverance against the demon's forehead."[6] Both of these were done in an attempt to "cast Jezebel out of the person." There is no biblical evidence for anything called a "Jezebel" spirit, even from Revelation 2:20 which is speaking of a human woman that is either named Jezebel[7] or that John is comparing to the Old Testament Jezebel. Yet many, due to goetic falsehood, have *created* a false demon out of that passage of scripture. Larson here is using both a *Bible* and something he refers to as *his* "Cross of Deliverance" to cast a demon out of someone. This use of a Bible and a Cross as "amulets" show not only the occultic origins that Larson is adopting this practice from, but looking at Trithemius's text, this practice is goetic in nature as well.

Paul does pray over handkerchiefs that are used to expel demons, (Acts 19:11-12) but the point of that text is show that God was with Paul and not the sons of Sceva. Seeing the number of times that Larson claims to have exorcised Jezebel in his public sessions, and not fleeing from him as James 4:8 states, this apparent Jezebel is challenging Larsons faulty authority over and over showing his authority is fallacious and anti-biblical. Also, the faulty theology surrounding spiritual gifts where many people claim to have certain gifts such as healing and never being able to verifty a single healing, again shows that this text needs to be reconsidered. It is a gifting that we do not have in our current day.

[p. 176; 1], [p. 177; 2], non-sensical goetic "angel tongues".

5. Bob Larson, *Jezebel*: *Defeating Your #1 Spiritual Enemy* (Shippensburg, Pennsylvania: Destiny Image, 2015), Logos Edition.

6. Larson, *Jezebel*, Logos Edition.

7. Names in this time were tribe and family oriented. Like in Luke 1:60–61 where with John it was clear that "John" was an odd name for the son of Rebecca and Zechariah. When people questioned Rebecca about it "his mother answered, 'No; he shall be called John.' And they said to her, 'None of your relatives is called by this name.'" (Luke 1:60–61 ESV) Since names were based on the family and not what the parents preferred like how infants today are named, the name Jezebel now being part of Judaic lineage would have been a family name in some tribes of Israel.

Chapter XI: Vsiel/Usiel

Whose spirit is the highest which is called Vsiel, dwelling in that region of the world, which we call Subcircium because of the wind blowing there. Who has under him forty leaders by day, and as many by night, who are above the treasury.

The ninety-first mansion of the whole world is called Subcircius in the wind. That is to say, which came quickly from that side. At this place there dwells a great prince called Vsiel, having under him forty princes who are in charge of the operations of the day, and forty who are in charge of the night operations. The duty of these is to announce hidden and underground treasures, and everything that seems to belong to the world of treasures. We will name a few of these, and as many as are sufficient in the operations of steganography at this point. And so, let us refer the rest with the others to be named in their proper chapter at the end of this book. And it is known that the leaders of that mansion, when called by the worker, were wanting to come willingly and with the greatest cheerfulness. And though they have many servants, yet I never saw that they brought any of them with them, at least visible. And if anyone wished to serve as servants, he could, since they are under princes, and are forced to obey them in everything. But only if the operator is such that he knows how to call them properly, or even compel them, if he wishes the spirits to appear more slowly.

Red.	Black.	R.	B.	R.	B.	R.	B.
Abaria	40.	*Saefar*	40.	*Amandiel*	30.	*Hissam*	30.
Ameta	40.	*Poriel*	40.	*Barsu*	30.	*Fabariel*	30.
Arnen	40.	*Saefar*	40.	*Garnatu*	30.	*Vsiniel*	30.
Herne	40.	*Maqui*	40.				

R.

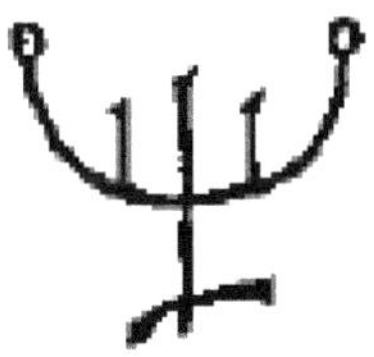

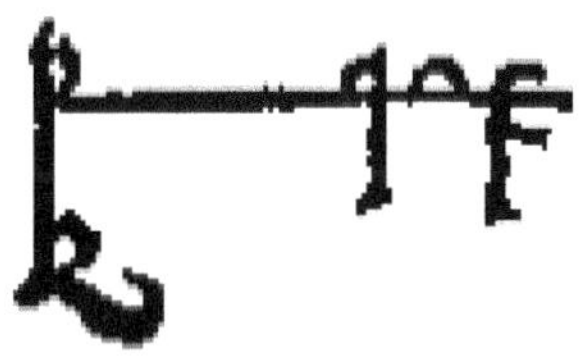

Black.	Red.	B.	R.	B.	R.	R.	B.
Ansoel	*40.*	*Saddiel*	*40.*	*Asuriel*	*20.*	*Pathyr*	*20.*
Godiel	*40.*	*Sobiel*	*40.*	*Almoel*	*20.*	*Marae*	*20.*
Barfos	*40.*	*Ossidiel*	*40.*				
Burfa	*40.*	*Adan*	*40.*	*Lapharon*	*10.*	*Ethiel*	*10.*

Of the forty Vsilian princes, who preside over the operations of the day, you have fourteen, with their servants, four hundred in number, and fourteen, who preside over the operations of the night, with four hundred forty of their servants, together with these others. Two signs of the order (to test and caution about the treasury, as you know, should a thief to be found in them) opposite to the eyes, to which we pray for the guard of the treasure, they find among them that the spirit is sent to a friend. So, when you wish to work through spirits in this business, if the business is the most important or belonging to a prince, call the leaders whom you wish from the order of the four, if proper. Out of three, if private and small. Out of two, if cheap and least. Then it should be done at night in the order of the solitary only.

> Vsiel parnothiel chameron briosy sthrubal brionear Caron sotronthi egyptia odiel Chelorsy mear Chadusy notiel ornych turbelsi paneras thorthay pean adresmo boma arnotiel Chelmodyn drusar loy sodiuiel Carson, eltrae myre notiel mesraym Venea dublearsy mauear melusyron chartulneas fabelmerusyn.

Having said these verses to Subcircium in silence, as time and place permit; do the rest that the art itself demands and commit to the already visible spirit the secret with the seal of the deep mysteries, without hesitating, for these guides are all good and faithful.

Let us suppose that you have such a mental secret as to confide to no one at all.

You have found the greatest treasure in Thecas of the dead, or in any other place in the earth, or you know for sure that it is hidden in secret. You alone are not sufficient to export it, and yet you do not trust anyone who lives around. You have a faithful friend, but absent at a distance, to whom you wish to reveal a mystery, but you do not trust to letters or news, or else you might fall into trouble and danger during the heat of the day and lose your profit. Then you call the spirit. The spirit comes, he brings the message, he calls his friend. He comes, he rejoices, he participates. I write letters, as you will, in which there is nothing at all to be feared.

I am sending you the speech I gave at the wedding of a friend of mine. God, the Creator of all, the Redeemer of humanity, the Saviour of all, that humanity should not perish, also instituted the sacrament of marriage. For we read that when the first man joined Eve to a woman, he said: Grow and Multiply,[1] establishing a law for the preservation of humanity. Afterwards God incarnate thought fit to sanctify the marriage by a miracle. Of God they deserve well those who serve the constitution, but they contribute more to men who assume a chaste marriage with zeal for children. You then, who assume an honest marriage, I would rightly praise the example of our Saviour. He does not use miracles, but I will praise the properly instituted sacrament of marriage with words. I think that if marriage is abolished, the whole human race will fail and collapse. For there is a human kind of marriage, however devastating, weak, and corruptible, which, however, would not continue without marriage. But you do this so that the fruitfulness of your marriage may be decorated with holy manners and conversation, and without causing offense to anyone. First of all, love the Goddess[2], be continually engaged in works of mercy with justice, flee from impiety, worship righteousness, love the good, praise God always, help the poor with alms, obey God's commandments. Do not forsake the truth, honour the ministers of God in the Churches, pay tithes, entertain strangers, deliver the innocent, feed the

1. A reference to Gensis 1:28.
2. Uyl – A reference to the Roman Cathoic Mary.

hungry, obey your elders, love your neighbors honestly, do no wrong to anyone, worship the Christian religion most devoutly. Abhor the vain, harmful and superstitious manners of the Gentiles. Keep the Gospel teachings and live according to the commandments of God. Run away from the pleasures of the flesh. Show yourselves honest and good, carefully guarding the purity of your mind and do not stain it. Remember, I beg you, what Christ our Lord cried out in the holy Gospel: "Blessed are the hearts of the world: those who keep the purity of their souls in a muddy body for God's sake."[3] But the purity of the heart should not be neglected by continuous and humble prayers. For prayer purifies the mind, cools the heated, and drives away the temptations of the devil. Hence the holy Apostle Paul teaches you to insist on diligent and devout prayers, so that you may be able to overcome harmful temptations. We join you in marriage, because you will construct the kind of clothing propagated by the decree of the law. You will not be obliged to flow into poisonous pleasures. For the pleasures of the flesh kill the soul and corrupt the noblest dignity of the human substance of the future. And so, remember these, knowing that you are travelers, returning to the country to which you have been called. So, live in marriage, that is, you may come to the kingdom of heaven after death, when it is exalted. John Trithemius, abbot of Spanheim, of the order of the Holy Father Benedict, I wrote on the day before the 2nd of March, in the year of the birth of our Lord Jesus Christ 1500.

When he receives these or any other letters to whom they are sent; knowing the sign of the great Vsielus, he secretly did as he knew to do by art: then he turned to Subcircium and Carmen.

> Vsiel asoyr paremon cruato madusyn sauepy mauayr realdo chameron ilco paneras thurmo pean elsoty fabelrusyn iltras charson frymasto chelmodyn.

With this said poem, the spirit will show himself visible, and unlock the commission. And if anything has been committed to him by him, he will report it to the sender.

3. Uyl – I am not sure what biblical reference Trithemius is making here.

Commentary: Chapter XI

[p. 181; 1] *Vsiel* [or, *Usiel, Uziel, Uzziel*] ... There is some debate over whether *Vsiel* is an angel or a demon. In kabbalistic literature, *Vsiel* appears as a "good" fallen angel that helped to sire the Nephilim in Genesis 6. A fallen angel is a demon, but some current scholarship have made the faulty assumption that demons and angels are two different types of supernatural being. In *The Book of the Angel Raziel*, Vsiel appears as an angel that stands before the throne of God.[1] *Vsiel* is also commonly called upon to protect treasure and other valuables, and to reveal precious objects hidden by someone else by a magical enchantment or spell.[2] This *Vsiel*, (or, *Uziel*) is different than the name of a human named Uziel that some have claimed appears in the Old Testament.

[p. 181; R1] More symbols used to draw in demonic spirits. See pp. 179–180 for a full explanation about how this faulty belief has found its way into Christian practice.

[p. 182; 1], [p. 182; 1], non-sensical goetic "angel tongues".

[p. 183; E], *First of all, love the Goddess*, ... The reference here to Mary as a "Goddess" should not be all that surprising. The way that the Roman Catholic Church, and Trithemius above, have believed that Jesus is submitted to Mary, that Trithemius calls Mary a "Goddess" is not a complete derivation from Roman Catholic Mariology.

In how the Roman Catholic tradition refers to Mary as the "queen of heaven", the following verses from Jeremiah are interesting to look at:

> Do you not see what they are doing in the cities of Judah and in the streets of Jerusalem? The children gather wood, the fathers kindle fire, and the women knead dough, to make cakes for the queen of heaven. And they pour out drink offerings to other gods, to provoke me to anger. Is it I whom they provoke? declares the LORD. Is it not themselves, to their own shame? Therefore thus says the Lord GOD: Behold, my anger and my wrath will be poured out on this place, upon man and beast, upon the trees of the field and the fruit of the ground; it will burn and not be quenched." (italics mine; Jeremiah 7:17–20 ESV)

We should see that Yahweh says that making cakes for the "queen of heaven" is detestable to Yahweh and will bring complete destruction to Jerusalem. The people of Judah, however, are determined to hold up their goetic vows to the "queen of heaven".

> "But we will do everything that we have vowed, make offerings to the queen of heaven and pour out drink offerings to her, as we did, both we and our fathers, our kings and our officials, in the cities of Judah and in the streets of Jerusalem. For then we had plenty of food, and prospered, and saw no disaster. But since we left off making offerings to the queen of heaven and pouring out drink offerings to her, we have lacked everything and have been consumed

1. Rosemary Ellen Guiley Ph.D., *The Encyclopedia of Demons & Demonology* (New York, New York: Checkmark Books, 2009), p. 260.

2. Michelle Belanger, *The Dictionary of Demons: Names of the Damned* (Woodbury, Minnesota: Llewellyn Publications, 2017), p. 112.

> by the sword and by famine." And the women said, "When we made offerings to the queen of heaven and poured out drink offerings to her, was it without our husbands' approval that we made cakes for her bearing her image and poured out drink offerings to her?" (italics mine; Jeremiah 44:17–19 ESV)

The judgment of Yahweh on Judah for making offerings to other gods, including gods by name of the "queen of heaven" is even more dreadful:

> Thus says the LORD of hosts, the God of Israel: You and your wives have declared with your mouths, and have fulfilled it with your hands, saying, 'We will surely perform our vows that we have made, to make offerings to the queen of heaven and to pour out drink offerings to her.' Then confirm your vows and perform your vows! Therefore hear the word of the LORD, all you of Judah who dwell in the land of Egypt: Behold, I have sworn by my great name, says the LORD, that my name shall no more be invoked by the mouth of any man of Judah in all the land of Egypt, saying, 'As the Lord GOD lives.' Behold, I am watching over them for disaster and not for good. (italics mine; Jeremiah 44:25–27 ESV)

We do need to take a minute to see who exactly this "queen of heaven" is. The Bible never gives a proper noun to identify this "queen of heaven" as a specific goddess, but there is enough textual archaeological evidence to show us who the "queen of heaven" was believed to be.

> The major Mesopotamian goddess of love, war, and the planet Venus is known primarily by the Sumerian name Inanna and the Akkadian name Ishtar. [...] The goddess is the spouse and lover of the king with whom she participates in the ritual of the sacred marriage. She provides the king with economic blessings as well as power and victory in war. Inanna/Ishtar is associated with the cults of many cities; she is particularly prominent in Uruk, Akkad, Kish, Nineveh, and Arbela. In Uruk, but particularly in Akkad and Assyria, she is a goddess of war and victory.[3]

The quote from T. Abusch shows a clear connection of Ishtar as the queen of "heaven" since she was the "spouse" or "wife" of the deific king. What we can also note is that Ishtar and the goddess Asherah that is mentioned in several places in the Old Testament were associated as the same goddess in the ancient world. T. Abusch again explains that "Ishtar derives from common Semitic ʿaṯtar. (A masculine god with this name appears in Southern Arabia and Ugarit [ʿaṯtar], though a feminine form [Astarte] is also attested in Canaanite literature and in the Bible.)"[4]

N. Wyatt then takes up the argument concerning Asherah in another interesting way.

> The conclusion many scholars have drawn that Asherah was the consort of Yahweh may be approached from another angle. If Yahweh developed out of local Palestinian forms of El, then we might expect a simple continuity of the old El-Asherah (Ilu-Athirat) relationship which appears to obtain at Ugarit. But it has been increasingly argued in recent years that Yahweh has 'baalistic' characteristics, or is even a form of Baal himself. It has been argued that Baal effectively usurps El's role at Ugarit, and takes El's consort at the same time.[5]

Asherah, which includes Ishtar, was falsely believed at some point to be the "consort/wife of Yahweh". Considering the goetic origins of the gods and goddesses in the biblical era, the Roman Catholic Church has adopted the goetic thought to "deify" Mary as

3. T. Abusch, "Ishtar," in *Dictionary of Deities and Demons in the Bible*, ed. Karel van der Toorn, Bob Becking, and Pieter W. van der Horst (Leiden, Netherlands: Brill, 1999), pp. 452–453.

4. Abusch, "Ishtar," p. 452.

5. N. Wyatt, "Asherah," in *Dictionary of Deities and Demons in the Bible*, ed. Karel van der Toorn, Bob Becking, and Pieter W. van der Horst (Leiden, Netherlands: Brill, 1999), p. 104.

the "queen of heaven". However, the Roman Catholic defense that since the mother of a "king" in the medieval world was still called "queen" therefore Mary is the "queen of heaven" is not defensible in this goetic context. In order for Mary to receive the name "queen of heaven" because she is Jesus' mother, she still would have needed to have been married to the Father. Even if Mary *could* be given the title of queen as being married to the Father, her proper title would still be "queen mother" after the son became king and not "queen of heaven". With that in mind, there is a clear connection to Mary as the "queen of heaven" and to Asherah/Ishtar as the wife/consort of Yahweh. The problems being faced by the Roman Catholic Church in the last few decades should not be alarming when looking at Yahweh's condemnation for worshipping the goetic "queen of heaven". Yet the Roman Catholic Church is trying to defend such worship as "holy" and "required for salvation". Yahweh also condemns such vows in the texts from Jeremiah 7 shown above.

Chapter XII: Cabariel

Whose spirit is the supreme emperor Cabariel who dwells at that quarter of the world, which is called Circius by wind, and has under him seven princes by day, and as many by night.

In the twelfth abode of the world described, which is towards that quarter, to which the wind Circius prevails, the great Emperor Cabariel dwells with infinite spirits, among whom are appointed for the operation of steganography. Fifty by day, and as many by night at all times, who preside over many servants and are very powerful. The secret duty of these is to invite friends, to reveal intrigues, and to warn the absent from whom it is most to be avoided. Of all these we will name a few.

Black.	Red.	B.	R.	B.	R.	B.	R.
Satifiel	50.	*Etymel*	50.	*Mador*	50.	*Ladiel*	50.
Parius	50.	*Clyssam*	50.	*Peniel*	50.	*Morias*	50.
Godiel	50.	*Elitel*	50.	*Cugiel*	50.	*Pandor*	50.
Taros	50.	*Aniel*	50.	*Thalbos*	50.	*Cazul*	50.
Asoriel	50.	*Cupher*	50.	*Orym*	50.	*Dubiel*	50.

You now have twenty of the great princes of Cabariel. Sufficing to you for the present, the first ten of whom are appointed for daily operations with five hundred servants, another ten for night, likewise with their five hundred servants. And you know that the spirits who preside over the operations of the day are much more benevolent than those of the night being more ready to obey. If you wish to work through the ministry of these spirits, turn yourself to that place which we have spoken of:

> Cabariel onear chameron fruani, parnaton fofiel bryosi nagreal fabelrontyn adiel thortay nofruau pena afefiel chusy.

When the poem is completed, if it is during the day, the spirit called will immediately attend without delay. But if he be in the night and there is a delay in the coming of the spirit whom you have called, rebuke him as often as possible, until he comes by the repetition of the song, which is usually very repulsive.

Let us suppose, for example, that there is a certain secret that no one trusts at all.

You have a faithful friend, whom you trust, as if to yourself, but who is absent far away, to whom you know that on your return there will be an ambush from a more powerful person on the road or in any other place or way. You desire to persuade him not to be secret, but the danger would be too great for you to persuade him if the secret should be made public. Therefore, the letters are not to be entrusted to be carried, and they are not to be read by anyone. Nor are they to be trusted to a man, in case they should be revealed.

So that you remain secure, and your friend is bold, you call the spirit, you commit the secret to the spirit, and it happens,

Send letters to a friend, family, or a devotional prayer that may be seen.

I had let you borrow my book (codex) of the deeds of the Lombards and the volume of Bede concerning the times, which I beg you to return. For it is appropriate for a wise man and a most Christian man to keep the faith which he has promised to keep. To forget the benefits of our divine and human institutions is the greatest crime. Do not bring on yourself such a sinful crime. I have sent you my volumes, that you may restore them at some time. I gave you Greek books free of charge, the perusal of which you deservedly and gratifyingly presented to us and the faithful. Farewell, from Spanheim, on the Ides of March,[1] in the year of the Lord 1500.

When a friend has received these or any other letters sent by you; knowing the sign of Cabariel, he turns to that part of the world from which the wind advances Circius; And after the usual preparations, he recites this prayer in silence.

Secret Song

Cabariel afiar paremon chiltan amedyn sayr pemadon chulty mouayr sauepor peatha mal frimaston dayr pean cothurno fabelrusyn elsoty chelmodyn.

When this song was spoken towards Circius, an angel would immediately appear visibly, unlocking the secret promise to him. He will report to you if he has committed anything.

1. Uyl – The Ides of March is the calendar date of March 15.

Commentary: Chapter XII

[p. 189; 1] *Cabariel* ... A demonic prince of the west whose daytime servants are good-natured and whose nighttime servants are deceitful, rebellious and evil.[1] This demon is also said to be difficult to see and prefers to show himself in remote locations. *Cabariel* is more likely to appear in stone crystal or scrying glass.[2]

[p. 189; 3], [p. 190; 3] non-sensical goetic "angel tongues".

[p. 190; 2] *For it is appropriate for a wise man and a most Christian man to keep the faith which he has promised to keep. To forget the benefits of our divine and human institutions is the greatest crime.* ... Trithemius here is connecting faith to the benefits of "divine and human institutions" which is implying the Roman Catholic Church. This attitude of "benefits" of the church as divine is an idea that is not present just within the Roman Catholic Church. While the traditions of the Roman Catholic Church do demand adherence and loyalty to the church over the Bible, the fact that it is a form of idolatry is undeniable. The "benefits" that Trithemius is claiming here are those of salvific faith. The benefit of faith is something the Bible is clear that only Jesus can provide and not the church, nor Mary.

In Protestant circles, this blind loyalty to the church is just as prevalent. Many in churches are too afraid to speak up when there are problems in teaching or the leadership. The reason for this fear is nothing more than a fear of man of which the Bible is clear we are not to have. (Matthew 10:28) Too many people are scared of being shunned or even excommunicated from a church for standing up against the sinful teachings of their leaders. This attitude of loyalty over biblical truth is cult-like in the way church leaders use it to free themselves of any responsibility of error. The argument from the leadership comes down to "most of the people do not have a problem with it, therefore this/these person(s) is/are wrong." However, it is never the majority that change the church in the way of biblical truth, but always the minority.

This loyalty to church over truth is a tradition that has been borrowed from the Roman Catholic Church. A loyalty so deeply rooted that people are afraid of losing the "benefits" of being part of a church for doing what the Bible says to correct other believers that are in error. Having grown up in the Dutch Reformed tradition myself, you never questioned the *Dominee* (doh-me-nay) which was how the Dutch tradition referred to a head pastor and/or minister. If the *Dominee* came to your house, it was like God himself was coming to your home. This same reverence for the church exists in not only the Dutch tradition but many churches where it is instilled in the congregation that you do not question the leadership. In one message I heard from a pastor, the pastor said (paraphrased) that "if

1. Rosemary Ellen Guiley Ph.D., *The Encyclopedia of Demons & Demonology* (New York, New York: Checkmark Books, 2009), p. 36.

2. Michelle Belanger, *The Dictionary of Demons: Names of the Damned* (Woodbury, Minnesota: Llewellyn Publications, 2017), p. 81.

God is with us, if you question us, you are immediately wrong and disobeying God." This is the attitude that many church leaders are putting into the minds of their congregants. This fear of the leadership is then passed down to fear of losing the benefits of being part of that church, or even of the faith in some more fundamentalist Protestant movements.

CHAPTER XIII: RAYSIEL

Whose prince is called Raysiel, dwelling directly to the north, under whom there are fifty chiefs, who are in charge of our day workers, and as many of those who work at night. Whose it is to narrate the traditions.

The third is the tenth mansion in the north, whose spirit and supreme commander is Raysiel, who has under his authority fifty captains who are in charge of the operations of the day, with many servants, and the same number who are in charge of the night with their servants. It is their duty, in these causes and traditions, which pertain to death, to encourage the friends of the worker, and to announce the secret. The leaders who preside over the operations of the day gladly obey those who call, and come cheerful, friendly, and most ready to obey. But those who preside at night are a little withdrawn because they greatly hate and detest the light. They do not easily obey, especially the novices less certified in art, whom they often laugh in the face, unless they are so constrained by the secrets of the worker, that they do not succeed in betraying the worker in this art. For he is very much afraid of secrets, and as if they were given to secrets more than the spirits of the day, and yet they obey when invited. But now from the number of all these let us set down the names of a few and the number of servants, how many are sufficient for us for the usual operation.

Black.	[1]	Red.		B.		R.	
Baciar	*50.*	*Astael*	*50.*	*Chanael*	*30.*	*Melcha*	*30.*
Thoac	*50.*	*Ramica*	*50.*	*Fursiel*	*30.*	*Tharas*	*30.*
Sequiel	*50.*	*Dubarus*	*50.*	*Betasiel*	*30.*	*Vuiel*	*30.*
Sadar	*50.*	*Armena*	*50.*				
Terath	*50.*	*Albhadur*	*50.*				

Red.	Black.	R.	B.	R.	B.	R.	B.
Thariel	*40.*	*Lazaba*	*40.*	*Lamas*	*10.*	*Thurcal*	*10.*
Paras	*40.*	*Aleasy*	*40.*				
Arayl	*40.*	*Sebach*	*40.*	*Belsay*	*20.*	*Sarach*	*20.*
Culmar	*40.*	*Quibda*	*40.*	*Morael*	*20.*	*Arepach*	*20.*

You now have a very good reader out of fifty daytime princes sixteen with six hundred seventy of their servants and out of fifty nighttime spirits fourteen with four hundred twenty servants in number, who will be sufficient for you for all the operations both at night and during the day. But when you wish to work through them according to the

1. Uyl – The empty cells in this table had symbols from the original Stenganographia which I did not include here. If you wish to see what these symbols were, there are plenty of free copies in the original Latin online for the reader to refer to.

hours intended, choose from the arranged order whom you wish, and call him to the north (since they all stay there) by this song.

Secret Prayer

> Raysiel afruano chameron fofiel onear Vemabi parnothon fruano Caspiel fufre bedarym bulifeor pean Curmaby Layr Vaymeor pesarym adorcus odiel Vernabi peatha darsum laspheno deuior Camedonton phorsy lasbenay to charmon druson olnays, Venouym lulefin, peorso fabelrontos thurno. Calephoy Vem, nabelron bural thorasyn charnoty Capelron.

Complete the prayer and when in silence, the spirit called will be present. Commit the secret securely, and he will carry out and report the commission. But if you preside over operations at night, as they are most willing to do, if you seem to slow down, address them by repeating the song powerfully, fearing nothing. For they will be forced to return to you as their master.

I have a secret, which I trust no one to convey, of this sort.

I suppose it is a case. A friend of mine is someone noble and educated, whom I knew to be secretly killed by some hired assassins. I dare not challenge them openly, because it is dangerous for me. In a more familiar and private matter, should the letters fall into the hands of others, I am afraid. I do not presume to trust a man who speaks with his mouth, because he who is with me today, perhaps tomorrow will stand against me. With freedom I take refuge in my usual art, to which I am not afraid that whatever I commit may become public, even if it should happen that I am tempted by the enemy.

I send letters to a familiar friend, in which I fear no danger.

The highest ornament of nobility is justice and philosophy. Disgrace defines ungodliness and ignorance as from ancient times. For what is more beautiful than to adorn the noble race that is in service with letters and virtues? We find many of the most noble men engaged in this and the rest and were active night and day in order to conquer the barbarians with arms, and to educate their people in righteousness and in their letters. By the example of these, Bumavv did not cease to highly praise the letters of humanity and the good arts in the most educated manner, with the beauty of arms and letters. And once upon a time the wisest princes were unwilling to include their wealth in their treasures, but rather to give it to themselves in literature. The happiness of justice is gained. A well studied knowledge of the scriptures makes leaders venerable to all and most feared. Ignorance of the scriptures, the so-called burial of a living man, used to bring disgrace and terrible calamity to princes and nobles. A man without letters is a two-footed ass, to be buried alive, indeed buried. The greatest, the nobles, and those governing the republic must be wise and notable for their knowledge of literature, ignorance of which leads to tyranny. The love of letters commends the deeds of noble princes forever. For we see that the ancient philosophers obtained the principality of memory, and having obtained immortality in name and immortality is more everlasting among all men by letters than by arms. For more by letters than by arms they restored the glorious, excellent sages, and ancient tyrants and princes, whose memory they bestowed with praise and titles with immortality. Let us add that the Christian study of literature is the highest and most honourable aid to the joy of heaven. For from the scriptures, we begin to contemplate the shining, honourable majesty of divine understandings, otherwise inaccessible to us. Thus Henry, the most learned soldier of letters, may you always live adorned with righteousness. Farewell, from Spanheim, Johannes Trithemius. March In the year 1500.

After these letters, or any other, a friend skilled in the art approaches, having recognized the sign of Raysiel, having given the customary statements, he turns to the north, and calls upon the spirit with this song.

Prayer of Conspiracy

Raysiel myltran, fruano fiar chasmy clymarso pean Sayr pultho chultusa medon vepursandly tusan axeyr afflon.

With these words, the sent spirit will immediately appear visible, and will report to you everything and everything that I have commanded to your ear. And I would have you know that some spirits, presiding over nighttime operations, do not willingly come to the operation at night, unless they are addressed with the greatest religious ceremonies and secret prayers. But those who, after they have come and been sent to a friend, are more willing to appear quickly and obey the caller, unless perhaps he himself, being deceived on every occasion, with something he would neglect the command in this art.

Commentary: Chapter XIII

[p. 193; 1] *Raysiel* ... Another demon that in goetic and kabbalistic belief is thought to have good-natured servants by day, but the nighttime servants are "evil, stubborn, and disobedient."[1] *Raysiel* is also a demon that is apparently hard to see and is best summoned in a glass vessel or scrying crystal. The goeticist is also warned to make sure the room that *Raysiel* is called into is protected so that no one may randomly, or intentionally, walk in without warning. *Raysiel* will apparently not like such "surprise" visits.[2]

[p. 194;1], [p. 195; 1] non-sensical goetic "angel tongues".

[p. 195, E], *The greatest, the nobles, and those governing the republic must be wise and notable for their knowledge of literature, ignorance of which leads to tyranny, ...* The implication of this statement can be seen in two different ways. The first, which deals with ecclesiological issues, is that many churches will demand that people be ignorant of the scriptures in order for them to push their false ideologies. In many charismatic, Prosperity, WOF and NAR movements, the teachers and adherents will literally push that knowing "too much" about the Bible is the basis of Gnosticism. This is a false analogy since the Bible always commands us to know the scriptures. (Joshua 1:8; Deuteronomy 11:18–23; Acts 17:11; John 5:39–40; John 8:32; Romans 15:4) Not only that, while the Greek word γνῶσις (gnōsis) does mean "seeking to know, inquiry, investigation"[3] there is another implication to the word with the Gnostic heresy that γνῶσις is also "higher, esoteric knowledge"[4] Thie "higher esoteric knowledge" that was gained from the Gnostic heresy was existential in origin. This special γνῶσις was not from study of the scriptures but of gaining special or "new" revelation about what secrets the scriptures contained. The basis of all Prosperity, WOF and NAR teaching that they claim is either "new" or "forgotten" teaching is existential in origin but that they as *false* "apostles" are brining to the church. The real Gnostic heretics are the Prosprity, WOF and NAR churches and *not* those that seek to study the Bible. Intentional study of the Bible will prove these false teachers wrong. Therefore, these leaders and their adherents will push people to trust them instead and mock anyone who can prove with the Bible that what they are saying and doing is *anti*-biblical. Often the defenders of these movements will call people that use Biblical evidence for their arguments "pedantic" meaning a critique of someone who takes something too literally for its intended meaning. Being pedantic" with the Bible is what the Bible commands. The Bible intends that we are to understand what it is trying to say, even within its figurative imagery and apply the intended meaning to our current lives. Charis-

1. Rosemary Ellen Guiley Ph.D., *The Encyclopedia of Demons & Demonology* (New York, New York: Checkmark Books, 2009), p. 209.

2. Michelle Belanger, *The Dictionary of Demons: Names of the Damned* (Woodbury, Minnesota: Llewellyn Publications, 2017), p. 258.

3. Henry George Liddell et al., *A Greek-English Lexicon* (Oxford, UK: Clarendon Press, 1996), p. 355.

4. Liddell, *Greek*, p. 355.

matic, Prosperity, WOF, NAR and Roman Catholic churches though cannot make a defense of their teachings from *within* the Bible with proper exegesis, so their only defense is to call people "pedantic" for sticking to the Biblical evidence. Personally, if someone calls me "pedantic" for taking the Bible too seriously, I consider that compliment.

The other application here is to what is happening politically. While the "rewriting" of history has been most common with the left-wing movements, the reality is that all political movements have been attempting in *some* way to rewrite historical events in their favour. What is happening in any political spheres, whether left or right wing, can all be corrected if people would simply open up the books and take seriously the lessons of history.

Trithemius, who was hiding messages in a goetic text, is making a statement here that I need to agree with. Even though the false image this text is showing is a goetic one, the reality is that many of the things we are learning in churches, in schools and in politics could all be reversed if people would simply take the texts that they are teaching from seriously. People need to take these texts seriously and do the research as to what *really* happened in the days and ages past. However, many refuse to do the research and will simply take the person behind the podium's word for it. This attitude of wilful ignorance is what is leading to "tyranny" in churches, school, politics and really all institutions in the world today. Many people would be shocked what the history books really have to say and tell us about our past histories, traditions, theologies and beliefs if they would simply do the research themselves.

Chapter XIV: Symiel

Whose supreme prince is called Symiel, who lives in the north, having ten princes under him. Those who are in charge of the daily operations, with many servants, whose duty it is to carry the family secret.

The fourteenth mansion is towards the north, distant from the beginning of the North by a little more than twenty-one degrees. The highest spirit of which is the emperor Symiel, who has under him ten leaders who are in charge of the operations of the day, with many of their servants. For the operations from the nighttime spirits there are many leaders, whose exact number I cannot find, since they also have many famous people under them. It is the duty of these to communicate among friends the most secret mysteries, which are not to be revealed to any man for all time. But you will be able to work through them, if necessary. I will explain to you ten of the daytime spirits, and the same number of the nighttime spirits, and that will suffice for the present.

Black.	Red.	B.	R.	B.	R.	B.	[1]
Asmyel	60.	*Larael*	60.	*Mafrus*	70.	*Marianu*	100.
Chrubas	100.	*Achot*	60.	*Apiel*	30.	*Narzael*	100.
Vastos	40.	*Banier*	90.	*Curiel*	40.	*Murahe*	30.
Malgron	20.	*Dagiel*	100.	*Molael*	10.	*Richel*	120.
Romiel	80.	*Musor*	110.	*Arafos*	50.	*Nalael*	130.

You now have ten chiefs appointed for the operations of the day with many servants and ten spirits for the night operations also with many servants, through whom you will be able to work securely and not at risk, just be well-versed in steganography. Let no one, who is not well trained in the operation of this art, presume to approach it according to its regulations, for not all princes obey. But you will want to work with this very knowledge, properly presupposed. Turn yourself to the north, and in the manner in which I delivered you I will send the secret plans that the prayer may come through this same way.

Song to the Spirit

Symiel myrno chamerony theor pasrõ adiueal fanerosthi sofear Carmedõ Charnothiel peasor sositran fabelrusy thyrno pamerosy trelno chabelron chymo churmabõ, asiel, peasor carmes nabeyros toys Camalthonty.

Having said these things, in the manner necessary, the spirit will come. You will call it to obey all your commands, especially if the spirits were to be stirred up during the night.

For example, let us say that every secret is completely committed to no one.

---

1. Uyl – The empty cell here had a symbol from the original Stenganographia which I did not include here. If you wish to see what this symbols was, there are plenty of free copies in the original Latin online for the reader to refer to.

You have some very secret business with a friend, which concerns you and him, the disclosure of which would cause you and him permanent damage or confusion. It is certain that the letters are not believed to be safe from being read by anyone, nor is a message sent that will spread to many. Our art is yours, so you will be safe, and your friend will know the secret.

Let us form for this purpose such letters as we please, in no way thoroughly suspect. John Trithemius, Abbot of Spanheim, of the Holy Order Blessed James Trithemius, the best young man, brother Charismus, S. D.

Leaning on the letter, he gathered the humility of the heart. Good manners adorn the youth and make them more illustrious than the nobles. The knowledge of letters adorns a young man who loves sanctity. Without the morals of justice, he will lack the knowledge of honour. A young man immersed in the delusion of sin, mocking of wisdom, does not love true wisdom, which you remember to be sought by moral goodness. The training of young learners is decorated with morals, since the honour of Heaven is conferred on the holy arts, and unfruitful knowledge will be tormented by eternal torments. The knowledge of virtues and letters prospers, neither does it fail to be tainted by sinful actions. Hope for pleasures, that you may understand the truth of wisdom by experience. Goodbye.

Receiving these letters, an expert in the art of steganography, as soon as he sees the character of the prince Symiel, he perceives by understanding what he must do. Turning, he says that he after having introduced the beliefs to the north, says a secret prayer.

Secret Prayer

Symiel marlos chameron pyrcohi pean fruary fabelronti gaelto siargoti melaflor hialbra penor olefy Aiulbrani ordu Casmeron omer vemabon.

When the prayer is complete, the spirit sent will faithfully fulfill the task entrusted to him.

Commentary: Chapter XIV

[p. 199; 1] *Symiel* ... According to goetic lore, *Symiel* is a demon king of the northeast. The dukes of *Symiel* are good-natured during the day, but the nighttime dukes are stubborn and resistant to commands.[1] The daytime dukes are far outnumbered by the dukes of the night.[2]

[p. 199; 3], [p. 200; 4] non-sensical goetic "angel tongues".

[p. 200; 2] *The training of young learners is decorated with morals, since the honour of Heaven is conferred on the holy arts, and unfruitful knowledge will be tormented by eternal torments*. Unlike what many in churches have believed, there is no requirement for pastors to go to a seminary to fulfill the role of pastor. What is required is that the person be trained and know the scriptures well. With the busy life that so many people are forced to live in order to survive in a family sense or even if the man is living on his own, the time to become well-trained in the scriptures is difficult so many churches have put the responsibility on seminaries to do the job for them that the church should really be doing itself. This being said, there are many churches that are still willing to promote to pastoral roles those that are unable to interpret or exegete the Bible properly for lack of any training at all. What this has resulted in is a movement by senior pastors to promote trusted friends, or even family members, over those that have the proper and adequate training.

There is another implicit problem within Trithemius's statement. The problem is where Trithemius states that "the honour of Heaven is conferred on the holy arts". This is a fallacious statement since so many seminaries are currently in a theological drift towards either Prosperity, WOF, NAR, liberal, or progressive theology. The assumption that "God's blessing is on us" simply because a church or school calls themselves a Christian one is a lie that many have fallen for.

Another problematic argument that arises out of Trithemius's statement here is that if a church, or person, does the "good acts" then the "blessings/honours of Heaven" will fall on them. Due to that thinking, many have believed that they can "declare" the reality of heaven down here on earth. This argument may seem like a good thing, the truth is that it is drawn from one of the most core occult philosophies that has existed for a very long time. This philosophy is what is known as "As Above, So Below". This "As Above, So Below", which is a paraphrase of the actual saying below, comes from an occult document written by Hermes Trismegistus, who is an anthropomorphizing of the Egyptian god Thoth. Hermes states this saying in the document infamously known as *The Emerald Tablet*.

---

1. Rosemary Ellen Guiley Ph.D., *The Encyclopedia of Demons & Demonology* (New York, New York: Checkmark Books, 2009), p. 253.

2. Michelle Belanger, *The Dictionary of Demons*: *Names of the Damned* (Woodbury, Minnesota: Llewellyn Publications, 2017), p. 289.

> *What is below corresponds to what is above, and what is above corresponds to what is below, accomplishing the miracle of the One Thing.* And as all things have come from the One, through the One, all things follow from this One Thing in the same way. [...] *It rises from Earth to Heaven, and then it descends again to the Earth, and receives power from above and from below. Thus you will have the Glory of the whole world.* All obscurity will flee from you. This is the strong power of all power because it overcomes everything thin and penetrates everything solid. (italics mine)[3]

These are interesting statements since the argument from Prosperity, WOF and NAR teachers is that when your "praises go up, blessings come down". When "praises", often interpreted as "singing" and less often "prayer", then the blessings of God will come down. There is no biblical teaching about that. God blesses those who are *faithful* which means living in faithful worship in everything that you do, not just when you sing, pray or "praise".

The idea that when "praises go up, blessings come down" is being drawn from hermetic occultism that is using *The Emerald Tablets* as the core of their philosophy. The whole concept of astrology is also based on the "As Above, So Below" concept since what is happening in the sky is a representation of what is either happening, or *going* to happen, on the earth. The most popular place that the saying of "As Above, So Below" has been in Eugene Peterson's perversion of the Bibile the paraphrase, *The Message*. Peterson's paraphrase is as follows: "Our Father in heaven, Reveal who you are. Set the world right; Do what's best—as above, so below." (Matthew 6:9–10 MSG) People may not see this as a problem, but it has introduced occultic and goetic ideology into many churches. Since the churches that are supporters of *The Message* as a legitimate Bible can all be noted as being involved in goetia, it is not an absurd idea to see that *The Message* has introduced goetia through its use of Hermes' *The Emerald Tablet* as legitimate for Christian practice.

The problem does not end there. If you refer back to page 168 of this volume where I explain what Satanism is, then theistic-Satanism and how that applies to the deification of Mary, also applies to the Prosperity, WOF, and NAR movements. See what Bill Johnson from Bethel Church in Redding, California has to say about Jesus.

> That means He didn't bring any special powers with Him when He came to earth. Even though Jesus was 100 percent God, He chose to live on earth as a regular person just like you. Why would He do that? Because He loves you. Jesus did many miracles, and He did them as a person, [...] If Jesus did all those miracles as God, then you couldn't do them, because you're human. But because Jesus healed the sick, raised the dead, and cast out demons as a person—you can too![4]

I brought up the greater problem of this teaching on pages 29–31 of this volume when explaining how many evangelicals are believing that Jesus did all his miracles as a man to show that you can do them too. As you can see, by putting that teaching about Christ, with the teachings of theistic-Satanists, people that believe that they can "do what Jesus did" and therefore "be Christ", are teaching a Christianized form of theistic-Satanism. Johnson pushes this deification of self forward by saying that you can

> [b]ring Heaven to earth. Your royal mission is to change the world! What did Jesus need for

3. Hermes, *The Emerald Tablet of Hermes* (Location of publication unknown: IAP, 2009), Kindle Locations 134-137, 139-142, Kindle Edition.

4. Bill Johnson and Mike Seth, *When Heaven Invades Earth for Teens: Your Guide to God's Supernatural Power* (Shippensburg, Pennsylvania: Destiny Image, 2014), Logos Edition.

> that kind of job? God's power. You Can Have Both! [...] When you obey and pray for them, the Holy Spirit does two things. [...] He will leak out of you and do the miracle.[5]

Johnson is trying to convince you that since you can do what Jesus did, and be what Jesus is, that you are able to pull heaven to earth. Understanding that the Prosperity, WOF and NAR movements are all part of a theistic-Satanic movement, I turn now to some evidence of a disturbing nature. I fully explain this issue in "Chapter IX: The Age of Aquarius, Klaus Schwab, the Order of Nine Angles, and the Eschatology of Prosperity, Word of Faith, and the New Apostolic Reformation Movements" in my book *The Emergence of the Neo-Satanist Church: The Reality of the Prosperity, Hillsong, Word-of-Faith, and New Apostolic Reformation Death Cult*, so will keep the commentary here short.

These statements below are all made by a pseudonym "Anton Long" who is believed to be David Myatt the founder of the Neo-Nazi theistic-Satanist group *The Order of Nine Angles* [ONA]. The goals of the ONA surprisingly match those of the Prosperity, WOF and NAR movements. First, Long explains how to open gateways or "nexions" to a realm he refers to as the "acausal" which is simply what he believes is a demonic realm of "non-being" (or "a" [non], "causal" [being]). Long says this power can

> result from events brought about by Satanic ritual and/or planning (such as wars). Voluntary sacrifice results from the traditional Satanist belief that our life on this planet is only a stage: a gateway or nexion to another existence. This other existence is in the acausal realm where the Dark Gods exist. The key to this other existence is not negation, but rather ecstasy.[6]

In performing such rituals, Long gives an example of an ONA ritual between a priest and priestess.

> She felt her crystal, [...] begin to respond and draw down power from the Abyss beyond. The power came to her, slowly, through the gates [...] Her consciousness was beginning to transcend to the acausal spaces where her Dark Gods waited and she sensed their longing to return, to fill again the spaces of her causal time. They were there, [...] ready to seep past the gate to feast upon the blood of humans.[7]

The connection from Johnson's argument to that of Long's is shown below.

> Our own sentient life [...] is therefore the largest intersection of these two universes. We access more of this specific acausal energy than any other organism we know. In effect, each individual is a nexion – that is, a connection or nexus between the two universes.[...] we possess the latent ability to directly access the acausal.[8]

Since Johnson says that we can do as Jesus did, and pull heaven down to earth by the Holy Spirit that is within us, the ONA Neo-Nazi theistic-Satanists are similarly saying that your own internal "acausal" power can open "nexions" to the "acausal". This "acausal" internal power will open these "nexions" to the dark gods to allow them to come forth and "feast upon the blood of humans." The ONA which consists of several other sub-"nexions" that work in the same way as terrorist cells, are also known for extreme acts of vampirism. Johnson's "acausal power" that he says is the "Holy Spirit" that is "within us" that allows us to "do as Jesus did and call heaven down", is the same "power" that ONA is calling on to draw their "heaven" down so that their "dark gods can feast

5. Johnson, *Heaven*, Logos Edition.
6. Anton Long, *The Temple of Satan—A Symphonic Allegory* (Gent, Belgium: Skull Press, 2003), p. 76.
7. Long, *The Temple of Satan*, p. 46.
8. Long, *The Temple of Satan*, pp. 45-46.

on human blood".

Putting this all together briefly, the idea of "As Above, So Below" that is being pushed by both the occult and goetic magicians, that the Prosperity, WOF and NAR movements are using as well, is also being used by the Neo-Nazi theistic-Satanist group the ONA to pull their demonic heaven down in the same way that the Prosperity, WOF and NAR groups are using their self-deity to pull down their "heaven". The idea of "As Above, So Below" has been suggested as a "Christian" idea here by Trithemius and pushed further as "Christian" by false teachers like Eugene Peterson. This teaching is spread across the entire spectrum of the Prosperity, WOF and NAR movements as well as a large number of charismatic and other more "centre-lined" evangelical churches. If this was not bad enough, Kenneth Copeland, in a mockery of communion, pretended to cut his hand open, along with one of his pastoral supporters. The two men then made it look like they mixed their blood in with grape juice, which Copeland proceeded to drink as a sign of "true communion". While it is clear the blood-letting is fake, the theistic-Satanism in the act of implied vampirism is upfront in the overt messaging of Copeland. The video can be found on YouTube.[9]

9. Revealing Truth, "Kenneth Copeland Takes Creepy to a Whole New Level," *YouTube*, November 4, 2024, https://www.youtube.com/watch?v=-At56s393Ko.

Chapter XV: Armadiel

Whose supreme commander is Armadiel, who dwells in that part of the world, from where Boreas used to blow the wind, having under him many princes.

The great emperor Armadiel dwells in the fifth mansion to the Boreal quarter, having under his command many generals and princes with their servants, to whom a hundred are given authority over the operations of the day and night indifferently and our daily activities in steganography at the will of the operator. The duty of these is to announce to princes and great men the most secret secrets of the working with the greatest fidelity and mystery. Of these we shall name some of the more important, which are sufficient for our purpose.

Red.	[1]R.	B.	R.	B.	R.	B.	R..	B.
Massar	50.	*Orariel*	*Pandiel*	10.	10.	60.	60.	50.
Parabiel	40.	*Oryn*	*Carasiba*	20.	20.	70.	70.	40.
Laiel	30.	*Samiel*	*Asbibiel*	30.	30.	80.	80.	30.
Caluarnya	20.	*Asmael*	*Mafayr*	40.	40.	70.	70.	20.
Alferiel	10.	*Iaziel*	*Oeniel*	50.	50.	60.	60.	10.

You have already from the spirits of Armadiel fifteen in number with their one thousand two hundred sixty servants who, according to the division of the twenty-four hours, are usually called to come to work in six parts with their leaders he willed himself, arranging his order in coming. When, therefore, you wish to work something in steganography through them, you must carefully observe the division of time according to this art, without which you will make no progress at all.

Secret Prayer

Armadiel marbeuo pelrusan neor chamyn aldron pemarson Cathornaor pean lyburmy Caueron Tharty abesmeron vear larso charnoty theor Caueos myat drupas Camedortys ly pa ruffes ernoty mesoryn elthi chaor atiel; messayn rouemu fable rusin, friatochasalon pheor thamorny mesardiel pelusy madiel baseroty sarreon prolsoyr asenosy cameltruson.

When you have completed this conspiracy as it should be, the spirit will soon be present, ready for your control.

Let us form an example to entrust such a secret to no one.

It is for me to share a certain secret with my prince. I do not dare to enjoin it in letters, or else through negligence or forgetfulness they should be read by others. I therefore like to

1. Uyl – This cell had a symbol from the original Stenganographia which I did not include here. If you wish to see what this symbols was, there are plenty of free copies in the original Latin online for the reader to refer to.

try the mystery of this art, by which my secret will always remain hidden.

Let us write letters, whatever we please, which should not be seen by anyone.

To the Most Serene Prince, Lord Philip, Count Palatine of the Rhine, Duke of Bavaria, Archdapifer of the Holy Roman Empire, Prince Elector, John Trithemius Abbot of Spanheim served with prayers.

The most illustrious prince with the submission of the most service. The kindness of your glorious leadership ordered me to write into letters some of the most secret matters, having been set forth in words. I would rejoice not far from faithful joy, if the strength equal to the will came to me, to distribute the favours presented to me in the most honourable and appropriate place, and to cause the obedience due to grace. The weakness of the heart will be restricted by the newness of undertaking the work without a previous path, for which I know that I am far from unequaled. For it will have an enormous and great work, and it will instill in me the greatest of my efforts. I will try my strength, I will obey your grace, I will without doubt approach the kindest judge, if my good will does not give me the opportunity to complete it. The most recent, is above all through the German Gymnasium. So, most clearly and most humanely, if I have anything or am a prince, I know that I am entirely subject to your kindness. And although there may be wiser than others, who could have done this work better or more ornately, and not in a mediocre way, nevertheless, I wanted to show my most faithful and righteous mind to your grace, and to try out new great things that I believe no one else has found. Dated 16th of April in the year of the Lord 1500.

Taking up these or any other letters, to whom they are sent by an expert in the art among the character of Armadiel, when he knows what he turns to, where the art commands him to turn, and says the following prayer.

Secret Prayer

Armadiel afran meson Casayr pelodyn, Cauoti chameron thersoruy marbeuon pheor Casoyn myruosy lyburmy deon fabelronton. Chubis archmarson.

This prayer having been properly completed, the sent spirit will appear in the open, and will faithfully reveal to the ear the secrets entrusted to him by the sender, adding nothing or taking anything away. And if anything is again committed to him by him, to refer to the ancients to whom he was sent. Let what is ordered by the art be done, and he will comply.

Commentary: Chapter XV

[p. 207; 1] *Armadiel* ... According to goetic lore, *Armadiel* is a demonic king of the northeast that serves under the demon king of the north. *Armadiel*'s servants, though demons, are said to be "good-natured" but can only be summoned at the correct time,[1] such as Bill Johnson teaches about angel visits at 3 am, or the "devil/witching hour", (see pages 76–79, this volume). While most demon rulers have many demonic lesser servants, *Armadiel* is believed to have much more select number of servants bringing the number of servants down quite a bit.[2]

[p. 207; 3], [p. 206, 4] non-sensical goetic "angel tongues".

[p. 207; 4] *ready for your control,* ... This is drawn from Merkavah Mysticism and is used by kabbalistic and goetic practice. This practice about being able to control spirits, or "angels", is also being used by many in churches who believe they can "pray for angel protection". The evidence has already been given many times about where this teaching is from, but it is helpful to note that people praying for angel protection are also assuming a deific ability to "control" these spirits by doing so.

---

1. Rosemary Ellen Guiley Ph.D., *The Encyclopedia of Demons & Demonology* (New York, New York: Checkmark Books, 2009), p. 18.

2. Michelle Belanger, *The Dictionary of Demons: Names of the Damned* (Woodbury, Minnesota: Llewellyn Publications, 2017), p. 39.

Chapter XVI: Baruchas

Whose prince Baruchas dwells in the quarter that the wind is most likely to blow, which is called the Vulturnum. Having under him many princes and his own, who are the chief commissioners of the lords' secret messengers.

But the great emperor Baruchas rules over the seventeenth mansion, situated to the windward of the Vulturnum. Who has under his command many princes, leaders, and other spirits, all whose duty it is to announce the hidden and most secret commissions of princes, nobles, and lords, to their subjects or friends. Of these I will name for you fifteen who will be sufficient for every worker in steganography. And they do not have divisions among themselves or orders for day and night like the others, but all have a commission about everything in general, so that every spirit, at any hour he is called by the worker, is forced to come.

Red.	Black.	R.	B.	R.	B.	R.	B.	R.
Quita	*Cartael*	*Monael*	*100.*	*10.*	*600.*	*60.*	*500.*	*50.*
Sarael	*Ianiel*	*Chubor*	*200.*	*20.*	*700.*	*70.*	*400.*	*40.*
Melchon	*Pharol*	*Lamael*	*300.*	*30.*	*800.*	*80.*	*300.*	*30.*
Couayr	*Baoxas*	*Dorael*	*400.*	*40.*	*700.*	*70.*	*200.*	*20.*
Aboc	*Geriel*	*Decaniel*	*500.*	*50.*	*600.*	*60.*	*100.*	*10.*

You have now from among the princes of Baruchas the great prince or the emperor named for the operation of steganography fifteen of his servants and seven thousand forty lower servants whose service is most sufficient for you for all the operation of this art. Guide,[1] observe the division of time according to the six hours of the day and night, and facing the Vulturnum, call him whom the hour concerns, carefully observing the letters of the servants, without whom they never proceed. And be careful not to make an error in their number, order, and dominion.

Secret Prayer

Baruchas maluear chemorsyn charnotiel bason ianocri medusyn aprilty casmyron sayr pean cauoty medason peroel chamyrsyn cherdiel auenos nosear penaon sayr chauelonti genayr pamelron frilcha madyrion onetiel fabelronthos.

With this conspiracy completed in silence as it should be, the one principal spirit will soon be present, whom you called with the attendants assigned to him according to the series of time. I have been entrusted with surveying the ranks, the Cœnobia and to improve and correct the wrongs done. So, I desire to send to a friend of the monks, who is far absent, such a secret that, having been published for him, the prison of the hatred of the pastor, would bring harm to me, and to the common good of the order. Whence it is

1. Uyl – a personal pronoun indicating the person performing the ritual.

not to be delivered to the letter, nor to be entrusted to any man. That we may both be safe, I the minister of art, bring the spirit to whom I trust the secret.

I WILL SEND SUCH LETTERS AS I WISH, WHICH I WILL NOT REFUSE TO MY SUBSCRIBERS.

John Trithemius, abbot of Spanheim, of the order of Saint Benedict, religious brother Nicolaus of Dureckheim, monk Cœnobia of Hirsaugi, of the same order, sincere charity in the Lord.

Let me know, my dearest brother, that you are a lover of the good arts. I am very pleased to exhort you, with as much as you would like to continue to search for and constantly rediscover the secrets of the scales, which show us the way to happiness. And to return by an easy path to the country which we have lost by sinning, to which the love of the gentlest and most merciful will be brought back hidden to us as in the holy scriptures of our Saviour. If we adorn our minds with good works, and training in holy study, it will be conferred without doubt. For what can be more wholesome and sweeter to those who wander in miserable exile than to devote themselves diligently to books, by the study of which our eyes are raised to seek the truth, and our minds are raised to the desire of future happiness. So, you despise the pleasures of the disorder of the world and spend day and night in literature. Since religion and good works are moderated by the good works done, and those same good works are enlightened by the involvement of these letters. So, he should neither choose letters without the adornment of noble good acts, neither let good works be successful without knowledge of the scriptures. And so, I exhort you, always give your attention to the study of literature. Farewell from Spanheim 16th of April in the year of the Lord 1500.

After he has received the letters, he to whom they are sent, knowing the sign of Baruchas, and setting forth the theory, to the region of the Vulturnum, which is near the eastern one, let him utter this secret prayer in silence.

SECRET PRAYER FOR THE SPIRIT.

Baruchas Mularchas chameron notiel pedarsy phroys lamasay myar chalemon phorsy fabelrontho theras capean Vear almonym lierno medusan thersiel peatha thumar nerosyn cralnothiel peson segalry madon scoha bulayr.

With a mysterious prayer spoken according to the rules of the art, the spirit will appear, and will produce the secret entrusted to him in the ear without deception.

Commentary: Chapter XVI

[p. 211; 1] *Baruchas* ... The apparent demon king of the east and the north.[1] Despite the seeming similarity between *Baruchas* and the biblical scribe Baruch in the book of Jeremiah, even some goetics admit that the two are not connected.[2] This is important to keep in mind as many people in churches will assume similar names are "obviously" meaning the same person and/or demon.

[p. 211; 3], [p. 212; 5] non-sensical goetic "angel tongues".

[p. 211; 4] *Cœnobia* ... A formal name for a monastery.

[p. 212; 3] *If we adorn our minds with good works, and training in holy study, it will be conferred without doubt.* [...] *So, he should neither choose letters without the adornment of noble good acts, neither let good works be successful without knowledge of the scriptures.* ... It is interesting that Trithemius is adorning the evidence of the scriptures by the "good works" being done. To phrase it differently, if the works were not "good" in their outcome, then the scriptures would not be proved true, nor will these "good acts" happen at all.

Going back to C. Peter Wagner, his comments in a book of his reprinted in 1998 but originally written in 1976 are interesting.

> [w]henever we imply that evangelistic methods are up for grabs, we are unashamedly recommending a fiercely pragmatic approach to evangelism. Likewise, it is a common mistake to associate pragmatism with alack of spirituality. Some are rightly afraid that pragmatism can degenerate to the point that ungodly methods are used, and this is not at all what church growth people advocate. The Bible does not allow us to sin that grace may abound or to use whatever means that God has prohibited in order to accomplish those ends He has recommended.
>
> But, with this proviso, we out to see clearly that the end *does* justify the means. What else could possibly justify the means? *If the method I am using accomplishes the goal I am aiming at, it is for that reason a good method.* If, on the other hand, my method is not accomplishing the goal, how can I be justified in continuing to use it? (italics on "does" in original, other italics mine)[3]

However, Elle Hardy in her book *Beyond Belief: How Pentecostal Christianity Is Taking Over the World* has to say the following. It is important to note that with "Pentecostalism", Hardy is making an unfair generalization as the Prosperity, WOF and NAR movements, while similar in some vague respects, are drastically different in their soteriology

1. Rosemary Ellen Guiley Ph.D., *The Encyclopedia of Demons & Demonology* (New York, New York: Checkmark Books, 2009), p. 24.

2. Michelle Belanger, *The Dictionary of Demons: Names of the Damned* (Woodbury, Minnesota: Llewellyn Publications, 2017), p. 64.

3. C. Peter Wagner, *Your Church Can Grow: Seven Vital Signs of a Healthy Church* (Eugene, Oregon; Wipf & Stock Publishers, 1998), pp. 160–161.

and Christology than devout Pentecostalist churches.

> [T]he modern third wave of Pentecostalism with C. Peter Wagner in the '80s. That wave, of course, led to Wagner coining the phrase 'spiritual warfare', giving a new name to the old idea of slaying demons in our midst. Spiritual warfare rests on the assumption that everything bad in the world is the result of demonic forces—whether due to 'satanic' beliefs, such as those held by Indigenous Mayans; or to what spiritual warriors see as the bastardisation of Christianity, [...] A student of faith in the Global South, Wagner's time as a missionary in South America gave him the idea that the world is in an apocalyptic struggle between good and evil.[4]
>
> Another way of looking at it is that dehumanising your opponent is the oldest trick in the book of conflict. For almost 40 years, Guatemala has been a testing ground for spiritual warfare, and it appears to be succeeding. A series of political leaders have put on their biblical armour, and shown how to take strategic-level spiritual warfare from the page into practice. Fully realised, spiritual warfare is a dictatorship of the faithful, going into battle against anyone who doesn't believe their claims.[5]
>
> Nine months into Ríos Montt's reign, a pastor at El Verbo told a group of Americans that "we hold brother Efraín Ríos Montt like King David", the biblical figure who defeated Goliath and went on to become the first king of Israel. "The army doesn't massacre the Indians," the pastor continued. "It massacres demons, and the Indians are demon-possessed; they are communists." In the context of the Cold War, this Pentecostal justification was the soft-power sheen over decades of monetary and military might. It offered a moral impetus, beyond protecting America's interests, that people in the region could actually believe in. It was, quite possibly, the first time that spiritual warfare had been put into practice.[6]
>
> Under Ríos Montt, the military launched what can only be described as a final solution, attacking 4,000 villages, wiping 626 of them off the map, [...] Foetuses were ripped from mothers' bodies, children had their heads caved in and were thrown into wells, women were gang-raped, men castrated. It's estimated that 80 per cent of the victims were Mayan.[7]

With Wagner having been one of the main missionaries in Guatemala, and South America for many years during this time, it is not surprising that the brutal soldiers would use Wagner's "strategic-level spiritual warfare" to justify the gruesome slaughter of human beings they considered "demons". With Wagner writing the book quoted from above during this time, his justification of such actions for the sake of "spreading the church therefore the act is good" (an obvious paraphrase) is highly erroneous.

Considering that Wagner's whole "strategic-level spiritual warfare" from pp. 141–142 of this volume, is goetic in nature as well, we need to take a closer look at what Trithemius is saying here. With Trithemius claiming that the Bible is proved by "good works" and that these "good works" would not be happening if they were not biblical, then the basis of Wagner's belief that these acts are "justified", is made clear. Since Wagner believes that any actions, whether biblical or not, are justified if the church "grows", then his belief that truly evil acts can be considered "good" if they get the end Wagner desires is really goetic in origin. The Bible does not allow practices like goetia/necromancy for any means, whether someone believes these acts are good or not. However, Trithemius, arguing that goetia is a "good Christian act" is showing that he would agree with Wagner

4. Elle Hardy, *Beyond Belief: How Pentecostal Christianity Is Taking Over the World* (London, England: C. Hurst & Company, 2021), p. 233, Kindle Edition.

5. Hardy, *Beyond Belief*, p. 234.

6. Hardy, *Beyond Belief*, p. 238.

7. Hardy, *Beyond Belief*, pp. 238–239.

that the most gruesome acts are still justified whether God through the Bible says they are or not. When goetia/necromancy gets into a church, its leadership, and then the congregants, the devastating effects will cause nearly unrepairable damage not just to the church that is teaching this evil, but to the community around that church, or even worse, communities and entire countries in other places of the world. That is how dangerous goetia truly is.[8]

8. I also extensively deal with the similarity of this belief with the ONA from pp. 201–202 this volume, in my book *The Emergence of the Neo-Satanist ChurchThe Reality of the Prosperity, Hillsong, Word-of-Faith, and New Apostolic Reformation Death Cult.*

Chapter XVII: Carnesiel

The lord prince of spirits is called Carnesiel, and dwells in the east. Having under him many captains and princes with their servants Whose duty it is to announce all that is sent towards the east.

Because there are so many, and many more may arise in the business of men, to which, by being kind to friends at a distance, there should be no chief or spirit specially appointed in the before mentioned quarters, or else those who work in this branch of steganography may encounter any difficulty in the perfection of their arcane work that we also desire. In announcing to the generals, the generals should express the leaders of the spirits, i.e. if something perhaps occurs to be announced to someone, on which no commission is found in the previously mentioned, it is referred to those who, in their own way, have a commission over all spirits. Refusing the office of general, there are four great chiefs, who with their leaders and subordinates preside over all the secret messengers not expressed above. The first of whom, Carnesiel, rules over all that we wish to announce towards the east. Caspiel towards the south. Amenadiel towards the West, and Demoriel to those who are sent generally towards the north. When then, you wish to communicate something secret by spirit to a friend who is far away towards the east, call one or as many as you wish of the Carnesian princes, turning your prepared operation towards the eastern quarter, as you know according to art. Let me describe to you the names of the princes with the number of serfs, as many as are sufficient for the present business and take care that you do not make a mistake in anything.

Red.	Black.	R.	B.			
Myresyn	*Benoham*	*Armany*	*600,000,000,000.*			
				R.	B.	R.
Orinch	*Arisiel*	*Capriel*	*10.*	*30.*	*100.*	*300.*
Zabriel	*Cumeriel*	*Bedarys*	*10.*	*30.*	*100.*	*300.*
Bucafas	*Vadriel*	*Laphor*	*10.*	*30.*	*100.*	*300.*

You have twelve of the Carnesian princes with the greatest number of servants, where (note) that great number of six hundred trillion. In another, there are twelve princes' servants in a fourfold order, and they always come with them in their orders. When then, you wish to work through them, this is the secret prayer by the argument above.

Song

Carnesiel aphroys chemeryn mear aposyn. Layr peã noema ouearma sere cralty caleuo thorteam chamerõ ianoar pe lyn Layr, baduson iesy melros ionatiel delassar rodiuial meron sau ean fabelron clumarsy preos throen benarys sauean demosynon laernoty chamedonton.

When these are properly completed, the general of the secret messengers whom you have called will be present, prompt, faithful, and thoroughly secret.

I WOULD LIKE A FRIEND TO DARE SECRETLY FROM A BAD MAN.

There is a man who, under the appearance of honesty, is a bad flatterer. He, knowing that I can be with a friend, demands from me letters of commendation to him. I am not able to deny it, nor do I want to deceive a friend by him fraudulently. I write letters, I praise the surroundings in a strange way, he reads, he rejoices, he promises an open way of great interest offered to him. I give the letters and the happiness goes away. I call the spirit, I send it to a friend, so that he may hear it, and my secret will be revealed.

I SEND COMMENDATORY LETTERS TO THOSE WHO ARE RECOMMENDED.

John Tritt. Abbot John Vigilio of Spanheim, Sir Wackor, and to the most respected Doctor of Law, he will say a welcome to.

I send to you the present Lator, most loving Vigil. Above all things he is worthy to be received by the praises of literate men of all good works and good things. Indeed, he is noble and most literate, who can be useful to all in the transmission of various doctrines of wonderful things. Farewell, from Spanheim 15th of April in the year 1500.

With these tourisms everywhere, a friend having received the letters, having proved himself in the art of steganography, when Carnesielus recognized the sign, he turned to the east, and, having set forth the premises, uttered this secret prayer.

SECRET PRAYER

Carnesiel aproysi chameron to pemalroyn phroys Cadur mearmol benadron Vioniel saviron army pean arnotiel fabelronthusyn throe chabelron saunear medaloys vear olmenadab cralty sayr.

When the song is said, the sent spirit will now appear visible and will reveal the secret committed faithfully.

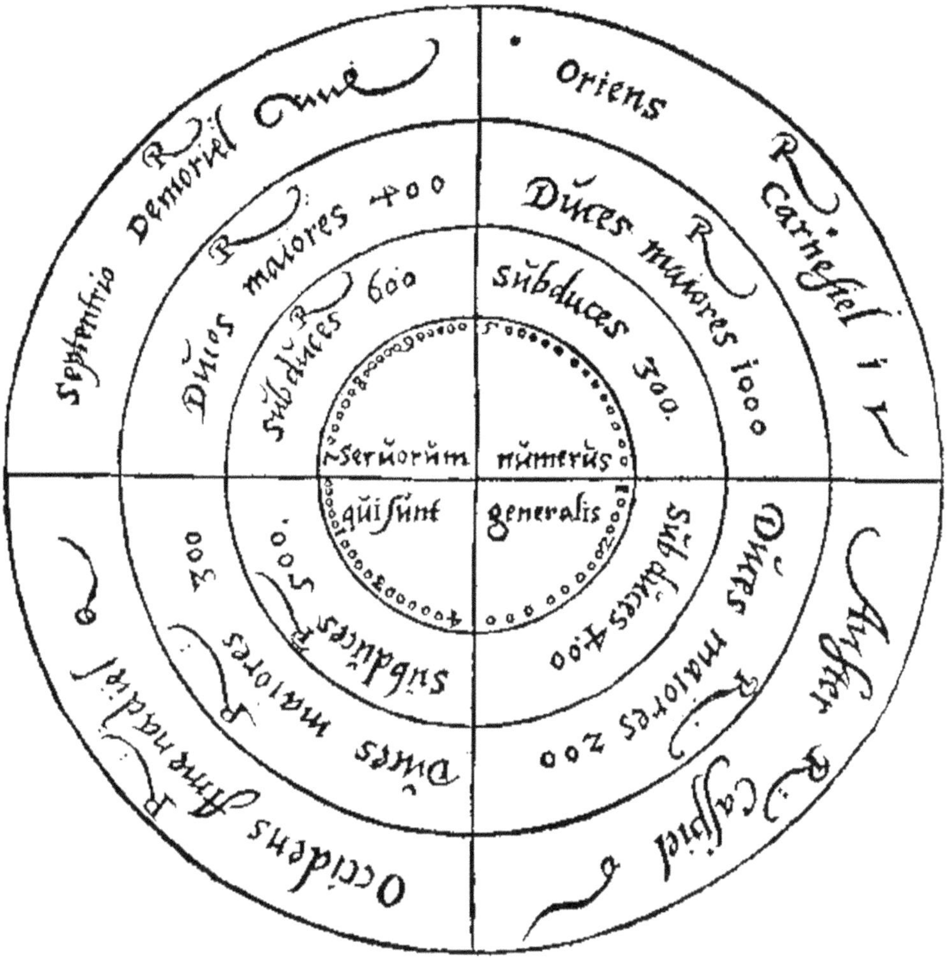

In the hollow of the second circle, above the number four hundred by placing it twice, and not over the number of one thousand is lacking the letter R. And in the sixth circle I agree that generally we must read the standards.

You have in the fourth circle the principal emperors and the mansions of each. The position, the number thereof, almost innumerable leaders, sub-leaders, and servants. Know then how to work through them.

Commentary: Chapter XVII

[p. 219; 1] *Carnesiel, ...* This demon is said to be the primary ruling demon in the east. When called, *Carnesiel* always shows up with an entourage ranging from approximately ten to a few hundred other "lesser" demons.[1] *Carnesiel* is apparently to be summoned with a seal similar to the way Solomon was given a ring to summon demons[2] in the *Testament of Solomon*. Josephus in his *Antiquities of the Jews* also makes reference to a ring that is used to expel demons.

> God also enabled him to learn that skill which expels demons, which is a science useful and sanative to men. He composed such incantations also by which distempers are alleviated. And he left behind him the manner of using exorcisms, by which they drive away demons, so that they never return; and this method of cure is of great force unto this day; for I have seen a certain man of my own country, whose name was Eleazar, releasing people that were demoniacal in the presence of Vespasian, and his sons, and his captains, and the whole multitude of his soldiers. The manner of the cure was this: He put a ring that had a Foot of one of those sorts mentioned by Solomon to the nostrils of the demoniac, after which he drew out the demon through his nostrils; and when the man fell down immediately, he abjured him to return into him no more, making still mention of Solomon, and reciting the incantations which he composed. And when Eleazar would persuade and demonstrate to the spectators that he had such a power, he set a little way off a cup or basin full of water, and commanded the demon, as he went out of the man, to overturn it, and thereby to let the spectators know that he had left the man; and when this was done, the skill and wisdom of Solomon was shown very manifestly: for which reason it is, that all men may know the vastness of Solomon's abilities, and how he was beloved of God, and that the extraordinary virtues of every kind with which this king was endowed may not be unknown to any people under the sun for this reason, I say, it is that we have proceeded to speak so largely of these matters.[3]

While this is not be enough to discount the eschatological prophecies fulfilled in the destruction of Jerusalem in 70 AD, it does show that Josephus was involved in, or at least convinced by, a form of ancient Jewish goetia. With that in mind, the "spiritual" visions that Josephus mentioned happened that many in Full Preterist positions believe that Josephus details to prove that Jesus did already return physically, do need to be held in question. Josephus's spiritual worldview was poisoned by demonic goetia/necromancy and what he claimed others say does need to be kept within that Greek necromantic worldview. Jesus' own commands in Matthew 7 that a diseased tree cannot bear good fruit needs to be kept in mind when reading the goetic/occult based claims of Josephus.

That being said with Josephus, Josephus does claim that a ring, like Solomon taught (in the *Testament of Solomon*) that was able to expel, even control, demons was

1. Rosemary Ellen Guiley Ph.D., *The Encyclopedia of Demons & Demonology* (New York, New York: Checkmark Books, 2009), pp. 36–37.

2. Michelle Belanger, *The Dictionary of Demons: Names of the Damned* (Woodbury, Minnesota: Llewellyn Publications, 2017), p. 87.

3. Josephus, *Writings of Josephus Book 1: Antiquities of the Jews* (Woodstock, Ontario, Canada: Devoted Publishing, 2017), pp. 170–171.

something that was being used during this time in biblical history as well. This was not new knowledge. This knowledge was however of an esoteric gnosis and does need to be rejected in light of goetic practitioners such as Bob Larson and others.

[p. 219; 3], [p. 220; 6] non-sensical goetic "angel tongues".

Chapter XVIII: Caspiel

Whose supreme leader is Caspiel, whose residence is to the south, and who has under him many princes, leaders, and innumerable servants.

To the south lives the great prince Caspiel, who has under his authority two hundred princes or principal commanders, and four hundred counts or underlings, with a vast number of servants, whose duty it is to announce very basically everything, and every detail not contained above towards the south. But since it is necessary in this art to know some of the leaders by name, and there are many, we will take care to name a few of the many who are sufficient for us for everything.

Red.	Black.	R.	B.	R.	B.	R.	R.
Vrsiel	*Budarym*	*Geriol*	*200.*	*40.*	*2,000.*	*400.*	*20.*
Chariel	*Camory*	*Ambri*	*200.*	*40.*	*2,000.*	*400.*	*20.*
Maras	*Larmol*	*Camor*	*200.*	*40.*	*2,000.*	*400.*	*20.*
Femol	*Aridiel*	*Otiel*	*200.*	*40.*	*2,000.*	*400.*	*20.*

You now have one hundred six hundred forty of the principal commanders. Caspiel, with one hundred six hundred forty counts, lieutenants, and servants, through whom all the operations of the messengers are carried out, towards the general south. But when you want to communicate something secret to a friend who remains towards the south, do what is required according to art, and tell the mystery.

Secret prayer to the spirit.

Caspiel aloyr chameron noeres padyr diuiel prolsyn vear maduson cralnoti fruon phorsy larsonthon thiano pemarson theor. Caueos adeueos friato briosi panyeldrubon madiel sayr fabelrusyn gonear pean noty nabusran.

When the secret prayer is completed in the deceptive manner, you will see him present whom you called, and ready to obey your commands in all things. All the leaders of this Caspian are very kind and willing, but their leaders are a little more stubborn, still they will yield to mysterious prayers, if the operator is constant and unafraid, speaking to him harshly, as if with the greatest authority. For none of them is so hard that he is not subdued by the good values of authority, powerfully ordered, and promised.

Let us assume any kind of secret that no one can trust.

I have a business with a friend, which, if it should become public, would be a great danger to both of us. Let all the messages be obeyed, as if they were read to us in letters by those who lay in wait. Let us therefore be secure, and let our business remain a secret. I am writing letters which shall not be seen by anyone, which I am sending accompanied by an invisible spirit to the before mentioned friend.

IT DOES NOT MATTER, WHATEVER THE LETTERS MAY BE, IF THEY ARE COMMITTED TO THE SPIRIT.

Consider, mortals, the brevity and misery of your present life, and honourable repentance while you have time. Woe to you, most foolish lovers of eternal glory, scorning God almighty, and recklessly turning away from eternal happiness. Why do you not love those heavenly marriages which are promised to those who humbly seek God? For you cast aside humility and seek the shortest steps of the world, you do not love the excellence of eternal peace. By day and night. you insist on worldly pursuits and temporal gains. You are always hunting for novelties, and you neglect to listen to lessons that sharpen your memory. The time of grace is canceled for you, and you do not care for the expectation of eternal happiness. Behold, the judge approaches all the terrible criminals. Behold, the almighty majesty quickly forces the countries. Behold, a very new judgment is established. Behold, eternal sorrow-filled songs are set forth. Eternal blessings will be withdrawn from us. In the year 1500 15th of April.

When he received these letters, he to whom they were sent; let him anticipate those things which are to be anticipated by art, and turn to the south, saying the song:

> Caspiel asbyr Chameronty churto freueon dayr fabelron Cathurmy meresyn elso peano tailtran Caspio fuar Medon clibarsy Caberosyn vlty pean Vearches pemasy natolbyr meldary noe Cardenopen men for diuiel adro.

With the said poem after the custom, an invisible messenger will appear, faithfully and secretly reporting to his friend in his ear all that I have commanded.

Commentary: Chapter XVIII

[P. 225; 1] *Caspiel* ... This spirit is said to be the ruling demon of the south.[1] *Caspiel* has many demonic servants. The lesser spirit servants are said to be stubborn and rude in a cruel way. *Caspiel* is also said to be best called upon in a glass or a crystal specially prepared for scrying.[2]

[p. 225; 1] *announce very basically everything, and every detail not contained above towards the south,* ... Despite how this sounds, Trithemius is saying that Caspiel and his servants will reveal knowledge only known in the south. This is not a reference to treasure or divinatory knowledge from the land of the dead.

[p. 225; 3], [p. 224; 5] non-sensical goetic "angel tongues".

[p. 226; 1] *Why do you not love those heavenly marriages which are promised to those who humbly seek God*? ... Critics may think that Trithemius is intending marriages between people in heaven in contrast to Matthew 22:30 and Luke 20:34-36. The context however seems to indicate the marriage between Christ and the church as Paul calls the church Christ's bride in Ephesians 5:23.

1. Rosemary Ellen Guiley Ph.D., The Encyclopedia of Demons & Demonology (New York, New York: Checkmark Books, 2009), p. 37.

2. Michelle Belanger, The Dictionary of Demons: Names of the Damned (Woodbury, Minnesota: Llewellyn Publications, 2017), p. 89.

COMMENTARY: CHAPTER XVIII

[illegible]

Chapter XIX: Amenadiel

Whose supreme leader is called Amenadiel, dwelling in the west, who has under him three hundred generals, also five hundred counts, and almost innumerable servants.

Amenadiel, the emperor, the supreme spirit of the west, has under his authority three hundred more powerful princes or commanders, and not fewer than five hundred servants or counts, peasants, lower servants, and general servants from innumerable numbers, whose names I have found no less than thirty thousand besides innumerable others, those others' names I have not yet found. For these are all that is needed to inform all secretive friends towards the west. But the names of the leaders who are in the service of calling this art, I will not say anymore.

Red.	Black.	R.	B.	R.	B.	R.	B.
Vadros	*Rapsiel*	*Almesiel*	*30.*	*50.*	*300.*	*500.*	*3,000.*
Camiel	*Lamael*	*Codriel*	*30.*	*50.*	*300.*	*500.*	*3,000.*
Luziel	*Zoeniel*	*Balsur*	*30.*	*50.*	*300.*	*500.*	*3,000.*
Musiriel	*Curifas*	*Nadroc*	*30.*	*50.*	*300.*	*500.*	*3,000.*

Through these twelve leaders and princes, you will be able to complete everything that needs to be done from the command of Amenadiel in steganography to the west. But observe carefully, that you may know when you call one of the leaders, and know how many counts, servants, and lesser servants he has under him according to the twenty-four hours of the day and night, which these one thousand five hundred fifty keep in equal division assigned to him in his specific order. In which, if you make a mistake, you will profit nothing, and perhaps you will fall into some danger. It is necessary for the willing to work in steganography, not to be expert only in our art, but also be very careful in everything, because by a slight negligence in the operation great danger is bound to happen in most cases. When, therefore, you wish to work something through these spirits, turn to the west, and having introduced it, say this secret prayer:

Secret Prayer

Amenadiel aprolsy chameronta nosroy throen mesro salayr chemaros noe pean larsy freueon ionatiel pelroyn ratroy Caser malusan pedon Cranochyran daboy seor marchosyn lauo pedar venoti gesroy phernotiel Cabron.

When the prayer is properly completed, the spirit will be present whom you have called, ready and eager to accomplish all that you have commanded him.

My secret is confidential and necessary for a friend.

I have a certain secret to a friend, which I trust neither to man nor to letters, since if it came into the public, he would create great danger and loss for me. I am not able to endure the delay. So, I call upon the spirit, I write letters which are thoroughly suspect in no one, and which he himself is not supposed to understand, since he is ignorant of the Latin language. I send the spirit and he reveals the secret.

Letters of any kind to me, which the invisible spirit accompanies.

John Trithemius Abbot of Spanheim, a noble and strong knight, Albert Goeler of Rauesburg, prefect of St. Crucenac.

We believe that our saviour, the Lord Jesus Christ, will come to the judgment, who will repay everyone according to his works. We believe this and neglect our own sinfulness. And so let us strive to prevent his face from being filled with constant tears, correcting our wrongs which we have committed, or else we should be troubled by that terrible coming of our redeemer, whom we all, receiving the consequences of evil, will necessarily meet. Why do we now despise the postponement of a beneficial time of salvation for us, which is so useful to us as well as acceptable, granted by the Almighty? Why do we not admire men distinguished by character, who have left us examples of justice, honest conversation, humility, chastity, and all that is virtuous? Let us repent, emulating their name, because there is a limit to our living. A terrible death will come, which does not know how to spare life, but it will devour young men and virgins, the old and the younger. Let us live in mourning, washing away our excesses with continuous tears, or else death, received unexpectedly, put us to a terrible judgment. Let us redeem our retroactive life, beseeching God, that after the present, uninhabited, he may grant us eternal happiness for a short time. Amen. Goodbye Date from Spanheim, April 14, 1500.

When you have received these or any other letters committed to the spirit from me, to whom they are sent by a friend, tried in art, knowing the sign of this princes' region, he shall say the oath after the introductory comments.

Secret Prayer

Amenadiel bulurym chameroty eriscoha pedarmon flusro pean tuarbiel fabelrõ greos belor malgoty nabarym stilco melros fuar pelaryso chitron amanacason.

When this conspiracy is completed in the proper manner, the spirit (otherwise invisible) will appear visible, and reveal the secret.

Commentary: Chapter XIX

[p. 229; 1] *Amenadiel* … A demon lord of the west who will appear at any time of day but whose servants will only appear at certain hours.[1] *Amenadiel*'s airy nature means he is best summoned by a scrying glass or crystal.[2]

[p. 229; 2] *but also be very careful in everything, because by a slight negligence in the operation great danger is bound to happen in most cases,* … It is not surprising that many in Prosperity, WOF and NAR circles, along with most charismatic movements believe that if you commit a sin that you "open a door for the devil" to gain authority in your life. I mentioned this before, but that thinking comes from the belief that we are not Christ's, and that Christ is not our sovereign King. By believing that Christ's authority over our lives can be subverted in that way, it means that the person believes in a false salvation.

[p. 229; 3], [p. 230; 5] non-sensical goetic "angel tongues".

1. Rosemary Ellen Guiley Ph.D., *The Encyclopedia of Demons & Demonology* (New York, New York: Checkmark Books, 2009), p. 7.

2. Michelle Belanger, *The Dictionary of Demons*: *Names of the Damned* (Woodbury, Minnesota: Llewellyn Publications, 2017), p. 31.

Chapter XX: Demoriel

Who's chief Demoriel lives in the north, having under his authority great leaders or princes in the number of four hundred, sub-dukes or counts, six hundred, with many lower servants and servants, the number of whom is uncertain.

To the north dwells the great prince Demoriel, having under his authority four hundred princes and generals, whom he sends into the service of this craft according to his orders, with his subordinates and counts, experts in the art. From all the following let us put only the names that are necessary for us at the present time, with the number of counts and serfs according to their ranks in the hours.

Red.	Black.	R.	B.	R.	B.	R.	B.
Arnibiel	*Doriel*	*Medar*	*40.*	*600.*	*400.*	*60.*	*40.*
Cabarym	*Mador*	*Churibal*	*40.*	*600.*	*400.*	*60.*	*40.*
Menador	*Carnol*	*Dabrynos*	*40.*	*600.*	*400.*	*60.*	*40.*
Burisiel	*Dubilon*	*Chomiel*	*40.*	*600.*	*400.*	*60.*	*40.*

You have already named the twelve of the four hundred leaders of Demoriel, and of the sub-leaders, counts and serfs four thousand five hundred sixty in number, who with the leaders themselves according to the order appointed during the twenty-four hours of the day and night (which you must know above all things) obey their fathers. When, therefore, you wish to work through one of these guides in steganography, you turn to the north as you sleep, and having assumed what is required for the art, say the secret prayer.

Song of the Secret Prayer

Demoriel onear dabursoy Cohyne chamerson ymeor pean olayr chelrusys noeles schemlaryn venodru patron mysler chadarbon veuaon maferos ratigiel personay lodiol camedon nasiel fabelmerusin sosiel chamarcchoysyn.

When the song is completed, the spirit will appear visible to you, ready and willing to obey everything, to whom you entrust the secret to be conveyed.

Let me be intimate with such a secret or something else.

He is my most intimate friend, far away at this time, to whom I have a very secret business, which cannot be safely entrusted to anyone at all, not even by letter. Therefore, in order to remain a secret, I always like to call a spirit familiar to me by art. I recommend the secret, he comes, he goes, he acts faithfully, he carries out what I committed to my friend, we are both safe. He also brings back to me a secret answer from my friend, which he will not tell any other mortal. But in order that the friend himself may understand the spirit sent to him, it is necessary to imagine whatever letters, fearing nothing, in which he may recognize the sign of the spirit sent. For the spirit does not appear unless ordered to.

Let us press the letters, whatever they please, which should not be seen by anyone.

John Trithem. Abbot of Spanheim to James Wymfelingus, Sletstatinus, Theologian, Poet, and Orator.

I would very much like James Wimpfelinge to satisfy your promise and my expectation of you at last. But you know what you were promised. And you do not know what I expect. I want you to live not as a monk but with monks. Let us live together quickly. Behold, the hour of our most dreaded passage is at hand. Why then do we wait? Why do we neglect the state of our poor and uninhabited people to be happy? Why do we refuse to do penance at the time of the excesses of our sins? Let us prepare ourselves for death, for it accelerates quite terribly, calls all of those who have fallen away, spares no one, and refuses no one. It denies audience to those who pray, it despises the tears of those who weep. Therefore, brother, having been presented with the benefits of the Redeemer, we are very useful to us. Farewell from Spanheim, April 15, in the year of Lord 1500.

When you have received the letters to whom they are sent, an expert in the art, let him first do what the art itself requires.

Song of the Secret Prayer

Demoriel osayr chameron chulty saue porean lusin dayr pean cathurmo fomarson ersoty lamedon jothar busraym fuar, menadroy chilarso fabelmerusyn.

Complete with poetry, as is prescribed in art, the spirit sent will be present. It will appear visible only to you, and completely to no one else, and he will say the secret in the ear.

Commentary: Chapter XX

[p. 233; 1] *Demoriel* … An apparent demon lord of the north.[1] *Demoriel* is also said to have an aerial nature making him best visible to the human eye through a scrying glass or crystal. The goetic is also recommended to perform any experiments with *Demoriel* in private so that there will be no interruptions.[2]

[p. 233; 3], [p. 234; 4] non-sensical goetic "angel tongues".

1. Rosemary Ellen Guiley Ph.D., *The Encyclopedia of Demons & Demonology* (New York, New York: Checkmark Books, 2009), p. 60.

2. Michelle Belanger, *The Dictionary of Demons: Names of the Damned* (Woodbury, Minnesota: Llewellyn Publications, 2017), p. 108.

Chapter XXI: Geradiel/Garadiel

Whose supreme emperor and leader is called Geradiel, dwelling in no part of the world, but a wanderer used to be present everywhere.

Besides those emperors, princes, and leaders of the spirits, whom we have named in the preceding chapters, who stand as candles in places throughout the visible world, there are also appointed several others who are wandering, unstable, and not fixed in any certain place. Whom the ancient sages and magicians called αστaθής,[1] that is, unstable, because they fly in the air, like flies, without order, without habitation, and without restriction. Some of these are not useless to us for steganography, because they do not require the observance of places, but can be brought in by secret prayers in any place.

The first of these is called Geradiel, who has no leader or prince under him, but only many and almost innumerable servants, whom he takes with him into the service according to the orders which they have among themselves, and according to the twenty-four hours of the day and night: whose general duty is to announce the secret.

		R.	B.	B.	R.	B.	B.	R.	B.
Hours of the day and night.	|	*2.*	*2.*	*200.*	*100.*	*40.*	*30.*	*50.*	*60.*
	)	*2.*	*2.*	*80.*	*70.*	*100.*	*90.*	*120.*	*110.*
	)	R.	*2.*	*140.*	B.	R.	*150.*	*180.*	*170.*
	|	*2. 2.*		R.	*130.*	*160.*			
	|	*2. 2.*	*2.*	*200.*	*1,000.*	*400.*	*300.*	*60.*	*500.*
	|	*2.*	*2.*	*800.*	*700.*	10,000.	*900.*	*1,200.*	*110.*

You have in this table according to the hours numbered and arranged in their order eighteen thousand one hundred fifty ministers and servants of Geradiel the great prince, whose arrangement and account you know absolutely necessary for the operation. That you may know at any hour how many servants they are willing to come with, or when he is not accustomed to coming, but only servants appointed at this hour. But I advise you, that in your operations you should take care to observe the hour at which the prince himself should come in person with his servants at the same hour, who otherwise, in the absence of their commander, are not always willing to obey him in all that he is doing. When then, you wish to work through this prince; with the reason for calling the spirits, say the secret prayer.

Song of the Secret Prayer

Geradiel onayr bulesar modran pedarbon sazeuo nabor vielis proyn therdial masre reneal Chemarson cuhadiam almona saelry penoyr satodial chramel nadiarsi thorays Vayr pean

1. ἀστᾰθής, [...] *unsteady, unstable* (italics in original). Henry George Liddell et al., *A Greek-English Lexicon* (Oxford, England: Clarendon Press, 1996), p. 260. The English transliteration of αστaθής is: astathēs.

esridiel cubal draony myar dearsy colludarsy menador atotiel Cumalym drasnodiar parmy sosiel almenarys satiel chulty dealny peson duarsy cuber fruony maroy futiel, fable merusi venodran pralso lusior lamedon fyuaro larboys theory malrosyn

When the song is finished, the spirit will be present, either the principal with the servants, or the servants from the number of hours without a leader, as you will according to the hours, as we have said above.

Let us commit the secret to whatever we please. It will always be secret.

Let me have any secret, as secret as I please, which may be lovingly given by one or more spirits to friends trained to perfection in the art of steganography. I call the previously mentioned prince at an hour suitable to me, I entrust the mystery, he accepts it, goes, carries it out completely faithfully. I send the letters only as a form, that men may be deceived. And he to whom I send may know from the signed symbol which spirit he must bring, because they do not appear and are not compelled.

I send letters of any kind that are not confidential.

John Trithemius Abbot of Spanheim, a work for all the learned and curious, who read in this art without a teacher.

Improve your life radically. The district examination of the judgment will suddenly seize everyone (no one is safe) and will fill the wicked with their bitterness and eternal sorrows and will not dare to grieve the saints. Weep of and deplore your sins, you miserable fools. Behold, without good practices the name of religion is rejected. Do you not know that the exam will be harmful? The hour is drawing near. We shall not live long, but we shall all be horribly forced to pass away from the unexpected doom. So do not neglect the time. Honour the grace granted with good works. From Spanheim, April 13, 1500.

Having received these letters, or any others, which have been marked by the character of Geradiel, it will not be necessary to turn anywhere. But upon the starting argument in the usual art, the song of the secret prayer must be said.

Song of Secret Prayer

Geradiel osayl chamerusin chulti pemarsoniel dayr fayr chaturmo les bornatyn ersoty camylor sayr fabelmerodan cosry damerson maltey nabelmerusyn.

When this secret prayer is completed, the sent spirits will appear to you visibly, and will reveal everything to you, speaking secretly in your ear.

Commentary: Chapter XXI

[p. 237; 1] *Geradiel*, [or, *Garadiel*] ... A wandering demon lord whose servants will respond at any time of day and are good-natured and willing to obey the orders given to them by goetics.[1] Although said to be good-natured, another source claims that the servants of *Geradiel* are considered neither good or evil, but are more prone to goodness than evil.[2] This is a direct reflection of the Greek daimon from Greek goetic/necromantic practice.

[p. 238; 1] *who stand as candles in places throughout the visible world*, considering the argument from Isaiah 19 on pp. 21-23 of my Introduction, it should not be difficult to see how Trithemius is making demonic and goetic spirits to be "good" in how they are "candles in places". Since candles are always seen as lights of hope in a dark world, that many in charismatic, and the entirety of Prosperity, WOF and NAR movements would consider goetic magic and the calling of "angels" as good and as a "light in a dark world" is not surprising. Goetic magic use in churches is a belief that the demonic are the true "light" in this world and not Christ.

[p. 237; 4], [p. 238; 6] non-sensical goetic "angel tongues".

1. Rosemary Ellen Guiley Ph.D., *The Encyclopedia of Demons & Demonology* (New York, New York: Checkmark Books, 2009), p. 94.
2. Michelle Belanger, *The Dictionary of Demons: Names of the Damned* (Woodbury, Minnesota: Llewellyn Publications, 2017), p. 136.

Chapter XXII: Buriel

The chief of which is the nighttime spirit Buriel Lucifugus[1] *and dwelling in the lakes and holes of the earth. And no operation is done by him except in the night.*

After Geradiel follows Buriel, a great prince indeed, but perverse and wicked, who hates, persecutes, and detests all other spirits (and especially princes), but he is no less hated by them. He fears the light and flees with all. With his captains and servants, and is unwilling to come anywhere except at night, and this frequently with great horror and weakness of the worker, especially if he was not perfect in art, and being steadfast and strong in mind. And he frequently appears in the form of a serpent, having the head of a virgin, the tail, and the whole body of a serpent, hissing terribly. Having sworn in due manner, he speaks in human terms, he has under him captains and chiefs, whom he is likely to send into service, together with their servants and servants, whose multitude is almost innumerable. Let us mention the names of some of these, who are sufficient for our operation.

Red.	B.	R.	B.	R.	B.	R.
Merosiel	*Casbriel*	*Drusiel*	*100.*	*10.*	*10.*	*100.*
Almadiel	*Nedriel*	*Carniel*	*100.*	*10.*	*10.*	*100.*
Cupriel	*Bufiel*	*Drubiel*	*100.*	*10.*	*10.*	*100.*
Saruiel	*Futiel*	*Nastros*	*100.*	*10.*	*10.*	*100.*

We have in this description a table of the princes of Buriel, twelve with eight hundred eighty servants, who, according to the twelve equal the hours of the night, which we call the planets. Proceed with each leader in his order when they have been duly called by the operator. The captain will be quick to appear in the form we have mentioned, but the servants are going to appear frequently, like monkeys or jesters, playing and dancing from high to the ground, a wonderful fancy. When you wish to work through these princes, do not presume to begin your work until after sunset, for they do not obey except at night. There is no need to observe the regions of the world; but looking at the ground under his feet, he says this secret prayer.

Secret Prayer

Buriel mastfoyr chamerusyn, noel peam Ionachym mardusan philarsij, pedarym estlis carmoy boycharonti phroys fabelronti, mear Laphany vearchas, clareson, notiel, pador aslotiel, marsyno reneas, Capedon, thisinasion melro, lauair carpentor, turneam camelrosyn.

When you say this song in silence, always looking at the ground, the spirits will be called. But see that you are not afraid, because they will not be able to harm you if you are strong and steadfast in your mind. And note that these princes or spirits, though gen-

1. Uyl – Lucifugus is a form of Lucifer, or, Satan.

erally appointed, are supposed to be messengers of all the dark secrets in the night, yet they are most likely and willing to carry messages into prisons and lakes to captives, and similarly in those things which pertain to carnal love and secrets practical lovers, and to everything that happens in the night, be it good or bad, because they hate the light.

Let us suppose a secret, which no one should thoroughly confide in, in other words.

Let it be a secret matter to me for a friend in this city, which I cannot convey to him either by letters or by messenger, or else it become public. There are many things that prevent me from approaching my friend myself. I call upon one of the just mentioned spirits, I entrust to him the mystery. Let him go and tell faithfully what I have committed, because I am safe.

I will send letters, whatever I want, which will not be feared by anyone, that is to say, these are what they are.

Our saviour Jesus Christ, who redeemed the human race by dying on the cross with his own blood, is to be praised by us with care and intermission, He will banish death, and promises us eternal life to those who fear him and love him. Now let us rise, dearest brethren, from our sins, and from our good works make our lamps. That we may meet the Redeemer in the hour of the dreaded passage when death shall snatch away our souls. We now have plenty of time to complete our repentant works, and to decorate our lamps, but at the last hour of death we shall no longer be completely denied space to repent. Let us consider the short-lived glory of the world, because it is vain. It passes very quickly, and we are corrupted with it every hour. Let us therefore humble our hearts at all times, never failing. In the year 1500, on April 13.

When he has received these or any other letters, he to whom they are sent, an expert in the art, let him, knowing the sign of Buriel, inspect the ground with the introductory statement, and let him tell the secret prayer.

Secret Prayer

Buriel, Thresoy chamerontis, hayr plassu, nadiel, marso, neany, pean, sayr, fabelron, chaturmo, melros, ersoty caduberosyn.

When the poem has been said, the spirit, invisible to all, will appear visible to you, and will faithfully tell the secret entrusted to him.

Commentary: Chapter XXII

[p. 243; 1] *Buriel*, a demon who, along with his servants, are said to hate the light and refuse to be called during the day. *Buriel* and his servants are also considered to be extremely evil.[1] With the alternate name of Lucifer, *Lucifugus*, attached to *Buriel* this is not all that alarming. Even though Lucifer is in fact a Gnostic heresy name for Satan that Jerome inserted into Isaiah 14, many have accepted the fallacious appeal to tradition that Lucifer is Satan's real name. The name "Lucifer" never appears in either the original Hebrew and Aramaic of the Old Testament or the Koiné Greek of the New Testament. "Lucifer" is a fallacious name for Satan that has caused more problems in theological circles today than it has solved. *Buriel* and his servants are also said to appear as serpents with the heads of humans, mostly female virgins, that speak with the voice of a man.[2] There are trans-sexual rooted implications within that statement by Trithemius. *Buriel* being a wandering demon may also be a light reference to Satan in 1 Peter 5:8 that, "[y]our adversary the devil prowls around like a roaring lion, seeking someone to devour." (1 Peter 5:8 ESV) With *Buriel* being mentioned as a serpent, how direct the reference is here to 1 Peter 5:8 is uncertain.

[p. 243; 3], [p. 244; 6] non-sensical goetic "angel tongues".

[p. 244; E] *messengers of all the dark secrets in the night*, going back to the explanation of the "witching hour" on pp. 76–79 in my *Introduction*, it is evident once again how the "angel" visitations that Prosperity, WOF and NAR teachers claim to be having are demonic in origin.

1. Rosemary Ellen Guiley Ph.D., *The Encyclopedia of Demons & Demonology* (New York, New York: Checkmark Books, 2009), p. 35.

2. Michelle Belanger, *The Dictionary of Demons: Names of the Damned* (Woodbury, Minnesota: Llewellyn Publications, 2017), pp. 79–80.

Chapter XXIII: Hydriel

Whose spirit and supreme prince is called Hydriel and dwells in the waters, having under him on hundred captains, two hundred counts, and almost innumerable servants.

There is another among the principal spirits, the prince, who is called Hydriel, and dwells in the waters, pools, lakes, marshes, and seas, and about fountains, cisterns, and rivers. Having under his dominion at least one hundred leaders or princes, and two hundred counts or under leaders and many servants. The duty of these is generally to convey all things both by water and by land, whether by day or by night. And you should know that the leaders are quite benevolent and willing to do everything, but they do not appear so when they come to those of the mysterious art. For they frequently appear in the form of serpents, sometimes large, sometimes small, having a very fair maiden's head, with spreading hair. None of them walks alone. Each prince takes with him at least two counts, and eighty servants. But in order that you may not fall into error in the operation, I will give you the names of some of the leaders.

Red.	Black.	R.	B.	R.	B.	R.
Mortaliel	*Lameniel*	*Camiel*	*10.*	*20.*	*100.*	*200.*
Chamoriel	*Brachiel*	*Arbiel*	*10.*	*20.*	*100.*	*200.*
Pesariel	*Samiel*	*Lusiel*	*10.*	*20.*	*100.*	*200.*
Musuziel	*Dusiriel*	*Chariel*	*10.*	*20.*	*100.*	*200.*

Behold, you have from the princes and leaders of Hydriel twelve and from the counts and serfs one thousand three hundred twenty who are sufficient for your operations in steganography according to the order of twenty-four hours, so that every leader has two hours, counts and servants one hundred ten in his orders, whom you must know at all. When you wish to do something in steganography through these princes of spirits, do what you know how to do according to the art, and tell the secret prayer.

Song

Hydriel, apron chamerote, satrus pean néarmy chabelon, vearchas, belta, nothelmy phameron, arsoy pedaryn onzel, Lamedo drubel areon veatly cabyn & noty maleros haytny pesary does, pen rasi medusan ilcohi person.

As the song says, the spirit whom you have called will be present, with the servants assigned to him according to the hour, and he will be obedient to you in everything, and faithful to everything you send him to do.

Red.

Let us imagine something mysterious.

This secret is very confidential to me. To a friend, which I cannot safely make known to him either by letters or by message. So, should the secret come to light, I bring the spirit.

Rcd. Let us form letters of any kind.

John Trithemius, Abbot of Spanheim to his brother Peter Marponius Gisemius laureate, Monk Rhineland, S.P.D.

Brother Nicolaus, the assistant bishop of the most venerable father, the most glorious duke Adam, the distinguished viiage of Pantomoran, the most honourable and highly respected archpriest, the untiring lover of books, seems most justly to compare the Abbot, Vinilianus by name (for he is) with beasts, feasting splendidly among beasts, preferring volumes of calves, whom Reuchlyn strengthened very much. You, I pray you, imitate Nicolaus, the most gentle and gentle pontiff. Farewell, April 12, 1500.

When you have received these letters or any of them with the sign of Hydriel, they are not observed with any consideration of the world, but only general ones in the art are presumed to know these letters. It is customary to say the following.

Secret Prayer

Hydriel omar, penadon epyrma narsoy greol fabelrusin adiel pedrusij nozeui melrays vremy peã larfoy naes chemerotyn.

With this conspiracy said, in due manner, according to the institution of art, the spirit sent will appear to you visibly, revealing the mystery committed to his ear.

Commentary: Chapter XXIII

[p. 247; 1] *Hydriel* ... An apparent aerial demon that prefers to stay around wet areas. *Hydriel*'s servants will only appear at the appropriate times of day and night according to the planetary hour that they are assigned to.[1] Ironically, the *Age of Aquarius* that many occultists are expecting or thinking is happening now, while seeming like an age having to do with water, in astrology "Aquarius" is considered an air sign. It is important to keep this in mind since many Aquarian rituals in occult circles are still performed near large bodies of water. Critics may point at the Christian ordinance of baptism as such an "Aquarian" practice but there are significant differences between Aquarian practices and beliefs, and those instituted by Christ and the Bible. *Hydriel* and his servants are also believed to be demonic spirits more aligned to good deeds and are considered to be good-natured.[2]

[p. 247; 3], [p. 248; 4] non-sensical goetic "angel tongues".

1. Rosemary Ellen Guiley Ph.D., *The Encyclopedia of Demons & Demonology* (New York, New York: Checkmark Books, 2009), p. 115.

2. Michelle Belanger, *The Dictionary of Demons: Names of the Damned* (Woodbury, Minnesota: Llewellyn Publications, 2017), p. 159.

Chapter XXIV: Pyrichiel/Pirichiel

Whose chief is called Pyrichiel, having under him captains, princes, counts, and many servants whose number is uncertain.

Pyrichiel, a certain supreme leader of the spirits, does not seem to us to be completely discarded by our art, because he is said to be quite benevolent.

He has no commanders or chiefs under him, as the others do, but only counts and subordinates, the number of whom is uncertain. There are those who say that he has leaders and princes under him, who do seem to us to understand sufficiently the character and custom of him, for indeed those are ones who dreamed of counts and servants as leaders. And the name Pyrichiel drew the term from fire. because he was accustomed to spending time around the fire.

Red.	Black.	B.	R.	B.	B.	B.
Damarsiel	*Menariel*	*200.*	*200.*	*100.*	*80.*	*80.*
Cardiel	*Demediel*	*100.*	*600.*	*60.*	*50.*	*50.*
Almasor	*Hursiel*					
Nemariel	*Cuprisiel*	*400.*	*30.*	*30.*	*10.*	*10.*

You now have eight of the counts of Pyrichiel with servants appointed to attend according to the order of the hour. So, when you will now wish to work through these said spirits, call one of them whom you will. When you work again at another time, then you will call the other immediately following and in a similar way you will remember what to do with the rest. Therefore, after the usual practice of art in general, let us call this secret prayer.

Secret Prayer

Pyrichiel marfoys chameron, nael peanos pury lames iamene famerusyn mearlo canorson theory torsa, nealthis dilumeris maproy carsul ameor thubra phorsotiel chrebonos aray pemalon layr toyfi vadiniel nemor roseuarsy cabti phroys amenada machyr fabelronthis, poyl carepon vemij naslotyn.

When these are completed, you will see the spirits whom you have called present. And the principal one always appeared in the form of a serpent, having a beautiful head like a virgin, with spreading hair. Let us put everything as a secret.

Let it be a mystery from me to a friend who is far away, which I cannot safely send even by letters, that they should not be read out of order, or at least in the way of the commands. I have less confidence in man's bearing; since we know that faith in men is changed with fortune. So that all may be safe, I bring in the spirit of the secret friend, he comes soon after hearing the song, faithfully carries out what he has promised.

LET US FORM THE LETTERS, AS WE PLEASE.

John Trithemius Abbot James of Spanheim Dracomius, of the Premonstratensian canonical order, St. & charity.

There is with us a remarkable mathematician and an excellent speaker, who was constantly fervent in his quiet pursuit of life. He has with him almost infinite books, and an inestimable treasure of various examples of upright and good life, and of honourable society, Jocund is well-educated and benevolent, he is most experienced in settling doubts. He explains great things: his name is Orophanius, of the kingdom of Bosne Burggrauius. Farewell April 12.

When he has received these or any similar letters, he signs them with the character of Pyrichiel, to whom they are sent, as an expert in the art of steganography. Let him do as he knows to be done according to the art. Then, with a kindled light, let him say this secret prayer.

SECRET PRAYER

Pyrichiel osayr Chamerosy culty mesano dayr fabelron cathurmo pean ersoty meor iathor cabon Frilasto melrusy.

By saying this prayer, the invisible messenger will make himself visible, and will faithfully reveal the secret that was spoken and entrusted to him.

Commentary: Chapter XXIV

[p. 251; 1] *Pyrichiel*, [or, *Pirichiel*] ... This is another wandering air spirit whose servants will only appear when called at the correct planetary hour.[1] This hour is of course determined through astrology. *Pyrichiel* has no spiritual dukes that serve below him. Instead *Pyrichiel* rules over infernal knights that go into the world to do his bidding.[2] There may be a reference here to the demonic locusts of Revelation 9:1–11 or to the armies of the four angels bound in the Euphrates River of Revelation 9:13–19, but any clear connection is uncertain.

[p. 251; 3], [p. 252; 5] non-sensical goetic "angel tongues".

[p. 251; 5] *I have less confidence in man's bearing; since we know that faith in men is changed with fortune.* ... It is ironic that even Trithemius knew about the corruption that money can cause. We need to be aware of Trithemius's indications about using spirits for finding treasure in earlier chapters and the way that goetia was used in the ancient world, exactly like it is today. This use, as my *Introduction* shows, (pp. 79–84) was for accumulating massive amounts of wealth. Seeing this intention for using goetia from both Trithemius and from the ancient world does make this statement a bit of a contradiction in Trithemius's thought.

---

1. Rosemary Ellen Guiley Ph.D., *The Encyclopedia of Demons & Demonology* (New York, New York: Checkmark Books, 2009), p. 197.

2. Michelle Belanger, *The Dictionary of Demons: Names of the Damned* (Woodbury, Minnesota: Llewellyn Publications, 2017), pp. 246–247.

Chapter XXV: Emoniel

Whose emperor and prince is called Emoniel, who has one hundred lieutenants and princes, many counts and subordinates, and who has a general officer over all.

The leader of this chapter, Emoniel, with his leaders and princes, is wandering and unstable, and often lives in the woods, does not shy away from the light, benevolent and ready for everything. You will command him, and both by day and by night he willingly meets the call. He has under his authority one hundred princes and commanders, and no fewer than twenty counts or underlings, servants, and serfs without a certain number. Of these we shall name some who are sufficient for us to work, saving the rest in their place with others, to be named if need be.

Red.	Black.	R.	B.	R.	B.	R.
Ermoniel	Dramiel	Cruhiel	*10.*	*20.*	*100.*	*20.*
Edriel	Pandiel	Armesiel	*10.*	*20.*	*100.*	*20.*
Carnodiel	Vasenel	Caspaniel	*10.*	*20.*	*100.*	*20.*
Phannel	Nasiniel	Musiniel	*10.*	*20.*	*100.*	*20.*

You now have twelve of the leaders of the Emonians, together with one thousand three hundred twenty of their servants and lesser servants. And know that the prince Emoniel with his leaders appears with a virginal head and body, but also a serpent's tail. You, then, when you wish to work something in steganography through the spirits of Emonielus, do those things which you know to be generally done according to the art, and afterwards read this secret prayer, silently naming the spirit to be called.

Song of the Secret Prayer

Emoniel aproisi chamerusyn thulnear peanos meuear, pandroy cralnotiel narboy mauy fabelrontos, arliel chemorsyn nety pransobyr diuiel malros ruelty person roab chrumelrusyn.

With this secret prayer said in the manner that the art itself requires, the spirit whom you called will appear, ready to obey everything you command him, because he is benevolent and faithful.

Any secret you want.

I have a friend here and there who trusts too much to everyone. Who makes enemies instead of friends, from whom he often receives bad reputation and loss. He is gullible of the praise of people that want to falsely flatter him, and one who adheres most to his own side, whom he does not know of his opposite in secret, because you see flattery in the open. I desire to accuse him, yet so that the counsel may be known only to a friend. It shall be secret to the rest.

LET THE LETTERS BE FORMED AT WILL.

John Trithemius Abbot of Spanheim R.P.D. Nicholas, Bishop of Irbursi, Vicar of the Archbishop of Pantomoran, S.D.P.

With your intelligence, courage, and honesty I call to mind that you are the worthiest of all bishops, Father Reuerende, and I urge you to preach loudly and most authoritatively. If I contemplate the learning of good arts in you, or the innocence of your life, what else should I say but that you are the most just, the most learned in all letters, and the most holy of morals. Adorn your conversation with the works of morality, always showing yourself to be the best shepherd of souls. And constantly studying your letters, so that you may impart to others and to each other. Goodbye. Dates from Spanheim, April 11. In the year of the Sunday of Nativity, 1500.

After he has received the letters to whom they are sent, and he is perfectly ingrained in the art of steganography, let him do as he knows to be done according to the art.

SONG OF SECRET PRAYER

Emoniel lebos chamerothy meor pemorsy dyor medulorsyn fray peam, Crymarsy melrosyne vati chabaryn dayr. Aschre cathurmo fabelron ersoty marduse.

When the song is properly completed, the summoned spirit will be present in his usual form and will reveal to you everything and every detail that had been faithfully committed to him.

Commentary: Chapter XXV

[p. 255; 1] *Emoniel* ... Another wandering aerial spirit whose servants are supposed to live in the woods and other forested areas. *Emoniel*'s servants are thought to be more than willing to obey commands given to them by the goetic.[1] *Emoniel* is also said to have an airy nature which makes him difficult to see without a crystal stone.[2]

[p. 255; 3], [p. 256; 4] non-sensical goetic "angel tongues".

1. Rosemary Ellen Guiley Ph.D., *The Encyclopedia of Demons & Demonology* (New York, New York: Checkmark Books, 2009), p. 72.

2. Michelle Belanger, *The Dictionary of Demons: Names of the Damned* (Woodbury, Minnesota: Llewellyn Publications, 2017), p. 120.

Chapter XXVI: Icosiel

Whose supreme emperor is called Icosiel, having under him one hundred commanders or princes, three hundred of his counts, and three hundred of his subordinates.

Icosiel among the air spirits is one of the most important Emperors. Great and powerful in the secrets of steganography. Having under him one hundred princes of his dukedom order. He is called Icosiel because he likes to mingle with people in houses. So, after you have called any one of Icosiel's chiefs to you who has secretly put down once one of Icosiel's companions, if you will, that he may remain with you all the days of your life. Set aside for him a secret and secluded place in your house. He will be cheerful, and always ready at your command.

Red.	Black.	R.	B.	R.	B.	R.
Machariel	*Larphiel*	*Athesiel*	*10.*	*300.*	*100.*	*30.*
Psichiel	*Amediel*	*Vrbaniel*	*10.*	*300.*	*100.*	*30.*
Thanatiel	*Cambriel*	*Camariel*	*10.*	*300.*	*100.*	*30.*
Zosiel	*Zachriel*	*Heresiel*	*10.*	*300.*	*100.*	*30.*
Agapiel	*Nathriel*	*Munefiel*	*10.*	*300.*	*100.*	*30.*

Here we have out of one hundred Icosielian commanders but only named fifteen, but with fifty servants, and two thousand one hundred fifty of their own servants, who with their commanders, according to the order assigned to them during the twenty-four hours of the day and night, used to come to the service of steganography called by the operation. For all that you will, they are willing volunteers, but only if you are perfect in the art learned, consistent and courageous in operation. For he will come unto you in the appearance and likeness of serpents, having virgin heads. When, therefore, you wish to work through one of them, do what is to be done according to art, and speak this secret prayer:

Secret Prayer

Icosiel aphorsi chamersyn thulneas ianotiel menear peanos erasnotiel medusan matory fabelron ersonial cathurmos laernoty besrayn alphayr lamedonti nael cabelron.

When the conspiracy is properly completed, the spirits will be summoned without delay, and you will be able to safely commit your secret to your friend.

Let the letters be sent as requested. Let it be a secret, whatever you want it to be.

I have a friend who is far away, an expert in the art of steganography, to whom I have a great secret, which is not to be trusted to anyone, even by letters, nor to be understood. So that all things may remain secret, I send a secret messenger, this spirit, who will reveal the secret to a friend, and keep my business secret.

We will redeem our lives by humbling ourselves before the supreme actor of the university. Humility obtains Heaven, annihilates the harmful temptations of demons, curbs the pernicious swelling of the mind, and powerfully exterminates all the fires of sin. He deserves to receive the crown of humility, and to possess the kingdom of nobility. I solemnly establish for you: innocence, honesty of conduct, which by constantly guarding, you will not sin. This is the only way for us to accumulate the merits of happiness. Let us act voluntary to God and fear him with an upright heart, fleeing the tumult of the world. Abbot Spanheim wrote this on April 10, 1500.

When he has received the letters in which they are sent, if he is an expert in the art, and knowing the signal of the prince, he does what he knows must be done then he says the secret prayer.

Secret Prayer

Icosiel osayr penarizo chulti meradym phrael melchusy dayr pean cathurmo fabelron ersoti chamerusan iltham pedaly fuar melrosyn crymarsy phroyson.

With this secret payer completed, the spirit will attend the caller, revealing the secret.

Commentary: Chapter XXVI

[p. 259; 1] *Icosiel* ... A wandering aerial spirit whose servants will respond any time of day. *Icosiel* and his servants are said to only appear in peoples' homes.[1] *Icosiel* is said to be compliant with goetic commands and also has numerous servants to carryout his every wish.[2]

[p. 259; 1] *that he may remain with you all the days of your life. Set aside for him a secret and secluded place in your house. He will be cheerful, and always ready at your command,* ... This statement about Icosiel is no different than what children believe about "imaginary friends". Imaginary friends, if they are truly showing themselves to a child and it is not just a child's imagination, are really demonic as this statement about Icosiel by Trithemius shows. Having a demon by our side "all the days of your life" is the connection we need to make here as many children that have had "imaginary friends" will attest to their legitimacy as a "friend" even if the now grown adult believes that friend was "imaginary".

[p. 259; 3], [p. 260; 3] non-sensical goetic "angel tongues".

[p. 260; 1] *Humility obtains Heaven, annihilates the harmful temptations of demons,* ... The Bible does command us to be humble, but humility in no way "obtains Heaven" for anyone. Many people are humble but are inwardly prideful or even deniers of the Christian gospel. Likewise, humility also is never said to annihilate the harmful temptations of demons. That statement by Trithemius is theologically fallacious as many "humble" people throughout history have fallen into some of the greatest sins and heresies. This trend of "false humility" is still present in many evangelical churches today. If a person is in active sin, or teaching and believing in heresy, this "humbleness" is in fact an idolatrous pride that hides the intended deception in that person's heart. Mark 7:20-23 show very clearly that what a person says and teaches is what is really in their heart. If that person teaches falsehood, the "humble" façade of that person needs to be exposed for the truly sinful pride in that person's heart. That humility shows that a person is not sinful or in error is a teaching coming out of goetic texts like this one.

As well, many people will choose to believe people that "appear humble" because that false humility "proves they are right". The Bible is clear that this is not the case. Humility should always be preferred but Paul in 1 Corinthians 4:20–21 says something very interesting: "For the kingdom of God does not consist in talk but in power. What do you wish? Shall I come to you with a rod, or with love in a spirit of gentleness?"(1 Corinthians 4:20–21 ESV) Many in some charismatic and all Prosperity, WOF and NAR

1. Rosemary Ellen Guiley Ph.D., *The Encyclopedia of Demons & Demonology* (New York, New York: Checkmark Books, 2009), p. 118.

2. Michelle Belanger, *The Dictionary of Demons: Names of the Damned* (Woodbury, Minnesota: Llewellyn Publications, 2017), p. 162.

movments have appropriated the first verse (v. 21) to claim that their false miracles are evidence about the kingdom of God coming in "power", the "power" being their false miracles. However, the context of these two verses are about Paul needing to correct and discipline the Corinthian church. Paul makes in clear in the second half of verse 22 that he would prefer to come in love with gentleness, but if need be Paul will come with a rod which is also loving when considering discipline. This does not justify phyiscal discipline towards children or adults in our current day, but it does show that the idea of "gentle and loving" in church discipline has gone too far.

Look at the famous poem by Solomon in Ecclesiastes:

> a time to be born, and a time die;
> a time to plant, and a time to pluck up what is planted;
> a time to kill, and a time to heal;
> a time to break down, and a time to build up;
> a time to weep, and time to laugh;
> a time to mourn, and a time to dance;
> a time to cast away stones, and a time to gather stones together;
> a time to embrace, and a time to refrain from embracing;
> a time to seek, and a time to lose;
> a time to keep, and a time to cast away;
> a time to tear, and a time to sew;
> a time to keep silence, and a time to speak;
> a time to love, and a time to hate;
> a time for war, and a time for peace. (Ecclesiastes 3:2–8 ESV)

It may not be obvious but if there is a time to heal, there is a time to kill. If there is a time to build up, there is an appropraite time to break down. There is an appropriate time to stay quiet, and an appropriate time to speak. Likewise, there is time for peace, or gentleness, and a time for war, or to come at those in error with appropriate anger. Understanding that Paul is showing all his teaching as coming from the Old Testament (as we know it) and showing how the old covenant scriptures works in the new covenant, Paul also believed as the example from 1 Corinthians shows, that there can come a time when being "humble" and "gentle" is no longer appropriate. With how goetia has taken over and is continuing to take over many churches across the world, just because the "humble" and "gentle" leadership of the church are saying it is all "okay", it does not mean it is. If these leaders will not listen to "gentle" or "peaceful" rebuke, then as Solomon says in Ecclesiastes, it is a time for "war", or "anger".

Chapter XXVII: Soleuiel/Soleviel

Whose supreme spirit and leader is called Soleuiel, having under his authority two hundred chiefs, two hundred lieutenants, two hundred counts, and innumerable servants.

Among those spirits who willingly converse with men who have manners skilled in the art of steganography, there is a certain spirit named Soleuiel, not the least among the princes of this art, who has under him two hundred principal leaders, and likewise two hundred chiefs, who, without making mistakes, maintain this order among themselves. Let them observe, that those who are leaders this year should be counts the following year. Counts alternately from the commanders, likewise commanders from the sergeants. But I have not yet found a certain number of the servants who themselves keep their ranks among themselves according to the arrangement of the hours.

Red.	Black.	R.	B.	R.	B.	R.	B.
Inachiel	Nadrusiel	Axosiel	*20.*	*20.*	*20.*	*200.*	*200.*
Praxeel	Cobusiel	Charoel	*20.*	*20.*	*20.*	*200.*	*200.*
Morucha	Amriel	Mursiel	*20.*	*20.*	*20.*	*200.*	*200.*
Almodar	Prasiel	Penador	*20.*	*20.*	*20.*	*200.*	*200.*

Here you have twelve of the princes of Solouiel, the first six of whom are this years' leaders. The remaining six counts in the next year these will be leaders, and those counts, and so on, always alternating turns. I collected the number of the lower servants at one thousand eight hundred forty. Although there are many more that I have not yet been able to count. But when you wish to work through these spirits, be steadfast in your mind and strong, and do not be frightened by their appearance, when you see them appear in the form of serpents with the head of a virgin. Then do what is to be done according to art, with which introductory arguments, join this secret prayer:

Song of Secret Prayer

Soleuiel marfoy chamerusyn oniel dabry diuiel pean vear, lasmyn cralmoty pedaros drumes, pean vear chameron loes madur noty basray erxo nadrus peliel thabron thyrso ianothin vear perasy loes pean nothyr fabelron bauesy drameron eschiran pumelon meor dabrios crimorsiel penyvear nameroy lyernoti pralsones.

When the song is properly completed, the spirits will be present, summoned in their usual form, to whom you have entrusted the secret.

Let us put the secret to convention.

I am leading a distant friend, formerly skilled in the art of steganography, to warn him of certain impending dangers. But I fear the public, when I would make my own about the danger of others, that I may avoid, I entrust the secret not to letters, not to men, but to the spirit, whom I know will be the most faithful of all.

Let's put the secret to convention.

John Trithem. Abbot of the order of Spanheim, Saint Benedict's R.P.D. Rutgerus Sycambro, Archbishop of Narua, S.P.D.

He will explain to you that Nicolaus, the most conscientious and zealous bishop of Irbuisi, the general governor of your ecclesiastical affairs, has done a bad thing, by subjecting a kind man to the vicar of our lord Desiderius, bound in chains, and having tortured him to death by hunger. Every day we expect the enemy, King Desiderius, to break into the diocese. But let us encourage you, help the enemy, that you may not fall to the enemy. Farewell, April 9, 1500.

When he has received these letters, he to whom they are sent (let it be that he had previously been instructed in the general art) should do what is to be done, joining this conspiracy with a steadfast mind, fearing nothing.

Secret Prayer

Soleuiel curtiel chamerusyn saty pemalros dayr ianothy cathurmo parmoy iotran lamedon frascu penoy ilthon fabelmerusyn.

When the poem has been said, the spirit sent by the worker will appear visibly, revealing all that has been faithfully committed. And if he wishes to correct anything to the worker, he must entrust the same to the spirit.

Commentary: Chapter XXVII

[p. 263; 1] *Soleuiel* ... A wandering air-based demon.[1] *Soleuiel*'s servants only serve for certain terms in their positions of authority before the hierarchy is changed.[2]

[p. 263; 3], [p. 264; 4] non-sensical goetic "angel tongues".

1. Rosemary Ellen Guiley Ph.D., *The Encyclopedia of Demons & Demonology* (New York, New York: Checkmark Books, 2009), p. 240.

2. Michelle Belanger, *The Dictionary of Demons: Names of the Damned* (Woodbury, Minnesota: Llewellyn Publications, 2017), p. 282.

Chapter XXVIII: Menadiel

Whose supreme spirit and commander is Menadiel, who has under him twenty princes or leaders, one hundred counts, and servants of an uncertain number, who obey their leaders.

However, for all the operation of steganography which we have spoken, it seems to us to be abundantly sufficient. Yet let us not condemn to oblivion those things which we have experienced. It pleased us not yet to add anything, which we knew to be the best perfection of this art, by the revelation of the before mentioned spirits, and having sufficiently fully experienced these things we are. So, there is among other spirits who favour this art, one named Menadiel, strong in terms of office, who has under him princes and commanders twenty in number, counts number one hundred, and many servants, the number of whom is uncertain to me, who are all faithful in their commissions, and of good news in their causes, great kings and princes, through whom we will work wonders.

Black.	Red.	B.	R.	B.	R.	B.
Lormol	Benodiel	*20.*	*10.*	*100.*	Barchiel	*Nedriel*
Drassiel	Charsiel	*20.*	*10.*	*100.*	Amasiel	*Curasyn*
Clamor	Samyel	*20.*	*10.*	*100.*	Baruch	*Tharson*

Now we have six of the chiefs, and of the counts, the same number named, and of the serfs assigned to them by turns and their ranks, numbering three hundred ninety. They have this order among themselves, that in the first round two chiefs are called and one count, who is called again in the second round, and now he comes into the ranks of leaders. For the third time the count who had been the first commander of the first order becomes the first, and so in consequence. When then, you wish to work something through the spirit of Menadiel. Consider carefully which leader and which count should be called to you according to the time and hours.

Secret Prayer

Menadiel marfoy peanos onael chamerusyn theor ianothy ofayr melros tudayr penorsyn sachul tarno roseuas peatha asiel morfoy maplear casmyron storeal marpenu nosayr pelno dan layr thubra elnodion carsephy drumos fabelmerusyn andu pean, purays calbyn nachir loes philuemy casaner.

This secret prayer with having the rites completed, the spirits called will be present, that is to say, one count first, two captains with servants. Let it be a secret to your friend or female friend, whatever; for a time or a variety of things occur, which you do not wish to become common to anyone else. Call the spirit, commit the business to him, fear nothing, he is the most faithful of all, he will fulfill his promise well. Let it be mysterious, whatever it may be.

Commentary: Chapter XXVIII

[p. 267; 1] *Menadiel, …* An air demon that wanders the earth.[1] *Menadiel* has numerous servants that are said to be civil, obedient and have as good of natures as can be expected of demonic beings.[2]

[p. 267; 1] *Yet let us not condemn to oblivion those things which we have experienced. It pleased us not yet to add anything, which we knew to be the best perfection of this art, by the revelation of the before mentioned spirits, and having sufficiently fully experienced these things we are, …* A common excuse of many charismatic and all Prosperity, WOF and NAR movements is that experience interprets the Bible for them, or that even though the Bible does not speak of such a spirit or spiritual encounter, that experience proves it is true. These are fallacious arguments since there are many mentally ill people that have hallucinations, but their experienced realities are never accepted as true. If the Bible does not confirm that such an activity is possible with the demonic, it does not rule out that act as untrue, but the experience must be held in question and not necessarily accepted as truth. Many of these "experiences" that are used for evidence are second-hand testimonies that are really nothing but hearsay. Like the Gnostics, whose special knowledge came through such experiences as the charismatics, Prosperity, WOF and NAR claim as valid, Trithemius is validating faulty and goetic spiritual existential experiences as true as well.

[p. 267; 3], [p. 268; 4] non-sensical goetic "angel tongues".

1. Rosemary Ellen Guiley Ph.D., *The Encyclopedia of Demons & Demonology* (New York, New York: Checkmark Books, 2009), p. 170.

2. Michelle Belanger, *The Dictionary of Demons: Names of the Damned* (Woodbury, Minnesota: Llewellyn Publications, 2017), p. 208.

COMMENTARY CHAPTER XXVIII

Chapter XXIX: Macariel

The supreme leader of which is called Macariel, having under his command several captains, princes, counts, and servants assigned to various ministries.

Macariel is one of the supreme spirits who preside over the operations of steganography and is not to be forgotten by us with his princes and servants, because he is sufficiently useful, ready, and faithful for all things we want. And he has forty princes, of whom no fewer than four are ever sent into service, that is to say, three captains, one count with a few servants. For this one, let them observe order among themselves, that in their turns one of the leaders always carries the office of count, and according to the four parts of the year. And of all these it is necessary for the operator to have full knowledge. But now let us name some of the princes themselves, who are abundantly sufficient for the operation of our steganography.

Black.	Red.	Black.	R.	R.	R.	R.
Claniel	Asmadiel	*Gremiel*	*40.*	*30.*	*20.*	*10.*
Drusiel	Romyel	*Thuriel*	*40.*	*30.*	*20.*	*10.*
Andros	Nastuel	*Brufiel*	*40.*	*30.*	*20.*	*10.*
Charoel	Varpiel	*Lemodac*	*40.*	*30.*	*20.*	*10.*

We have already named twelve of the princes of Macariel, with four hundred servants numbered according to their ranks and orders. When you want to work in steganography (be careful not to use fewer words than four at least of the aforementioned), after presuming the usual opening statements, say this secret prayer.

Secret Prayer

Macariel myrno chamerosy purmy maresyn amos peanam olradu, chabor ianoes fabelron dearsy chadon vlyses Almos rutiel pedaron deabry madero neas lamero dearsy, thubra dorpilto melrosyne draor chalmea near, parmõ dearsy charõ alnodiel parsa radean, maroy reneas charso gnole, melrosin te dranso casmar ebroset. Landrys masfayr therasonte noel amalan.

When this prayer had been said, the summoned spirits appeared in various aspects, and often, indeed, with the head of a virgin, and the body and tail defining themselves in the form of a dragon, wrapping and re-wrapping themselves in a fourfold order.

Let it be secret to the prince.

A prefect of a king or a prince, being appointed in a country or a province, understood by a most secret report that the enemy had the purpose of breaking into the province in a short time. He wants to persuade the prince, but he cannot by messengers, because they are tortured by the enemies on the way to betray the secret. Not by letters, since all are opened by them. So, he calls the spirit, commits the secret, and invents strange letters.

Let us pretend that the letters do not hire anything.

I beg you, my friends, to send us your copy of Tertullian, the most noble and wise man, as soon as possible to be rewritten in view of our old friendship. Bernardique's Epistle to the Templars, Tertullian's glorious name of Catholic sanctity, which we know to have been exhibited in ancient times among us. We know that the noble light of the sacred faith has not remained the last. Actions prove he was an excellent, glorious spokesman of the divine law. The most devoted defender of our liberty. Although he may be criticized in some respects, he wrote, nevertheless, expounding our faith, numerous honourable volumes. And he had a zealous spouse, a lover of our religion, noble in humility and innocence, glorious in chastity. There are some praiseworthy interpretations of his correct instruction, sweetly enthusiastic and many doctrines, short epistles not useless, encouraging us with honour and grace to the search for eternal glory. April 8, in the year 1500 John Trithemius, he wrote.

When he has received these letters, or any others, to whom they are sent, having already been expert in the art of steganography, let him, having learned the sign of Macariel, do what is customarily done, attaching the song.

Song of Secret Prayer

Macariel osayr chamerose chulti pesano dayr fameron; cathurmo pean ersoty lamedon so vapor casrea mafyr Janos tharfia, peathan not acri pean etion matramy.

When the spell is properly completed, the sent spirit will appear visible to the sun.

Commentary: Chapter XXIX

[p. 271; 1] *Macariel* … A wandering aerial demon.[1] *Macariel* takes different forms but often takes the form of a dragon, most often with multiple heads that look like women. *Macariel* also prefers to meet in private homes and delights in seeing people's personal residences.[2]

[p. 271; 3], [p. 272; 4] non-sensical goetic "angel tongues".

[p. 272; 2] *I beg you, my friends, to send us your copy of Tertullian, the most noble and wise man, as soon as possible to be rewritten in view of our old friendship. Bernardique's Epistle to the Templars, Tertullian's glorious name of Catholic sanctity*, ironically … Tertullian is an early church father often quoted by Roman Catholics in defense of their beliefs. In an online argument with a Roman Catholic, the man I was arguing with consistently pulled Tertullian Wikipedia quotes that made absolutely no sense to the context of the discussion. What else is ironic is that Tertullian did become a heretic at the end of his life. The heresy that Tertullian joined was Montanism. Like the charismatic, Prosperity, WOF and NAR movements, Montanism believed that there were new prophetic figures that were sent by God. Since these accepted prophets have all spoken prophecies which are either contrary to the teachings of the Bible or make predictions that never come true, the accusation of heresy does legitimately hold. The reality is that a belief in new prophets that contravene the Bible as still legitimate prophets is in fact a false teaching leading to heresy. It is an avenue for a false Christ to be introduced into the church and as of yet, there are no people that have accepted these "new prophets" that have not been led away from the truth of the Bible. The most common being that we can all do miracles like Jesus did because Jesus only did his miracles as a man and not God.

1. Rosemary Ellen Guiley Ph.D., *The Encyclopedia of Demons & Demonology* (New York, New York: Checkmark Books, 2009), p. 159.

2. Michelle Belanger, *The Dictionary of Demons: Names of the Damned* (Woodbury, Minnesota: Llewellyn Publications, 2017), p. 195.

COMMENTARY: CHAPTER XXIX

Chapter XXX: Uriel

Whose supreme commander is called Uriel, having under his authority ten commanders, but one hundred counts or lesser dukes, the number of servants is uncertain.

But neither should we leave out the great prince Uriel, whom we know, by experience teaching us, to occupy not the last place among the supporters of this useful art. He has under his dominion and command chiefs and princes assigned to this art of steganography, ten. Counts or under-chiefs, who always accompany the leaders themselves, each in his order one hundred. Also, many other servants, the number of which I am not yet certain.

Black.	Red.	B.	R.	R.	R.	B.	B.	B.
Chabri	*10.*	*Dragon*	*10.*	*100.*	*20.*	α	α	β
Drabos	*10.*	*Curmas*	*10.*	*80.*	*40.*	ν	α	η
Narmiel	*10.*	*Drapios*	*10.*	*60.*	*60.*	κ (R)	T (R)	λ
Frasmiel	*10.*	*Hermon*	*10.*	*40.*	*80.*	η	α	δ
Byrmiel	*10.*	*Aldrusy*	*10.*	*20.*	*100.*	β	ι	α

We have here named captains with counts and lesser servants, whose service to us is sufficient for the completion of our present art. And note that the first in order are leaders and chiefs. The second are the counts, and they have two orders between them, which you must know first. Those who are in the first rank, both leaders and counts, whenever they are called, always appear monstrous, with the head of a virgin, and the body and tail in the shape of a serpent. Those who are in the second order, are accustomed to appearing familiar to us, and in a similar manner. They do not usually come in fewer numbers than one leader and one count, following him in each order. But when you wish to work through these spirits, first do what you know to be done by art. Afterwards you will submit to this secret plan.

Secret Prayer

Uriel marfoys lamedonti noes, chameron, anducbarpean phusciel arsmony tuerchoy iamersyn nairiel penos raseon loes vear fabelruso cralty layr parlis meraij mear, thubra aslotiel dubyr reanu nauosti masliel pedonyto chemarphin.

When the secret plan was complete, the spirits were summoned, each one in order, ready and cheerful to obey in all things.

The secret is very great.

Let me tell a certain secret to a prince, or to a friend, the revelation of which would bring danger to me, and no small loss to him. So let all things remain secret between me and him. Note that I commend the mystery to man, not to the letter, but to the spirit.

THEY SHOULD LITERALLY BE AFRAID OF NOTHING.

Begin, my dearest brethren, to make amends for your negligence, wiping away your past sins with constant tears, and asking the Saviour of all the living for the rest of the time. Hear, Oh Lord, the groaning of those who weep constantly, forgive the sins, the lover of the innocent. Give life to those who mourn, give life to the innocent, and do not despise people who are exiles. To pity very much the best of men Christ Jesus our most noble Saviour, free the weak souls of the exile. Most kindly save the wretched and grant us forgiveness. Hear us the humble and the weakest, in the hour of death, grant the light that is pleasant, the comforter of all, the norm and the humble. In the year 1500, April 7. I wrote this, John Trithemius, Abbot Spanheim.

After receiving these or any other letters, signed at the end by the sign of Prince Uriel, he to whom they are sent, an expert in the art, shall first of all do what he knows to be done according to the art, and speak the secret prayer.

SECRET PRAYER

Uriel Aflan pemason cosayr chameron, chulty fabelmerõ deyr pean, cathurmo merosyn ersoti chalmon sauepo Meduse rean lamerosyn.

When the song has been said, the invisible spirit sent will appear in his usual form. In everything he will faithfully reveal what has been entrusted to him by the worker or the sender, and in the utmost secrecy. So that none of those around him can perceive or hear anything, and it will always remain a secret.

Commentary: Chapter XXX

[p. 275; 1] *Uriel* … Yet another aerial demon that is said to wander the earth. *Uriel*'s servants are known to be evil, liars, and do not want to obey the commands of exorcists or goetics.[1]

Uriel is also an angel that appears in the *Book of 1 Enoch*[2] and the book of *4* [*2*] *Esdras*. In the *Book of 1 Enoch*, *Uriel* is an angel that accompanies angels such as Michael, Gabriel and Raphael. In *4 Esdras*, *Uriel* is the angel that speaks the messages from God to Esdras and whom Esdras consistently asks God to send so that Esdras can speak to him. Since *4 Esdras* was included in the Bible by the original 1611 KJV, it is not a surprise that people want to accept asking for angels for various tasks as biblical. The 1611 KJV noted that these books should not be considered canonical, but since the books were in the official version, people still took them seriously. *4 Esdras* was not officially removed from the KJV until 1885.

Uriel as an angel is said to have guided Enoch through heaven in Enochic literature, to be guarding the gates of Eden, and being sent to punish Moses for not circumcising his sons (Exodus 4:24–26). The angelic *Uriel* is also credited with taking Abel's dead body after it was spit out of the earth and setting it on a rock and preserving it until Abel and Adam could be buried at Hebron. Along with the kabbalistic Enoch, the goetic archangel Metatron, *Uriel* along with Metatron are said to have given the *Kabbalah* to humanity.[3] Remembering that I pointed out in my *Introduction* that Jake Stratton-Kent recognized that goetia is the core of all magic (p. 11, this volume), it should not be surprising that kabbalists believe the *Kabbalah* was given to them by goetic/necromantic beings in Metatron and *Uriel*.

[p. 275; 3], [p. 276; 4] non-sensical goetic "angel tongues".

---

1. Rosemary Ellen Guiley Ph.D., *The Encyclopedia of Demons & Demonology* (New York, New York: Checkmark Books, 2009), p. 260.

2. Michelle Belanger, *The Dictionary of Demons: Names of the Damned* (Woodbury, Minnesota: Llewellyn Publications, 2017), p. 304.

3. Rosemary Ellen Guiley Ph.D., *The Encyclopedia of Angels, Second Edition* (New York, New York: Checkmark Books, 2004), p. 360–361.

Commentary: Chapter XXX

[illegible]

Chapter XXXI: Bydiel/Bidiel

Whose supreme leader is called Bydiel, having under his authority twenty commanders, but two hundred counts, the number of servants is uncertain as they are very many.

Still, one remains and the highest of spirits, assigned to us for the operation of steganography. We are indeed at the last in the order, but with the first in dignity, whose name is called Bydiel because of his office, having under his command twenty captains, counts or underlings, two hundred servants and many lesser servants. These captains and their companions have a certain order among themselves and whenever they are called by the operator, two captains come with twenty companions, and appear in human form, calm and ready for everything. They alternate with each other, for in the first year the leaders were called, afterwards the counts, in the second the counts are called for the leaders.

Black.	Red.	B.	R.	B.	R.	B.	R.
Mudriel	*20.*	*20.*	*200.*	*20.*	*200.*	*Charobiel*	*20.*
Cruchan	*20.*	*20.*	*200.*	*20.*	*200.*	*Andrucha*	*20.*
Bramsiel	*20.*	*20.*	*200.*	*20.*	*200.*	*Merasiel*	*20.*
Armoniel	*20.*	*20.*	*200.*	*20.*	*200.*	*Parsifiel*	*20.*
Lameniel	*20.*	*20.*	*200.*	*20.*	*200.*	*Chremoas*	*20.*

We have already here ten of the princes and counts of Bydiel signed with their names, who are sufficient for us as present for all our operations in the art of steganography, together with many servants who knew how to observe their order according to the command of the dukes and princes. But when you wish to work through them in this art, by presuming the introductory argument, call it a secret prayer.

Song of Secret Prayer

Bydiel marchan chamerosi philtres maduse vear casmyren cralnoti: pean deuoon fableros eltida camean veor. Oniel vear thyrso liernoty: ianos prolsato chanos elasry peanon elsatha melros notiel pen soes probys chyras lesbroy mauear iothan liernoti chrymarson.[1]

When the song is said as it should be, the spirits called will immediately appear visible, walking beautifully, and leading each other like friends, embracing each other, and they will be willingly obedient to you in everything.

It is a mystery to me, whatever it may be.

It is mysterious to me that I desire to know a very secret absent friend. It concerns a hid-

1. Uyl – There was a symbol from the original Stenganographia which I did not include after the Secret Prayer. If you wish to see what the symbol was, there are plenty of free copies in the original Latin online for the reader to refer to.

den substance, which must be lost, if the mystery should in any way happen to be made public. So, I entrust it not to man, not to letters, but only to spirits, whom I know to be secure and faithful.

John Trithemius, Abbot of Spanheim, Rutgerus Sicambro S.D. And the present great Basilius should say a little prayer.

The glory of indescribable eternal bliss is acquired by good and humble practices. Now wipe away mortal errors with tears, love God, adoring his holy name. Learn to follow the path of the humble Jesus Christ, humbly crucified, always paying him honour, burning sweetly with the love of our most gracious saviour. Glorify and exalt his praiseworthy goodness. Bless his holy name. Be zealous for the fire of goodness. Despise pointless honours. Learn to return praises in adversity. Love the exercise of devotion. Cultivate the most noble humility and exalt Jesus who redeems us from death and saves us. Goodbye. April in the year of the Nativity of our Lord 1500.

But the friend receiving the letters, already an expert in the art of steganography, having known the character of Bydiel, after presupposing those things which are to be already known by custom, let him speak generally of the secret prayer.

Secret Prayer

Bydiel maslo chameron theory madias near fabelron thiamy marfoy vear pean liernoty calmea drules: Thubra pleory malresa teorty melchoy vemo chosray.

When the prayer is said, the spirit will be visible only to him who called him. He will report to you completely and faithfully what he entrusted.

Commentary: Chapter XXXI

[p. 279; 1] *Bydiel*, [or, *Bidiel*] ... This is another wandering aerial demon that has servants which switch when who gets called for different goetic purposes every year. *Bydiel* and his servants appear as attractive humans when summoned and are willing to obey exorcists and goetics.[1] *Bydiel* is said to be of a good nature and is even-tempered to deal with.[2]

[p. 279; 3], [p. 280; 4] non-sensical goetic "angel tongues".

[p. 280; 1] *The glory of indescribable eternal bliss is acquired by good and humble practices. Now wipe away mortal errors with tears*, ... The implications that good and humble practices will earn anyone heaven is theologically fallacious. Many secular people believe that they will go to heaven simply because they are "good people". Christians know that the claim about being "good" is nonsense since Paul states that "[n]one is righteous, no, not one." (Romans 3:10 ESV) Paul here is quoting Psalm 14:1, "They are corrupt, they do abominable deeds; there is none who does good." (Psalm 14:1 ESV) This verse is repeated in Psalm 53:1 "They are corrupt, doing abominable iniquity; there is none who does good." (Psalm 53:1 ESV) The belief that good works can erase sins, and that tears/mourning will wipe away "mortal errors" (sin, possibly original sin) again is a subverting of the gospel truth concerning Christ's death and resurrection. Believing that good works and tears can wipe away sins and not Christ's death and resurrection alone, is a belief in self-divinity and the denial of Christ's gospel.

[p. 280; 1] *Learn to follow the path of the humble Jesus Christ*, ... Seeing how Trithemius is wording this, it is a claim once again that "since Jesus did it, so can we." It is a rephrasing of the belief that "Jesus did his miracles as a man, therefore, so can we." It has just been taken one step forward to mean that we can earn our own forgiveness if we do exactly what Jesus did. It is again a claim to self-divinity.

1. Rosemary Ellen Guiley Ph.D., *The Encyclopedia of Demons & Demonology* (New York, New York: Checkmark Books, 2009), p. 28.

2. Michelle Belanger, *The Dictionary of Demons: Names of the Damned* (Woodbury, Minnesota: Llewellyn Publications, 2017), p. 71.

Commentary: Chapter XXXI

CHAPTER XXXII

In which a necessary restatement of the terms is made. Some cells are inserted, which are to be observed by those who wish to practice the art of steganography.

After that (praise be to the most blessed God) we have not without great and continuous labour described the offices of the supreme spirits of our steganography before the rest of those who favour us. So that those who wish to work through them should not make an error in order, names, characters, leaders, or counts. We have thought it necessary to make a general table of all for the sake of memory in this art to make this chart for this chapter. The following table is on this and the next page.

	Red.	[1]	R.	Black.	R.	B.	R.
1	*Pamersiel*		*1,000.*	10,000.	*100.*	*10.*	K
2	*Padiel* [*Pachiel*]		*1,000.*	200,000.	*100.*	*10.*	K
3	*Camuel*		*10.*	10.	*0.*	*100.*	K
4	*Aseliel*		*10.*	20.	*0.*	*200.*	K
5	*Barmiel*		*10.*	20.	*10.*	*200.*	K
6	*Gediel*		*20.*	20.	*00.*	*200.*	K
7	*Asyriel*		*20.*	20.	*10.*	*100.*	K
8	*Maseriel*		*30.*	30.	*00.*	*300.*	K
9	*Malgaras*		*30.*	30.	*10.*	*200.*	K
10	*Dorothiel*		*40.*	40.	*0.*	*400.*	K
11	*Vsiel*		*40.*	40.	*30.*	*300.*	K
12	*Cabariel*		*50.*	50.	*50.*	*500.*	K
13	*Rayfiel*		*50.*	50.	*40.*	*400.*	K
14	*Symiel*		*10.*	1,000.	*0.*	*4.*	K
15	*Armadiel*		*1,000.*	180.	*10.*	*800.*	K
16	*Baruchas*		*10.*	180/	*0.*	*100.*	K
17	*Carnesiel*		*1,000.*	300.	*1,000.*	*300.*	1,000.
18	*Caspiel*		*200.*	400.	*200.*	*400.*	200.
19	*Amenadiel*		*300.*	500.	*300.*	*500.*	300.
20	*Demoriel*		*400.*	600.	*400.*	*600.*	400.
21	*Geradiel*		*200.*	100.	*40.*	*30.*	60.
22	*Buriel*		*100.*	10.	*10.*	*100.*	θ
23	*Hydriel*		*10.*	20.	*100.*	*200.*	θ
24	*Pyrichiel*		*40.*	30.	*200.*	*10.*	θβ

1. This column in the original text had the symbols for the various spirits.

	Red.	R.	Black.	R.	B.	R.
25	*Emoniel*	*10.*	20.	*100.*	*20.*	θ
26	*Icosiel*	*10.*	300.	*100.*	*30.*	θ
27	*Soleuiel*	*20.*	20.	*20.*	*200.*	θ
28	*Menadiel*	*100.*	20.	*30.*	*10.*	θν
29	*Macariel*	*40.*	30.	*20.*	*10.*	θδ
30	*Uriel*	*20.*	10.	*40.*	*30.*	θκ
31	*Bidiel*	*30.*	40.	*100.*	*20.*	κβ

In this table we have placed thirty-one principal spirits, who assume, each in his office and in his order, all the operations of our steganography, of which we have spoken in this first book of ours. The character appropriated to him, the number and order of princes, dukes, counts, servants and lesser servants in their respective degrees. Joining together, or else anyone desiring to study this art fall into error because of the diversity of operations. Indeed, the great mysteries of this art can only be penetrated by the most studying of men, that is to say, those whom the love of secrets and nature promote to chase after, and who refuse to undergo any honourable and possible labour for the pursuit of knowledge. But men are lazy and ignorant, without intelligence, and whom neither love inflames to study the secrets of wisdom, nor nature helps, when they are unable to understand this most secret art of our approval. Not to be taught to us, but rather to be ascribed to their own misery, laziness, and hatred. Having a mind immersed in cares, they fail to spare themselves in going through them with care. Either they think they are wise or the most educated. They dislike our writings as unworthy of their lessons. They will also not come to any such former strangers. They stubbornly stand by traditions, that is, whatever they have not learned in them, they consider either impossible or superstitious. Those who are either unwilling or unable to understand the depths of this art are no more ignorant of the knowledge of this extremely deep art. Moreover, at the end of this book we decide to remind those who are both apt and willing to study in this art (if they are ones from in the future) so that they can make progress in learning the art. In the first place they are to be warned, in so far as they always keep the art itself secret, or else it should penetrate the hands and knowledge of the wicked, who would commit many and disgusting crimes by means of it. For even if the art of this action is truly good in itself, yet its practice will no less lead to evil through the wicked than to good through the righteous. Let it therefore remain secret among the good, that which would be harmful if published among the bad. And yet they will not have to despise this knowledge of the good on that account, because it is beneficial to the evil to do evil, just as the sword does not turn anyone away, which kills a man. Then the students of this art are to be advised not to make assumptions to go forward to work in this art. They must first be perfectly trained in all that is required for practical knowledge. For it does not escape me, how many dangers the matter is subjected to by those who are less experienced in attempting to work in it at some time.

Likewise, whoever is well-instructed in this knowledge wishes to work through it, he must carefully observe (according to what we have said both in the circle and in the individual tables and chapters) the difference, places, names, orders and offices of the supreme spirits, the guides and so on, of them, and how many counts there are in number; which order they will observe, and how many substitutes are present, as he knows how to express this in the oath. For unless the operator of the craft carefully guards all these things, he will not be able to make progress, and neither arrive at the effect of his intention. Again, let him pay careful attention, when anyone; and to what offices the spirit is to be called by secret faith, and to what part of the world he dwells, or else he should make error either in the places or in all the woes of some individuals whom he wills to call.

Likewise, let everyone who works in this knowledge be encouraged, that he attends most diligently, that he properly pronounces the words of the secret plans, in which the great power of our operation may consist of. But they are also completely reluctant. Consequently, he was warned let him not call one for the other, but each one, in their order, time, and office, just as we have in almost all the chapters of that book, it has been sufficiently said. For if, either by mistake or by any other negligence, he calls one for the other, he would profit nothing in his operation, but you would rather expose him to danger.

Likewise, in conspiracies, the spirit that is called, together with its equivalent replacements, is expressed by name, and the cause of the calling is previously established in the intention, let there not be an act of operation in light and profane matters, which one would otherwise be able to passionately say to the other without danger either by letters or by messengers. For this art is not to be resorted to except in great and difficult announcements, which are published or would bring loss or danger to the operator. Likewise, it is necessary for everyone who works in this art to know the natures of spirits, which are good, which are bad, which are ready and kind to obedience, and which are harsh rebels. Again, those who preside over the operations of the night, and those of the day, because unless he knows the nature of the spirits before he begins to work, he will succeed with the greatest difficulty, and will easily be turned into a stunned condition. Likewise, those spirits who are called appear visible before the worker, with the mysterious word given, he commits the secret of his mind to the leader or the companion with the words due and learned in silence, because there is no need for the spirit to speak with a loud voice, but rather a quiet voice. The operator and the recipient must also be extremely careful not to work in the presence of other people who do not know this art, and who do not belong to steganography, while they may have access to a secret place. And if they were unable to be alone, but forced to work among others, they acted so secretly, with great wisdom, and with such energy that none of the people around understood what the presence of the spirits are. All the spirits assigned to the ministry of this art are of such a nature and condition, that they thoroughly hate and are repulsed by the disturbance of men and hate public conversation. Likewise, we must be careful. It is for the worker not to direct the spirit without letters, or at least with the character of his emperor, since he does not see the character himself impressed there. He completely despises the one who calls him to obey and the secret to be suffered through. But we send letters for a double reason, although we could communicate the secret without letters through the spirit alone. Namely, we will guard the character from suspicion of the people who carry it, and we will constrain the spirit bound by the character itself to obey the friend.

Commentary: Chapter XXXII

[p. 284; 1] *Indeed, the great mysteries of this art can only be penetrated by the most studying of men, that is to say, those whom the love of secrets and nature promote to chase after, and who refuse to undergo any honourable and possible labour for the pursuit of knowledge. But men are lazy and ignorant, without intelligence, and whom neither love inflames to study the secrets of wisdom, nor nature helps, when they are unable to understand this most secret art of our approval. ...* Many people will refer once again to Deuteronomy 18:9 that we should not be learning the ways of necromancers and mediums in an attempt to scare people into not reading texts of this type or learning about these issues.

There is a flaw in that understanding of this Deuteronomy verse. The Hebrew word that is used for "learn" תלמד (tilmad) is what is known as a "Qal Imperfect". The Qal imperfect in its translation is said that the "*aspect in the Imperfect denotes incomplete action, whether in the past, present, or future.*" (italics original)[1] This may confuse some, but the explanation is pretty easy. The incomplete action and the next verb "following" indicates that the learning is for the purposes of "following" or "doing" the "abominable practices" of necromancy and mediumship.

With that explanation in mind, while it can be dangerous to study this material, we as Christians cannot be ignorant of it. As this first book and my *Introduction* has already shown, many Christians in all traditions are extremely and wilfully ignorant about necromancy and goetia. That ignorance has come because doing the proper research as to what goetia even is has been treated as forbidden for research purposes. Many have used the verse to take "no part in the unfruitful works of darkness, but instead expose them", (Ephesians 5:11 ESV) to mean that even studying these issues is "taking part in them". Again, this assumption is flawed since if you do not even *know* what the ways of darkness are, you will not be able to *discern* or *expose* what they are. Many charismatic, Prosperity, WOF and NAR church leaders have ignorantly assumed that they will simply "know" and have fallen into the gravest (pun intended) of errors in refusing to be aware of what practices like goetia, that the Bible tells us to avoid, even are. Being aware of that wilful ignorance, Trithemius in saying, "the great mysteries of this art can only be penetrated by the most studying of men" commands his followers to know these practices well. In knowing this "art" well, students do not need to be concerned since those that would persecute them for studying these arts do not have the determination to study them anyway.

[p. 284–285; 1] *In the first place they are to be warned, in so far as they always keep the art itself secret, or else it should penetrate the hands and knowledge of the wicked, who would commit many and disgusting crimes by means of it. For even if the art of this ac-*

1. Gary D. Pratico and Miles V. Van Pelt, *Basics of Biblical Hebrew Grammar, Third Edition* (Grand Rapids, Michigan: Zondervan, 2019), p. 155.

tion is truly good in itself, yet its practice will no less lead to evil through the wicked than to good through the righteous. Let it therefore remain secret among the good, that which would be harmful if published among the bad, … Trithemius is playing into the hands of the ignorant who use Ephesians 5:11 incorrectly as pointed out in the paragraph above. Trithemius knows that people will not want to be aware of the deceptive nature of goetia because it would mean being part of "the unfruitful works of darkness". People in churches have followed this assumption and play on their own ignorance to the advantage of not just goetics, but the occult in general. It is also ironic that Trithemius recognizes that this art coming to the knowledge of the "wicked" will give the wicked the ability to "commit many and disgusting crimes by means of it." Considering how Prosperity, WOF and NAR movements use goetia specifically for the purposes of taking financial advantage of those who simply "want to believe" goetia is biblical, the warning here from Trithemius is worth taking note of.

The first book of the Steganography of John Trithemius, Abbot of Spanheim, is finished this April 6, 1500.

Book II

The book of the sequential steganography of John Trithemius Abbot of Spanheim to the Most Serene Prince, Lord Philip, Count Palatine of the Rhine, Duke of Bavaria, Arch-dapifer of the Holy Empire, and Prince Elector.

PREFACE

In the preceding book, relying on the help of the most high God, we have spoken in order of thirty-one of the supreme spirits of our art. Our Emperors with their leaders, counts, and servants, necessary to our operation, not without great sweat, whose services, if for the announcement of all mysteries, no matter how secret, ministers abundantly to all let them be sufficient for the workman. But however, we should seem to remove any of those things which may be employed for the perfection of this art. We decided to join the first book with the second. But since at each hour of the day and of the night the spirits are each, by some wise tradition, assigned to various operations, and with various and wonderful effects, it pleased us to copy their order only, and not their superstition. For let us take from them, without injury to the Christian name, what leads us to our purpose. The rest indeed, let us pass through as if full of magical arts, and rejecting the opposites of our faith. We shall proceed, therefore, at each hour of the day as well as of the night, appointed by the secret of Solomon, known as Hermes in his volume of magic, the spirit, as the supreme commanders of the art, with other officials, necessary to us for the purposed operation. Let them reveal to their friends the secrets and secret thinking of their minds every hour with a safer plan. For every prince presides over his spirits, guides, companions, and servants as a watchman, to whose command those called to us come with a legitimate song They carry out secret commissions and show themselves obedient to us and ready in all things. But when I am about to mention the spirits again, I think I should say again, nothing in this art of ours should be treated as petty, nothing contrary to the evangelical tradition or to the Catholic faith, nothing at all superstitious to tradition. For all that we have either said in the preceding volume, or are about to say in the following, are based on natural, lawful, and honourable principles, and the mystery veiled only by strange institutions, and the words shrouded in the names of spirits, require a learned reader. For we use the ministry of the Spirit to cover the secret, which would hurt the heretic when published. And let no one fail in the calculation of the hours by mistake. Let him know that we have received the hours of the planets both in the day and in the night.

Commentary: Preface

[p. 293; 1] *But since at each hour of the day and of the night the spirits are each, by some wise tradition, assigned to various operations, and with various and wonderful effects, it pleased us to copy their order only, and not their superstition. ...* There are entire charts and comparisons that can be found on various pro-occult websites that will attempt to pinpoint which hours each of the demons in *Book 2* are assigned to. The reason this ambiguity exists is because Trithemius never defines when the first hour of day is with the first demon, Samael.

While we may think we know the answers to "the first hour of night", in kabbalistic Judaism, the "first hour of night" was determined to be six o'clock PM by our modern clocks, or 1800 hours. Meanwhile, in Greek magic and goetia, the hour of night is never directly defined. All that is known is that the "witching hour" began at midnight.

Since Trithemius makes several references to the Kabbalah in different chapters within this entire volume, it is fair to say that Trithemius indicated six o'clock PM as the time of the "first hour of night". This conclusion needs a lot more evidence for verification, but considering the arguments already given to us about this books' basis in kabbalism, it is the conclusion I will be working from.

[p. 293; 1] *We shall proceed, therefore, at each hour of the day as well as of the night, appointed by the secret of Solomon, known as Hermes in his volume of magic, the spirit, as the supreme commanders of the art, with other officials, necessary to us for the purposed operation. ...* The reference to Solomon here as Hermes is something that the occult claims, however we also know that Hermes is a reference to Thoth, Hermes being the anthropomorphizing of the Egyptian god Thoth. That the occult would associate Solomon and Thoth together is not something that is overly surprising because Judaic occultism often falsely associated Hermes with Solomon through texts like the *Testament of Solomon*, where Solomon is referenced by that name. As faithful researchers, demonologists and occult researchers working within Christian beliefs to expose occult practices within the church, we need to be aware of these twisting of biblical and historical facts to fit occult purposes. This is something that also happens regularly in some charismatic and all Prosperity, WOF and NAR movements.

Translator and Commentators Note: The angels and demons mentioned in *Book 2* are repeated in another later and in *Part 3* of an equally infamous goetic text the *Lemegeton* more popularly known as *The Lesser Key of Solomon*. The text in this volume references more information on each angel and/or demon than the *Lemegeton*: *Part 3*. If there is any other information from other goetic, kabbalistic or occult texts, the additional information will be given.

Chapter I: Samael

Samael, supreme emperor, who presides over the first hour. Who has under his command several captains, counts, and servants, whom he sends at this hour only to be summoned to work by someone experienced in steganography.

At the first hour of the day, which begins at the rising of the sun, the spirit and emperor Samael[1] is called. Who has under his command a great number of captains, counts, and subordinates, who are called by the operative at this hour only in steganography. They carry the secret that is commanded them, but to come beyond the hour they will despise coming completely. And note that the leaders and chieftains of the Samaelians are rarely sent by him in the service of the house of science, since they are charged with the duty of exciting men with magical and nighttime illusions.

Now the counts with their servants are specially assigned to the service of this art, in which they are sent more frequently even without the presence of leaders. Who being of the highest order among spirits, are most likely to present themselves somewhat proud and rebellious to those who call them, and it is not easy for anyone but the most skilled in the art of steganography. And let them perish in danger, for they are disrespectful, and hateful of illusions. The most prepared of men, they ridicule. And they condemn especially those whom they have found to be less expert in the art of steganography. But those whom they regard as bold, steadfast, and experienced in the art itself, the spirits are turned away from them, and the spirits are afraid of them. They always obey commands with trembling and reluctance. Now we will mention the names of those who are necessary for us in the operations of stenography at this hour.

Red.	Black.	R.	R.	R.	B.	B.
Ameniel	*Brumiel*	10.	100.	1,000.	μ	ν
Charpon	*Nestoriel*	10.	100.	1,000.	α	β
Darosiel	*Chremas*	10.	100.	1,000.	10.	20.
Monasiel	*Meresyn*	10.	100.	1,000.	20.	10.

We now have from the leaders of the great Samael four. And from the counts as many, from the servants from the triple order four thousand four hundred forty whose service is abundantly sufficient for us for all the operation of the art of steganography, if it is done at the first hour of the day.

When, therefore, you wish to work in the art in the first hour of the day, write the character of the ascendant lord in the card first, then the moon afterwards of all the remaining moons according to the usual order, and in the sign without the character of the ascendant at the same hour. And when you have finished this, write on the back of the

1. Uyl – Samael is the old Jewish name for Satan that is used in Kabbalism. In Kabbalism, Samael is the demon that rescued the Jewish Lilith (different from the Assyrian Lilith) from Eden and impregnated her. It is still believed in Kabbalism that Samael/Satan is the husband of Lilith.

same card this secret prayer with silence, being silent.

Secret Prayer

Samael afluar onayr mylco layr madiel cuhiel naniel nabruys satiel atharbiel nadian naslon, ranyalcoha pemarson.

With this secret prayer written on a card, it is preferable, to send beautiful, clear, and distinct letters to him whom you wish to know the secret. You will fit the letters in whatever form you please because it does not matter by what kind of letters (as long as the letters to be sent do not contain any secret) they were formed. Then, with the letters also written, call one or two of the companions according to order, if you work many times at this very hour, and say the secret prayer prescribed from the same card, with the strongest intention, fearing nothing. When it is duly completed, the spirits called will immediately appear visible to you in a familiar form, accustomed to each other, placid, benevolent, meeting with all the promptest services. To whom appears commit your secret to the chief among them, saying, "Ameniel I command thee by the secret power of this mysterious prayer, in other words to Albertus Goëler de Rauenspurg, prefect in Creutzenach, as soon as possible go on, and tell him in my name thus or thus." Add to these words a secret word, which must not be written, and the spirit will immediately fly. But send the letters sealed in Samael's handwriting (as is the custom) by a messenger, in which no secret shall be contained, and which shall not be seen by anyone.

Let it be mysterious, whatever it may be.

It is a great mystery, and a difficult secret, in any case; for the time it occurs, and such, that it should not be communicated to anyone. Neither to believe in letters, nor in reports. Because it is not in this art, especially in the spirit of this second volume, to work for a few little ones, for reasons which may be communicated in other letters.

You will form the letters upon these at will.

The majesty of the Catholic faith, to be firmly served by all, pledges the happiness of eternal life to those who love Christ. Hold the Catholic Christian faith, glorify the Almighty, fleeing the turmoil of self love. No one will have the blessed power of good works. A faithful man should follow Christ along the path of goodness. Integrity is adorned with good works, and the Catholic name is preserved by Christian faithfulness. For the poor man clouded his faith. Christ hates the reckless, but loves Christians practicing Catholic activities, worshiping peacefully.

John Trithemius, abbot of Spanheim, I published April in the year of the Lord 1500 –.

When the person to whom they are sent has received the letters, an expert in the art shall introduce those which are to be done before in the general instruction of the art when expressed. But as soon as he has completed the prayer, he will see the spirit present, and when he sees it, he will fearlessly say:

+ penador auenal + solemn panu + sauear caschanti hernoty maduran Amen.

Having said these things, let him be silent, and stop the spirit approaching him, and secretly and securely bring back to his ear the mysterious secret, which he should hear without fear, with great energy, as if someone were sitting around, that by a gesture or a word the spirit present be indicated.

Commentary: Chapter I

[p. 297; 1] *Samael* ... A name used for a demon and also as a pseudonym for Gentiles in Jewish myth and esotericism. *Samael* is often associated with Satan, but this is not always the case. *Samael* is always associated as being the husband of Lilith.[1]

One of the implications coming from the *Otzar Midrashim*, a kabbalistic text, was that *Samael* was the angel of death that stood before God and was sent to take the soul of Moses when Moses died. Even though *Samael* was possibly considered the angel of death, in contrast to the popular belief that the angel of death is the Islamic angel Azrael, *Samael* was still not an angel that Moses was wanting to have his soul carried to heaven by. The following are all my own translations.

> "Samael the taker of souls," [...] "to take the soul of the righteous" Then Moses asks that "it be your will, O my God and the God of my fathers, that you do not deliver me into the hand of this angel."

While fulfilling God's orders as the angel of death, *Samael* was still considered to be evil and a servant of Satan as well by kabbalists.

> The wicked Samael, the head of Satan, was expecting the death of Moses at every moment and said, "when will that moment come that I will come down to kill him and take his soul?"

As I stated above, *Samael* was also a pseudonym for Gentiles in kabbalistic literature. The following text from the *Sefer haZohar* is especially interesting in light of dispensational beliefs about the restoration of the Jewish state of Israel.

> The Shekinah [a "God" spirit often associated as either the "wife" or "daughter" spirit of Yahweh], [...] protects them, and spreads her wings over them like a mother over her sons, and from this we bought a tent of peace for us. And because of this in the seventh month, in which all these commandments are fulfilled, (Song of Songs 8) many waters [Gentiles] will not be able to quench the love of the people of Israel for their father in heaven. And there is no abundant water [Gentiles] but all the nations and their inhabitants. If a man, who is Samael [a Gentile], gives everything he has in this world, so that he may participate in these commands with Israel, he will be despised.

Once we understand that one of the key "commands" that Israel was to observe was that concerning the temple, we can understand that no matter how much money or support is sent to national Israel to reconstruct the temple, "Gentiles" will still never have a part of that temple. Any temple that is constructed at this point in salvific history by Israel will be a pagan temple. Yet, many people are more than willing to send millions of dollars per year to Israel to rebuild a temple that these same Christians will have no part of if it is ever built. Christians will likely try to be part of temple celebrations and cultus, but the rabbinic authorities, most of whom are also highly trained in kabbalism, will make sure

1. Michelle Belanger, *The Dictionary of Demons: Names of the Damned* (Woodbury, Minnesota: Llewellyn Publications, 2017), p. 269.

they are forbidden from entry.

[p. 297; 1] *And note that the leaders and chieftains of the Samaelians are rarely sent by him in the service of the house of science, since they are charged with the duty of exciting men with magical and nighttime illusions. …* While Samael is said to be the demon to call in the "first hour of the day, which begins at the rising sun", it is noteworthy that Samael's servants are responsible for causing "nighttime illusions". This helps to confirm the reality of the "witching hour", more specifically the "devil's hour", being at three o'clock am (pp. 76–79, this volume) and how many charismatic, and all Prosperity, WOF and NAR leaders have taught that "Jesus" will appear at the "devil's hour" and interact with these leaders in a clearly *anti*-biblical way. Even goetics recognize these "illusions" for what they are. Yet false Christians are completely convinced by these deceptions. *Samael* is also named in the *Lemegeton* under the name *Samuel*, but as an angel and not a demon.[2]

[p. 298; 1], [p. 299; 3] non-sensical goetic "angel tongues".

[p. 298; 6] T*he majesty of the Catholic faith, to be firmly served by all, pledges the happiness of eternal life to those who love Christ. …* No church, or institution of any kind, including people or members of that institution, have any biblical authority to "pledge" "happiness of eternal life" to anyone. That guarantee of eternal life is given to us by the confidence of our salvation given to Christians by Christ through our faith. If the Bible does not affirm the confidence of your salvation, a church will never be able to.

[p. 299; E] *Christ hates the reckless, but loves Christians practicing Catholic activities, worshiping peacefully. …* Keeping in mind the goetic idolatry involved in the Roma Catholic Church, this guarantee by Trithemius that Christ "love Christians practicing Catholic activities" is a theological fallacy. That Christ apparently loves Christians practicing these activities, also shows that the idea of "saved by works" is in view here. Works show a persons' faith but works themselves can not save anyone. Salvation is only attained though faith in Christ and no one and nothing else including a church or institution can make that promise or guarantee.

2. Rosemary Ellen Guiley Ph.D., *The Encyclopedia of Angels: Second Edition* (New York, New York: Checkmark Books, 2004), p. 43.

Chapter II: Anael/Anafiel/Aniel/Anyiel/ Ariel/Ausiel/Hamiel/Haniel/Onoel

The second hour of the day is called Ceuorym. whose chief and supreme spirit is Anael, who has under his command ten commanders, one hundred counts, centurions, and presidents.

President and emperor in the second hour of the day, the principal is called Anael, who has under his command appointed in the service of this art of steganography ten commanders. Anael also has one hundred counts, centurions, and presidents with all their other spirits. The number of servants is still not certain to me. Now the second hour of the day is called Ceuorym, in which changeable operations are performed which are astonishing to all men. The spirits of this emperor are all quite happy, pleasant, cheerful, and very willing to obey the worker in the art. Only let him be skilled in the art, strong in mind, steadfast, and well-intelligent.

Black.	Red.	B.	R.	B.	R.	B.
Menarchos	*Orphiel*	*Quosiel*	10.	100.	G.	n.
Archiel	*Cursiel*	*Ermaziel*	10.	100.	G.	n.
Chardiel	*Elmoym*	*Granyel*	10.	100.	G.	n.

In this table we have placed from the leaders of Anael as numbering three, from the company six, and from the servants three hundred thirty who are sufficient for us for all the operation of steganography at this second hour of the day by sending them through their ranks.

When, therefore, at this hour you wish to work on something in steganography, write on a clean sheet the character of the ascendant lord, and in the order following it, the other planets, and most notably the sign of the twelfth house, with an ink burned into the letter and made of the material of that art. Then write this secret prayer on the back of the previously mentioned card in silence, with your face turned towards the sun.

Song of the Secret Prayer

Anael otiel aproisy rachimas, thulnear layr meuear theor cralnotiel amersoty mouear phroys lierto mear vrnesa elty famelron.

Having written the conspiracy, do the rest, which you know how to do according to art. Then recite the hymn in silence, and you will soon see the spirit present, cheerful, pleasant, and benevolent to all things to whom you entrust the mystery securely.

Let us put it as a mystery.

It is a mystery to us somehow, for the time occurring, which neither seems to be useful for the letter nor to be committed to the post office. One or the other of them shall be called from the spirits of Anael, the leader and the comrade, as he pleases. Let the principal be entrusted with the secret in a due manner, as it should be according to the precepts of art, and faithfully bear it.

LET THE TENOR OF LETTERS BE FAMILIAR.
John Trithemius, Abbot of Spanheim, William Salute to Veldicus, Canon of St. Augustine in the Franconian valley with the philosopher.

I would be glad to answer your letters, so may Christ make me rejoice. I would transmit the requested volumes, if at last I had them. I am zealous for the greatest secret caretakers of nature with the good zeal which the most ancient philosophers had. And I owe you many and immortal thanks, my sweetest brother, who have made thin the glue of the loan. I have clearly learned this from the family business, which you seem to have taken care of with the greatest modesty, which I praise, I have the thanks that will never die. And so, I would most desire to behave according to your requests, if I had demands (Christ knew). I have recently seen various Latin translations done, Pico Mirandulani, the most excellent man, I have read many brilliant volumes, Hippolytus I have seen the Greek, whether it has been completely translated, I do not know the ultimate truth, Christ whom nothing of darkness can kill, what from the heart I desire to give to you in prayer. I plead with you adamantly for the virtue of the zeal of righteousness, despise praises, honours, and perishables. I consider it praiseworthy to imitate the true predecessor of Christ. Do, I pray you, as far as you are a priest by works, love Christ and all the time you live. A true lover of Christ will serve the zeal of justice. The true rest of the soul, and the knowledge of the saviour, the loving observance of the Catholic apostates, prepares eternal glory for all. Jesus Christ, the glorious giver of all good things, grant you eternal love, making you a Catholic priest of Christians. Goodbye. April 4, in the year 1500.

When the person to whom they were sent has received the letters, he is requested in this art, with the generally customary introductory statements, that he orders the lord of the ascendant with the rest, which are usually on the chart, and tells the prescribed conspiracy. Having said this, the sent spirit will appear visible to whom he turned in surprise and said:

Fabelmerusyn passoriel liertos ryneas melchus thyrmo nydran vear padroys.

Having completed this song, the spirit will soon be flattered to approach, and faithfully report the mystery committed. And let everyone who works in this art beware, both he who sends the spirit, and he to whom it was determined to go to, or else they should be killed in public or among others who are not of this art. To presume to work at all, for all the spirits of the schedule love the secret and detest the public and they will not go without danger.

Commentary: Chapter II

[p. 303; 1] *Anael*, [or, *Anafiel*, *Aniel*, *Anyiel*, *Ariel*, *Ausiel*, *Hamiel*, *Haniel*, *Onoel*] ... This a demon that is called a spirit of power who reveals secrets from the past, present and future.[1] This is not surprising considering the divinatory nature of goetia and the desire to find mysteries such as lost treasure. In other sources, *Anael* is considered to be an angel that goes by a variety of other names (see above). One of the names, *Ariel* is also a named used for the city of Jerusalem in the prophetic book of Isaiah:

> Ah, Ariel, Ariel, the city where David encamped! Add year to year; let the feasts run their round. Yet I will distress Ariel, and there shall be moaning and lamentation, and she shall be to me like an Ariel. And the multitude of all the nations that fight against Ariel, all that fight against her and her stronghold and distress her, shall be like a dream, a vision of the night. (Isaiah 29: 1–2, 7 ESV)

As an angel, *Anael* is said to be in charge of the plant Venus, human sexuality, the second heaven, and possibly the moon. *Anael* is also responsible for ascending prayers from the first heaven and is one of the seven angels of creation.[2] *Anael* is also named in the *Lemegeton*, but as an angel and not a demon.[3]

[p. 303; 4], [304; 4] non-sensical goetic "angel tongues".

[p. 304–305; 5] *And let everyone who works in this art beware, both he who sends the spirit, and he to whom it was determined to go to, or else they should be killed in public or among others who are not of this art. ...* Despite what many believe, the demonic have no ability to take life. God is the only one who is able to determine when someone lives or dies. God's ability to determine when someone dies applies to both believers and non-believers. Job 14:5 tells us that "his days are determined, and the number of his months is with you, and you have appointed his limits that he cannot pass." (Job 14:5 ESV). Likewise, in Deuteronomy 32:39 Yahweh, through Moses, says "that I, even I, am he, and there is no god beside me; I kill and I make alive; I wound and I heal; and there is none that can deliver out of my hand." (Deuteronomy 32:39 ESV). The power over life and death is God's alone and belongs to no one else. Trithemius claiming that Anael will kill anyone that is not careful when using goetia is theologically fallacious. The idea that the demonic have the power to kill, apart from God's will, is goetic in origin and *anti*-biblical.

---

1. Michelle Belanger, *The Dictionary of Demons: Names of the Damned* (Woodbury, Minnesota: Llewellyn Publications, 2017), p. 32–33.
2. Rosemary Ellen Guiley Ph.D., *The Encyclopedia of Demons & Demonology* (New York, New York: Checkmark Books, 2009), p. 17.
3. Rosemary Ellen Guiley Ph.D., *The Encyclopedia of Angels: Second Edition* (New York, New York: Checkmark Books, 2004), p. 43.

Commentary Chapter II

Chapter III: Vequaniel

The hour of which is called Dansur/Danzur,[1] *and his spirit is the supreme commander, Vequaniel, who has under his authority twenty commanders, two hundred counts, and there is no number of servants.*

The third hour is called Dansur, whose supreme spirit and emperor is called Vequaniel, having under his command twenty generals and two hundred counts. The number of the servants is uncertain. The duty of these is general for all things, and they are quite ready and benevolent in all things, whatever are committed to them, and faithful and secure, nor are they unwilling to obey. But they can at least be called in public without injury or danger to the caller. For they love secrecy, like all the others who are in charge of the hours and their operations. I do not know the true names of all, but only of a few, which are enough for us to reveal them in this table.

Red.	Black.	R.	B.	R.	B.	R.
Asmiel	*Drelmech*	*Gemarij*	20.	20.	200.	200.
Persiel	*Sadiniel*	*Xantiel*	20.	20.	200.	200.
Mursiel	*Parniel*	*Seruiel*	20.	20.	200.	200.
Zoesiel	*Comadiel*	*Furiel*	20.	20.	200.	200.

In this table we have named four captains, eight counts, and one thousand seven hundred thirty of the unnumbered amounts of servants, who are sufficient for us for all the operations of this art at the third hour of the day. When, therefore, at this hour you wish to call the spirit to a friend for some message, no fewer than two captains at least, the same number of counts as their servants shall be called. But if you wish to call more or fewer, indeed you will be able, but it will be necessary to have a secret request with the universal emperor, without whose command they do not violate the order of the spirit. So, write on a new piece of paper, the character of the ascendant lord, moreover, in the order of the planners, with the sign of the twelfth house, in the manner that the training of the art requires. Write this secret prayer on the back of the paper.

Secret Prayer

Vequaniel, odiel mesrij reuoij sotiel mear iamy otiel aslofian yrsoti breotion drearij fable merusin.

The written secret prayer was merged with those things which are required by art. Say it in a low voice, so that no one overhears it and immediately the summoned spirits will come, whom you see, commit the secret to the superior, which you will easily recognize from their habit. Because he who is first among the rest of the spirits always appears crowned.

---

1. Uyl – the *dance.*

Let it be mysterious in any way.

Let it be a secret to you, to an absent friend, that the letters are not to be read to anyone, as a commission, nor the courier, or else, on any occasion, nor may price, corruption, or fear, betray you to the public. Call the spirit assigned to this hour, commit the mystery to him, fearing nothing. He will bear it faithfully.

You will shape the shores at will.

John Trithemius Arnold, Abbot of Spanheim. Bostia; To the Carmelites of Ghent, the Conphilosopher, greetings and charity.

Since I know you to be a lover of the arts of humanity, a devoted worshiper of the Christian faith, the greatest supporter of all philosophers, I gladly grant your requests, led by the wonderful pleasure of friendship. Behold, I am sending you a book of writers, pre-ordained for Catholic ecclesiastics and teachers, to encourage you, so that you may have something to entertain your mind. And the book of Hermetius, the books of Dionysius on spirits, and the great work of Euencius on winter questions, have been returned to me. May Christ deign to adorn the eyes of our hearts with the most fervent zeal of his love. May he make us love heavenly goods and teach us to hate self-loving honours stripped of our lowest desires, in so far as we may understand the most excellent art, the great secrets of nature, and have a continuous desire for philosophy, to purify our affections, by which we always establish the Catholic faith with honesty and morals. Hold on to a great word. You are a philosopher. Let go of everything and you will find to suspect the hour approaching death in so far as you are ready to meet it. Goodbye. April 3, 1500.

With each letter you received the seal with the character of Vequaniel, write the figure of the ascendant lord, and the twelfth house. with the rest that are required for the art in the new card, and on the back of it the secret prayer just mentioned, and immediately the spirit sent will appear visible, when you soon see him then say this song:

Song of the Secret Prayer

Fameron aprois liernoti stadiuear diuiel sauean Lamersy.

Having said this, receive the word from the mouth of the spirit without fear, because he is faithful enough. And be careful not to work in public in front of others.

Commentary: Chapter III

[p. 309; 1] *Vequaniel* ... Beyond what is mentioned in this chapter, there is not much information from outside sources about the angel or demon *Vequaniel. Vequaniel* is mentioned in the *Lemegeton,*[1] but no other information about the angel or demon is mentioned in that text.

[p. 309; 3], [p. 310; 5] non-sensical goetic "angel tongues".

[p. 310; 3] *the books of Dionysius on spirits.* ... The books of Pseudo-Dionysius, *Celestial Hierarchy* and *On the Divine Names and the Mystical Theology* are what Trithemius is referencing here. While these two books by Pseudo-Dionysius (we do not know who really wrote these books) are considered highly fallacious in their interpretation of the Bible, these two books have been main source texts by many angelologists throughout history.

1. Rosemary Ellen Guiley Ph.D., *The Encyclopedia of Angels: Second Edition* (New York, New York: Checkmark Books, 2004), p. 43.

COMMENTARY: CHAPTER III

[illegible]

[illegible]

[illegible]

[illegible]

Chapter IV: Vathmiel

The hour of which is called Elechym, and the supreme spirit of the hour is called Vathmiel, who has under his command ten counts and one hundred commanders. The number of servants is not certain, by whom the operation is done in the fourth hour.

The fourth hour of the day is called Elechym, whose highest angel is prepared, Vathmiel, who has under him appointed for this art of steganography the most named leaders, ten counts, but one hundred commanders, the number of servants is infinite. They have the duty of announcing in general all things secret, and they are very good, benevolent, and obedient to all things, every one of them are ordered. It is true that lovers of privacy greatly hate the commotion of men. So, take care, that having been appointed among others, who are not skilled in the art, you attempt to work something through them, for they would not easily approach the conspirators, and they would not leave without your own danger. Keep all that we command you, and you will make great progress in this knowledge.

Red.	Black.	R.	B.	R.	B.	R.
Ammyel	*Emarfiel*	*Iermiel*	10.	100.	100.	100.
Larmich	*Permiel*	*Thuroz*	10.	100.	100.	100.
Marfiel	*Queriel*	*Vanesiel*	10.	100.	100.	100.
Ormyel	*Strubiel*	*Zasuiel*	10.	100.	100.	100.
Zardiel	*Diuiel*	*Hermiel*	10.	100.	100.	100.

We have in this table five of the leaders of Vathmiel, ten of the leaders, and one thousand five hundred fifty servants, whose service is sufficient for us for all the operations of steganography until the fourth hour. Therefore, when you wish to work at this hour, write the character of the lord of the ascendant and the twelfth house with the rest on a new piece of paper, and on the back of it this mysterious prayer, as it should be.

Secret Prayer

Vathmiel adres rheareso raper rheotij venosi sayr fatiel cafa irsoti verotiel does ro fabel merusin

Then, after you have said those things which are customary to say, say the same secret prayer in a low voice, and immediately the summoned spirits will come, at least one leader and one count, with their servants ready to obey your commands.

The subject of privacy now.

It is a secret of any kind, great and very secret, of which you would like to know none at all except one. Call the appointed spirits of the hour, as many as you will, and commit the secret to the principal. Write letters, in whatever form you choose in which there is nothing secret, and which should not be seen by anyone at all.

John Trith. Abb. Spanish of the order of Saint Benedict, Rutgero Vencaius Sicambro, Canon of the order of the divine father Augustine Cœnobius Dametensis, St.

With the help of Christ, I resolved those things which you proposed to be paid to me. Well, you, who proposed, carry the opinion. I will briefly relate to you a wonderful thing that happened. Recently, a brother, a friend, also one, we did not look back, reported to me that a young man had been resurrected, referring to the raising of Christ from the dead. They have always existed ungrateful to Christ, those who suffered horribly and were known to be ungrateful by virtues, not by living well, and blinded by sins, they neglected future joys, pursuing the pleasures of the world, who cried out most bitterly, repenting of their negligence. We deserve these things, who have always been ungrateful to the redemption of humanity, Christians in name, Gentiles in action. We have always sought earthly comforts for the wretched, and so you receive the due retribution of eternal damnation. Alas, we who are most unhappy, why have we stumbled upon Christ? Why have we despised the cancellation of time? When the young man recovered, he reported to us many other things, which I am not able to write completely now, he is most hindered by important business. So, let us zealously follow the footsteps of Christ's brother, always giving thanks to our most gentle Saviour, asking him to forgive us the sins committed against us. Goodbye. Warming. April 3.

When he has received the letters to whom they are sent, an expert in the art, he observes the lord of the ascendant at the same hour, and the sign of the twelfth house, and writes their characters with the rest on paper, together with others that are required for the operation, and afterwards says the above-mentioned mysterious prayer, and saying these words in the spirit.

thulnear venean maueas fabelron

Having said these things, the sent spirit will approach, and faithfully and without danger will reveal the secret entrusted to him.

Commentary: Chapter IV

[p. 313; 1] *Vathmiel*, [or, *Vahrmiel*] ... Beyond what is mentioned in this chapter, there is not much information from outside sources about the angel or demon *Vathmiel*. *Vathmiel* is mentioned in the *Lemegeton* by the name *Vahrmiel*,[1] but no other information about the angel or demon is mentioned in that text.

[p. 313; 3], [p. 315; 4] non-sensical goetic "angel tongues".

[p. 314; 2] a *friend, also one, we did not look back, reported to me that a young man had been resurrected, referring to the raising of Christ from the dead.* ... This reference is not a literal raising of the dead, like Prosperity, WOF and NAR churches have been notorious for claiming to be able to do and always failing. When Trithemius is saying "had been resurrected" he is referring to a resurrection into salvation. That is why the raising of Christ from the dead is mentioned immediately afterwards.

[p. 314; 2] *Christians in name, Gentiles in action.* ... Paul says that there "is neither Jew nor Greek, there is neither slave nor free, there is no male and female, for you are all one in Christ Jesus." (Galatians 3:28 ESV) There is no difference between Jews and Gentiles anymore under Christ. The fact that people still believe there is a difference is one of the big problems in theological circles today. All people are now one people all of whom have been offered salvation. To believe there is still a difference between Jews and Gentiles is to continue to divide when Christ came to unify. The goetic suggestion behind this kind of division is continued in beliefs about Cain being a literal son of Satan and not Adam, or the current divisions between different cultural groups all over the world. We are one people and one human race. There are no longer any divisions.

[p. 314; 2] *So, let us zealously follow the footsteps of Christ's brother, always giving thanks to our most gentle Saviour, asking him to forgive us the sins committed against us.* ... Trithemius's flaw here is that *we* are required to forgive. We cannot ask Christ to forgive someone on our behalf. If someone repents, which is required *first*, then we are required to forgive. Getting someone else, including Christ, to forgive when we are not willing to ourselves is a meaningless and *anti*-biblical form of "forgiveness".

1. Rosemary Ellen Guiley Ph.D., *The Encyclopedia of Angels*: *Second Edition* (New York, New York: Checkmark Books, 2004), p. 43.

Chapter V: Sasquiel

The hour of which is called Fealech, and the supreme spirit and emperor is called Sasquiel, having under his command the greatest number of captains, ten counts, and one hundred servants.

The fifth hour of the day is called Fealech, and his spirit is named Sasquiel, a great and powerful emperor, who has under his dominion, among many leaders, ten counts, with their one hundred servants, assigned to the service of our various and most secret arts and this science. And it is to be noted that the captains are seldom called at the fifth hour for the operations of steganography, because they are not always necessary. Since the counts alone with the servants assigned to them are abundantly sufficient for us for all operations. However, if one should see some of the leaders, the power if he wills of them, he can call one, two, or more, and they will come without delay, who are sufficiently kind and ready to obey those who work.

Black.	Red.	B.	R.	R.	R.
Damiel	*Iameriel*	*Omerach*	10.	100.	1,000.
Araniel	*Futiniel*	*Lameros*	10.	100.	1,000.
Maroch	*Rameriel*	*Zachiel*	10.	100.	1,000.
Sarapiel	*Amisiel*	*Fustiel*	10.	100.	1,000.
Putifiel	*Vraniel*	*Camiel*	10.	100.	1,000.

Of the leaders of Sasquiel, we have already named five, and ten of the counts, and five thousand five hundred fifty of the servants, whose service is sufficient for all the operations of the present hour. So, when you wish to work steganography by any of the before mentioned at that hour of the day, write the character of the ascendant lord, the twelfth house with the rest, those required for the art on a clean sheet of paper, and on its back this secret prayer, in the way you know.

Secret Prayer

Sasquiel adres rhetroseti rosiel emelto satu olmeniel irsoti sauear nauediel liernoti chameson.

Having completed these, the rest, having joined the necessary things, say the conspiracy itself, as it should be. Immediately you will see the spirit whom you have called, visibly present, to whom you can safely commit the mystery.

The subject of the secret message.

Let it be a secret to us of some kind, to a friend, that we would wish no one to know it beyond him, let it be such that no letter can be safely committed, not even by a courier. Let us call one of the previously mentioned companions of Sasquiel, let us commit to him the secret, and let us attach letters signed in his character, and we shall be safe.

TENOR OF LETTERS TO CUSTOM.

John Trithemius, abbot of Spanheim, to his religious brother, Nicholas Baselius of Durckheim, the monk of Hirsaugiense, St.

Holy obedience, good brother, you neglect humility, the constitutions of the blessed are undermined. From the report of all who met successively, I learned that you had a good hatred of Zela, to forsake the rule of religion, Catholicism, and obedience, to occupy yourself with secular works and arts. Good brother, what are you doing? You have disturbed us, and foolish zealous bilinguals. You love hatred, bitterness, quarrels, contentions, you hate goodness, you are double-minded, contentious, and proud. What are you doing? The time has come to speedily, according to justice, zealously correct these negligence's of yours, and devotion to bitterness with the whips of humility, unless you run humbly to break us. We are compelled by duty to be zealous against all that activity attempting to undermine the Catholic faith and morals. Farewell from Spain. April in the year 1500.

When he received the letters, he to whom they were sent, an expert in the art, having known the character of Sasquiel, the foregoing, after the custom, let him say the abovementioned conspiracy, and immediately the spirit sent will appear and present himself visibly. When he sees this, he should immediately say these words:

Fabelmerusyn aueual vear plyan cralti penason.

Hearing these words, the spirit soon approaching will reveal the mystery.

Commentary: Chapter V

[p. 317; 1] *Sasquiel,* ... Beyond what is mentioned in this chapter, there is not much information from outside sources about the angel or demon *Sasquiel. Sasquiel* is mentioned in the *Lemegeton,*[1] but no other information about the angel or demon is mentioned in that text.

[p. 317; 3], [p. 318; 4] non-sensical goetic "angel tongues".

1. Rosemary Ellen Guiley Ph.D., *The Encyclopedia of Angels*: *Second Edition* (New York, New York: Checkmark Books, 2004), p. 43.

Chapter VI: Samiel

Whose hour is called Genapherym, and his spirit the supreme commander is called Samiel, who has under him one hundred ten generals and counts with many servants.

The sixth hour of the day is called Genapherym, and his angel is Samiel, great and powerful in his operations, who has under his command ten captains, one hundred counts, and five thousand five hundred fifty servants assigned to the ministry of various operations. Who for us, in all things which we intend to work with steganography at this hour, is sufficient.

Leaders, however, are rarely called, although they are ready and very willing to obey our commands, because their companions are accustomed to performing their duties to a great extent when they are often occupied in other magical experiments.

Black.	Red.	B.	R.	R.	R.
Arnebiel	*Gamyel*	*Nedabar*	10.	100.	100.
Charuch	*Ienotriel*	*Permon*	10.	100.	100.
Medusiel	*Sameon*	*Brasiel*	10.	100.	100.
Nathmiel	*Trasiel*	*Camosiel*	10.	100.	100.
Pemiel	*Xamyon*	*Euador*	10.	100.	100.

We have here named five of the commanders of the Samians, ten of the counts, and five thousand five hundred fifty of the servants, by whom the steganography is performed at the sixth hour of the day. So, when you wish to work through these spirits, let it be entirely in a secret place. If you wish to call one or more leaders, let it be in your power, although there is no need, because the counts are sufficient for us to be comfortable with everything. So, write on a clean chart the usual characters of the planets and signs, and on the back of it the plot.

Secret Prayer

Samiel asiel thebrean pothijr ersoty mear pornys layr moas, famerosyn.

Then, after making the preliminaries, say the same conspiracy in the manner you know and immediately the spirit called will be present, ready, and eager for everything, whom you send to a friend far or near, so that he can bear the secret.

Privacy Policy

Any secret you will have, to whom, in the art of steganography you can safely send an expert in the art of steganography through the spirit of Samiel at the sixth hour of the day.

The form of the letters, as you like.

Praying with humble lamentations, we shall obtain the grace of forgiveness with groanings, and we shall receive freedom from our sins. People who constantly repent will receive joy with merit, adorning Catholic faithfulness with works of justice, they will keep the law of kindness of Catholic praise. All will be delivered by the most righteous Saviour, who will forgive and forgive sins to those who seek indulgence, and only those who follow the path of the Catholic religion will perceive the joys of exaltedness. The good power of liberty to those who block the path of the law, they will triumph gloriously, they will obtain bright happiness in the light of the Trinity. In the year 1500, April John Trithemius Abbot wrote this chapter.

When he received these letters, he to whom they were sent, already an expert in the art, having said the foregoing, let him say the mysterious prayer:

Charmes pormeniel vear saseuij liernoty noty ersy melron.

With these words, as is prescribed in the art, the spirit will come nearer, and will faithfully and privately reveal the secret entrusted to him.

Commentary: Chapter VI

[p. 321; 1] *Samiel*, ... Beyond what is mentioned in this chapter, there is not much information from outside sources about the angel or demon *Samiel*. *Samiel* is mentioned in the *Lemegeton*.[1] One other reference in *The Sybilline Oracles* is that *Samiel* is one of the five angels who lead souls to judgment.[2]

[p. 321; 4], [p. 322; 3] non-sensical goetic "angel tongues".

[p. 322; 1] *only those who follow the path of the Catholic religion will perceive the joys of exaltedness*. ... Considering the goetic theology of the Roman Catholic Church, the joys of "exaltedness" will not be given to those who openly defy the commands of the Bible to not be involved in the occult. The Vatican II council and also Pope Francis have made universalist statements that salvation is open to all no matter what form of "God" they worship. The statement here by Trithemius shows once more that when salvation is taken out of the hands of Christ, and put into goetic spirits like Mary, or human agencies such as the Roman Catholic Church, deviances in soteriology will continue to get worse over time.

1. Rosemary Ellen Guiley Ph.D., *The Encyclopedia of Angels*: *Second Edition* (New York, New York: Checkmark Books, 2004), p. 64.

2. Rosemary Ellen Guiley Ph.D., *The Encyclopedia of Angels*: *Second Edition* (New York, New York: Checkmark Books, 2004), p. 309.

Commentary: Chapter VI

Chapter VII: Barquiel/Barachiel/Barakel/ Barkiel/Barakiel/Barqiel/Barchiel/Barbiel

Whose hour is called Hamarym, and his spirit Barquiel, having under his command ten captains, one hundred counts, and servants, but their number is not certain to me.

The seventh hour of the day is called Hamarym, and his angel is called Barquiel, who has under his command ten captains, one hundred counts, and a great and uncertain number of servants. The services of all of whom, by their turns and orders, are abundantly sufficient for us for all the operation of steganography at the seventh hour of the day. But when you wish to work by the spirit of the previously mentioned emperor in the seventh hour: you will require no fewer voices than at least one leader and one count, who have servants assigned to them, each in his order. But you should have at hand the names of some of the leaders and counts through whom you may work. Pay attention to the table below.

Red.	Black.	R.	B.	R.	B.
Abrasiel	*Harmiel*	*Pasriel*	10.	10.	100.
Farmos	*Nastrus*	*Venesiel*	10.	10.	100.
Nestorii	*Varmay*	*Euarym*	10.	10.	100.
Manuel	*Tulmas*	*Drufiel*	10.	10.	100.
Sagiel	*Crosiel*	*Kathos*	10.	10.	100.

Here you now have those named from the leaders five, from the counts ten, and numbered from the order of six hundred servants. So, when you will want to work through them, write on a clean piece of paper the characters of the lord of the twelfth ascendant house with the rest of the custom, and on its back, you write this secret prayer according to the rules of art, as you know.

Secret Prayer

Lamedon mosco vrsoty tharuean: dayr Lays emel thebrean rasoty bamerson.

Then, having joined those things which are to be joined according to the custom of the art, say the mysterious prayer itself with a strong intention, as it should be, and immediately the spirits called will appear visible. The secret is not a count but a leader's commission, unless perhaps you have called a count without a leader, which, although I do not deny that it can be done, yet according to the laws of the art, at least one leader with his companions is to be called as you will.

Argument of secrecy, as you wish.

Let it be a mystery to you and to a friend that you would not wish to have in common with any other. As a result, neither letters nor couriers are to be trusted, because fraud can intervene in both. Call of the spirits just mentioned, as many as you will. Commit the secret to the superior, fearing nothing, because they are good and faithful in all things.

LET THE FORM OF THE LETTERS BE AS DESIRED.

John Trithemius, Abbot of Spain, gives an informal greeting to the valiant soldier Henry de Bunano, with the most studious philosopher. he says:

I had lent you my books on the condition that you should restore them, my dear soldier Bunane. But behold, you have not restored those which you ought to have returned in short order. You are doing contrary to the law which the Catholic faith has sanctioned concerning the promise. Do not delay what you have promised to pay to all. It is not fitting for a good and honourable man, born to great and noble parents, to violate a promise. But you had promised to restore it with the utmost care. It is as Leuita's promise to defer to Calendas Grecias. Have I not waited long enough with great benevolence? It is most shameful to promise the greatest and to pay the least. Good faith adorns a soldier. It is a graver crime to deny a guaranteed promise. Now the constitution of the Christian law commands to keep a promise, to repay a loan, and what you desire to be done to yourself, you must also willingly do to others. I will send out my books, which I had adapted to your request, and I will release the longer excuses which you sent to Calendas Grecias instead. You hold my mind in pieces. Consider your name honourable and the race of Buna Wensii, send me my volumes. Farewell from Spain. The ninth of April. In the year of the Lord 1500.

When you have received these letters, or any others, from him who sent the spirit to you, having known the sign of Barquiel, observe at the same hour the lord of the ascendant, and write his character with the rest on a clean piece of paper, and read the secret prayer written on the back privately, as it should be. And immediately the messenger will appear, whom you will soon see, and say these words to him.

Mefarim burne; theor alueas casuean cralti lierto aply charmoys.

Having said these things, the sent spirit, approaching nearer, will reveal to you the secret entrusted to him faithfully. But see that you are strong, steadfast, and fearless in everything.

Commentary: Chapter VII

[p. 325; 1] *Barquiel* [or, *Barachiel, Barakel, Barakiel, Barkiel, Barqiel, Barchiel, Barbiel*] ... A demon that is said to be the ruler of lighting and also to rule the planet Jupiter. This is appropriate considering Jupiter's association with the Roman Jupiter, the Greek Zeus who had the power of a lightning bolt. *Barquiel* is also believed to be one of the four chief seraphim, the ruler of confessors and an angel called on for luck with gambling.[1] Barquiel is also mentioned in the *Lemegeton*.[2]

[p. 325; 3], [p. 326; 5] non-sensical goetic "angel tongues".

[p. 326; 3] *You are doing contrary to the law which the Catholic faith has sanctioned concerning the promise. ...* Interestingly, Trithemius here appeals to Catholic law rather than the command from Christ to let "what you say be simply 'Yes' or 'No'; anything more than this comes from evil." (Matthew 5:37 ESV) The compromising of Christ's commands here by Bunane should be enough to convict him. Instead, Trithemius appeals to a fallacious authority in the Roman Catholic Church. The Bible should be enough here. For this devout Roman Catholic, the goetic Trithemius, the Bible is not enough.

1. Rosemary Ellen Guiley Ph.D., *The Encyclopedia of Angels: Second Edition* (New York, New York: Checkmark Books, 2004), p. 64.

2. Guiley, *Angels*, p. 43.

COMMENTARY CHAPTER VII

Chapter VIII: Osmadiel

Whose hour is called Janfanym, and his angel is called Osmadiel, who has under his command ten commanders, one hundred counts, and an uncertain number of servants.

The eighth hour of the day is called Jafanym, and its principal spirit is called Osmadiel, according to Picatrix in magic, who has under his command ten captains, one hundred counts, and innumerable servants assigned not only to the operation of our steganography, but also to many magical experiments. And Solomon the Jew, surnamed Hermes, in his book on the nature of spirits, says that all these, obedient and subject to the first-named Osmadiel, leaders and companions, were likely to come in various transformations at the will of the worker, just as they were commanded by the worker. But let us now mention the names of some.

Red.	Black.	R.	B.	R.	B.	R.
Sarfiel	*Demarot*	*Mariel*	10.	10.	100.	100.
Amalym	*Ianofiel*	*Remasyn*	10.	10.	100.	100.
Chroel	*Larfuty*	*Theoriel*	10.	10.	100.	100.
Mesial	*Vemael*	*Framion*	10.	10.	100.	100.
Lantrhotz	*Thribiel*	*Ermiel*	10.	10.	100.	100.

Of the five leaders and of the ten counts we have already named in the board, who are sufficient for us for all the operations of this hour. And when you wish to work through them in steganography, write on a clean sheet of paper with the usual characters and mysterious prayers, and first of all attaching them, say the written secret prayer itself, which is like this:

Secret Prayer

Osmodael aneor ersoty neas, hays layr Caphrayn thelreas mear penarsy.

When this song of secret prayer is said, the spirits will be summoned, ready and obedient to everything. The commission of the secret leader, not the count, unless he is absent, because he must always be recommended to the chief among those who come.

Argument of privacy to the agreement.

Let it be a mystery to us, (that we wish to know a friend who is absent far away) and such that we do not wish to come to the notice of anyone else, and it may often happen. Then do not let either the carrier reveal the mystery on any occasion, or let the letters reach foreign hands. We will work, and through the spirit we will be secure.

John Trithemius Abbot Spanish of the order of Saint Blessed Lord Conrad Abb. Saints Stephen Herbipolensi, S.D.

A rumor went out about the Abbot of Lympurge, that he had dismissed his brother John of Rielsdorf, a faithful man, and most expert in temporal matters, and that he had introduced new Pantimoran monks, and himself had deputed officials to him. I am greatly surprised at the fact that it was useless. But when I recall the custom of the Limburgians, I do not know what to say. They are indeed temporal, and therefore they let go of the faithful man, because he recounted their deeds, who ought to have thanked our saviour Jesus Christ for the faithfulness of such a brother, who was able to reveal their needs. Evil sinners, why do you repel a good and necessary helper? What shall I say? I do not praise the withdrawal of such a useful brother, and most expert in temporal matters, who had come to the Limpurgians as soon as possible. I deeply regret that the monks of Limburg have thus lost the best man, and the monks, who have absolutely no power in temporal matters, have been appointed as financiers. Machari Abba, this was not the way a man should be. At first you praised, but now you reject a man who is much needed by you, and who is nowhere to be put off. I confess that if Christ had given him to me, as befits a Christian, I would now give the greatest thanks. I would take care that he should never depart. But you, being ungrateful to Christ, chose to let go a faithful man, exhausted by the foolish counsel of the stupid, or else it should be seen that there was hope of recovery in your deserted affairs. From Spain. April 1500

When he has received these letters or any others, sealed with the sign of Osmadiel, he to whom they are sent, already an expert in the art, with the opening statements, shall say the prescribed secret prayer, and as soon the sent spirit appears visible, whom you will see, say:

Menason aproysy elmano thulneas assierto mauear veneas cralnoti permason.

His having said this, the spirit of the messenger will reveal the mystery to you.

COMMENTARY: CHAPTER VIII

[p. 329; 1] *Osmadiel* ... Beyond what is mentioned in this chapter, there is not much information from outside sources about the angel or demon *Osmadiel. Osmadiel* is mentioned in the *Lemegeton,*[1] but no other information about the angel or demon is mentioned in that text.

[p. 329; 1] *according to Picatrix in magic. ... Picatrix* is an originally Arabic astrological and talismanic book written in the 11th century. Different modern versions of this text have been translated from the Arabic and the Latin text. The Latin text was a reconstruction from a Spanish translation that Trithemius most likely used. Current translations have no reference to the name of Osmadiel or any variants of that name.

[p. 329; 1] *And Solomon the Jew, surnamed Hermes, in his book on the nature of spirits, says that all these, obedient and subject to the first-named Osmadiel. ...* While Osmadiel is named in *Part 3* of the *Lemegeton*, or *The Lesser Key of Solomon*, we know that the *Lemegeton* is a later goetic work. Trithemius may have had access to manuscripts that fallaciously claimed to be written by Solomon, but if such texts did exist, they are now missing or destroyed. No other historical works, that have survived through history, that are falsely claimed to have been written by Solomon mention the angel or demon Osmadiel.

[p. 329; 3], [p. 330; 3] non-sensical goetic "angel tongues".

1. Rosemary Ellen Guiley Ph.D., *The Encyclopedia of Angels*: *Second Edition* (New York, New York: Checkmark Books, 2004), p. 43.

Commentary Chapter VIII

[illegible]

[illegible]

[illegible]

[illegible]

[illegible]

[illegible]

Chapter IX: Quabriel

Whose hour is called Karron, and the name of its highest angel is Quabriel, having under his authority ten commanders and one hundred counts, but the number of servants is not determined.

The ninth hour of the day is called Karron, and its principal spirit is called Quabriel, who has under his authority many and almost innumerable leaders, counts, and serfs, and to whom are assigned to the service of this art of our steganography from the ten leaders and from the one hundred counts who are assigned servants that they have many of in their ranks. In the first order there are ten, in the second twenty, in the third thirty, in the fourth forty, in the fifth five hundred, in the sixth six hundred, in the seventh seven hundred, in the eighth one thousand and eighty, in the ninth ninety thousand. All ranks are called spirits, and if they were called, not all, but some, with their leaders and companions, were likely to come according to the command of the emperor. And Raziel the great said in his book[1] on royalty and transformations, that the number of these spirits is the greatest, and they keep their orders most diligently in all ministries and offices. And Solomon Hermes the Jew says of the nature of spirits that these usually appear in that form, in which they work in the art described by his will. But now let us explain the names of some leaders and committees.

Red.	Black.	R.	B.	R.	B.	R.
Astroniel	*Kranos*	*Trubas*	10.	10.	100.	100.
Charmy	*Menas*	*Xermiel*	10.	10.	100.	100.
Pamory	*Brasiel*	*Lameson*	10.	10.	100.	100.
Damyel	*Nefarym*	*Zaznor*	10.	10.	100.	100.
Nadriel	*Zoymiel*	*Iandiel*	10.	10.	100.	100.

Here we have already named five commanders, ten counts, and numbered six hundred fifty of his servants appointed, who will be sufficient for us. And when, at the ninth hour of the day, you wish to work through these spirits, observe the lord of the ascendant, and write on a clean paper those things which are prescribed according to the instruction of the art, and on his back the mysterious prayer.

Quabriel, odiel, amear, cayn alco mean chyr pareos payr peray, thubro menasry.

Then, after opening statements as usual, say the secret prayer itself, as is ordered in the art, and immediately the summoned spirits will be present, in whatever form you choose, ready and faithful to everything. Entrust the secret to the most important spirit.

1. Uyl – Most likely referring to the 13th century book ספר רזיאל המלאך (Sefer Raziel HaMalackh) which has only been found in Latin so far and is called *Liber Razielis Archangeli*, or *The Book of Raziel the* [*Arch*] *Angel*.

Privacy Policy.

Let it be a secret to us, whatever it may be to a friend, that which we wish to be most secret, and to be revealed to no one but himself in any way. So, let us call one or two of the previously mentioned captains and companions, according to the establishment of the art, and let us commit to a better secret.

Let us form the letters at will.

John Three times. Abbot of Spain Ord. St. Ben. To the Religious Father, John Hugh the Guardian, of the Friars Minor of Saint Francis in Creucenach, Health and charity.

Religiously venerable father, I know that you willingly grant everything adapted to your friends. So, I humbly beg you, in so far as, in view of Catholic faithfulness, you do not bring your zealous brothers detained with us any longer with the utmost charity. For it was necessary for them, begging me, to remain. It was a glorious joy for us. We all rejoiced without fault. We rejoiced in the lord's spiritual joy, giving thanks to the Almighty God with zeal for good. What, I pray you, is more religious than this conversation? Where nothing is said to be idle, nothing is unjustly zealous, Christ Jesus the saviour of all may make us rejoice in eternal glory. The glorious zealots of the righteous acts set nothing before the truth. We rejoice with holy joy, praying that you receive the brothers we already mentioned in peace, and put away all bitterness of jealousy. Farewell from Spain. 3rd of April in the year of the Lord 1500.

When he has received these or any other letters, written in the character of Quabriel, already being an expert in the art, having said them, let him say the determined secret prayer, whereupon you shall soon see the spirit destined, whom he will see, and let him say these words:

> Mesraym pasloriel vear reneam cralty thio phroysy ma mear hamorsy.

Having said these things, the sent spirit will calmly approach you and tell you the secret mission.

Commentary: Chapter IX

[p. 333; 1] *Quabriel* … Beyond what is mentioned in this chapter, there is not much information from outside sources about the angel or demon *Quabriel*. *Quabriel* is mentioned in the *Lemegeton*,[1] but no other information about the angel or demon is mentioned in that text.

[p. 333; 1] *And Raziel* […] *And Solomon Hermes* … While references are mentioned, there is no spirit by the name of Quabriel in either of these texts. Quabriel is not mentioned in *The Book of Raziel the Angel* or any fallaciously ascribed Solomonic text written before this book.

[p. 333; 3], [p. 334; 6] non-sensical goetic "angel tongues".

1. Rosemary Ellen Guiley Ph.D., *The Encyclopedia of Angels: Second Edition* (New York, New York: Checkmark Books, 2004), p. 43.

Chapter X: Oriel

At the hour of which Lamarhon was resurrected, and his commander was called the supreme spirit Oriel, who has under his commandment many leaders, counts, and servants.

The tenth hour of the day is called Lamarhon, and his chief angel is called Oriel, a great and powerful emperor, who, according to Solomon the Jew, has many leaders under his command, through whom there are wonderful experiments in magic at the tenth hour of the day. Now those ten captains, and those counts, who are assigned to the operation of steganography, with their servants, have ranks among themselves. In the first row there are ten, in the second twenty, in the third thirty, in the fourth forty, in the fifth five hundred, in the sixth six hundred, in the seventh seven hundred, in the eighth eight hundred, in the ninth nine hundred, and in the tenth one thousand. But from the last we are content to assume only five leaders in our operations, if it pleases him to know the names of more, let him call one of those named on the board, and question him, and he will hear whatever he wants. And as much as he wills to know, he will know perfectly from that.

Red.	Black.	R.	B.	R.	B.	R.
Armosy	*Lemur*	*Xantros*	10.	10.	100.	100.
Drabiel	*Ormas*	*Basilon*	10.	10.	100.	100.
Penaly	*Charny*	*Nameron*	10.	10.	100.	100.
Mesriel	*Zazyor*	*Kranoti*	10.	10.	100.	100.
Choreb	*Naueron*	*Alfrael*	10.	10.	100.	100.

We have here five of the chiefs of Oriel and ten of the counts, together with the servants assigned to them by their turns, in the number of one thousand one hundred, who are sufficient for us for all the operations of this hour. But when you wish to work through them at this hour of the day, after the usual opening statements, and the writings being written on clean paper, and with this secret prayer arranged on his back, do the rest, as you know.

Secret Prayer

Oriel burnadiel irasmny crismean pormy ersoti amear medusen.

After you have completed this secret prayer according to the correct instruction of the art, you will see the leader present with the other spirits called, to whom you will entrust the secret.

Constitution of Arcana.

Let him be a friend to whom we wish good. We fear that he should be supplanted and surrounded by someone. So, we want to be bold. We cannot do so with open words through messengers, or through letters, should they fall into the hands of anyone, we dare not want to know these things. So, let us be safe, and let our secret always remain a secret. Let us call upon the spirit to guide one to the least of the previously mentioned. He comes, he obeys, he delivers the message faithfully.

THE LETTER WILL BE FORMED AS REQUESTED.

John Tritthem. Abbot of Spain He salutes Henri de Banau, the Golden Knight, a distinguished philosopher and mathematician.

You are very interested in the arts of humanity. I think you will be glad, very much, that you have found a new study partner. He who will present these letters to you is a man of great learning, a supreme philosopher, a most subtle arithmetician, a most eloquent speaker, and most excellently learned in all things. He speaks very elegantly, and Tulliana shines with fluency. If I had not been your best friend, I would have kept the man completely, since I have experienced him as a very learned philosopher. I am most pleased with you that you gratefully receive the philosopher whom I am sending you with a singular love. Would that all our students were like that, who despise noble knowledge with a timid heart. This man's study of philosophy and other sciences, of the highest and most profound nature, is constantly scrutinized, continually treated, and most acutely penetrated. So, you remember to treat the man Heinrich Bunavv with a liberal face for Christ. Farewell from Spain. 2nd of November in the year of our Lord 1500.

When a friend has received the letters to whom they are sent, an expert in the science of steganography, let him do all that is to be done according to the art, and join the ordered secret prayer, as is customary. And when he sees the sent spirit present, let him say these words to him who is superior among the spirits.

Camyn aparsy aslotiel omear reneas vean triamy cralty penason.

When these are brought forth, the spirit will immediately approach nearer, and will reveal to him the secret.

Commentary: Chapter X

[p. 337; 1] *Oriel* … Beyond what is mentioned in this chapter, there is not much information from outside sources about the angel or demon *Oriel. Oriel* is mentioned in the *Lemegeton*,[1] but no other information about the angel or demon is mentioned in that text.

[p. 337; 1] *according to Solomon the Jew* … Oriel is not mentioned in any fallaciously ascribed Solomonic text other than the *Lemegeton* which was written after this book

[p. 337; 3], [p. 338; 4] non-sensical goetic "angel tongues".

1. Rosemary Ellen Guiley Ph.D., *The Encyclopedia of Angels: Second Edition* (New York, New York: Checkmark Books, 2004), p. 43.

CHAPTER XI: BARIEL

At the hour of which Maneloim was resurrected, and his supreme commander is called Bariel, who has under his rule many princes, leaders, counts, and servants.

The eleventh hour of the day is called Maneloim, and his chief angel is called Bariel, who, as Hermes the Jew writes, has many under his command of the spirit, through whom wonders are wrought at the eleventh hour of the day, in various experiments. Many of these were assigned to the operation of steganography through their ranks. In the first order there are ten, in the second twenty, in the third thirty, in the fourth forty, in the fifth five hundred, in the sixth six hundred, in the seventh seven hundred, in the eighth eight hundred, in the ninth nine hundred, in the tenth one thousand. They are sent to the service of this art, among whom are captains and counts with their servants, very many, whose names it is not easy to find out, it is not even necessary, when it is sufficient to know the names of a few, and working in the art always from the relation of one spirit to know the names of many others can. And note that, according to Raziel, all these spirits form and transform themselves at the will of the worker. So, in whatever form he wishes to see them, he commands before the mysterious prayer in the manner that art dictates, and he obeys him most readily in all things. But now let us explain the names of some that are sufficient for us.

Red.	Black.	R.	B.	R.	B.	R.
Almarizel	*Menafiel*	*Almas*	10.	10.	100.	100.
Prasiniel	*Demasor*	*Perman*	10.	10.	100.	100.
Chadros	*Omary*	*Comial*	10.	10.	100.	100.
Turmiel	*Helmas*	*Temas*	10.	10.	100.	100.
Lamiel	*Zemoel*	*Lanifiel*	10.	10.	100.	100.

Here we have already named fifteen of the spirits of Bariel, of whom five are commanders and ten counts, who have a number of one thousand one hundred servants, who are sufficient for our operations of eleven hours a day in steganography. So, when you wish to work through these spirits, observe the lord of the ascendant with the rest, according to what we have said above, and write this secret message with the others on clean paper, as you die in this knowledge.

SECRET PRAYER

Bariel mylan theory madruson alfayr dreschym taparoys mear moas layr penason.

Having made promises, tell the secret message as it should be, and immediately the spirits will appear whom you have called. Commit to them whatever secret you have.

THE CONSTITUTION OF ANY MYSTERY.

It is a mystery to us to a friend, or to any other expert in our art, that neither through letters nor other means, that we can express it by means of a letter, because we fear danger on every side. So, we call on the spirit, we commend to that spirit the most important secret, and we are safe in all things.

THE CONTENT OF THE LETTERS AS AGREED.[1]

John Trith. Abbot of Spain of the order of the divine Benedict, brother of Quirinus, monk of Corbeiensi in France, St.

Concerning the mother of the Ever-Virgin Mary, I transmit my prayer, which you recently requested to Quirine. O most kind mother Anna, the most radiant parent of the Virgin Mary. You are the most faithful helper of all who call on you. You are the noble refuge of those who seek you, the quiet blessing of holiness. Salutation to the poor, brought to you by the most gentle consoler of the groaning, the most beautiful, the most beautiful storehouse of virtue. Alas for the sad unrevived Judas, the most salutary medicine of the sick, the most famous promoter of the faithful Christians, obtain forgiveness for us in sorrow, appease the terrible judge Christ. Intercede for your servants, that we may obtain happiness, we ask you by your intercession to receive the poor. Amen. 8th of April. In the year of the Lord 1500.

When he has received the letters to whom they are sent as an expert in the art, let him pay attention first of all to the character of the hours attached to the letters. When he knows this, he will work through the lord of the ascendant of the hour in which he received the letters, with the rest of the instructions in the art. Then let him add the prescribed prayer, in the manner and order in which it is necessary, and soon the sent spirits will appear. Those whom you see, these words are to be said to the chief among them:

chamerusin maslotiel vear reneas liernoty trismy penason.

When these words have been spoken to the spirit superior among others, who is easily recognized by his habit and crown, and always precedes others, he will soon reveal the secret to his ear.

1. Uyl – There was a symbol from the original Stenganographia which I did not include after the Secret Prayer. If you wish to see what the symbol was, there are plenty of free copies in the original Latin online for the reader to refer to.

Commentary: Chapter XI

[p. 341; 1] *Bariel* ... Beyond what is mentioned in this chapter, there is not much information from outside sources about the angel or demon *Bariel*. *Bariel* is mentioned in the *Lemegeton*,[1] but no other information about the angel or demon is mentioned in that text.

[p. 341; 1] *as Hermes the Jew writes... according to Raziel* ... Bariel is not mentioned in any fallaciously ascribed Solomonic text other than the *Lemegeton* which was written after this book. *The Book of the Angel Raziel* also does not mention any angel or demon by the name of Bariel.

[p. 341; 3], [p. 342; 5] non-sensical goetic "angel tongues".

[p. 342; 3] *Concerning the mother of the Ever-Virgin Mary, I transmit my prayer, which you recently requested to Quirine. O most kind mother Anna, the most radiant parent of the Virgin Mary. You are the most faithful helper of all who call on you.* [...] *Intercede for your servants, that we may obtain happiness, we ask you by your intercession to receive the poor.* ... Anna being the mother of Mary comes from a book fallaciously attributed to James called *The Infancy Gospel of James*.

> And behold an angel of the Lord appeared, saying unto her: Anna, Anna, the Lord hath hearkened unto thy prayer, and thou shalt conceive and bear, and thy seed shall be spoken of in the whole world. And Anna said: As the Lord my God liveth, if I bring forth either male or female, I will bring it for a gift unto the Lord my God, and it shall be ministering unto him all the days of its life.
>
> And behold there came two messengers saying unto her: Behold Ioacim thy husband cometh with his flocks: for an angel of the Lord came down unto him saying: Ioacim, Ioacim, the Lord God hath hearkened unto thy prayer. Get thee down hence, for behold thy wife Anna hath conceived. And Ioacim gat him down and called his herdsmen saying: Bring me hither ten lambs without blemish and without spot, and they shall be for the Lord my God; and bring me twelve tender calves, and they shall be for the priests and for the assembly of the elders; and an hundred kids for the whole people.
>
> And behold Ioacim came with his flocks, and Anna stood at the gate and saw Ioacim coming, and ran and hung upon his neck, saying: Now know I that the Lord God hath greatly blessed me: for behold the widow is no more a widow, and she that was childless shall conceive. And Ioacim rested the first day in his house.
>
> And on the morrow he offered his gifts, saying in himself: If the Lord God be reconciled unto me, the plate that is upon the forehead of the priest will make it manifest unto me. And Ioacim offered his gifts and looked earnestly upon the plate of the priest when he went up unto the altar of the Lord, and he saw no sin in himself. And Ioacim said: Now know I that the Lord is become propitious unto me and hath forgiven all my sins. And he went down from the temple of the Lord justified, and went unto his house.
>
> And her months were fulfilled, and in the ninth month Anna brought forth. And she said

---

1. Rosemary Ellen Guiley Ph.D., *The Encyclopedia of Angels: Second Edition* (New York, New York: Checkmark Books, 2004), p. 43.

unto the midwife: What have I brought forth? And she said: A female. And Anna said: My soul is magnified this day, and she laid herself down. And when the days were fulfilled, Anna purified herself and gave suck to the child and called her name Mary.

And day by day the child waxed strong, and when she was six months old her mother stood her upon the ground to try if she would stand; and she walked seven steps and returned unto her bosom. And she caught her up, saying: As the Lord my God liveth, thou shalt walk no more upon this ground, until I bring thee into the temple of the Lord. And she made a sanctuary in her bedchamber and suffered nothing common or unclean to pass through it. And she called for the daughters of the Hebrews that were undefiled, and they carried her hither and thither. (The Infancy Gospel of James 4:1–6:1)[2]

We see here from this fallacious *Infancy Gospel of James* that Mary was born in as equally a divine way as Jesus was. The divination of Mary after seeing the text from *The Infancy Gospel of James* as a "Goddess" above (pp. 183–185, this volume) should not be surprising. That Mary never even touched the ground, so that she would not be unclean, puts Mary as a divine being *above* Christ himself. Anna and Ioachim are never mentioned as the parents of Mary by any biblical or legitimate sources. Hippolytus of Rome and Origen of Alexandria both refer to the book and tenets of James as a gnostic source. Many are undecided on whether this infancy gospel is gnostic instead arguing that Hippolytus and Origen might be referring to the *Gospel of Thomas* instead.

Looking at the statements by Hippolytus we see what Gnostics of that day believed.

But since it so appears expedient, let us begin first from the public worshippers of the serpent. The Naasseni call the first principle of the universe a Man, and that the same also is a Son of Man; and they divide this man into three portions. For they say one part of him is rational, and another psychical, but a third earthly. And they style him Adamas, and suppose that the knowledge appertaining to him is the originating cause of the capacity of knowing God. And the Naassene asserts that all these rational, and psychical, and earthly qualities have retired into Jesus, and that through Him these three substances simultaneously have spoken unto the three genera of the universe. These allege that there are three kinds of existence—angelic, psychical, and earthly; and that there are three churches—angelic, psychical, and earthly; and that the names for these are—chosen, called, and captive. These are the heads of doctrine advanced by them, as far as one may briefly comprehend them. They affirm that James, the brother of the Lord, delivered these tenets to Mariamne, by such a statement belying both.[3]

The Naasseni were a known gnostic sect and the Naassene do claim that a fallacious James delivered heretical tenets to Mariamne, or Mary. While these gnostic connections are questionable, it does raise the true origins of the Roman Catholic "traditions" that are claimed about Mary. Hippolytus may have a strong point and that point shows that many of the Mariology traditions held onto by the Roman Catholic Church are very possibly gnostic in origin.

That Anna is believed to be able to intercede for anyone, as Mary is, shows that the divinization of Mary goes back into her ancestors according to Roman Catholics as well. Since Mary is not in fact of the line of David, and neither is Anna, this claim is fallacious in every way. Joseph was the descendant of David and Jesus was the Messianic fulfillment of that promise. That promise ended with Jesus when Jesus was resurrected and all authority

2. Montague Rhodes James, ed., *The Apocryphal New Testament: Being the Apocryphal Gospels, Acts, Epistles, and Apocalypses* (Oxford, England: Clarendon Press, 1924), pp. 40–41.

3. Hippolytus of Rome, "The Refutation of All Heresies," in *Fathers of the Third Century: Hippolytus, Cyprian, Novatian, Appendix, ed. Alexander Roberts, James Donaldson, and A. Cleveland Coxe, trans. J. H. MacMahon, vol. 5, The Ante-Nicene Fathers* (Buffalo, New York: Christian Literature Company, 1886), pp. 141–142.

was given to him. (Matthew 28:18) Anna, and especially Mary, never had that authority or ancestory to make any claim of that sort. The website *Got Quesionts* attempts to claim that Mary was a descendant of David but as their own website claims, "Luke's genealogy shows that Heli, whom we *assume* to be Mary's father, was a direct descendant of Judah, not Levi." (italics mine)[4] The use of "assume" here is a big hermeneutical problem. *Got Questions* claims that Elizabeth and Mary are being identified as descendants of Levi because the daughters of a family took the ancestery of their father. However, this is also true of the wife. The wife of a husband in a Jewish family at that time, became an official part of that tribe and family. Therefore, even if Elizabeth was of the line of Levi as Luke 1:5 states in "in the days of Herod, king of Judea, there was a priest named Zechariah, of the division of Abijah. And he had a wife from the daughters of Aaron, and her name was Elizabeth," (Luke 1:5 ESV) and Mary is identifed as a member of Elizabeth's family in Luke 1:36, "And behold, your relative Elizabeth in her old age has also conceived a son, and this is the sixth month with her who was called barren," it does not mean that Mary was genetically of the family of David. Since Mary and Elizabeth are identifed as relatives, and Mary would have been considered of the line of Judah, and the family of David by marrying Joseph, it means that Jesus is genetically of the line of David *because* of Jospeh. *Got Questions* own admission of making an assumption to connect Mary to David is a big part of the problem in proving that Mary was genetically connected to David.

4. Author Unknown, "What was Mary's lineage?" *Got Questions*, accessed November 15, 2024, https://www.gotquestions.org/Mary-lineage.html.

Book II Commentary Chapter XVII

was given to him (Matthew 1:16; Luke 3:23), and especially Mary, [illegible] with no intention or ambition to make any claim of that sort [illegible]. [illegible] claim that Mary was a descendant of David [illegible] their own [illegible] claims [illegible] that Heli [illegible] 3:23 [illegible] of Judah, not Levi. [illegible] there is a [illegible] claim that [illegible] Mary are being identified as descendants of Levi because the daughters of [illegible] family [illegible] however, [illegible] also [illegible] family [illegible] Luke states [illegible] "In the days of Herod, king of Judea, there was a priest named Zechariah, of the division of Abijah. And he had a wife from the daughters of Aaron, and her name was Elizabeth" (Luke 1:5 ESV), and Mary [illegible] identified as a kinswoman of Elizabeth's family in Luke 1:36: "And behold, your relative Elizabeth in her old age has also conceived a son, and this is the sixth month with her who was called barren." It does not mean that Mary was genealogically of the family of David. Since Mary and Elizabeth are identified as relatives, and Mary would have been considered of the line of Aaron, and the family of David by [illegible] means that [illegible] genealogically [illegible] of Joseph [illegible] own [illegible] proving that Jesus was [illegible] connected to David.

[illegible]

CHAPTER XII: BERATIEL

Whose spirit the great emperor has under his authority many princes, generals, counts, and servants. The hour is called Nahalon, and its spirit is Beratiel.

The twelfth hour of the day is called Nahalon, and its supreme angel the emperor is called Beratiel, who, according to Solomon, a Jew under the empire, has under him spirits assigned to various operations almost innumerable. From all these, they were assigned to the operation of steganography in different orders. In the first order there are ten commanders and counts, in the second twenty, in the third thirty, in the fourth forty, in the fifth five hundred, in the sixth six hundred, in the seventh seven hundred, in the eighth eight hundred, in the ninth nine hundred, in the tenth one hundred, in the eleventh two hundred, and in the twelfth three hundred. All these, in their turns and ranks, with an infinite number of servants, are assigned to the operations of this art, an intelligent and perfect operator in the art, whom he will be able to bring in as many as he will at the twelfth hour of the day. Now all the princes, leaders, and counts of this hour (according to Raziel's opinion) assume forms at the pleasure of the operator.

Red.	Black.	R.	B.	R.	B.	R.
Camaron	*Plamiel*	*Edriel*	10.	100.	10.	100.
Astrofiel	*Nerostiel*	*Choriel*	10.	100.	10.	100.
Penatiel	*Emarson*	*Romiel*	10.	100.	10.	100.
Demarac	*Quirix*	*Fenosiel*	10.	100.	10.	100.
Famaras	*Sameron*	*Hamary*	10.	100.	10.	100.

Here we have already named fifteen of the spirits of Beratiel, five of whom are leaders in as many orders, and ten counts, who are joined to them, are one thousand one hundred servants for various operations in the secrets of magic. So, when you wish to work through any of them at the last hour of the day, observe the lord of the ascendant of that hour and the twelfth house, and the character of the other, write on a clean sheet of paper with the other necessities, and this secret prayer on his back.

SECRET PRAYER

Berathiel Odiel irsoti rodu dreor rauezo melros ethiel aty nodiel hayres penason

Then, having introduced all the rules as usual, say this secret prayer in the proper manner, and immediately the spirits called will appear. Then you shall give priority to the secret, according to the instruction of art and be faithful in obeying all things.

ARGUMENT OF THE PRIVACY OF ANYONE WHO MEETS THE AGREEMENT.

We have a friend who is far away, and we know that he is in danger, because he himself is hidden. We want to meet him, but for certain reasons we do not dare in the open. We therefore call the second hour the spirits assigned to this operation and we recommend the secret securely.

WE CLOSE THE LETTERS, FORMED ACCORDING TO CUSTOM, BY THE SIGN OF THE SPIRIT.

Anyone who glories in temporal things can by no means be called righteous, and he who loves temporary things cannot be a lover of justice, since Catholic integrity detests a man who is encumbered by worldly loves. For the holy religion of the Christian faith forbids the love of the world to its people because he who loves worldly joys loses heavenly happiness. It is argued that a Catholic who does not live as a Catholic has denied Christ, and he who loves temporal things is not said to be a good Catholic. He who loves the Creator seeks the joys of spiritual things. The lover of Christ despises all the lusts of the world, and cares not for glory, for the rich and unstable. But the lover of the world hates the righteous things, he cares nothing for future joys. Alas, what are you doing, Christians, intent on self-loving things? Thoughts which are not honest, acts contrary to religion. Do not, I beseech the poor, do not love the soon-to-be-perished self-pleasures of this world. Rather, take care to love Christ, so far as he receives us to the heavenly kingdoms. John Trithemius, Abbot.

When an expert in the art has undertaken this directed speech, or any others sealed with the character of Beratiel, let him faithfully do all that is ordered in the art; and say the secret prayer. However, the spirits that will come without delay, he sees that they are present, he says to the superior who walks crowned:

Famerulyn melysno alny vemoby dreary drymes charsony.

Having said this, let the spirit approach nearer, and faithfully speak the secret into the ear of the worker. But he must be constant, and not afraid, because they are good spirits, and they do no harm to anyone who is well trained in this art. But if anyone presumes to approach with no experience, he will not escape danger.

Commentary: Chapter XII

[p. 347; 1] *Beratiel* ... Beyond what is mentioned in this chapter, there is not much information from outside sources about the angel or demon *Beratiel*. *Beratiel* is mentioned in the *Lemegeton*,[1] but no other information about the angel or demon is mentioned in that text.

[p. 347; 1] *according to Solomon, a Jew under the empire ... according to Raziel's opinion* ... Beratiel is not mentioned in any fallaciously ascribed Solomonic text other than the *Lemegeton* which was written after this book. *The Book of the Angel Raziel* also does not mention any angel or demon by the name of Beratiel.

[p. 347; 3], [p. 348; 4] non-sensical goetic "angel tongues".

[p. 348; 2] *Anyone who glories in temporal things can by no means be called righteous, and he who loves temporary things cannot be a lover of justice, since Catholic integrity detests a man who is encumbered by worldly loves. For the holy religion of the Christian faith forbids the love of the world to its people because he who loves worldly joys loses heavenly happiness.* ... Two things need to be noted here. First, it is true that a Christian who loves the sinful things of the world are separated from the righteousness of Christ. However, understanding that Christ will return one day and restore the world so that there is no longer any taint of sin left in this world, there is a certain love of the world that is needed in order to carry out Christ's command to spread the gospel to every person and nation. Considering also that this world will be our eternal home after Christ's return, to detest everything about it, and to shun the world in favour of only heavenly desires is gnostic in origin. Gnostic eschatology believed that all "believers" would ascend to a certain heaven, while the "illuminated" (or, illuminati)[2] would ascend to the highest heaven to be merged with Bythos (from the Greek βυθός [bythos, or buthos], meaning "deep" as in the תהו ובהו [tōhu wabōhu, or, formless and void] of Genesis 1:2). The others who were not of the "illuminati" would only ascend to a lower heaven while the unbelievers would be destroyed with the material world. Believing that Heaven is our eternal home and not this earth has gnostic roots.

---

1. Rosemary Ellen Guiley Ph.D., *The Encyclopedia of Angels: Second Edition* (New York, New York: Checkmark Books, 2004), p. 43.

2. We need to be aware that there is no legitimate evidence of a secret organization called *The Illuminati* ever in history. All of the "evidence" that has been given has all been circumstantial in nature and based in false analogies. The real origins of *The Illuminati* are from the gnostic heresies that have been taken too far.

COMMENTARY: CHAPTER XIV

p. 342. [1] *Bartzabel*. Beyond what is mentioned in this chapter, little is known of [illegible] [illegible] besides that he is a spirit or demon [illegible]. He is also mentioned in the *Lemegeton*, but no other information upon the [illegible] is mentioned in [illegible].

[illegible] [illegible] that [illegible] are [illegible]. According to Crowley's [illegible], Bartzabel is not mentioned in any [illegible] ascribed to Solomon, [illegible] the [illegible] which [illegible] after this [illegible]. In [illegible] of the [illegible] also does [illegible] mention the name of Bartzabel.

p. 342. [illegible] [illegible] [illegible] [illegible].

p. 343. [illegible] [illegible] [illegible] [illegible] [illegible] [illegible] [illegible] [illegible] [illegible] [illegible] who loves the simple things [illegible] separated from the [illegible] Heaven of understanding [illegible] [illegible] [illegible] [illegible] [illegible] [illegible] [illegible] [illegible] [illegible] [illegible] Considering [illegible]

[illegible]

[illegible]

Chapter XIII: Sabrathan

The hour of which is called Omalharien, and his highest angel is called Sabrathan, who has under his command many princes, chiefs, counts, and servants.

The first hour of the night is called Omalharien, and his angel is called Sabrathan, who has many other spirits under him, performing various magical operations in their times and orders, as Hermes Solomon, a Jew most experienced in magic, testifies. Many of these have been assigned to the operation of our art in their turns and orders. For in the first order there are ten, in the second twenty, in the third thirty, in the fourth forty, in the fifth five hundred, in the sixth six hundred, in the seventh seventy, in the eighth eighty, in the ninth ninety, in the tenth one hundred. Their turns and secret orders, of which we have neither full knowledge, nor do we speak.

Red.	Black.	R.	B.	R.	B.	R.
Domaros	*Ramesiel*	*Hayzoym*	100.	100.	100.	100.
Amerany	*Omedriel*	*Emalon*	100.	100.	100.	100.
Penoles	*Franedoc*	*Turtiel*	100.	100.	100.	100.
Mardiel	*Chrasiel*	*Quenol*	100.	100.	100.	100.
Nastul	*Dornason*	*Rymaliel*	100.	100.	100.	100.

Here we already have from the Sabrathan spirits five leaders, and ten counts named, who have two thousand servants assigned to them by turns and orders. If you wish to work through them, observe the lord of the ascendant, and write his character with the other necessary things on a clean sheet, and this secret prayer on the back.

Secret Prayer

Sabrathan odiel melros rhupis othian elroz adiel methiel mear nasutiel lafian irsoti brestion dreor chamerson.

Then, after the custom of foretelling, as soon as you say that the secret prayer as directed, you will see that the spirits are present, with whom you do according to the teachings of the art, whatever you will.

Let it be secret at will.

It is a great secret, and a difficult secret, which is harmful when published, and for this reason neither letters nor couriers should be entrusted, but the service of the spirits who preside over the hour in which you are working. It is not safe to invoke the spirit in light causes, but where human ministrations fail, their skill is required.

Let the content of the letters be as agreed.

John Trithemius, Abbot of Spanheim, to Brother Nicolaus Basselius, the monk of

Hirsaugiens, he should say the present prayer with his salvation.

> Almighty God, the supreme Creator of all, who redeems us Christians through Christ, has given his zeal to Catholic love, suggesting the forgiveness of sins to those who believe by the light of faith. And he most liberally gave his beloved son, a gracious light to deliver us all who believe from the power of the mournful king of Tartarus, and to destroy the dark and cruel prison of Zabulum. What will we Christians be able to do worthily to the sufferings of Christ, weak men, professing the Catholic faith without works of righteousness? Therefore, praying most devoutly, we praise you, our redeemer, with the highest praises, saying, I praise you, eternal light, most kindly Saviour of all, who redeemed us with your blood. Strengthen our weakness with the zeal of your love. Hail to us the sweetest Saviour Jesus and pour into our hearts the zeal of the Catholic faith. Your zeal is holy, it works guilt into the hearts of those who seek you, Christ the Saviour most kindly. O Eternal Light, sweetest Jesus, illuminate the darkness of your servants with the usual goodness. Saviour Jesus, eternally save our souls. Grant us eternal joys, Christ, hear your humble servants, and forgive the sins of all who are exhorting. Saviour, save us poor, though most unworthy. Grant us good devotion in humbly asking, Amen. We wrote on the 18th of May in the Year of our Lord, 1500.

When he has received the letters, if he to whom they are sent is an expert in the art, he then observes and writes the lord of the ascendant of that hour with the rest of the precepts in this art. In advance, let him say the ordered secret prayer, and at once the sent spirits will appear to him visible, whom he sees and as soon as he observes them, he says these words of priority:

> chameros burnean aslotiel vear reneas cralty triomy penason.

Having said these things, he will reveal the secret to his ear.

Commentary: Chapter XIII

[p. 351; 1] *Sabrathan* ... Beyond what is mentioned in this chapter, there is not much information from outside sources about the angel or demon *Sabrathan*. *Sabrathan* is mentioned in the *Lemegeton*,[1] but no other information about the angel or demon is mentioned in that text.

[p. 351; 1] *as Hermes Solomon, a Jew most experienced in magic, testifies* ... Sabrathan is not mentioned in any fallaciously ascribed Solomonic text other than the *Lemegeton* which was written after this book.

[p. 351; 3], [p. 352; 3] non-sensical goetic "angel tongues".

[p. 352; 1] *a gracious light to deliver us all who believe from the power of the mournful king of Tartarus, and to destroy the dark and cruel prison of Zabulum.* ... The problem here with Trithemius's claim that there is a "mournful king of Tartarus" that we are to be delivered from is that Hell (Tartarus) is a prison for the demonic as laid out in 2 Peter 2:4. "For if God did not spare angels when they sinned, but cast them into hell and committed them to chains of gloomy darkness to be kept until the judgment." (2 Peter 2:4 ESV) Michael S. Heiser's faulty thought that this verse is speaking about angels that intermingled with human women in Genesis 6,[2] when reading through the entirety of the context, while Noah is mentioned as being "saved", the text is really speaking of all evil in the world. That Peter is speaking of all evil that will come to judgment is evident from verse 6 where Peter speaks about the judgment on Sodom and Gomorrah. Sodom and Gomorrah had absolutely *nothing* to do with angels/demons intermarrying with human women and having children by them. To take 2 Peter 2:4 to say that Peter was indicating the "sin of the watchers" from *1 Enoch* and Genesis 6 is pulling that verse out of its context for faulty exegesis. 2 Peter 2:4 is talking about the judgment of the angels/demons for their sin and being sentenced to Hell (or, Tartarus) for their violations against God. That Hell is a place where the demonic are held in "chains of gloomy darkness to be kept until judgment" shows that the demonic, Satan included, do not want to be there and as Matthew 28:18 tells us, once more, that since Jesus has all authority in heaven and on earth, Jesus is the king of Hell just as he is the king of all things. To try to claim that Satan still has some authority as a "true king" would be to implicate Gnostic dualism along with the goetic notions of the demonic that are independent of any heavenly or Yahweh type authority.

The reference to Zabulum (zābulum) is the accusative singular of the Latin zābulus which is an alternate spelling for diabolus, or devil, meaning Satan.

---

1. Rosemary Ellen Guiley Ph.D., *The Encyclopedia of Angels: Second Edition* (New York, New York: Checkmark Books, 2004), p. 316.

2. Michael S. Heiser, *Demons: What the Bible Really Says about the Powers of Darkness* (Bellingham, Washington: Lexham Press, 2020), pp. 111–112.

COMMENTARY: CHAPTER XIII

Chapter XIV: Tartys

The hour of which is called Panezur, and his angel the supreme commander is called Tartys, who has under him many princes, generals, counts, and serfs.

The second hour of the night is called Panezur, and his angel is called Tartys, having under his command many princes, commanders, counts, and subordinates, whom he called to various ministries working in the hidden secrets of nature by turns and orders, he was accustomed to send his own. Of these twelve orders are assigned to our knowledge of steganography which are sufficient for us for all operations. In the first place, in order there are ten, in the second twenty, in the third thirty, in the fourth forty, in the fifth fifty, in the sixth sixty, in the seventh seventy, in the eighth eighty, in the ninth ninety, in the tenth one hundred, in the eleventh one thousand, in the twelfth one hundred thousand.

It rarely happens, however, that an operation is done through all these spirits, because there is no need to occupy ourselves with the higher things. Since the weak are abundantly sufficient for us for everything, unless someone well trained in this art and is completely perfect, wishes to see the leaders of all the prescribed orders, and to know their names, he could lead them all in order.

Red.	Black.	R.	B.	R.	B.	R.
Almodar	*Permaz*	*Gabrynoz*	100.	10.	100.	10.
Famoriel	*Vameroz*	*Mercoph*	100.	10.	100.	10.
Nedroz	*Emaryel*	*Tameriel*	100.	10.	100.	10.
Ormezyn	*Fromyzn*	*Venomiel*	100.	10.	100.	10.
Chabriz	*Ramaziel*	*Iennziel*	100.	10.	100.	10.
Praxiel	*Granozyn*	*Xemyzin*	100.	10.	100.	10.

Here we have named from the leaders of Tartys six, from the counts twelve, servants, so that they were numbered by turns and distributed in ranks, one thousand three hundred twenty, which are sufficient for us to try our art at this hour. And note that (according to Solomon and Raziel) all these leaders and princes of the Tartys are kind and most ready for obedience, and in whatever form they are commanded to appear, they willingly assume it. So, when you wish to work in this knowledge carefully observe the lord of the ascendant with the rest that we command and write all that is to be written with this secret prayer.

Secret Prayer

Tartys chrybes faziel yrsoti haelnot dreor aduear afy mearo Vény satu pemerson.

Then, having completed everything with the utmost care, and read the secret prayer in the proper way as it should be, the summoned spirits will soon come ready for your control.

LET IT BE A MYSTERY, WHATEVER IT MAY BE THAT CONFRONTS US, GREAT AND ARDUOUS.

The secret that we wish to carefully tell a friend through the spirits may be of whatever kind according to the time and the variety of affairs that may occur to us, so that it may not be light, and such as may otherwise be securely announced.

John Trithemius, to the sanctimonious on Mount Rupert's Alm, adorning the Catholic faith with bright virginity, eternal happiness is continually earned by the most holy zeal of religion.

By the mercy of the Eternal King, we providentially send you, at the long-awaited time, a man of great experience in temporal affairs, John of Raunenstat, a reverend of the monastery of Violsdorp, and a zealous Abbot for a long time, and freely resigning the same Abbey. I went on his behalf, as I had promised you, to the monastery of Lunapurgense, where he was serving Christ, busy with continuous prayers and reading the holy scriptures, with the monks of the same monastery. And I asked him to come down to your abbess, and take care of the temporal things, and become a steward and storekeeper. The abbot of Limburg, with his usual instability, changed his mind, and I was able to let him go with his consent. At last, inspired by Christ, he consented, though timidly, because he was afraid to serve the nuns, who change very slightly. He is not without reason to fear, since, as experience has taught us, the nuns have often given back to their financiers an uncommendable reward for their benefactions. A woman's mind is suddenly changed by jealousy and bitterness. And giving to Christ, I know that he is useful to you. He is a Christian, he is a monk, he fears the saviour, he has a good understanding. Accustom yourself to control a woman's changeability in this way, as much as you can remember that she is constant, receiving her with holy honour and sincere charity, laying aside all the lightness of a woman's mind, especially when she can help you, and recover the collapsed state of your temporal affairs in the monastery aiding Christ the Redeemer, who is zealous for charity. Farewell, from Spain. May 17, in the year of our Lord Jesus Christ, 1500.

When he receives the letters marked with the character of Tartys, he to whom they are sent, an expert in our art, he observes the master of the ascendant, and does everything and every detail that needs to be done with the utmost care and joins the usual mysterious prayer. And when he sees that the sent spirits are present, he says to the chief these words:

Chabor massotiel tuseuo reneas porean trismeny penarson

And when he had said these words with a strong intention to the principal leader, he immediately approaches calmly and reveals the secret.

Commentary: Chapter XIV

[p. 355; 1] *Tartys* ... Beyond what is mentioned in this chapter, there is not much information from outside sources about the angel or demon *Tartys*. *Tartys* is mentioned in the *Lemegeton*,[1] but no other information about the angel or demon is mentioned in that text.

[p. 355; 3] *according to Solomon and Raziel*... Tartys is not mentioned in any fallaciously ascribed Solomonic text other than the *Lemegeton* which was written after this book. *The Book of the Angel Raziel* also does not mention any angel or demon by the name of Tartys.

[p. 355; 4], [p. 356; 6] non-sensical goetic "angel tongues".

1. Rosemary Ellen Guiley Ph.D., *The Encyclopedia of Angels*: *Second Edition* (New York, New York: Checkmark Books, 2004), p. 345.

Chapter XV: Serquanich/Serguanich

Whose hour is called Quabrion, and the angel of his supreme spirit is called Serquanich, having under his government a prince, leaders, counts, and many more servants without number.

The third hour of the night is called Quabrion, whose Emperor and supreme angel is Serquanich, having princes under his empire, many commanders and counts in twelve ranks, with many continuous servants separated. For in the first order there are ten, in the second twenty, in the third thirty, in the fourth forty, in the fifth fifty, in the sixth sixty, in the seventh seventy, in the eighth eighty, in the ninth ninety, in the tenth one hundred, in the eleventh one thousand, in the twelfth ten thousand.

Red.	Black.	R.	B.	R.	B.	R.
Menarym	*Euanuel*	*Vanosyr*	10.	10.	100.	100.
Chrusiel	*Sarmozyn*	*Lemaron*	10.	10.	100.	100.
Penargoz	*Haylon*	*Almonoyz*	10.	10.	100.	100.
Amriel	*Quabriel*	*Ianothyel*	10.	10.	100.	100.
Demanoz	*Thurmytz*	*Melrotz*	10.	10.	100.	100.
Nestoroz	*Fronyzon*	*Xanthyoz*	10.	10.	100.	100.

Here we have already named twelve of the more important spirits of Serquanich, from whose order there is one, who, according to their turns, assume the rank of duke and count. The remaining six never change their job but are always leaders. But he who wishes to know the names of many, can easily obtain his purpose through those whom we have named. So, when you wish to work through them, observe the lord of the ascendant and write his character with the other necessary things on a clean sheet of paper, and on his back this secret prayer.

Secret Prayer

Serquarnich osiel theory dreochy amersoty omear, pornis layr mear penarson.

Then, having joined together, and having read the conspiracy, the spirits who were summoned will soon come ready to obey, with whom it is prescribed to act according to the rules of art.

A secret argument.

We desire to warn our friend of imminent danger, but we fear the danger itself, because if we had dared him, it would have been noted and he would have been subjected to no less inconvenience. Therefore, since neither letters nor messengers are to be trusted, we have now decided to trust the spirit.

Let the content of the letters be as agreed.

John Trithemius, Spanish of the Order of Saint Benedict to the Pastor of the Church of the Valley of the Almonds, he says Salutations.

Of the ecclesiastical writers I have made a great catalog, which I have lately exhibited to your fraternity to see. Concluding too suddenly, I confess that I have passed over some of the most famous men, only from envy, which is most false. I wrote about the conception of the most holy mother of God, and I affirmed that it was always the most beautiful without any new original excess, which a puffed-up thinker, wanting to rebuke with a puff, said, that the most brilliant virgin was stained with the guilt of the original sin (contrary to Catholic observance with the most vain rashness). It is reckless to wish to disfigure the most blessed maiden. And the most eminent doctors of Cologne, desiring to completely root out and destroy the opinion of the mad brother contrary to the truth, forced him to recall his vain fables, asserting that the most blessed virgin, and affirming also, that according to the statute it should be believed most pure, had in no time (however brief) succumbed to the original sinfulness. I wanted to write these things to you, because you love the truth, just as much as you despise the mockers of the most blessed virgin. Farewell, 16th of May 1500.

But when he receives the letters to whom they are sent, he who is skilled in the art, should attend to the sign of the principal spirit, that he may know whom he ought to lead according to the shifts of the hour. Then he will observe the lord of the ascendant at the very hour in which he receives the letters, with the rest of the disposition of the sky through the twelve houses of the Zodiac, omitting nothing at all of those which are ordered. Having said the secret prayer, when he sees the spirit present, he should say the following words:

> chamerusyn maslotiel vean reneas cralty thyrmo venear penarson.

Having said these things to the principal spirit, the spirit will soon approach nearer, and will reveal to his ear the secret that was committed to him.

Commentary: Chapter XV

[p. 361; 1] *Serquanich* [or, *Serguanich*] ... Beyond what is mentioned in this chapter, there is not much information from outside sources about the angel or demon *Serquanich*. *Serquanich* is mentioned in the *Lemegeton* by the name *Serguanich,*[1] but no other information about the angel or demon is mentioned in that text.

[p. 361; 3], [p. 360; 5] non-sensical goetic "angel tongues".

[p. 362; 3] *I wrote about the conception of the most holy mother of God, and I affirmed that it was always the most beautiful without any new original excess, which a puffed-up thinker, wanting to rebuke with a puff, said, that the most brilliant virgin was stained with the guilt of the original sin (contrary to Catholic observance with the most vain rashness). It is reckless to wish to disfigure the most blessed maiden. ...* Despite the argument of the Roman Catholic Church, if Mary were free of original sin, then the sacrifice of Christ and his redemption would have been pointless since it would be possible for people to be "free of sin" without him. Since Jesus came to redeem the sins of those that repent and believe, if even *one* person was not required to repent of sin, then Jesus' death was not necessary. That Mary was not stained with original sin would make her the saviour and not Christ. In reality, as Mark 3:22–35 shows, Mary at that time did not believe in who Jesus was either despite what Gabriel had told her in the infancy narrative. (Luke 1: 26, 27) Instead of repeating the argument here, I will refer you to *Book 1* and *Commentary*: *Chapter XI* on pp. 185–187 on this volume. Because Mary did not believe that Jesus was Yahweh come to earth in human flesh even for that chapter in Mark, she was indeed afflicted with original sin. The goetic nature of a human that is able to be divine, as Mary is argued to be by the Roman Catholic Church, at this point in this commentary is self-evident. For more argumentation about the divinization of a human as being based in goetia, see my *Introdution* pp. 29–31 and p. 84.

1. Rosemary Ellen Guiley Ph.D., The Encyclopedia of Angels: Second Edition (New York, New York: Checkmark Books, 2004), p. 326.

CHAPTER XVI: JEFISCHA

Whose hour is called Rameryz, and his supreme angel is called Jephisha, who has under his rule many princes, leaders, counties, and ministerial spirits.

The fourth hour of the night is called Ramerzy, whose angel is called Jefischa, having under his command many princes, leaders, counts, and ministerial spirits, who, like those whom we have described in the previous chapter, are distributed in twelve ranks and orders. In the first place, in order they are ten, in the second twenty, in the third thirty, in the fourth forty, in the fifth fifty, in the sixth sixty, in the seventh seventy, in the eighth eighty, in the ninth ninety, in the tenth one hundred, in the eleventh one thousand, and in the twelfth ten thousand. And from in these twelve orders, by their turns, the spirits are sent to serve us in the operations of the art of steganography, of which we shall now mention some.

Red.	Black.	R.	B.	R.	B.	R.
Armosiel	*Rayziel*	*Lamediel*	10.	100.	100.	1,000.
Nedruan	*Gemezin*	*Adroziel*	10.	100.	100.	1,000.
Maneyloz	*Fremiel*	*Zodiel*	10.	100.	100.	1,000.
Ormael	*Hamayz*	*Bramiel*	10.	100.	100.	1,000.
Phorsiel	*Iapuriel*	*Coreziel*	10.	100.	100.	1,000.
Rimezyn	*Iasphiel*	*Enatriel*	10.	100.	100.	1,000.

Here we already have six leaders named from the spirit of Jefischa and twelve counts to whom seven thousand two hundred sixty ministers are assigned, who are sent by their turns and orders to the service of the worker in the art. Now these princes, according to the saying of Solomon the Philosopher, are mule-like, and they assume whatever forms they have been ordered to take. When, therefore, you wish to work through them at the fourth hour of the night, observe the lord of the ascendant and the shape of the wheel of heaven, and do everything according to what we command you, writing everything on a clean sheet, and on the back of it this secret prayer.

SECRET PRAYER

Jefischa osiel mear pathyr lays mean theor dreochis fazan moab lofeas orsoti breo pornys tayr penarson.

Then to join the ones already brought together, when you say the secret prayer itself in the due manner, form and order, spirits in which the greatest form will appear visible, ready and willing to do everything.

LET IT BE SECRET AT WILL.

Whatever mystery occurs to you for the time being, which you would like to know about the absence at this hour of the night, the fourth, you can safely commit to the spirits. Only let it be such that you cannot send it safely either by letters or by messengers. For those things which we can send without danger either by letters or by messengers, we must by no means also have sent by the ministry of spirits. If anyone has tried to bring the spirit on account of light and secret matters, which can be delivered without danger by means of letters or messengers; without doubt it will bear loss and inconvenience with danger.

THE CONTENT OF THE LETTERS AS AGREED.

To the venerable father in Christ, the Oeconomist of the Limpurges, the religious master, called John [Weißdorffen], the humble abbot John Ouilis of Spanheim, the joys of heaven.

The nuns of St. Rupert covet their governor with excessive and greedy eagerness, and they ask you with humble benevolence, in so far as you undertake the government of the temporal affairs of the monastery itself. To serve the devoted virgins of Christ is praiseworthy and worthy of merit. You have the good fortune of the most famous visitor of the spiritual affairs of the same Cœnobius, who embraces you with the greatest honour, high in character, adorned with virtues, careful in counsel, in everything well-loved, well-known for the conversation of the monastic religion, and notable to all men (whose life is most pleasing to Christ by merit), the best abbot of the monastery of St. John. He is the most literate of the letters of both Christians and Gentiles, who greatly exceeds the wisdom of all men. He knew very well how to rule the flock entrusted to him, and he is the guardian of the virgins of Christ, whose nunnery he guards most firmly. Do not be afraid to serve under him such honourable nuns, who knows how to govern the brides of Christ according to the monastic law with the best discretion, who with the virtue and devotion of the Christian faith will gladly come to you in need. Since you have this man so illustrious, kind, and generous as a family member, I request that you willingly take the helm of such religious virgins. Christ will reward your labour with eternal joys. May the spouse, guardian, and most kind rewarder of the nuns grant you better zeal for good zeal. Farewell, from Spain. 15th of May, in the year 1500.

When the letters marked with the character of Jefischa were received by him to whom they were sent, already an expert in the art, he observes in the first place the lord of the ascendant at that hour with the whole figure of heaven, and writes it down on a clean sheet, and on the back of it the prescribed secret prayer, which he said when, having predicted, and saw the spirits sent to him there and then present to him, he says in order of precedence as follows:

chamerusin aphroys aslotiel mean reneas vear tryamo cralti penason.

Having duly said these things to the principal spirit, he will approach nearer, and will reveal to his ear the secret which he had committed to him.

Commentary: Chapter XVI

[p. 365; 1] *Jefischa* … Beyond what is mentioned in this chapter, there is not much information from outside sources about the angel or demon *Jefischa*. *Jefischa* is mentioned in the *Lemegeton*,[1] but no other information about the angel or demon is mentioned in that text.

[p. 365; 2] *according to the saying of Solomon the Philosopher* … Jefischa is not mentioned in any fallaciously ascribed Solomonic text other than the *Lemegeton* which was written after this book.

[p. 365; 3], [p. 367; 1] non-sensical goetic "angel tongues".

1. Rosemary Ellen Guiley Ph.D., *The Encyclopedia of Angels*: *Second Edition* (New York, New York: Checkmark Books, 2004), p. 43.

CHAPTER XVII: ABASDARHON

Whose hour is called Sanayfar, and his supreme angel is called Abasdarhon, who has under his dominion many leaders, counts, and servants.

The fifth hour of the night is called Sanayfar, whose first and supreme angel is called Abasdarhon, who has under his authority princes, commanders, counts, and many ministers, distributed in twelve ranks and shifts, like the former whom he sends to the service of various arts and experiments to operators duly appointed that they are used to. In the first row there are ten, in the second twenty, in the third thirty, in the fourth forty, in the fifth fifty, in the sixth sixty, in the seventh seventy, in the eighth eighty, in the ninth ninety, in the tenth one hundred, in the eleventh one thousand, in the twelfth one hundred thousand. And by these all the operation of steganography is done at the fifth hour of the night.

Red.	Black.	R.	B.	R.	B.	R.
Meniel	*Gemarii*	*Barmas*	100.	100.	100.	100.
Charaby	*Vanescor*	*Platiel*	100.	100.	100.	100.
Appiniel	*Sameryn*	*Neszomy*	100.	100.	100.	100.
Deinatz	*Xantropy*	*Quesdor*	100.	100.	100.	100.
Nechorym	*Herphatz*	*Caremaz*	100.	100.	100.	100.
Hameriel	*Chrymas*	*Vmariel*	100.	100.	100.	100.
Vulcaniel	*Patrozyn*	*Kralyn*	100.	100.	100.	100.
Samelon	*Nameton*	*Habalon*	100.	100.	100.	100.

Here we have already named forty of the spirits of Abasdarhon, of whom the first twelve are leaders in their ranks, while the remaining twelve are counts, and there are two of each rank, namely one leader and one count. We have three thousand two hundred ministerial deputies who take turns in various magical operations. But Solomon and Raziel, wise men and most experienced in magic, say that the princes of Abasdarhon are wont to appear in every place, they have been ordered in form by him who works, which, since we have frequently experienced it, we confess it is supported by the truth. So, when you wish to work through them in steganography at the fifth hour of the night, observe the lord of the ascendant, and write him as well as the whole arrangement of Heaven on a clean sheet with the rest that we have taught, and on the back this secret prayer.

SECRET PRAYER

Abasdarhon morca lafias tharuean buel dreschin tayr moab ersoty layr pornys theori mean asar penason.

Then, having joined together, as soon as you have said the secret prayer itself, the spirits whom you have called will appear to you, ready to do all that you have ordered them to do.

The topic of meeting privacy.

Every secret you have, because otherwise you are not able to make it known to a friend at a distance or near, without danger, entrust to the better of the spirits that form to whom it is necessary according to art, fearing nothing, for they are benevolent and faithful.

Literally, they are made to order.

Let the Catholic faith save no one who despises the eagerness of divine love. Now many men are found to boast of the Catholic faith, but few have the works of the Christian faith, but have a lazy faith that dies. Many believe, but very few obey the commandments of God. Alas, they believe that the weak are zealous, how much stronger can even unbelieving people be, and many are strong. Gentiles who do not believe that our Saviour, made man, became the Son of the Almighty, will be tormented by the punishments of Hell. They will torture, but with greater punishments all those who believe that the Son of God came into the world, made man, for the zeal of human redemption, but they do not in the least practice the Christian faith with holy works. They prefer the honours of the world to eternal bliss, always unloved by the sins of the world. zealous for ungodly actions, defiling the purity of faith by bad behaviour against obedience. But the lovers of God, who have the right zeal of the Christian faith, prefer nothing to God, exactly follow Christ, shun sins, and despise the rich honours of the world. Now then pay attention to these words which boast of faith, love God and you will have the reward of happiness and be zealous for righteousness. If you love the self-love of the age against the honour of God, you will receive the shame of the zealous sins, the horrors of hell. I wrote this on the 15th of May, in the year of the Lord 1500.

When he receives the letters signed in the character of Abasdarhon, he to whom they are sent, already an expert in the art, he immediately considers the lord of the ascendant, and the whole arrangement of the heavens, observes and writes with the tenor of the conspiracy and other necessary things in a clean slate. Let him say these words more to the advantage:

Chameron massotiel taseuij renean pornas thilmeuij penason.

Having said these things, he will soon approach nearer, and will faithfully reveal the secret entrusted to him to the ear of the worker.

Commentary: Chapter XVII

[p. 371; 1] *Abasdarhon* … Beyond what is mentioned in this chapter, there is not much information from outside sources about the angel or demon *Abasdarhon*. *Abasdarhon* is mentioned in the *Lemegeton*,[1] but no other information about the angel or demon is mentioned in that text.

[p. 371; 2] *But Solomon and Raziel, wise men and most experienced in magic* … Abasdarhon is not mentioned in any fallaciously ascribed Solomonic text other than the *Lemegeton* which was written after this book. *The Book of the Angel Raziel* also does not mention any angel or demon by the name of Abasdarhon.

[p. 371; 3], [p. 372; 6] non-sensical goetic "angel tongues".

[p. 372; 3] *became the Son of the Almighty* … Saying that Jesus "became" the Son of God, or the Almighty, is a heretical statement. Jesus has always been the Son of God, meaning Jesus as the second person of the triune-Godhead. To say that Jesus "became" God is again a belief in the possibility of a human becoming "like God" as the serpent in Genesis 3:5 tempted Adam and Eve to believe.

---

1. Rosemary Ellen Guiley Ph.D., *The Encyclopedia of Angels: Second Edition* (New York, New York: Checkmark Books, 2004), p. 2.

COMMENTARY CHAPTER XVII

[illegible] beyond what is mentioned in this chapter [illegible] information from outside sources about [illegible] mentioned in [illegible] but no other information about [illegible]

[illegible]

[illegible]

[illegible]

[illegible]

Chapter XVIII: Zaazenach

Whose hour is called Thaazaron, and his angel is called Zaazenach, a spirit presiding over many.

The sixth hour of the night is called Thaazaron, and the name of his angel is Zaazenach, who has under his authority almost innumerable princes and commanders, counts and ministers, who preside over various magical operations by turns and orders. In the first row there are ten, in the second twenty, in the third thirty, in the fourth forty, in the fifth fifty, in the sixth sixty, in the seventh seventy, in the eighth eighty, in the ninth ninety, in the tenth one hundred, in the eleventh one thousand, in the twelfth ten thousand. But when you wish to call them, in any case if it pleases you, they are ready and completely obedient, as the previously mentioned wise men testify, and we have experienced it.

Red.	Black.	R.	B.	R.	B.	R.
Amonazii	*Tuberiel*	*Pammon*	100.	100.	100.	100.
Menoriel	*Humaziel*	*Dracon*	100.	100.	100.	100.
Prenostix	*Lanoziel*	*Gematz*	100.	100.	100.	100.
Namedor	*Lamerotz*	*Enariel*	100.	100.	100.	100.
Cherasiel	*Xerphiel*	*Rudefor*	100.	100.	100.	100.
Dramaz	*Zeziel*	*Sarmon*	100.	100.	100.	100.

Here we already have from the twelve ranks of the spirits of Zaazenach, twelve named captains and six counts with their servants, duly assigned by order to the number of one thousand eight hundred sixty, who are abundantly sufficient for us at the sixth hour of the night for all the operation of steganography. So, when you wish to work at this hour of the night, observe the lord of the ascendant, and write him, as well as the whole arrangement of heaven, with the rest of the necessary things, in a clean slate and secret prayer.

Secret Prayer

Zaazenach eneos fari neabdiel lasmy chyrmean ersoty layr pornys theor mean penason.

Then, after having been duly joined, and by the said secret prayer, the summoned spirits will appear without delay, calm and benevolent, ready for everything.

The subject of privacy of any meeting.

No matter what kind of mystery we encounter, what not by messengers, neither by letters we can safely send to a friend, at the sixth hour of the night one of the prescribed leaders, or even the counts, if the leader is not present, which can often happen. Let us commit ourselves in the manner and order in which there is a direction in this art, fearing nothing at all for they are all good and they are faithful in all that has been entrusted to them by the worker, and they leave nothing behind.

THE TENOR OF THE LETTERS IS SET AT THE PLEASURE OF THE OPERATOR, OR OF THE PRESENT BUSINESS.

John Trithemius, Abbot, Spanish Salute and charity to the master of arts and philosophy from the solitude of the washerman.

Be mindful of the promise you made to Christ when you accepted the Catholic faith. Did you offer the solemn vow of eternal happiness to whom it was promised? Repentant or dirty? Undoubtedly, the temporal pleasures and joys of the present life are promised in view of the future of eternal rest and to those who despise them, and those who love God eternally. We know that the best rewards are promised to the lovers of God, but to the lovers of the world, to Christians and reprobates, God has prepared the bitterest punishments of Hell. He who has faith, but he neglects to have divine love, he is unfaithful, and his faith is what he presupposes in vain. Zealot of divine love, who does not cease to adorn the Christian faith with devoted and good works every day, training himself humbly in the arts of faithfulness. Farewell. 14th of May, in the year Lord incarnate 1500.

When he has received the letters, consigned to the hour by the character of the spirit, if he to whom they are sent is an expert in the art, and he is observing first of all the figures of the sky, let him inscribe it with the rest of the necessary things, by the prescribed conspiracy, when the spirit appears visibly, he should say:

Chamerufi fetion notiel aseuomy rean, badian, laso sear vaobry hastoripeson.

Having said these things, the spirit will reveal the secret entrusted to him faithfully and secretly into the ear of the worker.

Commentary: Chapter XVIII

[p. 375; 1] *Zaazenach* beyond what is mentioned in this chapter, there is not much information from outside sources about the angel or demon *Zaazenach. Zaazenach* is mentioned in the *Lemegeton*,[1] but no other information about the angel or demon is mentioned in that text.

[p. 375; 3], [p. 376; 5] non-sensical goetic "angel tongues".

1. Rosemary Ellen Guiley Ph.D., *The Encyclopedia of Angels*: *Second Edition* (New York, New York: Checkmark Books, 2004), p. 43.

COMMENTARY, CHAPTER XVIII

[illegible]

[illegible]

[illegible]

Chapter XIX: Mendrion

Whose hour is called Venaydor, and his angel is called Mendrion, having under his rule the principles, daughter, counts, and ministers which are non-numberable.

The seventh hour is called Venaydor, whose angel and supreme spirit is called Mendrion, who has under his command many other spirits, as princes, leaders, counts, and ministers, who are assigned to various operations in magic. From these to steganography and other operations at the seventh hour of the night, by turns and orders, their chiefs, commanders, and counts, with their servants, were now appointed in great numbers. In the first row there are ten, in the second twenty, in the third thirty, in the fourth forty, in the fifth fifty, in the sixth sixty, in the seventh seventy, in the eighth eighty, in the ninth ninety, in the tenth one hundred, in the eleventh one thousand, in the twelfth one hundred thousand. All these are called by turns and come to work.

Red.	Black.	R.	B.	R.	B.	R.
Ammiel	*Ventariel*	*Rayziel*	10.	100.	100.	100.
Choriel	*Zachariel*	*Tarmytz*	10.	100.	100.	100.
Genarytz	*Dubraz*	*Anapion*	10.	100.	100.	100.
Pandroz	*Marchiel*	*Imonyel*	10.	100.	100.	100.
Menesiel	*Ionadriel*	*Framoth*	10.	100.	100.	100.
Sameriel	*Pemoniel*	*Machmag*	10.	100.	100.	100.

Here we have from the twelve orders of spirits of the highest angel at the hour of the seventh night Mendrion twelve leaders and six counts who are sufficient for us at this time for all operations with their subordinates. And these spirits come, as Hermes the Hebrew and Raziel the Arab testify, in whatever form they have been commanded by him who works according to this art. But he who has not been perfected in our art will not be given obedience, but danger and inconvenience, if he approaches the work. And you, when at the seventh hour of the night you wish to work something through these spirits observe the lord of the ascendant, and the figure of the whole heaven, which you write with the rest of the commands in the art on clean paper, including this secret prayer behind his back.

Secret Prayer

Mendrion suriaco breotnirus ersoy neuo, omear nyco lays ersota theory pornys Azan mean lafias asto penason.

Then, having been joined together, the spirits will immediately appear to you, ready for everything, as they should be.

Let it be a secret of any kind.

As for announcing a secret near or far away to a friend previously skilled in this art of spirits, it matters little what kind it may be, as long as it is not light, or such as could otherwise be safely announced by messengers or letters. Nor are we concerned with the letters, what they are, only that they have the character of the principal angel of that hour in which the operation takes place, and no secret at all.

LET US FORM THE LETTERS AT WILL.

John Trithemius Abbot Nicholas Basselius monk S.D. and he transmits this prayer to the great Nicholas.

First of all created was the man, Adam, the founder, reformer and maker of all things, to whom he married the most beautiful woman named Eve, the mother of all living, foreshadowing the Catholic Church to be united to the shepherds, shining beautifully in the morals of righteousness, to give birth to good children of works, men who perceive the kingdoms of the heavens without end in humility. Christ redeems us by his kindness, humbling himself for our sake. It is necessary for us to love most kindly, who gave us the Catholic faith, those who truly love them will obtain angelic happiness by right. So, every day we all honour our almighty founder, conversing in the true religion and living the Catholic life. Lord Jesus, most gracious Saviour, who mercifully redeemed us all from the barrow of death, kindly attending to our frailty and infirmity, conform us to the Catholic faith, so that as we deserve to have eternal rest of consolation and happiness after our transitory life, Amen. 14th of May 1500.

When he has received these letters signed in the character of Mendrio, he to whom it is said, if he is an expert in our art, he will observe the master of the ascendant and so he writes the whole arrangement of heaven on a clean slate, and on the back of it a mysterious prayer. Then, having joined all the others, and having finished the song, as soon as the spirit appears to him, he says these words to the spirit:

Chamerusyn merion nodiel burmy raueto badria sauepo elayreas penason.

When these truths have resounded to him, who among the rest of the spirits appears to be the most prominent, he will soon, calmly approaching, reveal the secret that was committed to him.

Commentary: Chapter XIX

[p. 379; 1] *Mendrion* ... Beyond what is mentioned in this chapter, there is not much information from outside sources about the angel or demon *Mendrion. Mendrion* is mentioned in the *Lemegeton*,[1] but no other information about the angel or demon is mentioned in that text.

[p. 379; 2] *as Hermes* [Solomon] *the Hebrew and Raziel the Arab testify* ... Mendrion is not mentioned in any fallaciously ascribed Solomonic text other than the Lemegeton which was written after this book. *The Book of the Angel Raziel* also does not mention any angel or demon by the name of Mendrion.

[p. 379; 3], [p. 380; 6] non-sensical goetic "angel tongues".

[p. 380; 5] *It is necessary for us to love most kindly, who gave us the Catholic faith, those who truly love them will obtain angelic happiness by right.* ... This is really no different than Muslim claims that Adam was really a Muslim and that the religion of Islam began at the Garden of Eden. This faulty claim about Islam is based on an Islamic version of an appeal to tradition. Likewise, Adam and Eve knew nothing about the Catholic faith when they were created, or after they fell. For Trithemius to make a claim that Adam and Eve "gave us the Catholic faith" is based on a fallacious appeal to tradition and nothing more. This same appeal to tradition is commonly referred to when it comes to kabbalism as well. Many in kabbalistic circles, or in deep and erroneous conspiracy theory circles will attempt to claim that the *Kabbalah* truly came from Enoch. This claim is based on the faulty authorship claims of texts like 1, 2 and 3 Enoch. All of the books of Enoch are rooted in Jewish Merkavah Mysticism and goeticism. Some of these kabbalists and conspiracy theory activists have also attempted to say that Solomon's temple in 1 Kings was really built as a kabbalistic ritual temple. This belief is rooted in an appeal to tradition and to Masonic beliefs based in tradition as well. To believe that these books were written before the flood by Enoch is a fallacious claim that has been proven to be untrue, likewise with the claims about Solomon's temple. The only way to continue to believe that the three books of Enoch, along with the *Kabbalah*, were written by the biblical Enoch in Genesis 5:21–24 is by an appeal to tradition. As I already mentioned, this fallacious appeal to kabbalistic tradition has been proven to be false many times.

---

1. Rosemary Ellen Guiley Ph.D., *The Encyclopedia of Angels*: *Second Edition* (New York, New York: Checkmark Books, 2004), p. 238.

Commentary: Chapter XIX

In 420 at Arezzo: [illegible] is mentioned in this chapter, there is no [illegible] information from outside sources about the angel or [illegible]. [illegible] in the [illegible] no other information about the [illegible] is mentioned in this text.

In [illegible]. Nothing [illegible] is [illegible] mentioned in any [illegible] other than the [illegible] which was written after this book. [illegible] any [illegible] by the name of [illegible].

19. [illegible] of Phoenician [illegible] gods and tongues

[illegible]

[illegible] Catholic [illegible] to make a claim that [illegible] the Catholic [illegible] to [illegible]

[illegible]

[illegible] *The* [illegible] (New York: [illegible], 2008), [illegible].

Chapter XX: Narcoriel/Narcariel

Whose hour is called Xymalim, and his chief angel is called Narcoriel, having under him a prince, generals, counts, and servants.

At the eighth hour of the night Xymalim will be called, and his angel the emperor, the first and supreme, will be called Narcoriel, who has under his command many other spirits, princes, leaders, counts, and ministers who are called by their ranks to various effects by those who work in secret philosophy. And of all these there are twelve ranks of those who abandon steganography. In the first row there are ten, in the second twenty, in the third thirty, in the fourth forty, in the fifth fifty, in the sixth sixty, in the seventh seventy, in the eighth eighty, in the ninth ninety, in the tenth one hundred, in the eleventh one thousand, and in the twelfth ten thousand. All these should observe their orders in such a way that no one can work safely through them unless he is fully trained in everything. For whoever does not observe the due order, exposes himself to danger, and will be frustrated in the desired effect.

Red.	Black.	R.	B.	R.	B.	R.
Cambiel	*Amelzon*	*Xanoryz*	100.	100.	1,000.	1,000.
Nedarym	*Lemozar*	*Iastrion*	100.	100.	1,000.	1,000.
Astrocon	*Xernifiel*	*Themaz*	100.	100.	1,000.	1,000.
Marifiel	*Kanorsiel*	*Hobrazym*	100.	100.	1,000.	1,000.
Dramozyn	*Bufanotz*	*Zymeloz*	100.	100.	1,000.	1,000.
Lustifon	*Iamedroz*	*Gamsiel*	100.	100.	1,000.	1,000.

Here we have already named twelve commanders and six counts, established in a secret arrangement through all the twelve orders, who have under them one thousand three hundred ministers who are sufficient for us for all the operations of the eight hours of the night. So, when you will wish to work through them in steganography at the eighth hour of the night, observe the lord of the ascendant, and write him as well as the whole disposition of Heaven on clean paper, and on his back with the rest you then say this secret prayer as usual.

Secret Prayer

Narconiel aples pornya my ship. Triomé ilneas azyfan lafias my bression ersoti penason.

Then, having been joined according to the custom of being joined, and by the so-called mysterious prayer, the summoned spirits will be present in that form which you ordered them to take, ready for everything.

A secret argument.

The secret that we want to know about a friend who is far away, if we trust neither letters nor messengers. At the eighth hour of the night let us commit to the superior of the spirits of Narcoriel, fearing nothing at all, since they are all faithful, and most ready to obey.

LET US FORM THE LETTERS AS WE PLEASE.

Oh, most merciful Jesus, I thank you for your most holy faithfulness, who reconciled the human race to the heavenly Father with your blood, hanging on the cross in a pitiful manner. For our sake you submitted the flowery youth of the most noble body to severe wounds, as if you were to revive a dead man. Let us therefore give the thanks we can to our Catholic Redeemer weeping and praising the memory of the passion of the Saviour of our race in Christian fashion. Have pity on me, most merciful Jesus, the fountain of mercy, the abyss of mercy, the glory of the saints, the light of the heavenly beings, and infuse me with the sweetest taste of your most holy love. Deliver me from all my suffering. Give me true joy of heart, that is exultation in your praises, glorifying you, how with the pain of your wounds you have healed me. What shall I repay for your mercy, my Redeemer, my reviver? I sympathize with your labours and tears and bless the most holy wounds of your body. I give immortal thanks to my most gracious Saviour Jesus, asking for the forgiveness of my sins. In the year of the Lord 1500, 13th of May. I have written this prayer. Ἐγωἰωαννχς τζιτχ́μι

When the letters, whatever they may be, consigned with the character of Narcoriel, he to whom they are sent, an expert in the art, shall observe the lord of the ascendant at the same hour, and he shall write them, together with the rest, on a clean slate, with all the necessary things according to custom, and by the so-called secret prayer. When the spirit sees the altar for himself, let him say these words to the superior spirit:

> Medaro Cassotiel va reneas thasny thyrmo thea penason.

Having said these things, according to the instruction of this art, the principal spirit will soon approach him, and tell the secret word.

COMMENTARY: CHAPTER XX

[p. 383; 1] *Narcoriel* [or, *Narcariel*] ... Beyond what is mentioned in this chapter, there is not much information from outside sources about the angel or demon *Narcoriel. Narcoriel* is mentioned in the *Lemegeton,*[1] but no other information about the angel or demon is mentioned in that text.

[p. 383; 3], [p. 384; 4] non-sensical goetic "angel tongues".

[p. 384; 2] *our Catholic Redeemer* ... Seeing the goetic roots of much of what is happening not only with the Roman Catholic Church, but also in many charismatic, and in all Prosperity, WOF and NAR movements, the claim to having Christ as a "Redeemer" is to be doubted. This claim to having Jesus as a Redeemer is erroneous by these larger groups.

[p. 384; 3] w*ith all the necessary things according to custom* ... A "custom" or "tradition" that is being used by the occult, here goetia, too. When traditions contradict the Bible as almost all do, we should not be surprised that it has led to the introduction to goetic "customs" or "traditions" into Christian practice.

1. Rosemary Ellen Guiley Ph.D., *The Encyclopedia of Angels*: *Second Edition* (New York, New York: Checkmark Books, 2004), p. 275.

COMMENTARY CHAPTER XXI

[illegible]

[illegible]

[illegible]

[illegible]

[illegible]

Chapter XXI: Pamiel/Pamyel

Whose hour is called Zeschar, and his spirit is called Pamiel, having many princes under him.

At the ninth hour of the night, he is called Zeschar, and his supreme angel is called Pamiel, who, after the manner of the preceding, has under his command many other spirits, good and bad, princes, leaders, and counts, and ministers appointed by turns and orders to him. In order they are ten, in the second twenty, in the third thirty, in the fourth forty, in the fifth fifty, in the sixth sixty, in the seventh seventy, in the eighth eighty, in the ninth ninety, in the tenth one hundred, in the eleventh one thousand, and in the twelfth one hundred thousand. In the operations of steganography, we do not need all these since a few are sufficient for us.

Red.	Black.	R.	B.	R.	B.	R.
Demaor	*Comary*	*Befranzij*	10.	100.	10.	100.
Nameal	*Matiel*	*Iachoroz*	10.	100.	10.	100.
Adrapon	*Zenoroz*	*Xanthir*	10.	100.	10.	100.
Chermel	*Brandiel*	*Armapy*	10.	100.	10.	100.
Fenadroz	*Euandiel*	*Druchas*	10.	100.	10.	100.
Vemastiel	*Tameriel*	*Saridel*	10.	100.	10.	100.

Here we have already from the spirits of Pamiel eighteen princes, who by their turns are sometimes leaders, sometimes counts. Whoever does not know their orders will labour in vain in this art. They have ministers assigned to them by turns and moments of the hour one thousand three hundred twenty with whom they work with wonderful results. So, when you wish to work through them in steganography at the ninth hour of the night, observe the lord of the ascendant at the same hour, and the whole figure of the sky, and write all this secret prayer on clean paper, and on the back of the same paper.

Secret Prayer

Pamiel lyraz Iafian mauelo breothis thirmoan ersoti layr pornis theory moar azas, penason.

Then, having completed all that is prescribed in the art, recite the secret prayer itself, carefully taking care not to miss anything due to those who are required for the completion of the operation. And when the conjuration is said, immediately the named spirits will appear visibly in that form which you have commanded them to wear. For all those whom we have named are benevolent, good, ready, and willing to obey, working properly, and faithful in their commissions.

Argument of Secrets.

Whatever happens to us, which otherwise we cannot safely make known to a friend by means of messengers, we entrust it first among the spirits appearing to us, and we are secure. But he is more distinguished from others by his habit and crown.

Literally, they are made to order.

Weep, mortals, who now laugh, and you despised the kindness of our glorious Redeemer with the most grievous sins and crimes in many ungrateful ways. Behold, the Turk, the mortal enemy of the Christians, will move an army from Hungary, and slaughter men like beasts. He crossed the Danube wild and was kindled by the zeal of impiety. So then, mourn the poor, you will die a horrible slaughter, you will die in the jealousy of bitterness, because your crimes will overtake you. You have despised the laws of God, your most gracious redeemer. So, deliver yourselves up to your most cruel enemies, who will devour you like locusts. By hearing we perceived how cruelly the Turk had invaded Hungary, Bohemia, and Poland, he destroyed the most powerful cities, women and virgins consecrated to God, holding chastity in the devotion of sanctity, he raped most publicly and disgracefully, horribly slaughtering the Catholics, whatever people they were, roaming everywhere like cruel beasts. You will feel his terrible cruelty in a moment, for he will suddenly disturb Germany with his most warlike army, unless the general defense of the princes resists without delay. Therefore, with groans, assume humility, reform your manners, pray to God with tears, to the extent that he may grant you the remission of offenses, and deliver us from the enemies who are most thirsty for our blood, I wrote 13th of May in the year of our Lord 1500, John Trithemius.

These letters, or any others, confirmed by the sign of Pamiel, receiving the person to whom they are sent, already an expert in the art, observes and writes the lord of the ascendant, and the whole figure of the sky as we have ordered, on clean paper, and does everything that is to be done according to the art and by the said secret prayer, with if he sees the sent spirits visibly alight, he should say to the superior:

Chasmeron apornys veto mean ilno vean aplois cralta ilso pamerson.

Having said these things to the principal, he will at once approach nearer, and will sensibly repeat in his ear the secret entrusted to him.

Commentary: Chapter XXI

[p. 387; 1] *Pamiel* [or, *Pamyel*] ... Beyond what is mentioned in this chapter, there is not much information from outside sources about the angel or demon *Pamiel. Pamiel* is mentioned in the *Lemegeton,*[1] but no other information about the angel or demon is mentioned in that text.

[p. 387; 3], [p. 386; 4] non-sensical goetic "angel tongues".

[p. 388; 2] *Behold, the Turk, the mortal enemy of the Christians, will move an army from Hungary, and slaughter men like beasts. He crossed the Danube wild and was kindled by the zeal of impiety.* [...] *By hearing we perceived how cruelly the Turk had invaded Hungary, Bohemia, and Poland,* [...] *You will feel his terrible cruelty in a moment, for he will suddenly disturb Germany with his most warlike army, unless the general defense of the princes resists without delay.* ... You will remember that in *Book 1 Commentary: Chapter III* I had mentioned how the pope and the king of France were planning to merge the two empires, and I had suggested it was most likely due to a coming Muslim invasion. The invasion, according to Trithemius did happen. We know that Vlad III managed to repel the Muslim armies before this book was written. Whether Trithemius was referring to this invasion as a hyperbolic reality about the Muslim threat is unknown.

1. Rosemary Ellen Guiley Ph.D., *The Encyclopedia of Angels: Second Edition* (New York, New York: Checkmark Books, 2004), p. 289.

COMMENTARY ON CHAPTER XXI

38.3 [illegible] — beyond what is mentioned in this volume, there is not much information from outside sources about the angel or demon [illegible] [illegible] in the [illegible], but no other information about the angel or demon is mentioned in that work.

[illegible] [illegible] [illegible] nonsensical [illegible] angel tongue.

[illegible] [illegible] [illegible] [illegible]

[illegible] [illegible] [illegible]

[illegible] [illegible] [illegible] [illegible] of the [illegible] in this book was [illegible] [illegible] this [illegible] about the [illegible] is [illegible].

[illegible] [illegible]

Chapter XXII: Jasguarim/Lssuarim

Whose hour is called Malcho, and his angel the emperor is called Jasguarim, who has under his authority many princes, commanders, and counts, and ministers.

At the tenth hour of the night, he is called Malcho, and his emperor the supreme angel is called Jasguarim, who has under his command many princes, chiefs, counts and ministers, assigned to miracles and various magical operations as Solomon, nicknamed Hermes, testifies in his Secret of Magic. One hundred commanders and one hundred counts of many ministers were assigned to steganography in their turns and orders, in other words.

Red.	Black.	R.	B.	R.	B.	R.
Lapheriel	*Chameray*	30.	10.	100.	100.	300.
Emarziel	*Hazaniel*	30.	10.	100.	100.	300.
Nameroyz	*Vraniel*	30.	10.	100.	100.	300.

And although there are many commanders and counts assigned to the operation of steganography at the tenth hour of the night, yet with us a few are sufficient for everything. We have placed three of the leaders, and likewise three of the counts, by name in this table, subjecting the number of servants to them, lawfully distributed by turns and ranks. But he who wishes to know the names of several, will bring one of the previously mentioned, and ask him about each one. But when you wish to work through these spirits at the tenth hour of the night, observe and do the things that are prescribed, writing everything very carefully on a clean sheet, and on the back of it this secret prayer, in the manner in which it is prescribed.

Secret Prayer

Jasguarim aprons vesale moes labiel throe. Tadrys asiel cachylos thubla nailso thirmiel vear. Turiel cralty solmys aslotiel naemes renhar, vear thirmo cralnoti saon dremion lauiel odres, notiel pornys. Pornis mear moab sayr aslotiel lo raytu lian aseuo, Bian eory churio bays astro penason.

Then, by joining together, and by the said secret prayer, as it should be, the spirits will soon be called.

The secret of any intention.

Let it be a mystery. Since you cannot communicate this by letters and messengers to a friend who exists near or far, call one or two of the spirits of Jasguarim and appoint your couriers, commit the secret, without doubting anything.

Literally, they are made to follow orders.

This is the prophecy of St. Nicholas Basselius of Irbusiensis, which he saw in the spirit. And he said, "This is what the Lord says to the pastors of the churches. You will quickly perish, since the greatest calamity will destroy your wide dominion, and scatter all Europe. Woe to the Ishmaelites, who break the covenants of the tabernacle, for they snatch the pastures with pride and recklessness. Behold, the dominion which you have will be broken, unless you hasten greater repentance by betraying and tearing apart. Alas, the whole Church is strewn with the worst of morals, hypocrisy has infested its ministers. Flee, do not look back, be desolate, and you will be drawn to the dogs. The whole earth will be strewn with blood. Seek repentance, inhabitants of the earth. Benjamen, the young man will experience troubles. Woe to the inhabitants of Gennesaret, which is Europe, for because of the multitude of their sins they shall perish at the hands of the Bulgarians." The prophet Nicholas makes it clear. 12th of May 1500.

When you have received letters of any kind pre-marked with the sign of Jasguarim, to whom they are sent an expert in the art, let him do all that is prescribed according to the art, and observe the order of the planets, write what is to be written. And the said conspiracy written above, as soon as the spirits sent forth appear, let him say to the former among them:

> Chamerusin othriel arnotiel solais elty. Naeles proy vear sato cralnoti, penason.

Having said this, the spirit immediately approaching will faithfully and calmly reveal the message committed to him.

Commentary: Chapter XXII

[p. 389; 1] *Jasguarim* [or, *Lssuarim*] ... Beyond what is mentioned in this chapter, there is not much information from outside sources about the angel or demon *Jasguarim*. Jasguarim is mentioned in the *Lemegeton* as *Lssuarim*,[1] but no other information about the angel or demon is mentioned in that text.

[p. 389; 1] *as Solomon, nicknamed Hermes, testifies in his Secret of Magic* ... Jasguarim is not mentioned in any fallaciously ascribed Solomonic text other than the *Lemegeton* which was written after this book.

[p. 389; 3], [p. 390; 4] non-sensical goetic "angel tongues".

[p. 390; 1] *This is the prophecy of St. Nicholas Basselius of Irbusiensis, which he saw in the spirit. And he said, "This is what the Lord says to the pastors of the churches. You will quickly perish, since the greatest calamity will destroy your wide dominion, and scatter all Europe.* [...]" ... The entirety of this "prophecy" does not need to be restated here. However, looking at what this saint is saying, it was undoubtedly true that many of these sins were happening in Roman Catholic Europe at that time. The problem of course that while the "Ishmaelites" (Muslims) did invade Europe, the kind of devastation being talked about in the entire prophecy never happened at Muslim hands. Napolean ravaged Europe from 1803–1815 and destroyed the Holy Roman Empire once and for all, but it was not the Muslims that did this destruction. This does make the prophecy made here false. A false prophecy being contained in a goetic book is not surprising considering that goetia was used for divinatory (or prophetic) purposes. Goetic divination was mostly done through a sheep's fleece [pp. 63–68 this volume], but it still does not make an excuse for the false prophecy that is being made. The prophecy, in being false, is goetic.

---

1. Rosemary Ellen Guiley Ph.D., *The Encyclopedia of Angels*: *Second Edition* (New York, New York: Checkmark Books, 2004), p. 43.

Chapter XXIII: Dardariel

Whose hour is called Aalacho, and his chief angel is called Dardariel, who has under his command many leaders, companies, and spirits.

At the eleventh hour of the night, it is called Aalacho, and its supreme emperor spirit is called Dardariel, having under his command many powerful princes and commanders, who preside over almost infinite counts and ministers. But the leaders themselves are exceedingly good-natured, cheerful, and pleasant, and they delight in conversing with men. And they are most obedient to those who work in the well-established art. And note that the number of these leaders is infinite, because almost the whole air is filled, and they cannot be numbered. And Solomon Hermes says, "And we have experienced that among the leaders, companions, and ministers of the spirit of Dardariel there are many good, useful, and most honourable men." They always desire to benefit you, always encouraging them by some invisible teaching to good, to honesty, peace, agreement, to the integrity of faith, to the love of God, and the observance of his commandments, to the contempt of the world, to the desire of heavenly happiness, and to all good. These are the good and most holy spirits who love, revere and have God, who delight in being with holy and God-fearing men, because they are their protectors appointed by God, the Creator of all. On the other hand, there are evil and worst heretics against God, enemies of all good things, who continually tempt mortals and lie in wait for men. And whatever the good spirits institute for the honour of God, these always try to destroy and recall it. And the air is full of these evil spirits, they run and run among men invisibly, always inciting them to evil, and they drag the unwary with them to hell. By means of these evil spirits of Dardariel, infinite mischief is wrought, not only among Christians, but also among unbelievers, and above all, they deceive young women, who are more ready to cause harm. And anyone, if they wish to persist in evils through them, they will be powerful in evils above all other evildoers, and worthy of eternal burning. But we who do not evil, but good, and always desire to teach and work for our strength, let us appoint a few messengers, not from evil, but from good spirits.

Red.	Black.	R.	B.	R.	B.	R.	B.
Cardiel	*Masriel*	*Nermas*	10.	20.	00.	20.	10.
Permon	*Hariaz*	*Druchas*	10.	20.	00.	20.	10.
Armiel	*Damar*	*Carman*	10.	20.	00.	20.	10.
Nastoriel	*Alachuc*	*Elamyz*	10.	20.	00.	20.	10.
Casmiroz	*Emeriel*	*Iatroziel*	10.	20.	00.	20.	10.
Dameriel	*Naueroz*	*Lamersy*	10.	20.	00.	20.	10.
Furamiel	*Alaphar*	*Hamarytz*	10.	20.	00.	20.	10.

Out of good things, we have here named fourteen captains of Dardariel's spirits, and seven counts, who are sufficient for us for all the operations of steganography for the eleventh hour of the night, with their numerous and almost infinite servants. So, when you wish to work through someone or some of them, do everything that is prescribed in the art of steganography and after you have completed everything, say this secret prayer with attention:

Secret Prayer

Dardariel pirno nadeuym pornis melto, nachir pheon pliros euali estafri thyrmano, Oniel maniel, vear raby cralnoti Vemy Throe orbasiel asar rauean. Purgiel near Iano Masiel Arlay.

If you have smelled the myrrhs of the merchul known as penason, then with this prayer completed with due attention, the spirits summoned will stand with benevolence.

A secret commission.

All the aforesaid leaders and comrades are good and faithful, doing absolutely no harm to anyone who loves God in truth. So, commit to them whatever you wish to announce at the eleventh hour of the night to a friend who is absent near or far, without hesitating anything according to this art.

John Trithemius, Abbot, Spanish Cornelius Gyrardi Gaudensi, Canon of Diu Augustus near Leiden, S.D.

Our Lord Jesus Christ, the most merciful Saviour of our souls, has promised us the happiness of eternal consolation, if we always keep his commandments with a pure heart. So, you my dearest brother, keep the commandments of God and the holy rules, carefully. Because unless you keep all the things that are forbidden unto death, which the almighty God has commanded you, you will perish eternally. So, I gave you the form and law of religious and holy conversation. But be careful that you do not give your heart through the desire of love to any mortal creature to possess. For no one comes to those supreme joys, except he who despises the world for God. Again, therefore, I exhort you by these letters of mine, as a most dear friend, you will observe my warnings which I have given you. For I consider myself happy when I have written something good at this sacred time, especially for the edification of the way of living well, by which you are always becoming better. I am now writing to you again for your good, because I fear your danger no less than mine. But I request of you, always watch, advancing daily in the fear of God, and living innocently, doing no harm to anyone, and persevering completely in your holy purpose. Trust not time, nor fortune, nor age, for they are nothing, but we are. Again, I love you in syncretism in Christ Jesus, praying that he may arrange himself for all that I am loved by you, and that I who am absent from you in body may always be present in spirit. Since I have a constant remembrance of you in my prayers, do not forget me either, I ask you eagerly. Goodbye. 12th of May in the year 1500.

Commentary: Chapter XXIII

[p. 395; 1] *Dardariel* ... Beyond what is mentioned in this chapter, there is not much information from outside sources about the angel or demon *Dardariel. Dardariel* is mentioned in the *Lemegeton,*[1] but no other information about the angel or demon is mentioned in that text.

[p. 395; 1] *And Solomon Hermes says* ... Dardariel is not mentioned in any fallaciously ascribed Solomonic text other than the *Lemegeton* which was written after this book. Where Trithemius is getting the quote, following this referenced text, from is unknown.

[p. 395; 1] *These are the good and most holy spirits who love, revere and have God, who delight in being with holy and God-fearing men, because they are their protectors appointed by God, the Creator of all.* ... While Matthew 18:10 does give a suggestion that young children have "guardian angels", the idea in its entirety is not conclusively proven by that verse. The reason being that Jesus in that verse says that "in *heaven* their angels always see the face of my Father who is in heaven." (italics mine; Matthew 18:10 ESV) The actual wording here suggests that these "guardian angels" are in heaven and not beside the children, or any adults, while "guarding them". The real source of the idea of "guardian angels" can be seen in Trimethius's statement here. Angels are not assigned to keep watch over us at all times here on earth. There is no biblical support for an ever-present guardian angel for all people, even children. The source of the "ever-present guardian angel" is goetic in nature.

[p. 396; 1] non-sensical goetic "angel tongues".

[p. 396; 2] *If you have smelled the myrrhs of the merchul known as penason, then with this prayer completed with due attention* ... Myrrh is a common summoning agent for goetics. As the *PGM* show you "inscribe in myrrh the following and set it in the same manner [along with the] hairs and fingernails, and plaster / it with [uncut] frankincense [and] old wine. [...] Good Daimon [...] Come to me, O holy Orion."[2] Myrrh can be used to both attract and repel goetic spirits, as can frankincense. Once again, Trithemius is taking a goetic practice and "Christianizing" it like charismatics have done with Psalm 91 and anointing their homes with anointing oil. This anointing oil also contains myrrh and frankincense which would make it a suitable catalyst for *PGM* spells like the one given in this paragraph. This does not mean the spell will work because of the use of anointing oil, but it does show that the practice of anointing a home with oil, at this point of any kind whether it has myrrh and/or frankincense at all, fulfills every requirement to classify the practice as goetic and *anti*-biblical.

1. Rosemary Ellen Guiley Ph.D., *The Encyclopedia of Angels: Second Edition* (New York, New York: Checkmark Books, 2004), p. 43.

2. E. N. O'Neil, "PGM I. 1–42", in *The Greek Magical Papyri in Translation Including the Demotic Spells* editor Hans Deiter Betz (Chicago, Illinois: The University of Chicago Press, 1986), p. 3. (3-4)

Chapter XXIV: Sarandiel

Whose hour is called Xephan, and his chief angel is called Sarandiel, having under him many princes, leaders, counts, and servants.

The twelfth hour of the night, which coincides with the dawn, is called Xephan, and his angel is called Sarandiel, who has under his command many spirits, good and bad, princes, leaders, counts, and ministers, who are appointed to various operations, both good and bad things. These princes (as says Hermes the Hebrew, who was called Solomon, in the fourth book on the offices of the spirits) frequently appear, usually in that form in which the Devil is read to have appeared to Eve, having one beautiful head like a virgin, with hair hanging down on each side, but two serpentine bodies, which, however, they always veil and hide under certain covers or leaves, so as not to be seen. But in the face, they are very beautiful, benevolent, and funny, and ready and cheerful for all the obedience of the worker.

Red.	Black.	R.	B.	R.	B.	B.	R.
Adoniel	*Marachy*	*Hardiel*	10.	20.	00.	20.	10.
Damasiel	*Chabrion*	*Nefrias*	10.	20.	00.	20.	10.
Ambriel	*Nestoriel*	*Irmanotz*	10.	20.	00.	20.	10.
Meriel	*Zachriel*	*Gerthiel*	10.	20.	00.	20.	10.
Denaryz	*Naueriel*	*Dromiel*	10.	20.	00.	20.	10.
Emarion	*Damery*	*Ladrotz*	10.	20.	00.	20.	10.
Kabriel	*Namael*	*Melanas*	10.	20.	00.	20.	10.

Here we already have from the good spirits of Sarandiel fourteen of the captains, and the seven of the counts. With many of their servants, who are sufficient for us at the twelfth hour of the night for all operations. When therefore you wish to work through them at the last hour of the night, observe and do all that we have commanded, carefully, and afterwards say the secret prayer.

Secret Prayer

Sarandiel marfo porno ioniel schendiel iano Nati chilpres joaschar meon prissi dyon volayr penason.

When the song is said, immediately the spirits summoned will stand ready for everything.

The constitution of the secret messenger.

When you see spirits appear in a form foreign to them, do not be afraid, because they are good, benevolent, harming no one and yet a monstrous form, but still as not to frighten anyone, as if they always hide it, appearing with a very beautiful face. Commit securely whatever you want your friend to know at night.

THEY ARE LITERALLY FORMED, AS YOU PLEASE.

Oh, miserable man, and truly miserable, why do you not pay attention to the instability of all temporal things? And why do you think that you will not die of a pitchfork? Remember what the first man earned, that he violated the commandment. May our soul die the death of the righteous, as Balaam wished, that we may be undefiled by the present pleasures and the pointless honours of the world, keeping ourselves from all sin. But we do not care how long we will finally fall into the terrible chains of death, of tormenting forever. I consider him lucky who thinks of these things. So, oh man, cast out the world as the Son of God did, and think how many evils follow us from his love. For he incurs many dangers to us. And since he is damnable to his lovers, he is deservedly despised. The lover of the world is truly worthy of eternal death. What good is this world to you, miserable man? While he is loved, he flees. While he is present, he passes away. While he exalts, he rejoices with God. While he is flattered, he deceives. While he blooms, he withers. While he sends his lovers away, he consigns them to perpetual miseries. In the year 1500, 12th of May.

Having received the letters, and knowing the sign of the principal spirit, let the expert in the art do what is customarily done. After the said and written mysterious prayer according to art, the spirits will appear, faithfully revealing what has been committed.

Commentary: Chapter XXIV

[p. 401; 1] *Sarandiel* … Beyond what is mentioned in this chapter, there is not much information from outside sources about the angel or demon *Sarandiel*. *Sarandiel* is mentioned in the *Lemegeton*,[1] but no other information about the angel or demon is mentioned in that text.

[p. 401; 1] *as says Hermes the Hebrew, who was called Solomon, in the fourth book on the offices of the spirits* … Sarandiel is not mentioned in any fallaciously ascribed Solomonic text other than the *Lemegeton* which was written after this book.

[p. 401; 3] non-sensical goetic "angel tongues".

[p. 401; 6] *When you see spirits appear in a form foreign to them, do not be afraid* … This is in defiance of the command by John to "not believe every spirit, but test the spirits to see whether they are from God, for many false prophets have gone out into the world." (1 John 4:1 ESV) Since many Prosperity, WOF and NAR teachers have never tested the spirits that they claim to see at three o'clock in the morning witching/devil hour (see pp. 76–79, this volume) or at other times during the day or night, it is obvious that these false teachers have gotten this idea to just trust the spirits from goetic "tradition".

1. Rosemary Ellen Guiley Ph.D., *The Encyclopedia of Angels: Second Edition* (New York, New York: Checkmark Books, 2004), p. 318.

COMMENTARY: CHAPTER XXV

p. 401, 2 [illegible] Beyond what is mentioned in this chapter, there is [illegible] information from outside sources about the angel [illegible] [illegible] provided [illegible] but no other information about the [illegible] is [illegible].

p. 401, [illegible] [illegible]

p. 401, [illegible] semical [illegible]

[illegible]

[illegible]

Chapter XXV

In which we will teach the method and general form of approaching this art of steganography, and of working in it without danger, with the most effort.

Whoever wishes to gain access to the knowledge of this secret art of ours, whoever wishes to work by it wonderful things and many advantageous dangers, in the first place he must be adorned with righteousness, and a clean conscience, and a good will, to God, to himself, and to his neighbor. Let him not be inclined that he should harm anyone, nor should he seek to engage in indecent dealings. Next, it is necessary that he should be somewhat filled with the good arts of literature, and especially in the knowledge of the stars, that he should know the general movements, courses, movements, changes, orders, natures, positions, risings, setting, and effects of the stars, signs, and planets. For without these no one with competent knowledge can have access to the depth of this art. Consequently, it is necessary that he should have a teacher who is perfect and experienced in the art. Because we believe that it is not possible, except in a few and in many of the most learned, and especially in magical experts, to come to this knowledge without a teacher. It is necessary for the teacher not only to be proven and experienced in knowledge, but also faithful, honest, and God-fearing, because the purer he is in good conversation with God, the more secure he will be in the operation of this knowledge, for spirits obey righteousness. So, if anyone is about to approach this art, let the teacher receive him and lead him to some secret and clean place. Let the time be calm and clear, and let the moon be in full opposition, with the sun shining brightly, and let Mercury in the ascendant be conjoined with Venus or Jupiter, if possible, Saturn and Mars are descendant, because if they or one of them were present when ascending, the establishment would not be perfect. The first oath to be instituted in the art of this oath is:

> I swear and promise by the power of Almighty God, by the blood of our Lord Jesus Christ, by the resurrection of the dead and the last judgment, and by the salvation of my soul in the holy Catholic faith to Almighty God, to the blessed Virgin Mary, to all the saints, and to you N., that this I will faithfully keep the art of steganography secret all the days of my life, and I will not teach it to anyone without your will and consent. Furthermore, I swear and promise in the same capacity that with this knowledge I will not go against God and his commandments, nor against the holy Roman and universal Church or its ministers, nor against justice and equity. I hope that shall God help me, and therefore save me in the last judgment.

Then the teacher reads the following conspiracy in the mystical language, and interprets it, and all the conspiracies contained in this work, before the student, or else it would be suspected that there is something diabolical, superstitious, or contrary to God, or that an agreement with demons, implicitly or explicitly, is in any way secretly hidden.

General secret prayer before approaching the art to be told by the Master.

> Mesari cosmeniel archea sameor critas.

Dricho mosayr visio noes veso tureas.
Abrithios naselion pyrno chyboyn ormon.
Cerualí myrbeuo lian saueao sayr.
Rhymano caue iapion nospiel saseuo rhaony.
Naty thirpolian ionayr chuleor nefris.
Mistriona nayr dauosy tyuamo turmy.
Pleon named Turias Bresne Nasephon
Adion sayr catros chyrosny aschyon ermy
Otyel layr romays theory naias atreuo.
Another measco trisna vseori jesaschor.
Bios pailon rauemy sear astropenason.

And after the master of this art has explained to his pupil the secret prayer, order, and sequence of all spirits, let him reveal to himself the most secret mysteries of this science, which are neither written nor to be written, forbidding, under the oath taken, that he should not repeat it to any one as long as he lives, unless he was worthy and skilled in the oath, also he does not write them in any way or for any reason. Then let him teach him the natures, names, places, numbers, offices, and properties of all the spirits who are assigned to this art. How, when, and where to work through them, and the rest of the mysteries that pertain to the perfection of this art, of which it is not necessary to write.

Commentary: Chapter XXV

[p. 405; 1] *Whoever wishes to gain access to the knowledge of this secret art of ours, whoever wishes to work by it wonderful things and many advantageous dangers, in the first place he must be adorned with righteousness* ... The idea that only those of the most righteousness, or even the right "level of faith", can do "miraculous" acts or even "be closer to God" is something born right out of occultism. Trithemius made it clear that much of what he says in this book is based on the *Kabbalah*. In the *Kabbalah*, the goal is to ascend the different "sefirot" or, "spheres" to gain unity with whatever it is the kabbalist, or occultist calls "God". Many of those in charismatic, Prosperity, WOF and NAR movements have over and over said that in order to gain more closeness with God you need to get to "new levels" or "new breakthroughs" with your faith.

The biblical reality of being able to have God work through us because of the "level of our faith" is flawed. As I showed in my *Introduction* that although Gideon performed a gross act of goetia in testing God, (pp. 63–68, this volume) God still used Gideon for his own purposes. Also, Nebuchadnezzar, Cyrus, and even Paul, who was sending Christians to be persecuted when Jesus appeared to him on the road to Damascus, (Acts 9:1–19) are other biblical examples. The whole idea that God will only work or be involved with those that are of an "appropriate level of faith" is a completely *anti*-biblical idea. Some of the biggest influences of the covenant promises of God in both the Old Testament and New Testament were men that committed gross acts of necromancy, were not even believers in Yahweh, or were determined to wipe the name of Christ out of existence. (*i.e.* Paul) Paul is the only of these examples that ended up becoming and staying a follower of Christ. Gideon apostacized, and the kings Nebuchadnezzar and Cyrus were identified as truly evil men their entire lives despite how Yahweh used them. The idea of your "level of faith" is nothing but kabbalism being repacked as a deceptive form of Christianity.

With Trithemius making the kabbalistic roots of his teachings in his goetia clear, his claim that these goetic rituals will only work with someone who is truly righteous is the same line of thought being taught by some charismatics, and all Prosperity, WOF and NAR movements about "levels of faith". God will use who he wants to use for what God wants to use that person for whether that person is a believer or not. God will also use a believer who these occult "Christians" believe has a "weak faith" as well if the use of that "weak faith" believer is the best way for God to be glorified.

[p. 405; 1] *especially in the knowledge of the stars, that he should know the general movements, courses, movements, changes, orders, natures, positions, risings, setting, and effects of the stars, signs, and planets.* ... Despite current beliefs about astrology, astrological practice was very common in the medieval and renaissance churches. John Dee, who had studied this text by Trithemius, was a member of Queen Elizabeth I's court as the court astrologer. Dee's job in the English court was to interpret the stars via astrology, and therefore the will of God, to the Queen. This astrology was believed to be biblical based off the apocryphal book of the *Wisdom of Solomon*:

> He it was who gave me sure knowledge of what exists, to understand the structure of the world and the action of the elements, the beginning, end and middle of the times, the alternation of the solstices and the succession of the seasons, the cycles of the year and the position of the stars. (Wisdom 7:17–19 NJB)

To us this may seem like a stretch to conclude that astrology was accepted in the medieval and renaissance church because of this verse. Pablo A. Torijano in his book *Solomon the Esoteric King*: *From King to Magus, Development of a Tradition* gives a good explanation of what is going on with the *Wisdom of Solomon* and why it caused the acceptance of astrology.

> In Wis 7:15–22, first the giver of the knowledge is identified, God himself is his teacher; thereafter, the exact nature of the promised knowledge is described in terms that point to a reinterpretation of the biblical source:
>
> The interpreters of the passage usually limit themselves either to furnishing Hellenistic and biblical parallels or to playing down the elements that do not correspond to what they suppose to be the 'correct' theology of the book. The text, however, is most interesting if we bear in mind the existence of later texts where Solomon, Hermetism and astrology appear in contact. The text states that the provider of the knowledge is God, whereas Solomon is only a disciple, who wishes to communicate the secrets handed down to him (Wis 7:15–16); this fact reminds us of the general structure of Hermetic writings where Hermes, the god, gives to a disciple exact knowledge about the universe. These two verses serve as an introduction to the catalogue of knowledge, which is then listed in detail.
>
> The exact nature of the knowledge is explicitly detailed in Wis 7:17: the knowledge is 'infallible' because it is divinely given and it encompasses the whole universe ("the things that are", its constitution ("the structure of the world") and the working of its ultimate components ("the activity of the elements"). The Greek term for elements (στοιχεία) is clearly related to the Greek doctrine of the four elements (earth, water, air, fire).[1]

We need to understand that astrology is one of the key parts of hermetic practice. With this in mind, since the *Wisdom of Solomon* does support the idea that the natural world gives us "infallible" knowledge[2] is important. While this book is rejected by Protestants, it was still included in the original 1611 KJV. That astrology would be so widely accepted still in this current day is not all that surprising with that consideration in mind. Many people are baffled when they learn that astrology was so widely accepted by Christians in the medieval and renaissance periods of history. Looking back at a text that fallaciously was, and still is, accepted as scripture by some churches, we again should not be surprised that a mostly uneducated group of people during that time, especially in theology, which was given only to the clergy, would believe astrology was a truly "Christian" practice that was noble in pursuing. A popular dispensationalist false prophet, John Hagee, makes similar claims about the natural world and the four blood moons in his book *The Four Blood Moons*: *Something is About To Change*.[3]

---

1. Pablo A. Torijano, *Solomon the Esoteric King*: *From King to Magus, Development of a Tradition* (Leiden, Netherlands; Brill, 2002), pp. 91–92.

2. "He it was who gave me sure knowledge of what exists, to understand the structure of the world and the action of the elements." (Wisdom 7:17, NJB) This does enforce Torijano's claim that this knowledge from the natural world, including the stars (astrology) was considered "infallible".

3. See: John Hagee, *The Four Blood Moons*: *Something Is About To Change* (Brentwood, Tennessee: Worthy Publishing, 2013).

[p. 405; 1] *Let the time be calm and clear, and let the moon be in full opposition, with the sun shining brightly, and let Mercury in the ascendant be conjoined with Venus or Jupiter, if possible, Saturn and Mars are descendant, because if they or one of them were present when ascending, the establishment would not be perfect.* ... With the explanation above, that Trithemius would reinforce astrological beliefs as important to goetia is not a surprise.

[p. 405; 3] *Then the teacher reads the following conspiracy in the mystical language, and interprets it, and all the conspiracies contained in this work, before the student, or else it would be suspected that there is something diabolical, superstitious, or contrary to God, or that an agreement with demons, implicitly or explicitly, is in any way secretly hidden.* ... With what my *Introduction* explains of what goetia/necromancy is from a biblical perspective, Trithemius's claims here are entirely flawed. Making use of the goetic side of this text is making an agreement with the demonic. As the book of Isaiah says:

> Because you have said, "We have made a covenant with death, and with Sheol we have an agreement, when the overwhelming whip passes through it will not come to us, for we have made lies our refuge, and in falsehood we have taken shelter" [...] Then your covenant with death will be annulled, and your agreement with Sheol will not stand; when the overwhelming scourge passes through, you will be beaten down by it. (Isaiah 28:15, 18 ESV)

What Trithemius is teaching and attempting to state in the quoted part of this commentary is rejected and annulled by Yahweh. Anyone who practices these arts, or any of the "Christianized" practices coming out of goetia, will face similar punishment.

[p. 405–406; 5] non-sensical goetic "angel tongues".

The second book of Steganography is finished.
John Tritthemius Abbot of Spanheim. 12th of May, in the year of our Lord, 1500.

Book III

The third book beginning of the Steganography of John Trithemius, Abbot of Spanheim, to serenity Prince, Lord Philip, Count Palatine of the Rhine, Duke of Bavaria, Prince Elector of the Holy Empire.

PREFACE

Afterwards, with the help of our Lord Jesus Christ, the Saviour of faithful souls, we have completed the first two books of our art, in which we have described our steganography. Having found in a certain book of an ancient philosopher, who was called Menastor, that it is possible, that by this art of our mind we may make it known to a friend, however absent, in twenty-four hours, without words, without books, and without notice, most perfectly, most widely, and most secretly. But when I was most enthusiastically led by the desire to know, I began to desire to test the truth of the sayings, and after many labours at last I found the knowledge itself proved by experience. The secret of this kind of art is great and is shrouded in such confusions that it cannot be easily discovered by anyone. For the Menastor has revealed the mystery very secretly and in a few words, with so much power that it should remain a secret, he has sought it, so that no one has yet been found after him who has dared to make his speech clearer by any document. I, however, fearing that such a wonderful work, because of its extreme secrecy, would be hated by the uninitiated, or at last burned in the fire, since I have already experienced many trials in it for a long time. So, I wanted to commend it to more open letters, that it might be possible, with the help of God, for learned men and those most studious in magic. To a certain extent it is impossible to become known, and yet it remains at all times hidden from the ignorant Rapophagi, and in no way known to their stupid understanding.

And Menastor said, "There are seven planets, seven of which are presided over by angels, and there are twenty-one spirits subject to them, through whom the mysteries are communicated." Let us explain the names of these in a table.

	Red.	Black.		R.	B.			B.
The mansions of the spirits with the planets vr.M.L.n.c.								
B.[1]	Red.		Red.			Red.		
		Sadael	1.	—	*675.*	*663.*	|	*651.*
	Oriffiel	*Poniel*	2.	—	*700.*	*688.*	|	*676.*
		Morisiel	3.	—	*725.*	*713.*	|	*701.*
		Floriel	1.	—	*575.*	*563.*	|	*551.*
	Zachariel	*Ariel*	2.	—	*600.*	*588.*	|	*576.*
		Raphael	3.	—	*625.*	*613.*	|	*601.*
		Amael	1.	—	*475.*	*463.*	|	*451.*
	Samael	*Asmael*	2.	—	*500.*	*488.*	|	*476.*
		Nebiel	3.	—	*525.*	*513.*	|	*501.*

1. This column in the original text contained the various symbols for the spirit in this table.

	Laniel	1.	—	*375.*	*363.*	)	*351.*
Michael	*Pasael*	2.	—	*300.*	*388.*	)	*376.*
	Vanriel	3.	—	*425.*	*413.*	|	*401.*
	Zabdiel	1.	—	*275.*	*263.*	|	*251.*
Anael	*Sacmiel*	2.	—	*300.*	*288.*	|	*276.*
	Adoniel	3.	—	*325.*	*313.*	|	*301.*
	Carmiel	1.	—	*175.*	*163.*	|	*151.*
Raphael	*Nabeyel*	2.	—	*200.*	*188.*	|	*176.*
	Pathiel	3.	—	*225.*	*213.*	|	*201.*
	Remafiel	1.	—	*75.*	*63.*	|	*51.*
Gabriel	*Tespiel*	2.	—	*100.*	*88.*	|	*76.*
	Theoriel	3.	—	*125.*	*113.*	|	*101.*

			Red.	Black.	R.	B.
S	*Aniel*	*Wenasor*	*631.*	*20.*	*642.*	*639.*
H	*Saturnus*	*Schamaro*	*627.*	*20.*	*638.*	*646.*
I	*Kraluotos*	*Thubrays*	*626.*	*20.*	*650.*	*634.*
	Ymarona	*Tzatzraym*	*628.*	*20.*	*639.*	

These are the seven angels of the planets according to the tradition of the ancient sages, each of whom leads the world for three hundred and fifty-four months twice in his order. Orifiel is the angel of Saturn, who at the beginning of creation ruled the world for 354 years and 4 months. Then Venus, then Jupiter, after that Mercury, and then Mars, then the Moon, and finally the Sun. It is described that each of the 354 years and 4 months of his angel had the dominion of the world written on a tablet common to him. And so, for a long time the sages say that Samael,[2] the angel of Mars, served as the ruler of the kingdom, Gabriel, the angel of the Moon, at the time of the confusion of tongues, Michael, the angel of the Sun, at the time of the exodus of Israel from Egypt. And indeed, if one applies faith to the previously mentioned truth, he will easily be able to know from the origin of the world the changes of the times, and the government of the angels, down to his own age in the prescribed order. But we, pursuing those which lead us to our purpose, subject to the seven angels of the planets, twenty-one, subject to other spirits, that is, we do not surround each of the three according to the instruction of our art of this kind, by whom we work the effect of our intention. We shall observe the usual order of the planets, beginning with Saturn, the highest of all, and proceeding to the Moon, first writing down the operation of any principal angel, and then the subordinate, and joining the chapters in order.

2. That is, Satan. The planet Mars in medieval goetic/necromantic texts was often considered to have a gateway to Hell on the planet itself.

Commentary: Preface

[p. 415; 2] *There are seven planets, seven of which are presided over by angels* ... Unlike in current understanding, back in the medieval and early renaissance, it was believed that there were only seven planets of which the sun and moon were two of those "planets". Since the term has shifted meaning in our current time, understanding that astronomy worked in a different way hundreds of years ago is required for this book.

[p. 417; E] *We shall observe the usual order of the planets, beginning with Saturn* ... This statement is important to remember when considering why Trithemius did not complete the writing of *Book 3*. Since the only chapter Trithemius did complete was on the planet Saturn, it would not be impossible for goetics to figure out what the processes were for the other six "planets", or even "planets" as we understand them in our current day. This is one reason we as Christians need to be aware of texts like this. While Trithemius did not give any definite answers of how to use goetia to "call on" or "summon" the angels of the other planets, there are many occultists with doctorates, or even those without, who are intelligent enough to figure out the rest of the unfinished book. Because of that reality, we need to be aware of where those determinations came from so that we can be aware of them.

Chapter I: Saturn; Oriffel/Orifel

Of Oriffiel, the first and priest angel of Saturn, and of the operations which are performed through him.

Saturn, the highest and supreme of all the planets, slow in motion by nature, cold, because it is remote, difficult, and high at the point of its beginning six hundred fifty years until the point of the first station in which it resides in any sign thirty moves by its own natural motion six hundred twenty-six. His first and supreme, the angel is called, according to the opinion of the ancients, Oriffiel, who has under him three other principal spirits, in other words, Sadael, Poniel, and Morifiel, of whom we shall speak in their own place and order. By means of him we can make known the secret of our mind to a friend, a knower of this art, wherever he may be, through letters if we please, or even without letters, and do many other wonderful things, which no one else understands, who is ignorant of this knowledge of ours. Therefore, wishing to work through this angel in steganography, especially on the day of Saturn, and in these matters, business, and causes that belong to Saturn. First of all, it is necessary that you know his various and diverse movements and the various first, pure, proper, mixed, upright, retrograde, and confused. And in all these it is necessary that he should know not only the general rules handed down by the astronomers (for although they are most conducive to this science of ours, they are not entirely sufficient), but also particular ones. So, as a basis for the tables below and rules about the motions of the planets, which it is absolutely necessary for anyone working in this art to know, we have added special rules and tables of precise movements throughout each chapter of this work, without observing which no one will be able to work in this art. And note that the day of any planet is divided into four equal parts, the first of which, *i.e.* three unequal hours, is occupied by the main angel of the planet itself, and the other three parts are succeeded by their substitutes in order. For example, on the day of Saturn, Oriffiel, his first angel, three unequal hours from the rising of the sun, which are called the hours of the planets, including, the second three, his first angel Sadael. Poniel the second holds the third, and Morifiel the angel of Oriffiel the third holds the fourth three hours. During the first three hours of the day, both of Saturn and of the other stars, in matters appropriated to Saturn, we must work through Oriffiel, under the second by Sadael, under the third through Poniele, and under the last three through Morisiel. And all operations according to the movement of Saturn either receive a successful result or a weak one. But now let us put a punctual table.

Punctual table.

R.		ἀλθα	B.				)		688	)			)		642		685	)	
Saturn		638	)		672	632	|		684	(		701	|		639		18	|	
644		633	|		657	696	|			(		725	|		633		693	|	
650		635	|		655	689	|		δέλτα	)	R.	719	|		643		696	|	
629		642	|		667	684	|		719			713	|		B.	R.	692	(	
650		632	(	R.	658	691	|		725			708	(		657		690	(	R.
645		640	(		673	692	|		704			710	(	R.	665		691	|	
635		637	|		675	699	|		725			717	|		674		692	|	
646		643	|		660	692	|		720			707	|		21		698	|	
636		638	|		651	698	|		710			715	|		672		993	|	
632		634	|		675	688	|		721			712	|		667		696	|	
646	βέτα	B.	|		669	684	|		712			718	|		671		69	δ)	
639		669	|		663	697	|		707			713	|		18		720	)	
634		675	|		658	682	|		721			709	)		654		707	|	
641		654	|		660	680	|		714			B.	)		656		710	|	
642		675	|		667	692	|		709			γ.ω.	|		671		17	|	
649		670	|		637	683	|		716			641	|		666		722	|	
642		660	|		665	698	(	R.	717			642	|		679		721	|	
648		675	|		662	700	(		723			649	|		671		710	|	
638		661	|		668	685	|		713			646	|				10	|	
634		651	|		663	676	|		709			635	(		23		712	|	
647		671	(	R.	659	700	|		722			24	(		[1] T. R.		713	|	
632		664	(		γάμμα	R. 694	|		707			644	|	R.	681		710	|	
630		659	|		694	688	|		705			646	|		700		708	(	
642		666	|		700	683	|		717			633	|		685		721	(	R.
633		667	|		679	685	|		708			635	|		683		714	|	
648		674	|		700	602	|		723			632	|		19		725	|	
650		667	|		695	682	|		725			631	|		682		715	|	
655		673	|		685	690	|		720			646	|		689		721	|	
626		663	|		696	687	|					635	|		684		714	|	
650		659	)		686	693	)					18	|		696			)	
644												643	)						

In the middle of Saturn's motion into the second day, having learned the degree and hour from the common tables, be careful to observe them first, whether it is direct or retrograde, pure, proper, mixed, or confused. But you will not find this from common tables. We have arranged a table prescribed in this circle, in which you will be able to find the point of the beginning and the end of its movement at any hour, by two steps running together in minute particles. So, that is to say, every minute is divided into two, three, or four hourly parts according to the proportion of pure or confused motion, that is, observed by the union and separation of other planes. For it is impossible either through the stars or through the spirits of the stars that you can achieve the effect of this art, by knowing and carefully observing punctual movement you will know how to precisely direct

1. Uyl – There was a symbol from the original Stenganographia which I did not include after the Secret Prayer. If you wish to see what the symbol was, there are plenty of free copies in the original Latin online for the reader to refer to.

your operations to the proper qualities of the planets. For in the various degrees, signs, days, hours, minutes, seconds, thirds, and fourths, the effects of the planets vary in many different ways, as regards this knowledge. For in each degree twenty-five we observed and found various changes, whence it seemed necessary to us to divide each degree into as many principal parts. But this division has no place in all degrees, but only in those in which the stars leading us to this art arise, with whom the operation is made to signify to the absent all that we will, by the service of spirits without letters, as we shall say. And so, the first table of the division of the degrees of Saturn's motion, which we have given, left out the first quarter of the day or night permanently in those things which pertain to the operation of Saturn and its beginning, but the second to the second for three hours, the third to the third, and the fourth to the fourth. Then we put the punctual order of the movement of Saturn himself in ascending, when he was in one of the first four signs, which are Aries, Taurus, Gemini, and Cancer. Of the remaining eight signs we shall also arrange the following table.

Table One

						9.		12.		12.		18		21.		
	B.	R.		B.		R.		B.		R.		*Lib.* B.		*Sag.* B.		
|	*3	*	|	‡· 6	|	♒	|	γ.	|	69	|	700	|	634	|	
|	639	693	|	16	|	700	|	647	|	716	|	692	|	♍ R.	|	
|	642	696	|	639	|	689	|	650	|	722	|	691	|	663	|	
|	633	685	|	638	|	697	|	634	(	721	|	21	(	673	|	
|	23	25	|	642	(R.	696	|	24	(R.	714	|	681	(R.	668	|	
)	641	679	(	633	(	691	(	642	|	24	|	696	|	18	)	
R.)	650	682	(B.	13	|	21	(B.	648	|	724	(	692	|	674	)	B.
|	642	22	|	644	|	682	|	643	|	710	(B.	684	|	671	|	
|	634	690	|	648	|	684	|		|	721	|	24	|	668	|	
|	24	692	|	643	|	24	|		|	714	|		|	675	|	
|	647	685	|	23	|	679	|		|	719	|		|	666	|	
|	632	25	|	0	|	682	|		|	721	|		|	658	|	

Table Two

	4.			7.		11.		13.		
	B.	R.		B.		R.		B.		
{	673		)		)	710	)	672	)	
|	663	706	|	668	|	717	|	667	|	
|	665	725	|	675	|	723	|	660	|	
|	665	714	|	674	|	718	|	20	|	
|	671	24	|	671	|	708	|	668	|	R.
|	659	717	|	21	|	721	|	675	|	
|	633	709	|	671	|	714	|	674	|	
|	23	19	(B.	667	|	24	|	24	)	

R.	|	664	722	(	664	(	R.	715	(	B.
	|	663	707	|	24	(		717	(	
	|	673	721	|	669	|		708		
	|	668	708	|	660	|		18		
	|	18	18	)	663	|		722		
	|	668			659	|		717		
	|	667			671	|		710		
	|	664			664	)		20		
	(	658								

16.	R.		19.	)		22.	|		24.	|		17.	|	
640	)		B.	|		R.	|		*Gem*. B.	|		R.	|	
642	|			|			|		694	|		675	|	
633	(		707	|		67	|		696	|		666	|	
23	(	B.	714	|		692	|		699	|		659	|	
647	|		722	(		684	|		696	(		19	|	B.
642	|		12	(	R.	24	(		689	(	R.	692	|	
635	)		709	|		700	(	B.	19	|		657	|	
			721	|		691	|		679	|				
20.			718	|		691	|		682	|				
Sag. B.			72	)		696	|							
	)					684	|		69 B.					
639	|						)							
632	|													
634	|		R.	|		5.	|		718			R.		
633	(	R.	724	|		*Sag*. R.	|		725			681. B.		
23	(		717	|		634	|							
632	|		17	(		646	|		8.					
636	|		722	(	B.	635	(	B.	*Aq*. B.					
635	|		717	|		646	(		695 R.					
646	)		710	|										

B.													R. The pure motion of the planets.					
649	)		549	)		333			|	Sat			650	|		626		
635	|		538	|		23	|		|	S	(		675	|		651		
646	|		534	|	B.	347	|		|	P	(	R.	700	}	B.	67	}	R.
639	|		546	|		342	|	R.	|	Vir	|		725	|		701	|	
644	|		535	|		348	|		|	[2]	|		550	|		526	|	
646	|		25	|		343	|		|	e	(		575	|		551	|	
635	|					♀ B.	|		|	a	(	B.	600	}	R.	576	}	B.
12	|		R.	)		245	|		|	r	|		625	|		601	|	
647	|		427	|		232	|		|	M.	|	R.	450	|		426	|	
642	(		450	|		235	|		|		(		475	|		451	|	
634	(	R.	441	|		25	|		|		(	R.	500	}	B.	476	}	R.
24	|		444	|		246	|		|		|		525	|		501	|	
649	|		24	|		240	|	R.	|	Sol	|		350	|		326	|	

2. Uyl – There was a symbol from the original Stenganographia which I did not include after the Secret Prayer. If you wish to see what the symbol was, there are plenty of free copies in the original Latin online for the reader to refer to.

<table>
<tr><td>635</td><td>|</td><td></td><td>432</td><td>|</td><td></td><td>246</td><td>|</td><td></td><td>|</td><td>L</td><td>(</td><td></td><td>375</td><td>|</td><td></td><td>351</td><td>|</td><td></td></tr>
<tr><td>642</td><td>|</td><td></td><td>439</td><td>|</td><td>B.</td><td>18</td><td>|</td><td></td><td>|</td><td>P</td><td>(</td><td>B.</td><td>400</td><td>}</td><td>R.</td><td>376</td><td>}</td><td>B.</td></tr>
<tr><td>646</td><td>|</td><td></td><td>447</td><td>|</td><td></td><td>246</td><td>|</td><td></td><td>|</td><td>V</td><td>|</td><td></td><td>425</td><td>|</td><td></td><td>401</td><td>|</td><td></td></tr>
<tr><td>645</td><td>|</td><td></td><td>17</td><td>|</td><td></td><td>235</td><td></td><td></td><td>|</td><td>Ve.</td><td>|</td><td></td><td>250</td><td>|</td><td></td><td></td><td>|</td><td></td></tr>
<tr><td>645</td><td>|</td><td></td><td>446</td><td>|</td><td></td><td>B.</td><td></td><td></td><td>|</td><td>Z</td><td>(</td><td></td><td>275</td><td>|</td><td></td><td></td><td>||</td><td></td></tr>
<tr><td>24</td><td>)</td><td></td><td>442</td><td>|</td><td></td><td>131</td><td>|</td><td></td><td>|</td><td>S</td><td>(</td><td>R.</td><td>300</td><td>}</td><td>B.</td><td></td><td>|</td><td></td></tr>
<tr><td></td><td></td><td></td><td>439</td><td>|</td><td></td><td>142</td><td>|</td><td></td><td>|</td><td>A</td><td>|</td><td></td><td>325</td><td>|</td><td></td><td>226</td><td>|</td><td></td></tr>
<tr><td>Iap. B.</td><td>)</td><td></td><td>20</td><td>|</td><td></td><td>135</td><td>|</td><td></td><td>|</td><td>M.</td><td>|</td><td></td><td>250</td><td>|</td><td></td><td>251</td><td>||</td><td></td></tr>
<tr><td>542</td><td>|</td><td></td><td></td><td>)</td><td></td><td>133</td><td>|</td><td></td><td>|</td><td>C</td><td>|</td><td></td><td>175</td><td>}</td><td>R.</td><td>276</td><td>}</td><td>R.</td></tr>
<tr><td>534</td><td>|</td><td></td><td>o</td><td>)</td><td></td><td>23</td><td>(</td><td></td><td>|</td><td></td><td>(</td><td>B.</td><td>200</td><td>|</td><td></td><td>301</td><td>|</td><td></td></tr>
<tr><td>533</td><td>(</td><td></td><td>R.</td><td>|</td><td></td><td>147</td><td>(</td><td>R.</td><td>|</td><td>p</td><td>(</td><td></td><td>225</td><td>|</td><td></td><td>126</td><td>|</td><td></td></tr>
<tr><td>23</td><td>(</td><td>R.</td><td>347</td><td>)</td><td></td><td>142</td><td>|</td><td></td><td>|</td><td></td><td>|</td><td></td><td>50</td><td>|</td><td></td><td>151</td><td>|</td><td></td></tr>
<tr><td>546</td><td>|</td><td></td><td>342</td><td>)</td><td>B.</td><td>148</td><td>|</td><td></td><td>|</td><td>R</td><td>|</td><td></td><td>75</td><td>}</td><td>B.</td><td>176</td><td>}</td><td>B.</td></tr>
<tr><td>542</td><td>|</td><td></td><td>346</td><td>|</td><td></td><td>143</td><td>|</td><td></td><td>|</td><td>I</td><td>(</td><td>R.</td><td>100</td><td>|</td><td></td><td>201</td><td>|</td><td></td></tr>
<tr><td>539</td><td>|</td><td></td><td>349</td><td>|</td><td></td><td>23</td><td>|</td><td></td><td>|</td><td></td><td>(</td><td></td><td>125</td><td>|</td><td></td><td>26</td><td>|</td><td></td></tr>
<tr><td>19</td><td>)</td><td></td><td>19</td><td>|</td><td></td><td>150</td><td>|</td><td></td><td>|</td><td></td><td></td><td></td><td>Punctua Table 26.</td><td></td><td></td><td></td><td>|</td><td></td></tr>
<tr><td></td><td></td><td></td><td>343</td><td>|</td><td></td><td>139</td><td>)</td><td></td><td>|</td><td></td><td></td><td></td><td>B.</td><td></td><td></td><td>76</td><td>}</td><td>R.</td></tr>
<tr><td></td><td></td><td></td><td>332</td><td>|</td><td></td><td></td><td></td><td></td><td>)</td><td></td><td></td><td></td><td></td><td></td><td></td><td>101</td><td></td><td></td></tr>
<tr><td></td><td></td><td></td><td>346</td><td>|</td><td></td><td></td><td></td><td></td><td></td><td></td><td></td><td></td><td></td><td></td><td></td><td></td><td></td><td></td></tr>
</table>

On the various motions of the Planets, and the interpretation of the Tables.

At any rate in the present chapter, we shall have a special treatise on the movements of Saturn and his spirits, and on the operations of steganography through them. Let us not, however, be forced to repeat what has once been said in any of the chapters, the reader should have been warned, that what we say in this very chapter, let him strive to be mindful even in the following. Now there are various motions of each planet, and they are all very subtly divided into various others. The pure and proper motion is manifold and is varied by the most subtle divisions. Direct, retrograde, mixed, and confused, they vary in almost as many points as they do at the beginning of their movement in the circle. What shall I say to you by the conjunction of the planets themselves? For, as Ptolemy says in *Gentiloquius*, there are one hundred and twenty conjunctions in the planets themselves, in other words, binary twenty-one, ternary thirty-five, quaternary thirty-five, quinary twenty-one, senary seven, and one septenary. And we will speak of these in their own place. But of the rest of the motions, however, we cannot give a definite term, on account of the infinite differences, in which the points which increase or decrease every day, are varied by the ignorant. Yet, as far as we could observe, we found more than three hundred thousand divisions, in which all the operations of this art, to what effect, they often vary. And unless one is very experienced in all these and knows perfectly the means of the motions of the planets themselves, and then the smallest punctual divisions, which come from the fourth, third, second minutes, and degrees, divided very finely into equal parts, he will easily fall into true troubles, and there is hardly any more serious danger to escape. So, for the perfect establishment of this science, we arranged three tables: in the first of which we reduced the movement of Saturn according to the four parts, both day and night, namely proper and pure, to the punctual root, and arranged to the true point of the ascendant of each sign. Beginning with the first degree of Aries, point six hundred forty-one, and sixty-nine. We have assembled the whole Zodiac in the second table. Then, in the same second table, the movement of Saturn in each of the twelve signs to all the quarters of the day and night we have them described in minute detail, in other words for every hour of the ascending degree in which Saturn himself was, when we know it, the root of the punctuality can be clearly seen. I do not know if our age can ever reach it, the table must be begun again at the head of its prince. In the third table we have reduced the septenary conjunction of Saturn with the other planets, which is unique, to the proportion of a point, by which all the one hundred twenty connections are easily brought to a point. In the same chart, the pure motion of all the planets is known by the punctual division, progression, and elongation of each principle from a point in each motion, if the mean of the motion is previously considered perfectly. For without knowledge of the medium's movement, it is impossible for anyone to approach the practice of this science. Again, even if you understand the motion of the medium and the truth in the same way perfectly, it will profit you nothing for the knowledge of this science, unless you understand the prescribed three tables for all the points of divisions in the motions of the planets taken equally by each minute detail. But now let us proceed to the operation.

But having known all, and having understood perfectly what we have said, and with the help of God, we are going to say, when you wish to work in this most profound observation, you must first of all know the rising, exaltation, and setting of all the stars of the eighth sphere, through which the work takes place, and how far each one is from another. But they are the stars, by means of which we work to announce any secret to the absent, either by words or in writing, and without a human messenger, are seven in number, whose names, places, risings, setting, elevations, distances, and return approaches we have described in a special book, which it would be too earnest to repeat here again by inserting. So, having observed the star in all things as it should be, and having known the point of the ascendant in which Saturn was at the same hour, if the operation is to be affected by him, consider very carefully the quality of its movement, if it is direct or retrograde, pure, or mixed, proper or combined with other hindrances of evil aspects, discreet or confused. Then write the point of the first movement in the same sign, both of Saturn itself and of the other planets conjoined to it, from the common tables, and those which we have given, very accurately and properly calculated on clean paper, and carefully observe how much it is progressed, how much it is elevated, or how much it is depressed. You will do the same thing in conjunction with the other planets, Saturn or the one through whom the operation takes place in union or sex. Because in them lies the greatest strength of this operation. Also, first of all, observe in which quarter Saturn is, not only for which day or night, but also for which sign he is in, and for which years from the beginning of the world, when he was in the house, his first creation, because all these things are necessary. And note, when Oriffiel, the angel of Saturn, rules the world in his order, that he will rule for three hundred fifty-four years and four months. Then all the operation of this most profound science, which pertains to the works of Saturn, and which is done through him, is done without great effort, it will achieve a clear result. And the same is to be observed about the other planets. Whoever, therefore, knowing the principles of this art, wishes to work by it without difficulty, shall work by that planet, whose principal angel at that time is found to govern the world by easy calculation. Therefore, having carefully calculated everything, proceed to the operation, observe which angel of Saturn presides over that fourth day or night and write his name with the name of the star through which you wish to work, which you need to see. And at all times you will be able to see the stars you need, by the art we have handed down, whether by day or by night. Then write on the same paper the rest, which you know to be most secret, having been carefully prepared for this in our manner as you know. Afterwards, place the very card which you have written before you on the table, and write on another piece of paper the concept of your mind which you want to know is absent, and fold these two cards one after the other, and place them in a more prominent place before you on the table or pulpit. And tell the secret plan to the spirit, through which to work, appropriated to him. Whether you prefer to communicate the secret through the spirit without writing at all, or without the spirit, it is at your discretion. For it is of the same operation, with the spirit or without the spirit, to communicate a secret to a friend, with a few alterations, as we shall say in its proper place. Now we will arrange the difference between the operations of Saturn and his angels according to the four principal quarters, with the conspiracies appropriated to each in order, to which we must seek, when the secret is announced by the spirit.

Of the first Angel of Saturn, who is chief, and is called Oriffiel, who observes the first quarter of Saturn.

The first and principal angel of Saturn, as we have said above, is called Oriffiel, who, together with the other angels of the planet in his order, rules the world for three hundred fifty-four years and four months. He has the first part both in the day and in the night, and through him the operation takes place from the rising of the sun in the day, and from the setting of the sun in the night, until the third hour inclusive, in all that pertains to Saturn, and in his day and night, as we have said. So, when in the first quarter of Saturn you wish to announce something to the absent person without words and without letters, then no other spirit of Saturn should be called to you than Oriffiel, because through him you will be able to announce everything perfectly. First of all, consider in what sign this Saturn is, and in what degree, and whether it is direct or retrograde, and with which planets it is conjunct. Let us take an example of the first: Behold, Saturn is already in the twenty-fifth degree. Taurus, on the twenty-eighth of April of the present year, which is the Lord's 1500. Now let us take twenty-five by twenty-five, and they become six hundred. Let us divide these into four equal quarters, and each quarter will remain one hundred fifty. Let us complete all the degrees of Saturn in the sign of Taurus, and there will be thirty. But let us take him three through twenty-five in all, and they become seven hundred fifty. Let us reject the four superfluous degrees in the middle of the third, the fourth, and six hundred fifty will remain. the elevation and setting of the angel Oriffiel with Saturn in the first quarter, knowing which, our operation will be easy.

Table.

B.	R.	B.	R.	R.	B.	R.)	B.	R.
Hora 1.	*Hor. 2.*	*hor. 3.*	*grad.*	*punct.*	*hor. 1.*	*hor. 2.*	*hor. 3.*	
640	635	22	25	634	632	632	632	650
642 } R.	646 } B.	647 } R.	3	646	32	640	640	640
634	25	646	2 } B.	648 }	640 } R.	24 } B.	633 } R.	646 } B.
646	640	632	1	632	650	647	632	639
635	646	634	4	639	644	638	632	650
646	642)	12)	1	647	639	639)	640)	626)
			5)	)	) *sat.*			R.

Having considered these very carefully, the angel Oriffiel of Saturn is found to be separated from Saturn by twenty-five degrees and fifteen minutes, and it is to the east, distant from the first point of Saturn's motion by six hundred twenty-five degrees, and from the end of its motion by twenty-five minutes. Having known these things, make an image of wax, or paint on paper a new figure of Oriffiel in the form of a bearded and naked man, standing on a bull of various colours, holding a book in his right hand, and a pen in his left, perfect and fit to communicate the secret of my mind to N. son of N. my friend securely, faithfully and completely, whom I love. Write your name on your forehead with a paste made of rose oil, and on your chest the name of your absent friend, saying,

> This is the image of N., the daughter of N., to whom the conception of my mind is announced through the angel of Saturn, Oriffiel, amen.

On the front of the image write *Merion* and, on the chest, *Troesda*. Then join both images together, saying,

> In the name of the Father and the Son and the Holy Spirit, amen. Hear Oriffiel, prince of the star Saturn, and by the virtues of the almighty God I admonish you, listen, I command and command you by the virtue of that image of yours, that you tell N. son of N. this intention of mine (let the intention be explained) as securely, secretly, and faithfully as possible, omitting nothing of the hearts, which I want him to know, and which I recommended to you. In the name of the Father and the Son and the Holy Spirit, amen.

Then wrap the images themselves joined as they are together in a clean cloth washed with white water, and place them in a movable vessel, which the sages of India call *pharnat alronda*. You will wish for a space of twenty-four hours and without any hesitation your desire will be perfectly fulfilled within those twenty-four hours. Let him know, your friend absent the intention in every form most perfectly, as you have said it above the image (however long it may have been) and whatever you wish to know from him, he will know in those twenty-four hours perfectly and most secretly, so that never in eternity will any man be able to perceive or know this without your will or that of your friends. And it is a great secret, which no wise man before us has ventured to commend to letters. But if that friend of yours wishes to inform you of any matter concerning his business, he can inform you with the same spirit within the same space of twenty-four hours, provided he is well perfected in this art. But you, after the twenty-four hours have passed, take the pictures from the place in which they were placed, and replace them, because you can work through them at all times of Oriffiel, not only for that friend of yours, but for anyone, others, changing only the name of the friend himself into the name of him whom you wish to know something about. And note that the images themselves need not be painted as beautiful or curious, but however much, if they were simple, it does not matter, as long as they have some proportional resemblance, so that they are known to be the images of men. But he who wills and will be able to paint them beautifully, will not be hindered by anything, nor will it profit.

Instead of the angel Sadael finding from the consideration of the fixed robed from the point of Saturn's motion, make images (in the manner in which we have said in the previous operation) of Oriffiel with the inscriptions, arguments, and other details that were said there. When these are completed, place the images themselves on the five, spread the branches of grass outside the house in a safe and secret place, and say over them:

> In the name of the Father and the Son and the Holy Spirit, amen. [They are ... red] Just as I placed these two images of the angel Sadael and N. the daughter of N. my friend joined together on these five movable branches, so I command you Sadael in the power of Oriffiel, your great prince, as the secret of my mind, which I committed to explaining to you, without delay to the notice of the aforesaid friend.

With these words, leave the images there for twenty-four hours; and what you wished will be done, and your friend will know everything that you said about the pictures, most perfectly and secretly. Likewise, if you wish to know about someone who is absent, how he is doing, and his true state in twenty-four hours, no matter how far he is, you will be able to know in this way.

AND ALL THAT TAKES PLACE IN THE WORLD BY OBSERVING THE CONSTELLATIONS, YOU WILL BE ABLE TO KNOW BY THIS ART.

OF THE THIRD ANGEL OF SATURN, WHO IS SECOND UNDER ORIFFIEL, AND IS CALLED POMIEL, PRESIDING OVER THE THIRD AND FOURTH OF SATURN.

The third angel of Saturn is called Pomiel, who is second in rank below Oriffiel, the principal angel of Saturn. He presides over the seventh, eighth, and ninth hours of Saturn, both day and night, in all that pertain to the operation of Saturn. Its place, since it moves with its own in order to the fixed stars twenty-five degrees from the east, you will find it in the tables arranged in its hours.

OF THE SECOND ANGEL OF SATURN, WHO IS THE FIRST UNDER ORIFFIEL, AND IS CALLED SADAEL, PRESIDING OVER THE SECOND GUARD OF SATURN.

Secondly, the angel of Saturn is called Sadael, who is the first placed in order under Oriffiel, and has a second part after his chief, both in the day and in the night, in the works and seasons of Saturn, that is, the fourth, fifth, and sixth unequal hours. When, therefore, in these three hours you wish to communicate something to a friend who has been absent for twenty-four hours, without letters, without words, and without a message, do it by all and in detail, which we have said in the previous operation and observe the point of the second movement of Saturn in its degrees to the sign, in which the planet itself moves, and what kind of movement it is, and where the spirit moving the star is, how much it recedes, and how much it is removed from the center of its movement, how much it is distant from any point of the entire circle or sphere. In order to obtain a knowledge of these, this table is:

R.			R.			B.			R.			B.			R.			B.			
Hora 54.			*hora 6.*			*hora 4.*			*hora 5.*			*hora 6.*			*hora 4.*			*hora 5.*			
669	)		634	)		673	)		655	)		669	)		658	)		668	)		
675	|		24	|		663	|		667	|		651	|		660	|		663	}	R.	R.
654	}	B.	666	}	B.	659	}	R.	658	}	B.	675	}	R.	667	}	B.	659	|	Saturn	
675	|		667	|		23	|		18	|		69	|		657	|		556	|		
25	|		674	|		673	|		673	|		663	|		665	|		653	|	B.	œ
670	)		667	)		675	)		675	)		23	)		662	)		652	)		

Having confirmed the movement of Saturn, and having found the punctual place of Pomielis, make two images, through all, as we have said.

Commentary: Chapter I

[p. 421; 1] *Oriffel* [or, *Orifel*] ... According to Cornelius Agrippa, *Oriffel* is the chief of throne spirits. According to kabbalistic lore and Eliphas Levi, *Oriffel* is the angel of the wilderness.[1] The wilderness in ancient Jewish biblical beliefs was the realm of demons. This is significant to remember when Jesus went out to the wilderness to be tempted by Satan after his baptism. (Mark 1:12–13) According to the *Lemegeton, Oriffel* serves under Anael. Paracelsus says that *Oriffel* is a talisman angel that replaces one of the Egyptian Genii.[2] This is the same way that Prosperity, WOF and NAR advocates call on angels to protect them from the demonic.

[p. 427; E] *Saturn or the one through whom the operation takes place in union or sex. Because in them lies the greatest strength of this operation.* ... We cannot know for certain if Trithemius is referring to sex magic as promoted in kabbalism[3] and by Aliester Crowley. There have been Prosperity, WOF and NAR movements that have believed that if a couple has sex in front of their congregation during a church service that they will conceive. There is a video of this literally happening on *YouTube*.[4]

[p. 427; E] *And note, when Oriffiel, the angel of Saturn, rules the world in his order* ... This "world" is referring to the rulership of the earth, not just the planet Saturn. That an "angel", really a "demon", is capable of taking rulership of the earth over Christ saying in Matthew 28:18 that all authority in heaven *and earth* is his, Trithemius saying this as a devout Roman Catholic, should give us all a clear warning about where the belief any demon can still rule the earth is coming from. The idea that Satan is currently ruling this world can be seen from this statement and this entire chapter as coming from goetia and not the Bible.

[p. 427; E] *that he will rule for three hundred fifty-four years and four months.* ... The *Age of Aquarius* is calculated in a similar way by astrologers and numerologists. While Aquarius is said to be associated with the planet Uranus. Uranus was not a recognized planet in the times that Trithemius's or the kabbalistic texts were written. Therefore, the application of Saturn to the *Age of Aquarius*, that many occultists believe we are either living in or about to enter into, is not out of order. The *Age of Aquarius* is believed to be headquartered in the United States of America where it will spread across the world.

---

1. Gustav Davidson, *A Dictionary of Angels including the fallen angels* (New York, New York: The Free Press, 1971), p. 215.

2. Rosemary Ellen Guiley Ph.D., The Encyclopedia of Angels: Second Edition (New York, New York: Checkmark Books, 2004), p. 283.

3. 1. See: Marla Segol, *Kabbalah and Sex Magic: A Mythical-Ritual Genealogy* (*Magic in History Book 23*) (University Park, Pennsylvania: The Pennsylvania State University Press, 2021).

4. 2. Solomon's Temple, "COUPLE TOLD TO CONCEIVE A BABY ON THE CHURCH ALTAR IN FRONT OF EVERYONE", *YouTube*, accessed November 17, 2024, https://www.youtube.com/watch?v=RHV7FAASd34.

In his troubling book about how the demonic Lilith with one day rule the world, Ed Russo states that

> I mentioned in chapter about esoteric instruction this eventually led to the founding of the New Atlantis who will unite the world under the Goddess [Lilith]. […] When General Washington had his unearthly encounter at Valley Forge the being laid out the plans for America's future as the New Atlantis. […] It put out a fire that couldn't be snuffed out by normal means due to how hot it was. It seems that for us to have world unity it first had to begin with the New Atlantis which is America.[5]

Considering how the two biggest occult based religious movements in the world right now, Dispensational Christianity and the Prosperity, WOF and NAR movements, were both founded and started in the United States of America, this is concerning. We also must realize that the founder of Hillsong Church in Sydney, Australia did come to the United States of America to learn Prosperity doctrine to take back to his then struggling church. Brian Houston's Hillsong Church is a direct product and child of the Prosperity movement, and the *Age of Aquarius* associated with it.

[p. 427; E] *pulpit* … a generic reference to a pulpit or podium. This does not indicate a pastor's or church's "pulpit".

[p. 428; 1 – p. 429; 3] There is too much to go over here. Therefore, all I will say is that the magical process that Trithemius is describing here for goetic purposes is very similar, if not exactly the same to, goetic spells within the *PGM.*

5. Ed Russo, *Lilith*: *The Power of the Woman's Spirit in the Age of Aquarius* (Research Triangle, North Carolina: Illuminated Publications [Lulu.com], 2014), pp. 118–119, Kindle Edition.

End of the third book.

APPENDIX

INTRODUCTION

By Anthony Uyl MTS

I remember when I was in what my church at that time called, "Children's Church" really an alternate name for "Sunday School". The pro-dispensational Children's Church leader that evening showed us a video of a man in a suit promoting something called "The Bible Code". I was not aware of the issues behind dispensational thought at the time, nor was I aware of the errors being shown as truth in this video.

The book written by Michael Drosnin (who during this time was a fundamentalist dispensational) claimed that he had met a scholar by the name of Eli Rips that claimed the following about the Hebrew Tanakh:

> Rips explained that each code is a case of adding every fourth of twelfth or fiftieth letter to form a word. Skip X spaces, and another X paces, and another X spaces, and the hidden message is spelled out.[1]

This seems rather odd. Throughout the chapter, Drosnin provides multiple examples of what he claims as evidence of predictions of events in the 1990's. When looking at the examples in the first chapter of his book,[2] There are very drastic discrepancies to the "number of spaces" that are counted between each word and even different words within the same text that Drosnin is trying to use to prove one event.

There is another very evident problem here. In the example on page 32, Drosnin attempts to show that the word אישנו indicates "president" where he tried to "predict" that Bill Clinton would become President. The problem is, there is no biblical Hebrew equivalent for אישנו. That "Hebrew" word simply never existed. What Drosnin has done, is read the word as ונשיא. When looking at the text, Drosnin seems to have missed that Hebrew is read from right-to-left, and not left-to-right. Even with that, there is no biblical Hebrew equivalent for ונשיא. So, Drosnin has imported the meaning from אביהו who was the son of Rehoboam, the king of Judah, Abijah. With that reading, Drosnin assumed that Abijah meaning, "Yah is father" to somehow mean the president of the United States of America. The same page, Drosnin tries to once again show the name "Clinton", but again, he is reading the Hebrew the wrong way.

On page 40, Drosnin cannot decide which way he wants to read his Hebrew. In the first example he claims that the ancient biblical Hebrew directly named Adolf Hitler. Drosnin circles the letters from different lines of Hebrew to form the word היטלר which when transliterated says "hytlr". Since biblical Hebrew did not use vowels in their writing, but vowels were used in their spoken language, other consonants could be used. Yod י could be used for an "i". But this still seems awkward that biblical Hebrew would spell out a German word. If this is not bad enough, Drosnin once again gets his Hebrew confused to spell out רצויצאנ (rtsvy[e/i]ts'n) as "Nazi and enemy". The נ which is the

1. Michael Drosnin, *The Bible Code* (New York, New York: Simon & Schuster, 1997), p. 25.
2. Drosnin, Code, pp. 15-17, 19, 27-29, 32-37, 40, 47-49.

English equivalent of a "n" is at the end of the word, not the beginning like Drosnin would need it to be. There is also no other נ is the rest of the text to support the use of the English word "enemy". Drosnin is again using the Hebrew to fallaciously spell out the name "Nazi". Even in biblical Hebrew there is no equivalent for וצר (vtsr) to mean "enemy". That is even allowing for Drosnin to read the word backwards as he already did.

Attempting to defend his belief, Drosnin quotes Rips as claiming that "The Bible code is a computer program,"[3] Since computers from the writing of this book (2024) have not even existed for one hundred years yet, the flaw in this argument is clear. The writers of the Bible would not have given us a "Bible Code" that could only be interpreted by computers thousands of years later.

Attempting to back up his claims, Drosnin tries to claim that someone else before the age of computers, Isaac Newton, tried to claim the same thing.

> Most of the million words in Newton's own handwriting were not about mathematics or astronomy, but esoteric theology. They revealed that the great physicist believed there was hidden in the Bible a prophecy of human history.[4]

While historical facts should have been enough for Drosnin to throw away this nonsense before giving into these lies, Drosnin once again tries to claim that an Israeli-American mathematician by the name of Robert J. Aumann said that "The Bible code is simply a fact."[5]

Not surprisingly, Drosnin's work was widely discredited by scholars. Drosnin attempted to write two further books to support his fallacious prophecies, but none of them have stood up to critique. As a result, Drosnin has pretty much been forgotten. Even when I attempt to question people that were in the same church at the time, none of them remember the "Bible Code" that this teacher was attempting to fool children into believing.

Why bring this all up?

I am not going to be commenting on anything within the books in the Appendicies, but if you choose to read through them, you will see how Trithemius says to take only certain letters within his messages, to switch them with other letters, according to the key he gives, and then interpret the letters in Teutonic (German). Within his text, Trithemius has many redundant letters that are to be skipped over, like Drosnin's "spaces", before getting to the appropriate letter of the hidden message.

Knowing that the *Steganographia* was used for goetic/occult purposes for hundreds of years, even up until 1997, and that the "rapture" ideology from dispensational thought comes from the goetic texts of Enochic Literature and not the early church, we need to question what Drosnin's true intentions were here. While we will never know whether Drosnin was attempting to push another form of goeticism into Christian practice, many people at that time did fall for it, even if they refuse to admit it, or even willingly remember. Drosnin does attempt to validate Newton's claim with the wording of "esoteric theology". Since no theology from a biblical perspective is "esoteric" in that it is to be kept "to a certain select few", the implications of an "esoteric theology" does imply a magical use of prophecy and not theology.

---

3. Drosnin, *Code*, p. 19.
4. Drosnin, *Code*, p. 21.
5. Drosnin, *Code*, p. 43. Robert J. Aumann is a Nobel Memorial Prize winner in Economics. Aumann is an Israeli-American mathematician.

We always need to be aware of where ideas like Drosnin's are coming from. If we continue to be wilfully ignorant, it will continue to cause problems. With the number of problems that have already been caused by texts like Books 1-3 of Trithemius's goetic work, we as faithful Christians need to start asking questions of our leaders and the teachings they are attempting to fallaciously push on wilfully ignorant people. Leaders will use the excuse "well they should know", however, leaders knowing that people sinfully choose to be ignorant of the Bible and other issues, need to be more careful of what they are allowing to pass through their pulpits, libraries and other ministry outlets. If leaders are not diligently knowing what is passing through their ministries, or where what they are teaching is coming from and what it means, their congregants, like people in the anciet world who *wanted* and even *preferred* to believe in goetia, will choose what they want to believe rather than what the Bible teaches.

The opening of Trithemius.

The ancient Philosophers of art and nature, who had discovered the secrets of the poor men, knew that they hid them in various ways and shapes. And Moses, the most famous leader of the Israelite nation, in the description of the creation of the heavens and the earth revealed the unknowable secrets of these mysteries in simple words that support the Jews. Hieronymus, the most well-educated among us, says that in the Apocalypse there are so many mysteries on the side, that the words, moreover, were of no little value to the wise men of the Greeks, who laboured to compose fables, partly to the unskilled, and partly to the wise, of a single narrative series with the most sensible reason. I am one of the most well-studied lovers of the wise, even though I cannot imitate them because of their originality. Yet I am amazed, and to the extent that I consider them to have succeeded above all other men who are the empty belly of memory, the empty stomach of knowledge, and if by some tiny aspect, maddened by the falling age of philosophers, I may in some way be able to fulfill them. However, neither did the opinion disappoint me as much as I think, since I learned many things which I did not know by the continuous labour of these many men, and I reserved access to my thoughts to search out the greater secrets of things in various ways. Although I am not of such a degree of learning or creativity, that I dare to confess that I have fully understood the secret method of the wise men of the ancients, which they used in concealing the majesty of Philosophy, yet certain methods, as it seems to me, of writing and concealing things secretly and completely without suspicion whatever you will, I devised. At the instance of the Most Serene Prince D. Philip, Count Palatine of the Rhine, Duke and Elector of Bavaria, and Prince Elector of the Roman Empire, to the most wise Philosopher of Mecaena, whom to me no one seemed more worthy, I handed over the letters, and in the following volume I copied them, not without great labour or else this great secret should fall into the ears of arrogant or ignorant men, or whoever may be the reader of this volume. By the sacred name of Jehovah, and by the blood of our Lord Jesus Christ, the saviour of faithful souls, I caution, but I also ask and plead of you, that you do not give the knowledge of writing this to anyone unworthy, rude, carnal, or to an old man intending evil. Since many evils can be done through it, among men, adulteries, fornications, conspiracies, murders, and other evil traditions, if what is missing has been made seen and known. A name like a good and honest home of his will, cutting the secret art of his will to another as often as it is necessary for his private benefit, or communicating it publicly without any suspicion of anyone, so perverse, rude, and blinded by carnal lust, he consents to the pleasure of his person as much as shamelessly and lustfully he expressed his evil desire by honest, modest, and holy words, by determining the place, time, and world of the meeting, as widely as he could without any suspicion. Neither will there be any safe journey for the married couple. While the woman seeing the will of her lover written in the best of words by her husband, and praising the most holy words, she can very easily understand without suspecting evil, and whatever you want to know about love, no matter how uneducated she may be in Latin words, wondering at her husband, and the messenger which is possible, by carrying out the delivered letter. Therefore, I will bring this knowledge to the notice of the Republic. If it should come to an end, the whole order would be disturbed, the public faith would perish, letters, instruments, writings, and all people themselves. The conversations of men would be turned into the most horrible suspicion. No one would now believe in letters, however good, holy, and honest they may be. Men shy of all things, and no less suspicious of mutual conversation than of any letters. But let someone object to me, you would say: If you really wanted this knowledge of yours to be hidden, why did you want to commit it to writing? To this I, if I had to answer, I say, because I neither had to and I could not hide the knowledge of the best principle, by which he could save his clients (of whom I am counting myself) from many dangers, should accidents happen to him. For through this science, he can write the ideas of his thinking to those whom he wants, secretly or privately, securely unknown, and without any knowledge, he can completely without fear of anyone. But if he wishes to write something by means of this art, he will carefully observe the manners, signs, and sizes of each one, which if he refuses to consider, he will easily be able to falsify what he has written. But now, with the help of the Lord, let us proceed to the demonstration.

Translator and Editor Note: You will see parapgraphs that are a single [...]. The [...] is because without the Latin text available, the letters that were mentioned to decipher the encrypted message will make no sense for tranferring these letters into the German [or, Teutonic]. Therefore these sections have been omitted.

Chapter I

Mode I

The first way of writing in secret is by the indicators of the first letters of singular words: of which this indicator is I.

The first way to write secretly is this: When you wish to write something to a friend, so that no one understands your will except when you speak, then take whatever Latin narrative you wish, which does not need to be hidden, let the letters of the sections make the word that you wish. I will teach you how in the present argument or by example, that this method of truth is not safe for the common man, because it might easily be discovered by an industrious man, as I have often tried. In the legend it is indeed easy, but it is filled with difficulty because it is a lot of work to find words suitable for the purpose always available. Let us give examples of this manner mentioned previously, the text of which is open Latin, but the message of the secret is found written in Teutonic,[1] that is to say:

An example of the first method.
The bright promise of eternal bliss, excellency, King, governor and guardian of the most robust of the universes faithfully vines of the vineyard, refugee due refuge, righteousness, acceptance, bond of all, joy of the mourners, holy joy of the sad, fragile life, nourisher of the needy, and the salvation of the afflicted. Helper of the poor, trumpeter of the noble, and administrator of thanks. Guide and rule the life of your servants, heal our sicknesses, saviour of all, beautifier of living souls, brightest light, and refuge of the hungry. Most kindly loving of the servants, the eternal rewarder of valor, the glorifier of used souls, those who serve you, we winemakers, Lord, as decorated with good morals, we rejoice unceasingly. True courage strengthens us, so that we may be restored to holiness in the victory. Help us God, our eternal redeemer. Deliver the lovers of your name, forgive all sin, extinguish the temptations of the guilty, give us a righteous life, with also the love of righteousness, and give us those who cry out. God is truly the winemaker of the lowly, the light of the mourners, hear us, so that we deserve to hold a righteous life. The winemaker is our saviour and king most merciful. Be the glorifier, zealous for the truth, and let us glorify the eternal king of the exalted, the humble, the merciful, and the exterminating of sins.

The message of the hidden secret
Dear faithful, you must be ready for next Monday as best you can and at around 5 o'clock at the country gate you must appear before me with our equipment.

And so, as a result, you will choose a quatrain.

Precautions to be taken.
It must be observed, however, that the method just mentioned, as we have said, does not mean that the writers' letter can be confidently safe in hard issues, because I suspect that

1. German

soon he will have something to do with these same letters, and the secret can easily be detected by the intelligent. The following methods are obviously safer. At the same time, if you write to someone in this or the other ways, and you are not well-educated in Latin, meaning that you do not want to make two points, then, if you wish: complete it with any secret word, so that the sense of the outer text is at seemingly not an issue. It seems safer, however, that neither dots nor commas should be made, and it is not in the word of the secret, but the sign of the period of the secular period that I like, that I do not put the last letter over the first letter or the first letter over the last one, which I did in the mad way above in the secret message.

An extension of this first method.
The very method of writing in secret, as in almost all cases, can be varied in many different ways, so that he who perfectly understands the previously mentioned order of secrecy may be able to get other secrets from it with difficulty, or even without difficulty. For any user may, at his own will, make this method different as well as with the rest in this volume. It is clear that the first line is aware of the secret, the second is not, or if it has been it is not now, and that consequently the concealer of the secret, as he wills, uses alternate lines, either wholly or half from the beginning of his letters, descending to the end, or from without ascending to the beginning. Also, add that descending from the correct side, and ascending the other side, as it were, you can obscure the opinions of your own, so that you may be both different and dual in love, so that Oedipus is needed in praising these. But the purpose of the name is to obtain the first simple days of writing, and to give those who are worthy, and worthy of learning much, an opportunity to move from the least to the greatest.

Mode II

The second way is to alternate dictionaries, wisely different in an easy and very safe overall language.
And the second way of writing without suspicion is that the text of the writers' letter varies in an different position that is clearly intended. So that when the first words of the first speech carry out a hidden test of the intention, the first words of the next will be secreted into the abyss. But as long as it is not empty of an answer, the fourth remains idle, and so in succession, always different sayings, not connected with secrecy, and according to the public practice, let them depart from the secret meaning in a sensible order, and this mode contains in all the worlds' easy languages, and seems to have been hidden enough to announce what you will, the secrets of which is such an example.

An example of the second method.
Deliver us, sweetest Jesus, the ultimate salvation of the blessed souls. And forgive our sins, weep for our sorrows. Soothe our afflicted ones, heal the old diseases of wickedness, grant us righteousness. Good Jesus, receive the exiles, restore, pardon, and mercifully forgive any of our excesses since we have sinned grievously and have often fallen back into sin. Our saviour Jesus Christ, save us with gentleness, let us be sorrowful to those who ask Jesus, and save us all as the servants of the beggar. We are the most loving people of Jesus, breaking the norm of justice, being merciful, of the highest good, because our constant unhappiness burns, and even so, I die. Jesus Christ, you knew this very early because you are the saviour. Look upon the humility of the faithful souls, and do not allow us to wander in the mud of the false security of temptation. Be a kind creator

more favourable to your servants, and show how quickly you will deliver us, the selfishness of the world has deceived us. Creator, saviour of humanity, and in the lowest voice of Jesus, hear us the humble ones crying out to you for freedom from present and future shipwreck, that we may live without end, would you look upon us, miserable exiles and castaways, because we are jealous of the travellers on foot. May Almighty God protect us with infinite love, inscribed with mercy, be our eternal protection, Amen.

The message of the previous secret.
Dear faithful bearer of this letter, if you have treated me badly, it is our command that you must be kept in custody until our arrival at 11.

An example of Secret Latin.
The lover of human salvation, who created man, has shown us the commandments of obedience, to which we are bound to obey and obey in all things. The highest gift of holy obedience is everlasting happiness for those who fear God. Let us be determined to copy Christ's obedience to all, so that we may gain entrance with the angels through the mercy of God. Let us act, while we may be patient. The time of life is short, death may stumble upon the learned, and suddenly consume the irresponsible. Let the judgment pass over the souls of our brothers in cries of forgiveness, for death will come sooner than any of you, which none of you can hold back for a long time. Therefore, look, as you go day by day, that you confess and repent when you have time, of which you have been failing at for a long time. Oh, the most terrible of deaths, how quickly you pity us, your uninhabited creature is more subject to the sign. Dear creator of humanity, grant to your servants that you will hear us and grant us forgiveness for our souls. Oh, most merciful Father, be merciful to us, heal our sicknesses, and help our weak souls. Father, with great extravagance, grant faithful rest to our souls. Unite with the angels who fear you and who you see fit to be present with you.

The hidden message of the previous.
Tonight, after twelve o'clock, I will come to you near the door, which will lead to sunrise, where you will wait for me, see that everything is ready.

Mode III

The third method is to use different expressions in such a way that the first line is always the signification of secrecy.

The third way of writing secretly arises from the previous, meaning, in which the saying alternately serves the secret, so as to convey the above intention differently, simply and with the last complete relating sentence or secret word at the end of which there is a gap with the following, which goes before the beginning of another word. And in this way, it is not easy to be safe from the ignorant, the ram is sure to be caught, and we will set an example of this kind.

An example of the third method.[2]
We all die, since we are all mortally guilty of the first sin. Everyone has lived to die; we are all bruised. Baptism forgives the original offense, making the daily routine boring but required. Yet the death of sadness remains as much as humility for fearing God, who saved us, because we lost our life by sinning. But by righteousness we are reborn in the divine light if we perceive the mercy of your death. Let us proudly praise our wretch-

2. In the natural alphabet, g is valid.

ed Creator, who, by his own humility, redeemed our sins with his own blood, or else we should be deprived of good things, and means that he gave eternal life to those who mourned nothing, but Jesus died while bearing the cross. Oh, most sweet recognition of Jesus, what shall I repay you? Jesus died innocent without sin for us. What is to be done when he comes to the examination of our lives? He will see in the end that if you pay the wages of each of the sisters for the works entrusted to them, everything will be wasted, and something innumerable will be passed, of which there is a horrible indication. Therefore, those who are coming should repent boldly, since the examination of the district cannot be stopped, and wipe away the crimes with tears. Have mercy on the children of the poor, lighten the tears, by being devoted to God. Lord, goodness surpasses forgiveness of crimes. I, while there is time, am filled with pity, and beat myself with repentance. Be grateful that his death has redeemed you, with holy humility supported by the fear of God, Amen. Johannes Trithemius

The message of the just mentioned secret.
Tomorrow at 8 a.m. I will be with you with 400 horses for a raid on the field near the court.

Mode IV

The fourth mode always takes in the first word in the open narrative, the two words that are missing from the secret, and after the complete word that similarly adds one that is not there. So that the first word of the following verb has nothing to do with the significance of the secret, which we have already said in the third way to be observed.

And with this mode it is possible to change it into many and various other methods, of which it would be in no way possible to discover the secret. Yet let us see an example of this, in which the mistake will not be popular, unless I carefully consider the quality of the mode itself, in which there is always one pesty empty sentence and two successively valid. For God is empty only in wordless mysteries; by two expertly completed writings, as will be evident.

An example of the fourth method.[3]
The passion of Jesus Christ, which is the saving of humanity, whose innocently afflicted life frees us from all catastrophes, because his humility will be saved for our need. But sinful acts will be disturbed, and the death of the good will therefore be abundant. Let us say, "Praise Christ Jesus who redeems our souls." Therefore, let us give our thanks to the most faithful redeemer, who redeems all that were subject to the Tyrant. All praise his blessed name as we are earning forgiveness for our sins. Every day we take care to live righteously in the love of the redeemer whose fearful awareness of what we do must justify us and make us gentler. I will change our lives with the meaning of grief, such that we shall gain the forgiveness of our sins by continually staying faithful with courage and humility. We shall not fail. Johannes Trithemius, Abbot.

The message of the previous secret.
I'll knock on the door at 11 tonight and let myself in.

3. L. is valid in the alphabet. II.

Mode V

The fifth mode, with the first vacancy through 2. Significantly starts and ends with another vacancy.

Since the manner is not much different from the fourth with the first blank, where the indicators usually start and end each word with a single blank without equals. Two significant expressions are always closed with a single blank.

An example of the fifth method.
In this case, the vine will achieve success, the cloud is gone, and the north will die elsewhere, where humility, and only rudeness will condemn. If you freely receive love, insistently gather together the greatest glory, and always be faithful pursuers of the truth. Do not annoy or give up on the youth of the world, since our time here is very short. Be a lover of Jesus Christ, our most merciful saviour. Cultivate all righteousness, flee from the sinful acts, and humble the innocence in the heart in order to keep being righteous. Love the Saviour of our souls, whose love is eternal life. Though all our joys suddenly pass away, the love of the beauty of the future give us its promises. The dog is always caught in the snare of the ancient enemy, whose poison is easily defeated by humility. Be on the watch, since the most intelligent and cunning enemy does not perish, and he is always on the watch, and whose most blasphemous determination is to be fiercely feared. Love God dearly, he always remains. The love of the age is quickly consumed. Honour, praise, and all other things will suddenly end. Determination to do evil is the way of damnation. Man, swollen with pride, will suffer the torture of mortal worms, and that miserable and unfortunate man will never be freed. A proud man, who is the worst of all, will burn without any brief pause, and he will never see the glory of eternal happiness. He will be thrown out with the demons, to also be tortured, and never delivered. Therefore, let us be proud of the eternal punishment of the lord of darkness, and horror will fill you. Oh, the failures of pride, which are followed by eternal cries of sadness. These are to be despised because they cloud the eternal judgment. Johannes Trithemius.

The message of the just mentioned secret.
On Thursday at one o'clock at night I must be sitting at the moat and when it is time to storm the castle I will be singing the Westermeller.

Mode VI

The sixth mode, after the two blanks, always receives the notifications, whether they be words or not.

The sixth way is also by way of the first two, to avoid suspicion. The empty spaces signify the two following in the order of the way to go, and if they have secretly completed the word by sayings of weak syllables, the word itself is customarily ended with two idle ones, or at least until it equality coincides in the narrative through two or more mysteries, where some word is missing the hidden term, as soon as what is said by the notifications begins. Let us offer an example of this mystery.

An example of the sixth method.
Bottom line, HG never dies. Righteousness is to God a pure love that will seek his glory in all things, and to despise the things of the world. The souls' humility will reign in heaven, pure innocence will be exalted, and the honest mind will be enlightened by the light. The fierceness of turning away from sin will be repaid while our divine actions will

be strengthened. The love of God tends to great works. The weak hates and disregards all future good, not faithfully restraining their sins, and they resist righteousness. As Christ said in the Gospel: "Let us not be burdened with unnecessary human cares, drunkenly," says the holy Apostle, "let us be content with such necessity." [Matthew 6:25–34] Let us therefore have Gods' love and faithfulness for the souls to whom life is written and let us find happiness after the terrible exit of the soul at death. We deserve to get for ourselves the humble conversations that finally lead to death. Let us be determined on doing good works so that sinful actions do not overwhelm us. Let us win more people innocently in one's religion than ten times more the number of Christians that will die. I will love God above all things, when he humbly pours into us with his holy commandments. He gave all good things to those who survived him. Therefore, let us defeat the various powers of the deceitful world, which destroy our honour, and corrupt all our intentions. To live righteously, to obey the commandments, to do wrong, to fear God, to give alms, to rule the family, to favour the good, to root out the sinful actions of the wicked, and to be free from sins. Also, despising the glory of the world and indulging the ones who seek forgiveness are the treasures of Christians. For the glory of the world is nothing but a failure, and only the false riches that we found will be all we leave to the children. The only intention is to make mortals beautiful. Let our glory and the ownership of our possessions continue with us for all time and let our minds' atonement to God never cease. Johannes Trithemius.

The hidden message of the previous secret.
Mercifully, you must eat here because while you are still in Spanheim, the castle will be taken by the Von Burtenbergs and the traitors.

Mode VII

The seventh mode concludes the mystical word by two and two according to the number of these syllables.

The seventh mode begins with two blanks and ends with any secret word of equal syllables through two indicators, one signifying equal syllables, and the other idle. This mode, like all the others, can be made different many times, so that it may be changed in such a way as to suit each industry for its own secret use. Let us give an example of such a way as follows.

An example of the seventh method.[4]
Jesus Christ, unfailing light of the blessedness of all the saints and creator of the universe and ruler, have mercy on us. We who are weak and crying, we ask you to grant us your mercy by the righteousness of the victory over the devil, so that we may deserve rest after hard labours. We pray to you with the desires of your family. Make us drool with the warmth of your love burning in us, you will give us a strong bond of brotherly love. Jesus, almighty King of the heavens, grant that we may be humble, diligently hating worldly things, so that we are always burning with your love. Oh, Preceptor of the humility of the gentlest Jesus, teach us to follow the doctrine, for we are subject to all kinds of evils, even though we are determined to do good. Lord, let us not die or even waste away in this life. Oh, supreme truth, strengthen us, sweet refuge of souls, be a tower of strength for us. For you are our strongest good thing, you are the true salvation of my soul and the healthiest recreation of my mind. You are the joy of the angels that we cannot under-

4. D. is valid in the alphabet 9.

stand, and the faithful rest of all. You are the holy happiness of lovers. Your name that cannot be understood is of the highest heavens. You are the resurrector of the dead, most merciful and sustaining, you, the sweetest Jesus. Help us to break our sinful ways, so that we deserve to walk on the right path along the path of truth without stumbling. Oh, Most Merciful God of Jesus, ease our harshest exile. And when the end of it is covered by our exile being completed, come near and come to our aid in a merciful way. Lord Jesus, we beg of you, by the power of your most noble sweet death, do not look down upon us on the day of our death, let your blood redeem and wash away each one of us, and let all our sins rest in the joys of our heavenly country, where you are waiting for us. Amen.

The message of the just mentioned secret.
Dear faithful, your soldiers understood our silence around March 9th so that we could get away from the enemy and defeat them..

Mode VIII

The eighth mode proceeds in a different way through three blanks and the same number of significant expressions.
Just as the sixth by two, so that any one mystical word of equal syllables clearly completes the sentence of the letter in such a way that without end there were three empty places following not from idle ones. But it will begin with three significant ones. If the secret word is in equal syllables, it will receive as many in its association, until the syllables before the period in some way finally become equal.

An example of the eighth method.
Omnipresent and ever-loving God, most graciously the saviour of the knight, who wished your son to be a sharer of our humanity, to redeem those who had long been set in miserable condemnation to hell of all men. The most holy and reverent Mary who is more prominent than all men and angels, gave birth to a king almighty God and man, by the urging of the manly consort at all unknown to the end of the disgrace. Always maintaining such high and immaculate the holy virgin mother of Jesus Christ. Done by the power of God, known to the lowly in every place, giving lovingly to others, to every land, always a permanent virgin. You are the most blessed of the angels, whom the son then accepts with the most generous condescension in all that he asks, and so that the mother should be revered as the most excellent of all creatures, who was accustomed to denying nothing to those who exhorted him, but he was suddenly a saint. He consents to his will, conceding all things, and is guided by the merits of this tendency of the poor. Therefore, venerating the merits of the most noble virgin Mary, we pray, Lady Emperor of the universe, that the light of truth be shed upon us. That you wash away the filth of crimes, that you bestow grace and most of all on those who are always afraid, that you take away temptations, that you grant us the courage to overcome those who hate you. That you clothe us with your love, chastity, and obedience, self-control, kindness, humility, self-restraint, and other righteous acts of omens that are marked by tears of exercise. Bestow upon us a poor heart. Amen.

The message of the just mentioned secret.
The person who brought this letter is making a big deal out of it, but I don't think much of it either; I'll just drag him away. Johannes Trithemius.

Mode IX

The ninth mode begins with three blanks and proceeds singularly through as many indicators in a different way.

The ninth mode begins with three blanks with the eighth, and running differently through as many indicators, each mystical word concludes before the period, with an equal syllable. That is, three and three are concluded by as many blanks, but unnecessary, if two by one, and if one by a similarly empty ends, so that the following mythical saying always begins with three blanks, so let us see in the following example.

An example of the ninth method.

Health and love to my dearest and most special friend, the bearer of the present, Euerhardon Rubicensis, the best of our friends, a generous and glorious man, whom I ask you to receive in a humane way. He will reveal to you his guilt and he will also relieve my former need and shortcomings that have fallen upon me that are better for him to make known. But with the Stuegrans, as it is more clearly evident to the light, exhausted by the damages and the various debts, of the determination of his faithfulness, I am strongly confident that friendship holds the required strength and bonds. Therefore, willingly present yourself to a friend as humanely as you have always been accustomed and also by helping a friend in need. And so, I asked him to subvert the Florentine leaders with certainty, since Manximain was appointed by necessity, and who, after being warned by you, was at last given the office. For what you have done, gives me immortal thanks that we may confirm your sincere love for us in your business. What you have done to him, if you wish to know that it has been done, I will take care to give you immortal thanks. But his friend Eurhardus himself will remain, that is to say, borrowed. For he will keep his promises in firm stability and will not deceive. Moreover, when you are glad to hear the news, I will tell you that it is surprising. I nourished the cane called Eris, the enemies of the peasants. So raw in learning and an expert in the memory of all things now that we see that the beast has been taken off and instead, he has put on a man. He understands Greek and knows Latin words. He humbly asks forgiveness for his offenses. Whatever he does to him, nodding to me with gestures, committed faithfully he guards, he divulges secrets to no one at random, which are put on him and believed by the one giving him bail. He loves to present himself as a determined man, he plays as a deceiver, and otherwise he does amazing things that are incredible to the ignorant. Wow.

The message of the just mentioned secret.

This man wants to borrow R. Gulden from you, my advice is to go to his own devices, he is totally corrupt and does not want to pay.

Mode X

The tenth mode begins with four blanks and ends with the indicators and blanks.

The tenth mode begins with four idle ones, and at the same time the significant one proceeds from the order of the eighth three. So that when a mystical word ends in a vowel the following one begins with the indicators. Had they continued, so many idlers might have been concluded, even in the number of the same indicators being dismissed. Let us see an example.

An example of the tenth method.

Since it is useful to know that it decorates the most honourable character, we shall say that ignorance is no worse a thing to happen to men. The empty things of the world are always opposed to the honour of the spirit, because the noble intellect swells with filth, clouds the memory, dissociates the memory, disturbs the senses, prostrates the discipline, weakens the body, effeminates the mind, and by the giving up of faithfulness, which the story had made of the man a fortress, he wastes time in all things that are doomed to failure. He seeks the comfort of the flesh, he transgresses in destroying all the brilliance of the Catholic institution, he does not deny God, but he despises men, he forgets the benefits, his conscience is disturbed by evils, he rejects eternal joys, the glory that he worships is human, he is pleasing self-fulfilling sin, and he is smeared with dirt and all-pervading filth. He remembers nothing of future good things stripped of his body, he eagerly loves only temporal things. But you, the best of friends, do not insist on matters that waste away, which you care for, but praise the faculty of reason in you by insisting on holy and good manners. Say what your connection is and hate the innermost part of your letters. Therefore, richly dress up your talent which nature has gifted, attempting to convince you to show what you have in outward possession, copying the humble with a true heart present what you have, since no one considers it acceptable that a good deed has been falsely explained which means he is not to be called a philosopher.

The message of the just mentioned secret.
At one o'clock the pastor of Rirchberg died, not so much with any devotion. Johannes Trithemius.

Mode XI

The eleventh mode runs differently through the four, and concludes the word with those signifying victory, with the empty.

An example of the eleventh method.
I am sending you the prayer that you said at the wedding of my friend: God, the creator of all things, the best redeemer of humanity, the best saviour, or else humanity itself will perish, even commanded marriage saying, "Grow and multiply," [Genesis 2] this the Law instructing the preservation of humanity. And in the Gospel, he consented to sanctify the marriages of those who are well-merited of God, preserving chastity, but he gives more on men who assume the determination to be without sex for humanity. I pray for you who have assumed a happy marriage by our example and by the command of the saviour who works miracles now and then. But I will establish the true institution of religion for the honour of marriage. We owe to you men, to whom marriages are started, and a great assembly of religious youths, which is the kind that preserves mankind. If the custom of marriages had not existed, the bed would have collapsed, and our race would have perished with no one living. Worship the Lord of peace, hate insults, always give a mule of pecans in alms to the poor. Live righteously, observe dedication to the end, love goodness, always praise God, and give alms of your own. Obey the commandments of God, do not abandon your vows, honour God's ministers, pay tithes to the churches, entertain the pilgrims, feed the innocent and feed the hungry. Obey your superiors, honour your neighbors and love them, do no wrong to anyone, worship the Christian religion devoutly, and do not follow any errors you find. Keep the teaching of the Gospels and live according to the commandments of God. Despise the pleasures of the flesh, show yourselves honourable and kind, and take on a purity of heart. There is nothing pleasing to those who love, by the remembrance of which he commanded in St. Evangelical C. Eno-

bis to teach us. Finally, the purity of the soul that we keep in the muddy body for Gods sake is why the holy Apostle says to you that you should always be intent on the sanctification of those who owe you should you fail yourself in some effort. Let us bring you to marriage, so that you will plant the generous offspring of your race, not that you should be obliged to give up our future dignity to harmful pleasures. Remember therefore, and know that you are travelers, and you will return to the country to which you have been called. For the burden which is the life of this age is quickly healed. Therefore, marry in this way, so that you may not be excluded from the kingdom of God. Goodbye.

The message of the just mentioned secret.
I have found a large, similar shawl in the ground. Come and help us to dig it up soon and get 100,000 guilders.

Mode XII

The twelfth mode begins its narrative with five blanks, and at the same time connects the indicators, starting differently, as we have shown in the tenth to be done by four.

An example of the twelth method.
For it is advantageous to a wise man to be a wall in what he promises, and to forget the stronger benefits. The injustice of business is twofold. That is to say, of want and ingratitude. Should you be ungrateful to the righteous who did not sow the promise, our Gracchus argues most gravely, because of your foolishness and sin, who, having been so often asked to restore the loan, dared to rashly take the promised faith according to us. Goodbye.

The message of the just mentioned secret.
Don’t trust this guy he likes to lie.

Mode XIII

He begins his narrative with five blanks, that the mystical word with as many indicators, if there were as many as one-hundred letters, it still concludes with the eleventh. The mystic word, however many indicators he has used from the five empty spots, may nevertheless begin. Let us imagine the following example of this also.

An example of the thirteenth method.
The great honour of the noble is the philosophy of the disgrace of the fire, the efficiency of the former is the cause of the evil. For what can be more beautiful than the good acts of letters that I strive to work with those who similarly strive. This Pliny, this list of the most noble men is found to have done, attacking the barbarians not only with arms but also with learning, and commending their inferior deeds to future generation. By the example of those who have been challenged by the example of humanely being encouraging with literature and cattle they show to also not cease from the determined pursuit of arms. Let all the ancient princes very wisely advise them not to hide treasures, but to contribute to the use of literature in the most honourable way to happiness, considering the benefit of literature, by which the Republic is made. I make strong men immortal from the weak men by the knowledge of the scriptures. He cooked them all. Ignorance is said to bury a man’s ear with wine. He brings humiliating disasters to men, and he has conspired to make the spirit of righteous acts cruelly mocked by the savages whom he

makes the same as true nobility. The fruit of literature is infinite, which shows the glory and sanctity of our souls compared to the heavens and the immortal earth. As the love of writing with loved ones burns, harm to the spirit is extinguished, knowledge alone is the best memory of those devoted philosophers who brought immortality to all generations, which is always praiseworthy to all men. And to the greater disciples of wisdom, he renders glorious and resplendent lovers of tranquillity, and gentle conquerors of the axes of the passions. It is easy for scorners of dishonour who despise the strongest to consent to God. Holy exercises of honesty, a model of all that is the normal acts of righteousness, glowing in the thinking of the sweetly exalted poets. The result of divine enlightenment is the honour of being dear to God, and to be respected by men. In imitation of this letter, you must devote yourself to contributing to the happiness of life by the right activities. Goodbye Johannes Trithemius, Abbot. Writing

The message that is hidden.
The people of Nuremberg have sent messengers to meet you in various guises before.

Mode XIV

Between the two, each of the words of the mystical mix is significant.
He always takes the beginning from a blank and proceeding properly through a significant order through one blank, the word concludes at the end by concealing the rest of the previous thirteen modes. Not only different but also enlarged, so that those who are educated in this art may be able to do so by these other numbers. Where we have reduced the demonstration three times beginning up to whatever number they will by 7, 8, 9, 10, or more, alternately, wherever they wish, let them rise up.

An example of the fourteenth method.
Letters bow down with humble submission. Be kind, carefully guard against ignorance, always seeking the learning of a wise institution, and being noble in honour. However, learning of illustrious manners, and being distinguished by honours is of little value. Knowledge steeped in sinful thoughts and actions is of little value. Determined learning always makes a life noble if it is also marked by righteousness, which is an honourable example. She will be subject to torments, but by righteous acts the winemaker in the cloistered knowledge of the friendly letters succeeds in spotting sins, depriving pleasures, instituting the exercises of righteousness or granting gentleness. Farewell from Spanheim 7. Calend. January, in the year of Christ 1498, Johannes Trithemius.

The message of the previous secret.
I beg you, let me know how the matter stands, you idiot.

Mode XV

It begins with the unit sign and proceeds alternately up to the eighth number.
One assumes the idle, the other adds the indicator, and when two different options follow then three will follow, and so we proceed from the eighth by seven, then by six, and so on until the first. For wholeness limits were necessary.

An example of the fifteenth method.
Greetings most illustrious prince with humble submission, good right to instruct the disciples, and natural righteousness that your leaders had let them hold fast and kept calm

those that they govern. For the most glorious authority of leaders is to lean on arms and letters at the same time, to exterminate the enemy by war, to decorate them with the arts of letters, and to rule at the same time with courage and wisdom. God, the enlightener, the most excellent, and the most kind gives the noble knowledge of all. To us I will take care of your grace for strength. He has a distinguished ministry, clearly understood by all men, to be concealed by death, that is to say, or else they should be commanded to make a bad use of the well-understood principles of this divine art. But those who tried to disturb the beast, those who are responsible these people disturb diligently, and with which they send letters securely in order to protect the things they are used to. Therefore, dearest and most honourable prince, I, being a man who loves the knowledge of secrets, with kindness and the best arts try to present this knowledge hidden from all to the light of the only lovable generation. But we are required to carry out things with complete dedication, and to devote ourselves to the movements that are holy so that we may deserve to enter the happiness of the predestined life arranged for us after death, and let that knowledge support us. Amen. Goodbye.

The message of the previous secret.
I beg your mercy, keep the room secret until you made the book and I found out about it orally.

Mode XVI

It agrees with the previous one in the process, but on the other hand it always starts from the empty ones.
The third way is from the previous one, which is closer to the beginning, because he first begins his narrative with the indicators. And this one from the idle, so to speak, is always idle, but the second is especially significant, and his rising from the first to the eighth is made by the rise from which the journey is sweet and the descent to the first, and this as often as the narrative ends, and let us imagine the consequent example of this high praise.

An example of the sixteenth method.
To the eternal life of the Son are the more uprightly risen up because those devoted to sins are in no way worthy in the kingdom of God and the pride of those who are shaken by the sinfulness of the demons. And the faithful were always troubled by the worms that will rebuke the cruel insults, and being conscious of whom will never rest for eternity but will be punished with stubborn axes of torments. Eternally forget this because there is no redemption in hell but only endless struggles and unshakable shooting forth of torment. And the fire will know how to wipe them out. Darkness and the night are always full of fear and the greatest suffering, cold and anguish, and there will be no step. For I am always afraid of eternal horrors, to bear the fire, or the cold, and the blameworthy devotion. Fleshly pleasure is a very short pleasure for those who do not want to be miserable, and they will begin with the greatest sufferings, but the salvation of ours remains steadfast. Dearest, Goodbye.

The message of the previous secret.
If he comes to you, put him in prison and put him under my protection

Mode XVII

The first way is to follow the individual words always in the letter beforehand.

The seventeenth method, like the first, begins with the first letters of each word, but cleverly arranges the letters of the alphabet. So that instead of a, take b. For. B., let c. and so, in consequence, until the end of the alphabet, let A be taken for z, and when you wish to write in such a way, that it is easier for you to follow the alphabet, consider that it has been to pass with your chin.

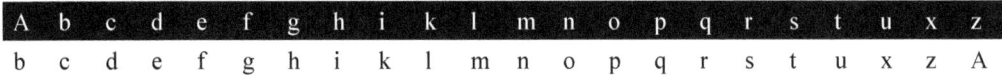

A	b	c	d	e	f	g	h	i	k	l	m	n	o	p	q	r	s	t	u	x	z
b	c	d	e	f	g	h	i	k	l	m	n	o	p	q	r	s	t	u	x	z	A

For a, let b be taken. the immediately following letter for b, c, for c, d, and so on, as is shown in the example.

An example of the seventeenth.

The Catholic majesty of the faith made stronger than all, the holy man, to men of everlasting life, in favour of Christ, promises to those who hold the Catholic faith. Christ the glorious almighty has chosen the future life, he will have life by the bread of works, the faithful man follows Christ. Holding power is declared to be good by works, and the Catholic name is saved by Christian faith. A self-focused man clouds his faith. Christ hates him with indecency, but the Christian loves the affections of the Catholics by righteously holding them.

The hidden message of the previous.

Dear faithful one, please call us next Monday according to your ability. And so, about the rest. This is the intent of privacy.

Mode XVIII

Converted letters are used as the previous ones in the indicators such as z.

The above, or in any other translation, uses literals, and like the second it has different indicators, but also has different idle ones so that the narration is from a significant saying whose first letter has not been converted, and which is idle and does nothing for the narration of the secret.

An example of the eighteenth method.

You have recently asked me very lovingly, brother, which of the favourable spirits I have. Unfortunately, I have lots of doubt since a deal of great learning was done in the fourth book, and I fear that by my kindness a thief has escaped who had been received in by my hospitality. The book was beautiful, and therefore pleasing to thieves. It was written in the most ornate manner, and it was decently painted and covered with reddish-yellow leather, but it escaped the Catholic thief, and the bearer mournfully complains that since, having been removed to the Greek Calendas, perhaps he will be restored to my kinsman at last. For what the Calendas had taken away at random from them will generally be restored. For as much as the best of the book that the worst man has stolen should have a punishment worthy of hanging. So much faithlessness with double merit by right finding the good based on the evils worse for those who are getting old, unworthy of the common time to be condemned by the most monstrous beasts ever to be torn apart in the burning abysses. Let Christ pursue with unappeasable hatred, as the demons of the most cruel beasts let him be deprived of more terrible joys than when the mercy of the blessed one is shaken. Faustinus, before the catalogue of the saint, should be mixed in with decoration. Christ Jesus will always be the face of the blessed because he carefully handled the bright and beautiful secrets of the great and mighty spirits. And so let that wicked thief be exterminated by eternal torments. Oh, my good friend Faustus, from every place that was close to me has blinded me. Goodbye.

The message of the previous secret.
Peter Kleipfenel bring you briefs is an evil spirit, full of terror and reverence for the name of God.

Mode XIX

Always after one blank space he places two significant letters translated in the previously mentioned manner.

He promises one empty one to which he always joins two of your indicators converted to the letter according to convention, so that always after one idle one is unconverted two indicators follow and are converted. Now this conversion can be different as if to infinity, as we shall see in what follows and as a result of this method let us set an example in which we observed the conversion of the letters mentioned above so that instead of any letter always following the same one is taken immediately.

An example of the nineteenth method.
The Catholic faith is to be strengthened by the most holy manners and by works which are always to be served. Divine love tests faith and strengthens the desire to last until the end. Good works with determined devotion, makes the Catholic doctrine the most beautiful, but eternal happiness is due to works. Although he loves his country, he shows the divine power of the Christian faith by his works.

The hidden message of the previous.
Dear faithful, today at ten o'clock we march with four hundred horses at the gate.

Mode XX

After moving the letters of the indicators, he always places the same number of indications after two empty spaces.

I found a secret ranch where they paid a hundred men to cast stone as gold.

An example of the twentieth method.
I am sending you, brother, my catalogue of the best enlightened men in Germany, the greatest defenders of the Catholic faith, with the number of many saints who are worthy to be mentioned in the catalogue. They were divinely enlightened, shining like the sun, showing that the way of salvation is the path of righteous acts. Whose glory was Christ, to despise earthly riches with love, to be taken up by the divine rather than by exercises, and therefore the riches of existence were written in the catalogue. Therefore, it is worthy that I transmit to you the code of my eager requests with the most faithful hand of the teachers who have instituted the good arts and that in time you may be able to live happily like a philosopher to decorate the Catholic faith with holy works. Humility befits Catholics and causes them to fear God who is the tower of strength and the foundation of all honours in which our faith remains safe. Keeping the commandments of God is truly Catholic. Goodbye.

The message of the previous secret.
I have found a secret ranch that doesn't pay for stone casting as planned.

Mode XXI

He uses different expressions with significant letters converted.

He uses different sayings, the first of which is empty, the second really significant, the third again empty, which is by no means idle, and so on until the end of the intended narrative, the letter in the significant saying is converted into the following second, so that for the letter a, let c be taken, for c, let e be taken and so on which brings you to the end of the alphabet, next for x, let a be taken instead of z. But the Greek υ is not necessary to us for a common name and must therefore be omitted in all the following alphabets.

An example of the twenty-first method.
I would like to answer your letter, so that Christ may make me rejoice. I should have passed on the volumes that were standing here. I think that I was jealous of the close and secret admirers in front of the good Zeto which the most accurate philosophers had. But I had thanks to you, my immortal tongue, my sweetest brother, who holds the mutual glory of love, for this family matter which you seem to have carefully cut off the modesty of the grain. I am well acquainted with those who would rather die with praise for their works, and for that reason I wish to act as soon as possible to your requests, if Christ knew that I had the demands. That is why your wild requests are already being upset, the supreme truth of your Christ no darkness hides, and the examiner of my heart could not be gratified to you. He proposes to the commandments of Christ, because he does not know the fear of God, the best determination of the soul, the love of peace, or about loving God passionately. For the true soul of the king is the knowledge of the saviour, the faithfulness of the observance of the Catholic faith, and to give thanks to the Almighty God Jesus Christ, glorious in all good things in abundance, may he give to you the love of eternity, and may he be written in the catalogue of the happy Christians. Goodbye.

The message of the previous secret.
Peter Dructer from Fridburg called Labsodel likes to drink strong wine. He is doctor of fools to Spanheim.

Mode XXII

After the conversion of the letters already mentioned, after two empty ones he places as many significant ones.

He begins with an empty word and immediately adds two more significant ones, so that through two blanks he significantly concludes the whole narrative, which is open, but which is also hidden. The letter of the first significant words are all placed in the third, so as to be taken. For b, to be taken d, for c, f and so in consequence until the end, as the first letter of the alphabet a, let x for b be taken, and for z, c taken in the kind of secret things the alphabet is displayed, the usual red being black this time hidden.

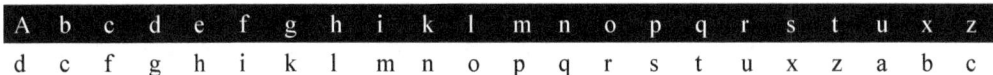

A	b	c	d	e	f	g	h	i	k	l	m	n	o	p	q	r	s	t	u	x	z
d	c	f	g	h	i	k	l	m	n	o	p	q	r	s	t	u	x	z	a	b	c

When you wish to write the stanza in the determined manner which follows, put the alphabet first, and see carefully that you keep the order before written, or else you will make a mistake to the speaker and to yourself. But let us give an example of this 22nd manner, which proceeds in two different ways.

An example of the twenty-second method.
Since I have declared you a lover of the humane arts, a cultivator of the Christian faith, and at the same time the most generous of all philosophers, willing to be fulfilled by your requests, and marveling at the vastness of friendship, I have brought you a book about the writers of the ecclesiastics and catholic doctors who are urging you on. I gave you a glorious one-turn from the canons in the books of stupidity about the spirits and the needy. I ask Christ to open our eyes with the devotion of his most holy love, that he may teach us to hate worthless honours, to the glory of the purified desire of the office, by which Catholicism always honours itself. Tumagnus, it is true that you are a Philosopher, that denies all things, and finds all things the time to look upon your soon to be death, even though he stumbles around like a wanderer. Goodbye.

The message of the previous secret.
What I have given you, you should keep and not give to anyone else but to me.

Mode XXIII

You always begin with an empty one, at each station you add a significant one, and so you proceed with different expressions, the first letter of which is always converted into the fourth, so that for a, e is taken, for b, f. for c, g and so on up to x, which it is received by as in the following alphabet we will clearly show an example.

A	b	c	d	e	f	g	h	i	k	l	m	n	o	p	q	r	s	t	u	x	z
e	f	g	h	i	k	l	m	n	o	p	q	r	s	t	u	x	z	A	b	c	d

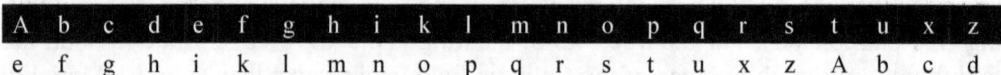

But this mode is dry, and all the others may be changed in many ways, so that as he already uses different ways, so in twos, threes, fours, or even more, the sign of this mode is then sought, and the others must always be observed as unchanging, so as not to reflect the variety of modes, but to show the order of the mysteries.

An example of the twenty-third method.
She, whom I had promised to pay for my debt, I met with Christ, and I would like you to make a decision for me, who then benefited me, and write the whole story back to me in brief. I am the witness of the Christians, the torments of those who, acting in the manner of the crucifixion of Christ, crucified his greatest criminals, who forgot the most precious benefit of redemption, and always remained ungrateful to Christ. They were asking for forgiveness more than he was, they neglected the future, following the pleasures of the world, and wept bitterly every day. Asking for forgiveness because of their negligence, "we are condemned, we are tormented, and we deserve to suffer cruel, cruel things. We have sought after earthly and worldly things; we have neglected Christ's command. We have despised the lowly, that is the retribution of sin, which we receive of eternal damnation. Sadly, we are unfortunate. Why have we denied Christ and why have we ignored our time in such a careless way? etc." He was raised to find many other wonderful things and so on. I cannot write more than a few letters. Goodbye.

The message of the previous secret.
At nine o'clock in the morning I will appear at the gates, secretly and silently, with 200

horses.

Mode XXIV

It receives all the indicators and converts each letter into the fifth following.

Like the first, take all the indicators of the narrative that comes before, but place the first letter of each word of the word in the fifth and next sequence, so that, for a, the receiver is f, for b, g, for c, b, and so on as we shall demonstrate in the second alphabet, where instead of the red letter, the black field is placed immediately above it.

A	b	c	d	e	f	g	h	i	k	l	m	n	o	p	q	r	s	t	u	x	z
f	g	h	i	k	l	m	n	o	p	q	r	s	t	u	x	z	A	b	c	d	e

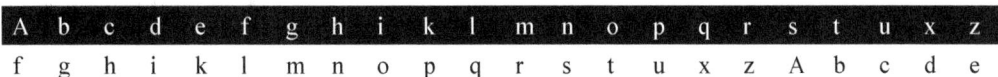

When, therefore, you wish to write in this manner, place this alphabet before you, and you will easily find all the signs of every kind.

An example of the twenty-fourth method.

Having resolved to ensure to offer good things, to remember the honesty of those offering gifts, and to remember the insults of the ones denying those gifts. I ask for the holy love of your brothers, who are devoted to good and to their honesty, who constantly decorate the holy works of our Catholic religion. But I ask you kindly brother, so that you will put away your fear of me, my double-minded brothers, the hatred of being loved, fighting and conflict, and separate goodness from evil works. The determination of the friends of the brothers, which is the best name for honesty, is the name of determination for the works of chastity of the body, which is also decorated with Catholic manners.

The message of the previous secret.

Don't pay attention to my word, I don't mean it that harshly, but it has to be that way, I will tell you the reason.

Mode XXV

Like the one before it, it receives all the indicators, but converts any of them into the sixth.

Like the one before it, it does not take up any empty space, but only the significant sayings which it admits. There is no need to insert any empty ones, since this does not happen in the world. Without the art of this book is someone able to find the secret notice written in these ways, nor anyone to a greater song if he wants the ability of also putting in two or more empty vessels of equal importance. We do not forbid it, especially since we know that every one of us can sail according to his pleasure, if he can, find sails, as he pleases, he is unchangeable. He causes others to commit error with him, so that if he writes in this way, because by each one and that 25. because the letters are converted to the sixth following, so as to show them in their place. They follow the 25. modes of the alphabet said above, in which g is taken for a, because it is sixth after a. For b, let h be taken and so on.

A	b	c	d	e	f	g	h	i	k	l	m	n	o	p	q	r	s	t	u	x	z
g	h	i	k	l	m	n	o	p	q	r	s	t	u	x	z	A	b	c	d	e	f

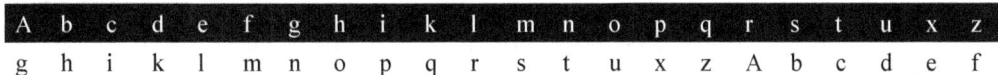

Therefore, if you want to write something in this way as well as in other ways, the first significant letters are written on a single sheet, arranged in an alphabet specially arranged for this purpose, put before you, which we make very consistently as an example.

An example of the hidden message.
Keep all the letters I send you secret and don't let anyone see them. Finally, let us imagine the narrative of this mystery.

[...]

An example of the twenty-fifth method.
Those who hold humble lamentations will obtain the grace of redemption. The grace of redemption restores freedom. But men repenting of their love, they are mercifully rebuked, the rules, the installing of which is painted by the most benevolent giver of liberty, the Catholic law that freed all, the most faithful saviour, the King of power, will show us all. He promised all things to be well to those who hold Catholic morality, the grace of happiness, and the good assurance of freedom. Those who hold the holy law will finally rejoice, they will kiss the most compassionate deliverer with light. Calm farewell, from Spain. 3. The ninth of January in the year 1498. John Trithemius Abbot.

Mode XXVI

It progresses with different expressions, and any letter of significance is transferred to 2.

It proceeds in the same way as the second, at first taking one empty place at the beginning, then the other significant one, and afterwards one empty place of the middle with a deep meaning, and so on until the end of the narrative. Furthermore, for each of the indicators, the first letter must be taken, afterwards he saw in the seventh order before a, h is taken for b, i for c, k, and so on, as will be seen in the following alphabet, two black letters are taken for red.

Rub. Nig.

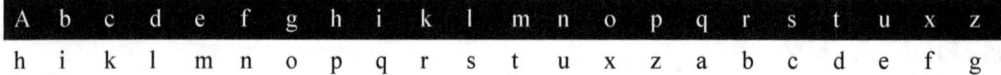

A	b	c	d	e	f	g	h	i	k	l	m	n	o	p	q	r	s	t	u	x	z
h	i	k	l	m	n	o	p	q	r	s	t	u	x	z	a	b	c	d	e	f	g

But in order that you may easily understand the art and know the manner of writing the secret narrative of the common people, I will now submit and show you the usual knowledge of their letters for the seventh conversion.

[...]

With this method you will want to write the letters of the empty words, as we have said, insert a blank letter beginning with the first letter to which you will soon connect the first meaning of the letters of the words, as you will prove that we have done in the example we are focusing on.

An example of the twenty-sixth method.
I had commended my books to you under the condition of restoring a thousand most precious moons. But behold, you have not restored the book in a wonderful way, which you should have sent payment for quickly. It is not fitting for a good and honourable man to violate the promise of the noble lineage of his ancestors, but you had promised to restore them with the utmost care. It is lightness every day to Calendas Greece, fulfill your promise.

Are we not sufficiently awaited with great kindness to promise great things? It is disgraceful to return the least effort possible, it decorates the promised soldier, and it is not fitting for a Christian not to wear the condition. And he commanded the Christians, who had promised to keep the constitution of the law, to pay back the money and what you trusted to happen, and having won over others, it is necessary to do liberally. I sent out my books, which I had commended to you who asked, but a longer apology than to Calendas Greece which I do not desire to reach. Let my mind be short, you hold the nobility, and are the son of the most honorable family. Bunnefind, consider your knees, let me have my volumes. Goodbye.

The message of the previous secret.
I wish you would let me miss the matter with the money and other things as you usually do.

This is the intention of the Secret.

Mode XXVII

He uses alternate expressions and will search for the letter of the indicators in the eighth sequence that is converted.

One argument being empty, he immediately submits to the other indicator, and so accordingly, the letter of the indicator of any saying proceeds by different numbers of turns, but the first transfer of the eighth later to the next, so that for the letter A, i is taken, for b, k, for c, l, and so consequently, as the following alphabet shows more clearly.

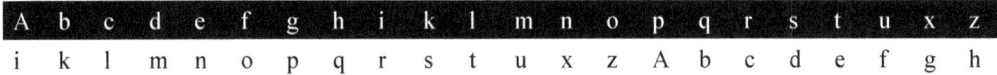

A	b	c	d	e	f	g	h	i	k	l	m	n	o	p	q	r	s	t	u	x	z
i	k	l	m	n	o	p	q	r	s	t	u	x	z	A	b	c	d	e	f	g	h

In order to demonstrate this following alphabet, I will give an example of the words that allow the secret letters to mean the first of the words, then an example.

[...]

Privacy Policy.
I wish you would let me go, the matter with the money and other things is up to you.

An example of the twenty-seventh method.
A rumour went out about the abbot of Limburg, who had released his brother from Felisdorf, a faithful man and experienced in the field of civil matters, and he had brought in new monks acting for the cause and themselves deputed to the office. He rebuked those who ought to have thanked our saviour Jesus Christ for the faithfulness of such a brother who had been able to recover their needs. Wretches, why do you reject a good and necessary administrator? What can I say? I do not praise the departure of such a useful brother of the civil experts of the Limpurgenses who came to the Limpurgenses so quickly. I am deeply sorry that the Limpurgenses have therefore lost the monks. I confess that if he had given Christ to me, I should have given him the greatest thanks, as suits a Christian, and I would have taken care that you should not depart until you, having stayed with Christ, chose to let go a faithful man exhausted by a good and bright counsel, or it should be seen that there is hope of recovering those that ran away from you. Goodbye. Not from Spanheim. Jah. The year of our Lord 1499. Johannes Trithemius Abbot.

Mode XXVIII

Like the preceding one, he uses different expressions, and reveals a less literal meaning.

Like the one before, he uses different expressions, the first of which is empty, the second significant, the third again empty, the fourth significant, and so on, but he changes any of the letters to the ninth following, so that instead of a, k is taken. For b, l, for c, m, and so on. As in the secret of the alphabet it must be known that this mode varies in many ways, as with all the rest, but when you want to give it to someone as a surprise to be read by someone who does not know what to do with it, I am sure you take each indicator as if it were another, to make this alphabet safe.

A	b	c	d	e	f	g	h	i	k	l	m	n	o	p	q	r	s	t	u	x	z
k	l	m	n	o	p	q	r	s	t	u	x	z	A	b	c	d	e	f	g	h	i

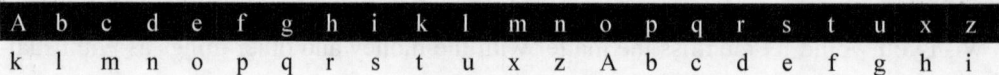

The message of secrecy.
Dear Guardian, these men, who are brothers, behaved very unchristianly with death and no mercy.

Meaningful letters.
[...]

An example of the twenty-eighth.
Religiously Reverend Father, I know that you freely give everything asked for by your friends, therefore I humbly ask you not to bring your devoted brothers with the most complete love into the touch of Catholic sin detained with us for a long time. We rejoiced in excitement, but most devoutly, in the marked joy of the appearance of God. The Apostle, bearing a good devotion, and the joyful knowledge was most faithful, so our joy too, is decorated with the righteousness of the all the different saints. A religious and Catholic brother beautifully decorated our blessedness with the discipline of the most holy devotion. For we praised without the devastation of the mind and always in the most religious manner. He was energetically shown to all of us by a very similar attack of prayer. I humbly ask you, what is going on in a religious meeting, where Catholic conversation flourishes, where nothing is said casually, and nothing unjustly concealed? May Christ Jesus, the Saviour of all, make us rejoice in the glory above, and may God's determined love revive all the true faithful of the truth. Brothers, we rejoiced with holy joy, praying and begging, that you may receive us in peace, and put away all bitterness of devotion. Farewell, from Spanheim, No. Jan. Anno & Domini 1498. Johannes Trithemius Abbot.

Mode XXIX

He uses different expressions, and the first letter of each indicator is transferred to the tenth.

In the same way, he uses different expressions as the ones before, beginning with one empty one, then the next significant one is soon joined with it. Again, one empty one, again one significant one, and so on until the end of the proposed narrative. However, the first letter of each significant expression is transferred to the eleventh following. So that instead of a, l is taken. for b, m, for, c, n, and so on as is evident in the alphabet itself.

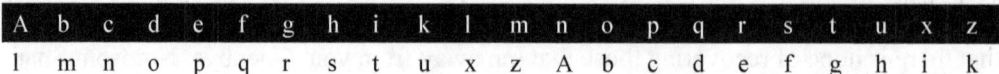

A	b	c	d	e	f	g	h	i	k	l	m	n	o	p	q	r	s	t	u	x	z
l	m	n	o	p	q	r	s	t	u	x	z	A	b	c	d	e	f	g	h	i	k

The message of secrecy.
Be careful, the person who brought these letters is an evil boy, don't worry, he's not looking for you, I'll kill him.

Meaningful letters.
[...]

An example of the twenty-ninth.
When you fix the most educated of the humane arts, I think you will certainly be glad, three times young new educated partner, this one who was there to drink letters is a man of much knowledge, the highest philosopher, the most subtle arithmetician. He is the most eloquent rhetorician, the most profound mathematician, and excellently learned in all things. He speaks most elegantly, noting Tulliana's eloquence. If I were only your friend, I would have completely withheld my husband. When, having experienced the familiar use of a learned philosopher, I am most grateful to receive the philosopher, whom I am sending to you under the influence of a singular friendship, and I saw in you some of the secrets of the arts, with the most decorated letters, the commandments of which he taught me to wonder at. To respond with the most important instructions that he had received was surprising. When he is able to answer the most important questions from the time he learned at home, he uses the dedications of a debate that is most suited for him. As far as I am concerned, we will teach this book in a different humane manner that you receive it with the courtesy and familiarity of all the good arts that we defend. Enimuero will be able to train you with mules, since the Philosopher is the most splendidly learned, an eminently skillful swordsman, a rhetoric too, and we will sharpen the Geometer. Oh, that ours were such as those who study, who despise the necessary study with a swollen breast. This man, a student of philosophy and other sciences and arts, deeply loves them, and constantly treats them. and it penetrates most acutely. Receive him with love, treat him with a generous expression, and strengthen him as a faithful Christian. Goodbye from Spanheim No. Now the year of our Lord 1499. Johannes Trithemius.

Mode XXX

It progresses in different sentences and the significant letter is converted to the eleventh. Beginning with one blank, he progresses through the different saying, so that always after one blank, he places another, significant letter, throughout the whole series of the narrative, which is very evident in the just shown manner and others. Further through the fourth letter of the significant lesson, the first following after the eleventh, and so on so that instead of a, take m, for b, n for c, o, and so on as is clear in the alphabet.

A	b	c	d	e	f	g	h	i	k	l	m	n	o	p	q	r	s	t	u	x	z
m	n	o	p	q	r	s	t	u	x	z	A	b	c	d	e	f	g	h	i	k	l

The message of secrecy.
They wrote to me that I should go to him but I don't want to go, you write to me beforehand.

Meaningful letters.
[...]

An example of the thirtieth.

I am sending you a prayer about the perpetual virgin Mary, as you recently requested: By whom you live, the most loving and kind mother, kind Mary, I purify the most radiant parent. You are also most grateful to the supreme unity, you are the most faithful helper of all the innocent, you are the noble refuge of those who seek you, for you sanctify every day the compassionate greeting of the poor. The gentlest advocate, the comforter of the afflicted, the most beautiful of righteousness, the most beautiful storehouse, the most kind comforter of the sad, and the most famous promoter of the faithful friends of Christ. Rejoice Anna comfort of the bereaved. Rejoice at the summit of nobility, hope of the faithful who are labouring, obtain forgiveness for those who belong to us, and appease the terrible Judge of Christianity. Comfort the apologetic in heart, take away our souls we ask you, sanctify them by your goodness. Blessed are you, virgin mother, most honourable, who gave birth to the most perfect virgin who gave birth to the almighty Saviour the son of God. Yet still remaining a virgin and always the purest, the messenger Gabriel greeted Jesus' mother with full grace and kindness. O mother, our fountain of extravagance, never tiring with faithfulness, shining with devotion, and the greatest magnitude of awards to all. Rush to intercede for your servants, decorate us with your righteousness, that we may obtain happiness after the end of this life by the kindness of the Saviour of all the faithful, Amen. Goodbye from Spanheim 7. Iduum January, year of our Lord 1499. Johannes Trithemius Abbot

Mode XXXI

So that different sayings are advanced, and the significant letter is changed into twelve.

From the empty one through all the different ones, the indicator properly comes first in turn, so that after one empty saying one indicator is always included. But for the first letter of any secret saying is the twelfth following after it is taken, so that for a, u, for c, p. Let us use the alphabet of this kind.

Alphabet.

A	b	c	d	e	f	g	h	i	k	l	m	n	o	p	q	r	s	t	u	x	z
n	o	p	q	r	s	t	u	x	z	A	b	c	d	e	f	g	h	i	k	l	m

The message of secrecy.

The old Upt von Fleischdorff had the Von Reinhartsborns' noses cut off.

This is the intention of the following mysteries.

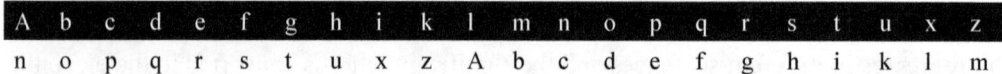

Meaningful letters.

[…]

An example of the thirty-first.

Why do you always make alms for temporal things and pure righteousness, and before a brief thing there cannot be a lover of sinfulness, since true love cannot be divided under any condition. The holy religion of the Christian faith forbids the love of the dumb to its people, because he who loves worldly joys loses eternal happiness. A Catholic who does not love Catholicly does not love Christ, and he who loves temporal things is not said to be a Catholic. He who loves the Creator gains in spiritual things, of Christ the lover despises the unsuccessful failures of the world and does not care for the joys of unrighteous men. The lover hates the holy things of the world by his righteousness, he cares nothing at all about future joys. Rather, take care to love Christ to the extent that you can receive him to the heavenly kingdoms. Goodbye Ex. Spanheim. 7. Iduum January, Year 1499. Johannes Trithemius Abbot.

Mode XXXII

It proceeds in turn through the different changes, and the first significant expression is transferred to the 13th.

In making the saying different like the previous ones, he uses a sweep in that the mystery begins with a blank space to which he always adds one significant turn, for the first letter and for the significant saying he takes 13 following the previous one in the order of the alphabet for a is taken o, for b, p, for c, q, and so on to show that it is clear.

A	b	c	d	e	f	g	h	i	k	l	m	n	o	p	q	r	s	t	u	x	z
o	p	q	r	s	t	u	x	z	A	b	c	d	e	f	g	h	i	k	l	m	n

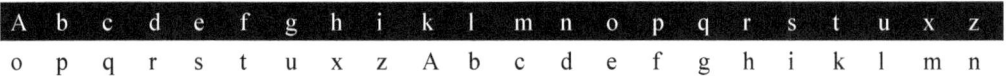

[The message of the secret.]
At around 9 a.m. you could still hear me whistling in the forest, respond with a key like that down to me. This intention is hidden secretly in the following narration.

Literary meaning.
[…]

An example of the thirty-second.
Almighty God, creator and eternal of all, who redeemed us Christians through his son Christ, and gave faithful devotion to Catholic love through the light of grace, that let them believe, but also giving us infinite faithfulness, and gave the most this liberally beloved man borne from prisons, and then scraping what should we be able to render worthily to Christians? Pour into our hearts the full devotion of faith. Holy is your joy, most graciously lighting up the remorse of works in the hearts of those who seek you Christ Jesus. Most graciously Christ Jesus the eternal light, lighten up the darkness of your usual goodness. Saviour Jesus, bestowing eternal joys on our souls, Christ your humble seed, and save all those who are exhorting you to forgive their sins. We your Christian servants, even though they are the worthiest, we humbly die in your determined devotion, Amen. Farewell, from Spanheim, 6. Iduues, January. In the year of our Lord 1499. Johannes Trithemius.

Mode XXXIII

Proceeding with the other sayings as above, the first significantly carries over into the 14th.

This begins the second narrative with a single blank and proceeds in reverse through the ones before it. But for the first significant letter of each sentence take the following letter after it converting it to the 14th, so that for a, p is taken, for b, q, for c, r, and so on according to the origin of the alphabet of this kind which follows.

Alphabet.

A	b	c	d	e	f	g	h	i	k	l	m	n	o	p	q	r	s	t	u	x	z
p	q	r	s	t	u	x	z	A	b	c	d	e	f	g	h	i	k	l	m	n	o

The message of secrecy.
He is still trying to get along well before he trusts you too much. He also likes to drink wine and is a glutton. This is the intention of this secret.

Meaningful letters.
[…]

An example of the thirty-third.
Johannes Trithemius, there was once a nun on the mountain of Rupert, who adorned the Catholic faith with playful virginity. He continued to worship the saints with the faithful memory of the father that raises up the greatest servant. We are sending a long-expected man, a great man, a more timeless man, John, known to your charities, and devoted to the religious determination of the Uleisdorfen monastery. For a long time, Abbot, I came to the new abbey freely dismissing it, therefore I had committed to you the monastery of Limpurgense, in which he served Christ with continuous prayers and being occupied with the holy readings of the scriptures with the monks. He would defend the superintendent, and take care of temporal affairs, the financial officer who would become the swifter Abbot of Limpurgensis. He who fears to serve nuns because they change slightly, fears not undeservedly, for as some experience has taught us, nuns have given back to their finances, for good deeds a woman's mind is suddenly changed to bitterness. It is a good understanding. Therefore, I warn you to control the changeability of women. Within the limits that you remember to be consistent, accepting with holy honour and sincere love all the lightness of the female mind, and putting down all the lightness of the female mind. Help us very much and recover the status of temporal things, which collapsed in your monastery. May it be useful to help Christ our redeemer, who is devoted to those who are chaste. Goodbye 7. Id. Johannes Trithemius

Mode XXXIV

In the same way he uses the previous changes and the first of each signifier is transferred in 15.

In this mode he begins with one blank as above and proceeds in the same way through the different ones, so that the first is an idle but significant cut, the third is again empty, which is the signifier of the repetition, and so on until the end of the prophetic narration. The first letter c is taken for each significant word, in the order of the alphabet of the following after it the 15th so that for a, q is taken for b, r, for c, s, and so on as is evident in the alphabet which follows.

A	b	c	d	e	f	g	h	i	k	l	m	n	o	p	q	r	s	t	u	x	z
q	r	s	t	u	x	z	A	b	c	d	e	f	g	h	i	k	l	m	n	o	p

A hidden message.
Tomorrow at 9 the umpteenth man will come and take away the farmers' peace, keep yours at home.

Meaningful letters.

[...]

An example of the thirty-fourth.

Of Ecclesiasticus the scribe I have made a great catalogue as I have lately seen of your brotherhood. And they conclude very suddenly that I confess that the men have read the most famous men and not in what turn of their rewards I would have seen the list as a heavy-handed. Swollen accuser with the most stupid words censuring the list, who thinks that I have not mentioned his men. This is only out of his own evil intentions, which is most false.

Of the Ecclesiastics, I have written a catalogue of the gradenificer, as I have lately exhibited to your faithfulness. And I have written the most holy conception of God's parentage and affirmed that it was the most beautiful woman without any original excesses, which the arrogant thinker most falsely wanting to reproach with other conceited men, said that the most brilliant virgin created by the original harm against Catholic observance was stained by the most failed recklessness. Recklessness intended to disturb the most blessed virgin in the town. But the most noble Doctors, wishing to be insane and fraudulently speaking their own thoughts contrary to the truth, are called on to put an end to their fables, compelled to back down, and asserting that the bliss of saintliness affirms that by law it is to be believed that the most pure has at no time been subjected to the original filth of pride. Goodbye.

Mode XXXV

He uses different sayings, and the first meaning of each 16th letter is converted.

Alphabet.

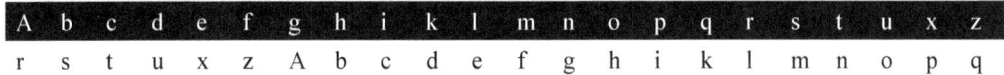

A	b	c	d	e	f	g	h	i	k	l	m	n	o	p	q	r	s	t	u	x	z
r	s	t	u	x	z	A	b	c	d	e	f	g	h	i	k	l	m	n	o	p	q

The message of secrecy.

The top of So John's Mountain maintains good communication with the Bavarians, but will not remain so for long.

Meaningful letters.

[...]

An example of the thirty-fifth.

I am admired in Christ, Father of the Limpugens and financier, with such a master as John of Vleisdorffensiris, to dedicate with a compliment with John, the humble abbot of Spanheim remaining in the joy of heaven. Nuns of St. Rupert contend their governor with excessive loudness rules the humble with goodness. As long as you accept another governor of the monastery it is praiseworthy to serve the holy virgins of Christ, but that the dead good of spiritual things was known to me as a noble and well-known life-giver. Embracing you in the honour of Christ, of a noble character, adorned with righteous acts, a wise man, and a noble abbot of all loved ones. Live a life deservedly acceptable to Christ, in the monastery of D. John, the best taster of letters, both Christian and Gentile. All wisdom is the most famous among the learned, whose wisdom we cannot think valuable. He knew very well how to feed the flock entrusted to him. I am now afraid to submit to the service of such honourable nuns, who know how to govern the monastic order with the best discretion according to the support of Christ. Who willingly submitted to me in the truth by the righteousness and devotion of the Christian faith. I made this righteous man the shepherd of Bingnon, a close friend of his family, who would willingly undertake your labours as the governor of such religious virgins. Goodbye 5. Ibid. January, in the year of our Lord 1499.

Mode XXXVI

Like the previous one, he uses different expressions, and the first meaning is passed over to the 17th letter.

When you begin with a blank, the indicator that connects it uses different expressions, and the first indicator of each expression in 17 past following it is changed, so that instead of a, s is taken, for b, t, for c, u, and so on until the end of the proposed narrative, as is evident in the following alphabet.

Alphabet.

A	b	c	d	e	f	g	h	i	k	l	m	n	o	p	q	r	s	t	u	x	z
s	t	u	x	z	A	b	c	d	e	f	g	h	i	k	l	m	n	o	p	q	r

The message of secrecy.
If one of S. Satharin's men leads Mandel away, you'll find him, so take him prisoner. This is the intention of the following mysteries.

[…]

An example of the thirty-sixth.
The Catholic faith does not save unless it is supported by the passion of the divine name. Belief and the faithfulness of the love of God does not here contribute anything at all to the redemption of the soul. For many men are found at once proudly telling of the Catholic faith, but there are few who do the works of the Christian faith. Without works faith dies, they believe a lot, but command very few gods are observed. Oh, the weak devotion of faith which I have. Men may be stronger in unbelief, with natural honesty, but the Gentiles will be tormented by the punishments of hell. God, who has the right determination of the Christian faith, will have Christ the Judge appeased by nothing, and will give them everlasting honour. I say this about these words, why do you boast in faith, love God and you will have the reward of happiness, and you will also have eagerness to rejoice. If you love failed starch against the honour of God, then you will receive a meal of the sins of the faithless, which are the honours of hell. Johannes Trithemius I wrote 4. Id. Jan. In 1499

Mode XXXVII

It proceeds in turn through the conversions, and the first of each indicator is changed to 18.

Alphabet.

A	b	c	d	e	f	g	h	i	k	l	m	n	o	p	q	r	s	t	u	x	z
t	u	x	z	A	b	c	d	e	f	g	h	i	k	l	m	n	o	p	q	r	s

The intention of the mystery.
Jacob Seum has now said that he will stab you as soon as he sees you before him.

Meaningful letters.
[…]

An example of the thirty-seventh.
By despising eternal life, we will obtain eternal happiness by using Catholic morals in truth. Hell is not prepared for those who love God, because those who are devoted to God are nothing but failures who condemn the joy of eternal majesty. The humble are exalted by the bitterness of jealousy. In serving Christ, not the devil, the lovers of the name of God are promised the best rewards, but for the lovers of the proud Christian world God has prepared the most bitter punishments of hell. I humbly ask you, what makes a Catholic man to nod his strength, I say, you who boast without devotion of divine love, and who claim to be a Christian do not show your dedication and faith worthy of Christian morals, because by humbly rejecting the Catholic tradition you believe that the old man is willing and faithful to the will of love. He has faith but he still neglects the divine love, he is faithless in his faith, and in absolute failure he presides over the divine love. He is a faithful devotee of divine love, who daily decorates the Christian faith with faithful and good works, and whose love is supported by humility. God, Johannes Trithemius 3. Id. Jan. In the year 1499

Mode XXXVIII

He alternately uses different ones, and the primary meaning of the word is transferred to the 19th letter.

The mode of 38 is through differing sayings in turns proceeding like the one before it. The first significant saying of which is transferred to the following one in 19. Thus, v. is taken for a, for b, x, for c, z, and so on as is evident in the alphabet below. You will be able to vary this method, so that you will be able to use not only different ones, but each two, three, four, opposing the calm modern signs.

Alphabet.

A	b	c	d	e	f	g	h	i	k	l	m	n	o	p	q	r	s	t	u	x	z
u	x	z	A	b	c	d	e	f	g	h	i	k	l	m	n	o	p	q	r	s	t

The intended message of privacy.
Know that Hans Schmerdt says a lot of bad things about you in your circle of friends and yet he acts like he is your almost good friend.

Meaningful letters.
[…]

An example of the thirty-eighth.
The father, king, and maker of all things first created man, Adam, to whom he joined his wife in the garden, a virgin, signifying that he shepherds the Catholic church as united.

Mode XXXIX

It also uses the different ones and the first significant word in 20 is converted.

This mode on the other hand uses different expressions, beginning with an empty one, or adding a significant one to the one before it, then again, an empty one, again a significant one, and so on until the end of the proposed narrative. Furthermore, the first letter of any significant expression is converted into the next one next to it, so that x is taken for a, for b, z, for c, a, and so on, as is evident in the alphabet itself.

Alphabet.

A	b	c	d	e	f	g	h	i	k	l	m	n	o	p	q	r	s	t	u	x	z
x	z	A	b	c	d	e	f	g	h	i	k	l	m	n	o	p	q	r	s	t	u

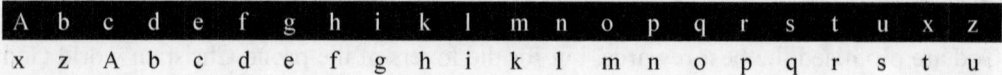

Privacy Policy.

My advice to those who have written to me is that you do not do anything; the evil thing is to have you banished or put in prison.

Meaningful letters.

[...]

An example of the thirty-ninth.

Oh, most kind Jesus, I thank you for your most holy mercy. Who restored humanity to your father with your blood, hanging on a pitifully strangled, broken body, sad soul, being spit on the face, and bearing our crimes through the faith of inexpressible love. Our bodies healed with the flowers of the body of youth for us with the most severe wounds. You have poured forth that man that you have made wine unto the dead having denied them too much love. You have laboriously desired to die restoring the communion of Catholics. I therefore give you all the thanks that I can to your dear Redeemer, weeping and mourning at the memory of your passion recalling Christ the Saviour. Oh, beloved Jesus, I greet you with your usual grace, and I ask you to pray for me in all things, because you take my glory and make me happy. My redeemer heals me. Sanctify me, oh Lord, the true light of the heart. I bless you, the most powerful protector of the world. King Christ, the saviour, the inextinguishable light, please purify my soul. The supporter of all, enlighten me. Christ, the lover of the faithful, look upon me with the glory of those who seek them, grant me eternal joys of happiness, and give me the most fervent fires of your love. Jesus of the saints is all healer of the world. Most merciful Jesus, through the pain of your blessed and most bitter passion grant me the light of understanding or let your humble pure conscience shine upon me like the rays of light. I was pitied by my good Jesus' mercy outside of faithfulness and the fullness of graces, the light of the spies of the people, and pour into me with the sweetest taste of your holy love. What reward do you reap from the redeemer of love, who is sympathetic to you, shedding tears, and blessing the holy wounds of your body with the most blessed passion? Oh, most kind immortal thanks, look upon your servant, Amen. Johannes Trithemius

Mode XL

He uses different sayings, and crosses over the first significant letter in the 21st.

Is converted to the next one in 21 so for b, a for c, b and so on, as is shown in the lower 40th alphabet of the mode which follows after. But this mode, like all the others, is changed in different ways, so that it uses either individual indicators, or different letters.

Alphabet.

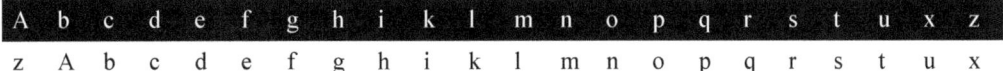

A	b	c	d	e	f	g	h	i	k	l	m	n	o	p	q	r	s	t	u	x	z
z	A	b	c	d	e	f	g	h	i	k	l	m	n	o	p	q	r	s	t	u	x

Meaning of letters
[...]

The intended secret.
It is still March 9th when the bridge strikes and I must look for you behind the trees.

An example of the fortieth.
Take pity on the wretched one, because now the greatest tribulations of our race have been endured by unbelieving men and the cruellest deaths. Consistency and definition are where? For a long time, through wrongs, the Christian kindness of yours has forsaken the Catholic faith. The faithfulness and ferocity of the divine love will be far removed. Therefore, the enemies of the Christian faith will kill and swear that men are like locusts. For we have heard how grievously Turens invaded Hungary, Bohemia, and Poland, destroyed the cities, gathered together and consecrated children, women, and virgins who had retained their chastity by the faith of God, and most shamefully raped and horribly killed any Catholics. All the annihilated cruelty of the one who overcomes men and beasts will all of a sudden disturb Germany with his most warlike army, unless the general defense of the kingdom be restored without delay. Deliver them to death. The year of our Lord, 1499, XI. Cal. March

Johannes Trithemius Abbot of Spanheim

Chapter II

The 11 Ways of Secret Writing, Which Are Considered Superior

In the previous chapters of this first book, Most Serene Prince, I have set forth in order the forty ways of our art of Steganography, the abundance of which may be sufficient for any secret concealment of anyone. To explain the modules, just as in the chapter just before, among the other 22 modes, we used the conversion of the letters of the alphabet, and we placed them in the following order. So now, according to one of the twenty-two letters of the alphabet, we only need to anticipate the five significant letters in the previous one, one by one. In which anticipation the first mode of that chapter will agree with the target of the previous one, the second with the second last one, and so as result up to the last target which will be the first of the chapter, the conversions changing the mode.

Mode I

The first method of this second chapter uses each significant letter, and each letter is taken as one.

The first method of this second chapter uses each significant expression, and each letter of the first of any expression is immediately moved to the one before. Indeed, in the 17th, the sequence is used immediately as if it were a significant letter. So here the previous one is taken first, but you must paint the alphabet in the circle in the same way as in all the following in which the letter is converted. So that z is taken here for a for b, a for b, c as is evident in the alphabet by the circle.

Now this manner, like all the rest, may be different here by the different changes, twos, threes, and fours, without more than one writing at the pleasure of the writer, yet so as to add signs agreeable to each one, otherwise he may easily forget what he has written, and no one will understand his meaning any better. And now, under the letters placed, a required number is indicated, so that each letter, b, a, which is the first in the alphabet of all languages, I will now sit down to explain this method of proceeding, using even more simple sentences than we used above.

Alphabet.

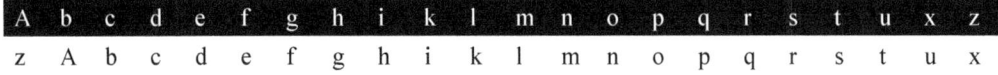

A	b	c	d	e	f	g	h	i	k	l	m	n	o	p	q	r	s	t	u	x	z
z	A	b	c	d	e	f	g	h	i	k	l	m	n	o	p	q	r	s	t	u	x

Privacy Policy.
Wait my morning at 9 with Semalt.

Significant letters.
[...]

An example of the first
The time is passing that we are sorry that you are sincere, and we humble our minds by mourning our mistakes every day. The time for mourning is here. The world will be destroyed. The world will be left behind. The fugitives will leave the laziness. Let us main-

tain the faithful devotion of Catholic holiness. Amen. Johannes Trithemius Abbot wrote on the 6th of Calend. March In the year of Sunday's incarnation. 1400

Mode II

The second mode uses other expressions, and the letters of significance are transferred to the second of the previous one.

The second mode of this chapter, beginning with a single empty spot, uses different expressions and meanings in order of the proposed narrative. The first letter of any meaning of the expression is moved into the immediately previous one that was second, so that x is taken for a, for b, z for c, a, and so in order, as is evident in the round table placed here than in the plain alphabet, which we have placed for the sake of an easier way of writing. Now the red letters are our usual alphabet, and every one of the letters in this was written in black, laid above the others in the round, is taken for the purpose of a mystical narrative.

Alphabet.

A	b	c	d	e	f	g	h	i	k	l	m	n	o	p	q	r	s	t	u	x	z
x	z	A	b	c	d	e	f	g	h	i	k	l	m	n	o	p	q	r	s	t	u

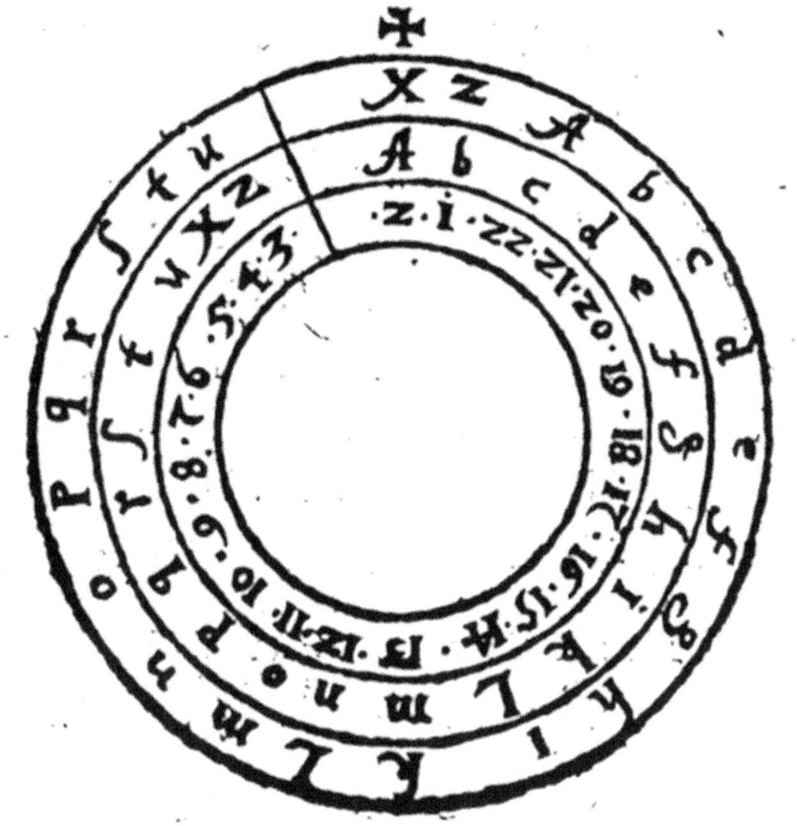

The message of the mystery.
I beg you to come to me immediately; it is very necessary.

Meaningful letters.
[…]

An example of the second.
Look, creator of humanity, God, guide your servants with the determination of righteousness, so that when we speak well, we may obtain a heavenly reward. Help us frail, and poor people with holy morals. We humbly ask the holy spirit of Catholic faithfulness, enlighten our minds with light, so that we remember your passion diligently with the tearful works of Jesus Christ. Saviour, deliver us by the power of your shed blood, leader of your Catholic unity, save your greatly afflicted people, whom you redeemed a long time ago by dying on the cross with your most blessed blood. Look at how greatly the people suffer under the cruelest Turks. Deliver us from the wretched by the grace with which you redeemed us, Amen. Johannes Trithemius, Abbot, in the year 1400.

Mode III

The third mode progresses through each of the meanings and is transferred to the previous one that was third by means of letters.

The third method of this second chapter progresses through each of the signified saying as the first, and the first letter of each saying is immediately moved to the third, so that v is taken for a, which is the third previous one to z, and so in order, as is evident from the very letters and numbers placed in the table. But this method can also be verified,

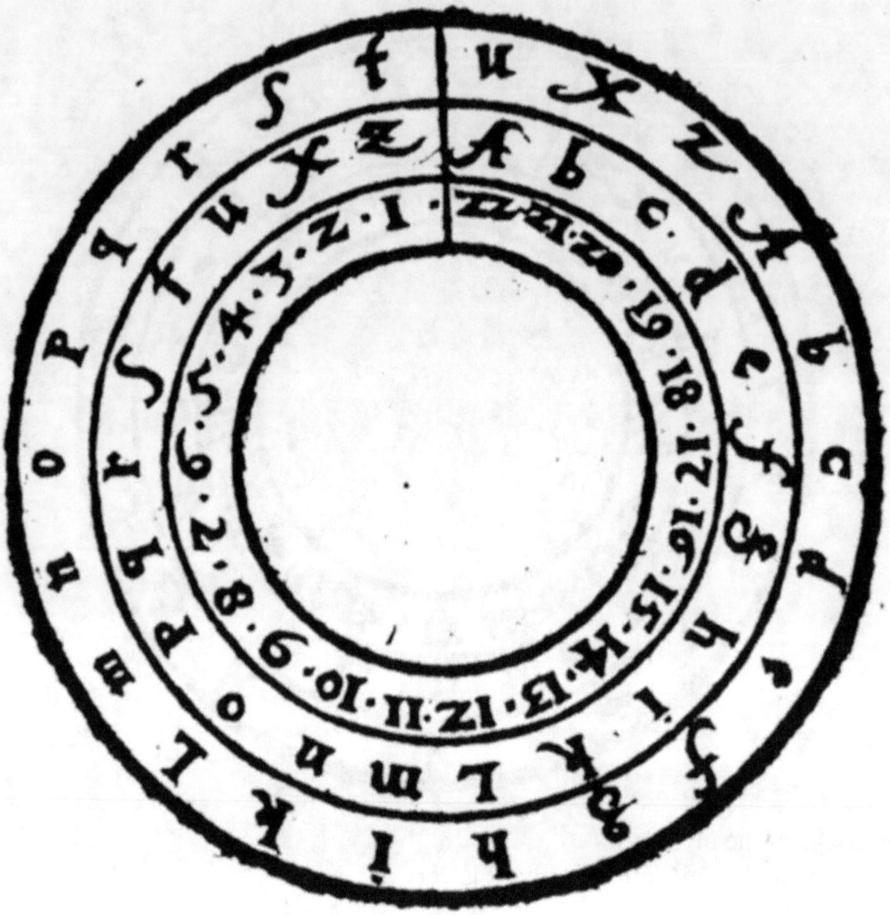

which very much, and the others, not only progressing through each significant one, but also through the different, twos, threes, and fours, as many as you please when writing.

Alphabet.

A	b	c	d	e	f	g	h	i	k	l	m	n	o	p	q	r	s	t	u	x	z
u	x	z	A	b	c	d	e	f	g	h	i	k	l	m	n	o	p	q	r	s	t

Privacy Policy.
Bring your letters, he's an evil boy, don't worry, it's too much for him.

Significant letters.
[…]

A third example.
The most excellent and kindest of the Catholics, by blessing the favourable time, let us worship Christ faithfully. Let us all do good loving works to those who are exiled from the way to faith. Lay down the cross of the persecution of the faith and rest in happiness. The Catholic faith praises Christ through good works. Rejoice, the Catholic victor, Christ, blesses the good Catholics, who have been drawn from the good Catholics every day. He will hold them receiving the reward of the most brilliant honour. Johannes

Trithemius. In the year of our Lord, 1499 successfully.

Mode IV

The fourth method uses each word meaning but the letters are moved to the previous quarter.

The fourth mode of this chapter proceeds in the same manner as the previous one, but the secret letters of the mystery are anticipated in the fourth immediately before, which is shown more clearly in the below table.

Here first the first letter of the alphabet a is taken t, which is the fourth in the cycle before it, for b, v, for c, x, and so on as is evident in the table. Now this method can be made different as with the others by differences in two, or more, but because by each significant procedure we can hide many more obvious secrets, we decided to adopt this method for the sake of beauty.

Alphabet.

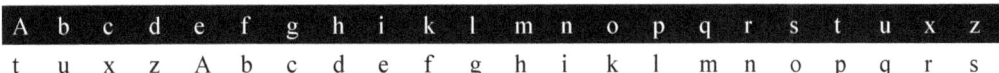

A	b	c	d	e	f	g	h	i	k	l	m	n	o	p	q	r	s	t	u	x	z
t	u	x	z	A	b	c	d	e	f	g	h	i	k	l	m	n	o	p	q	r	s

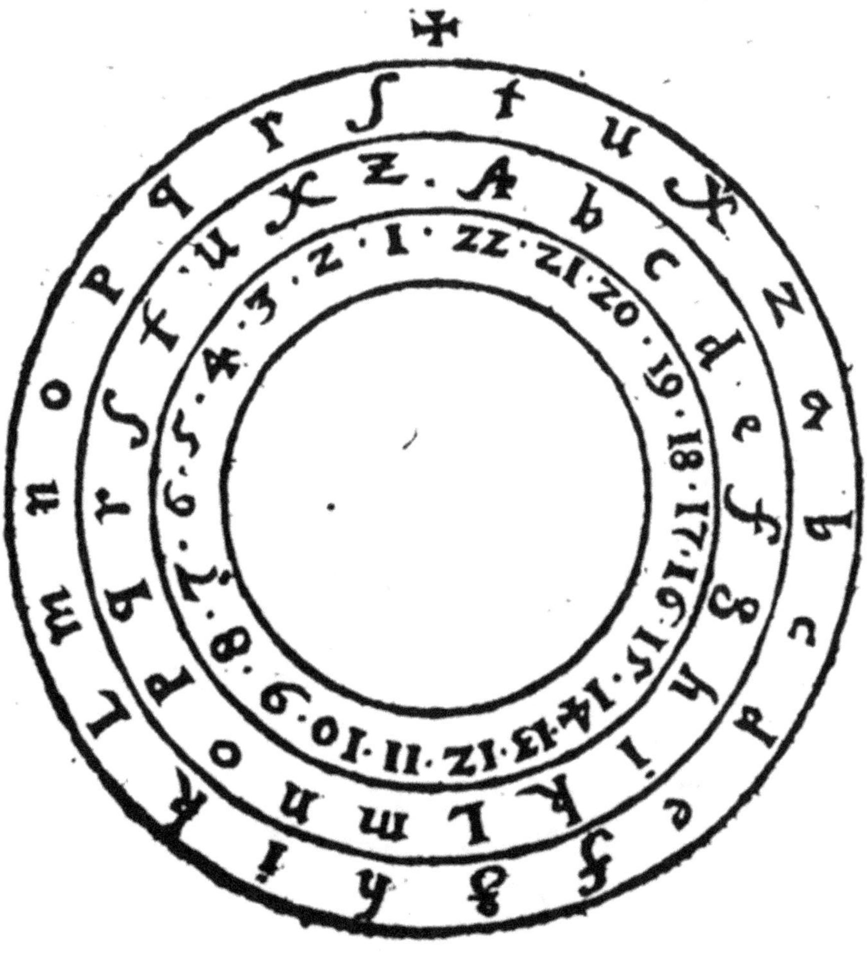

Privacy Policy.

The parish hall in Bing is one step different according to the parish. This is the intention of the following open narrative according to this method.

Meaningful letters.

[...]

A fourth example

In order to receive praise of divine love for the most devoted of our souls, let us continually approach every lie that has buried eternal failures desiring that all things pass away except God and laziness. Why do we love this life and desire to be immersed in destruction? Why do we lead ourselves away? We pray to Christ who is eternally dedicated to the devotion of love because we are daily scarred by great urges and temptations. Christ, give to us the sweet faithfulness of your love, and by your sweetness let sin not harm our souls, Amen. Johannes Trithemius scipsi 10. Calend. March, the year of our Lord 1500.

MODE V

The fifth mode makes use of each indicator, and the first letter is changed into the fifth before it.

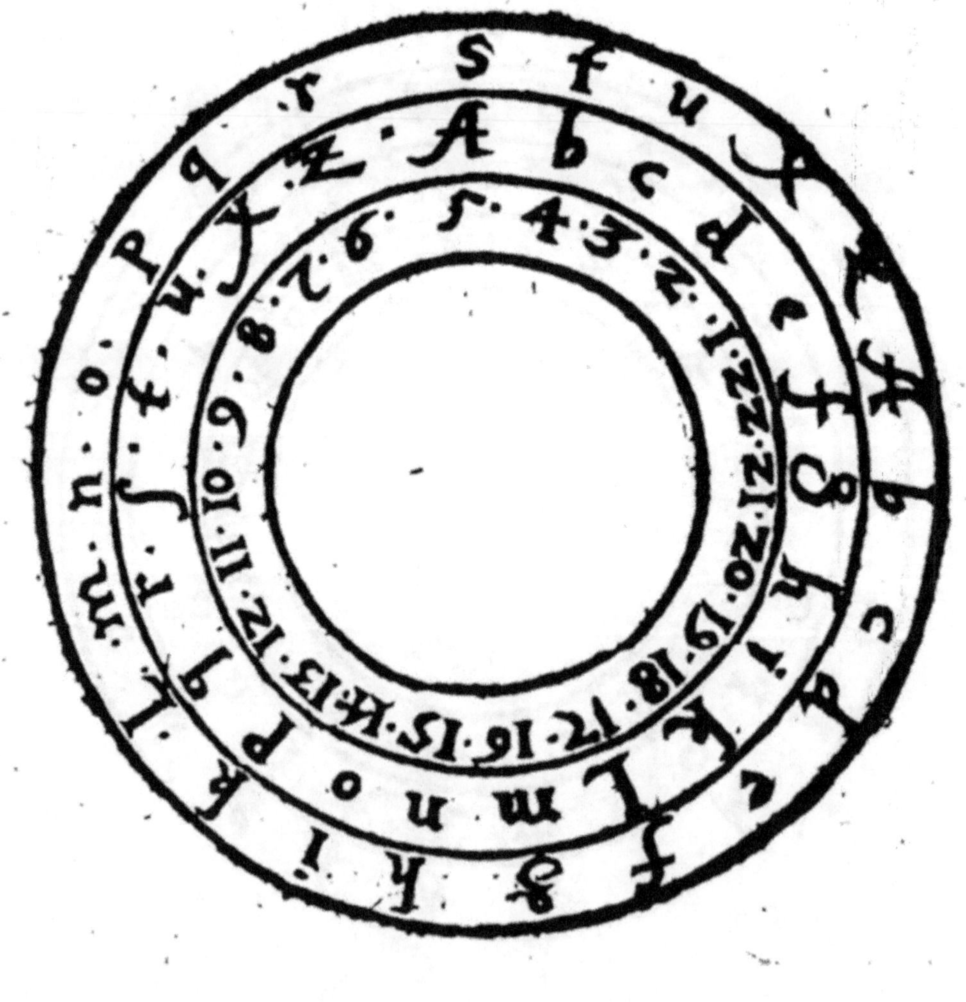

The fifth mode of this second chapter, like the previous one, receives empty deals, but through each significant mystery it passes away. Nor do I believe that any one ignorant of this art can ever find it hidden by these methods, while even a person who knows the art and is not well used to it is difficult to discover everything, which is in the table of the alphabet.

Fifth before it for b, t, for c, v and so on, as appears in the table. But he who wants this method by another two, or more, because it is not easy for everyone to go through each sign in writing, and do not remove any one inappropriately, otherwise he will easily fall into error, and knowingly cost the reader nothing of benefit.

Alphabet.

A	b	c	d	e	f	g	h	i	k	l	m	n	o	p	q	r	s	t	u	x	z
s	t	u	x	z	A	b	c	d	e	f	g	h	i	k	l	m	n	o	p	q	r

The intended message of the secret mystery.
Tomorrow at 7 am the scaffolding and mine at the Sreusch.

Meaningful letters.
[…]

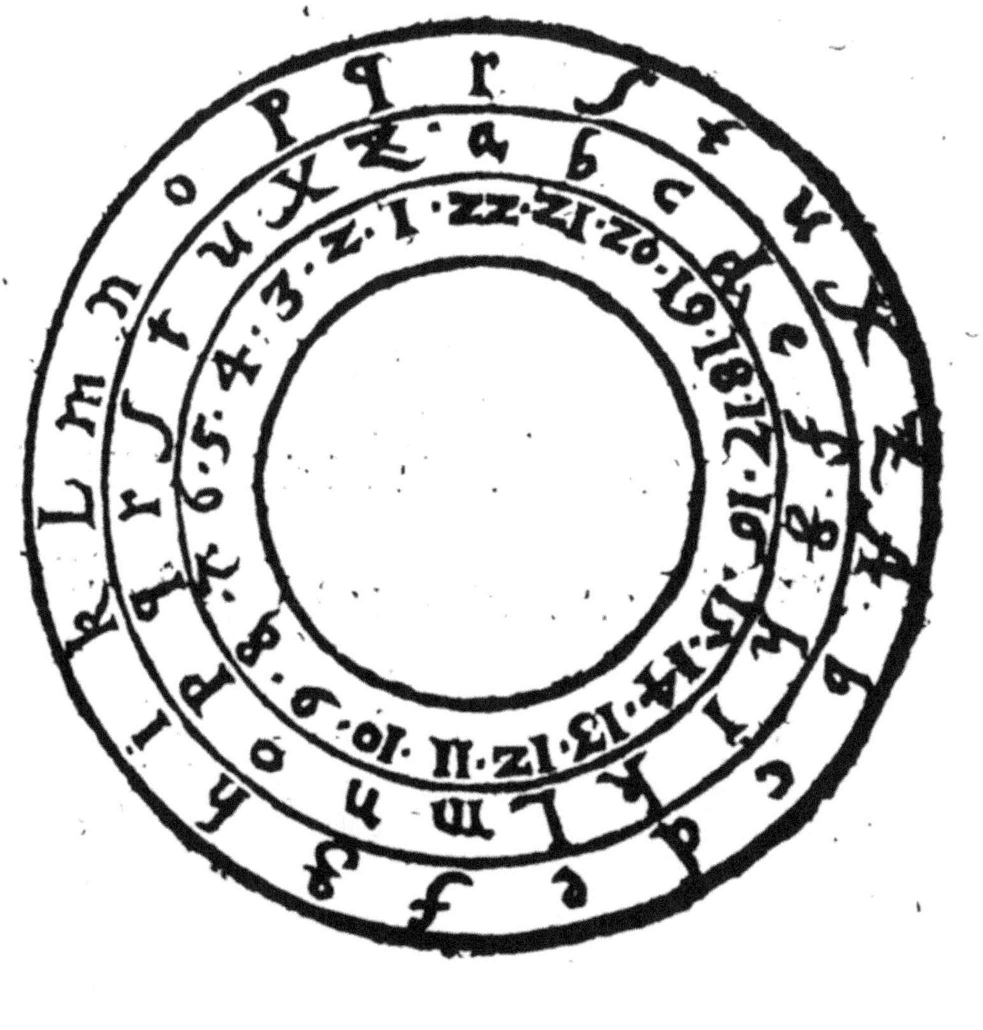

An example of the fifth
I humbly begged you for the burdens of your mind, the faithfulnes of the trinity, grant us goodness. Good faithful devotion pursues after defeating evil. I placed Johannes Trithemius Abbot 7. Calen. March, Anno 1400

Mode VI

The sixth mode progresses through all the indicators and each one is placed in the previous 6th.

The sixth mode of this chapter also progresses through all the significant saying like the previous one, admitting no empty space at all. All the letters of the secret mysteries are converted in such a way that for a, the sixth following in the roll is taken which is r, for b, s, for c, t, for d, t for e, x, for f, z for g, a, and so on according to the order of all the letters dwelling and placed in the book itself. By the supposed number of the alphabet, one can easily and without difficulty know how far each letter is from the other, and how much it is quoted in the order of the two alphabets. Now follows the table.

Alphabet.

A	b	c	d	e	f	g	h	i	k	l	m	n	o	p	q	r	s	t	u	x	z
r	s	t	u	x	z	A	b	c	d	e	f	g	h	i	k	l	m	n	o	p	q

The intended message of the mystery.
Do not take this man too seriously, he is a gentle man.

Meaningful letters.
[...]

An example of the sixth.
The glorious and merciful founder of our knowledge, the generator of the Christian world, the memory of Christ's actions, is being sold on the knees of humility at the same time. Why did we bother? Let us look at Christ cheering on his shoulders, the tree of majesty, the redemption of the servants, Christ nailed to the tree, and he dies for us. In the year of the Lord, 1500. 9. Claen, Martij, Johannes Trithemius, abbot.

Mode VII

The seventh mode progresses through all the indicators, and in the 7th the preceding letters are converted.

Now the seventh mode of this chapter receives no idleness but proceeds into the narrative of the hidden mystery by means of significant indicators. Truthfully τα` κα ´μμαλα all the secrets of the mysteries are converted into 7. whatever letter immediately precedes it, but this method can be changed in many ways, as we have taught in its place for each one. But all the letters are hidden mysteries. Therefore in 7 they are conveniently changed to the previous one, so that q is taken for a, which is the seventh distant from the place, counting backwards, as the supposed number clearly indicates, for b, r is taken, for c, s, and so on according to the order of the following table.

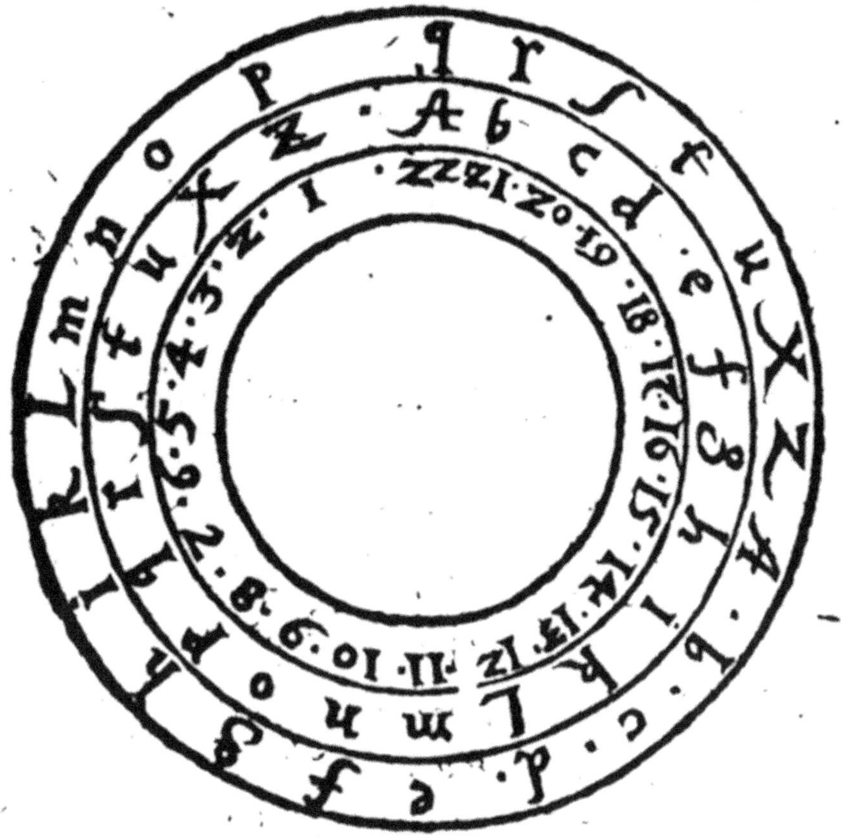

The alphabet is flat.

A	b	c	d	e	f	g	h	i	k	l	m	n	o	p	q	r	s	t	u	x	z
q	r	s	t	u	x	z	A	b	c	d	e	f	g	h	i	k	l	m	n	o	p

Intention of the secret mystery.
[...]

An example of the seventh
The time of other honours, the laziness of flattering and complimenting evil Christians wears out the peace of the moral laziness with various wars because the flesh is the failure of the criminal age. These are who recklessly hang on to the happiness of the future kingdom, not given to the wickedness of the good of no one, or the fiercest supporters of the beast. Although he is not followed, he loves purity, righteousness, goodness, shines temporary goods, hangs onto the cheap things of the world, and remembers the light of the future. Johannes Trithemius.

Mode VIII

The eight mode progresses through all the signifiers, and they are converted into the eighth letter.

The mode of the eighth truths in this capital, like the previous one, in the narrative of the mysteries, it uses expressions of significance throughout. Each of the hidden narratives is converted to the immediately preceding letter 8, so that instead of a, p,

which is to be numbered backwards and eighths distant from that bed, as is evident in the numbering roll. For b let q be taken, for c, r, and so on through the order of the whole alphabet. And this manner changes according to the pleasure of the one who knows the art by means of the other, two, three, four, or more sayings, as we may show in their proper place.

Alphabet.

A	b	c	d	e	f	g	h	i	k	l	m	n	o	p	q	r	s	t	u	x	z
p	q	r	s	t	u	x	z	A	b	c	d	e	f	g	h	i	k	l	m	n	o

The intended message of the secret mysteries.
Your friends are coming tomorrow with ten horses and I intend to get you ready.

Meaningful letters.
[…]

An example of the eighth.
Eternal saviour of souls by the power of the highest Father, comfort the sorrows of the poor, mitigate the tribulations of the innocent, and help in temptations. Stretch out your hand of defense to those who suffer in the need and desolation of the frail Jesus, since we deserve to be cleansed comforters of your laziness. Kindly, son of God, drive away the darkness of our sins, you are the sweet light of souls. I drive away reckless devotion in every way. Glorifier of the faithful, who eagerly wait for the sanctity of those who pursue

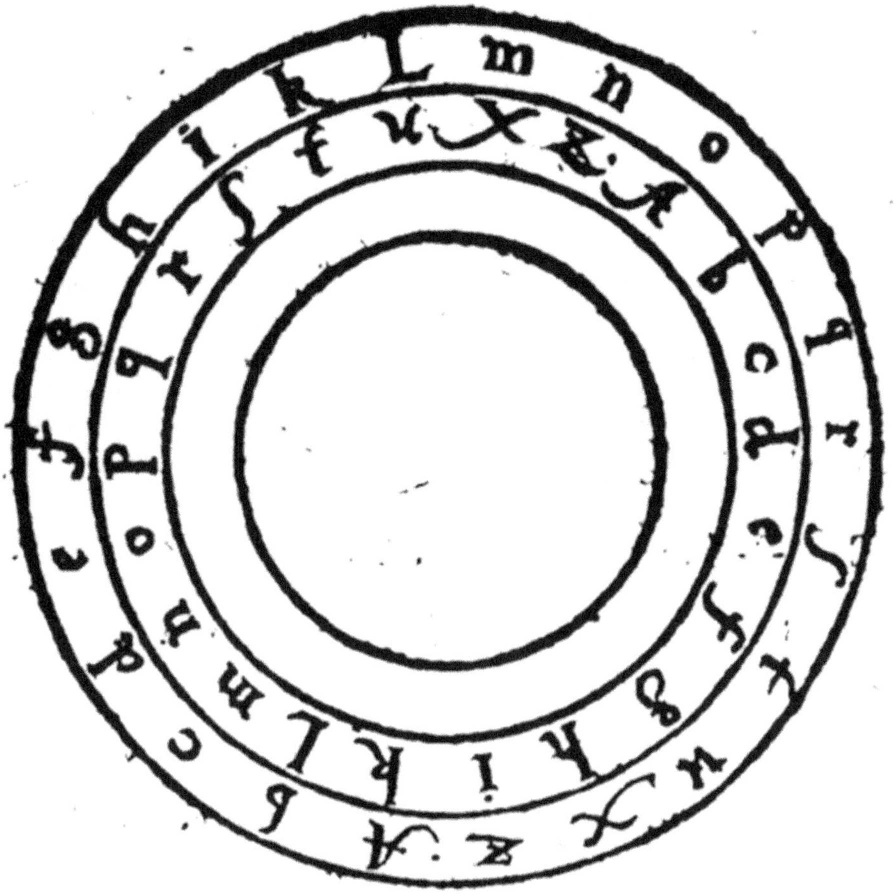

the part of the supporter, we powerfully grant the times of the most holy love with devoted praises. Oh, most gentle lover of Jesus examine the righteousness of the faithful's tears. In the year of the Lord, 1400. 8. Kal. March

Mode IX

The ninth method uses all the significant ones, and every letter is converted to the previous ninth.

The ninth mode of this previous chapter, in concealing the purpose of the mystery, directs it through all the significant products without order, and admits of no emptiness at all. But all the secret letters of the narrative are moved to the preceding 9 so that for a, let o be taken. which is ninth in the order of the alphabet before it, as is evident both in the scroll and in the flat alphabet. For b is taken p, for c, q, and so on. Now this mode is made, and all the rest can be changed into many others, not only by vast differences, by twos and threes, but also in other such different arrangements, that they can be made in any manner almost infinite.

The alphabet is flat.

A	b	c	d	e	f	g	h	i	k	l	m	n	o	p	q	r	s	t	u	x	z
o	p	q	r	s	t	u	x	z	A	b	c	d	e	f	g	h	i	k	l	m	n

Privacy Policy.
The people of Saxony collect a large number of bolts, not me, I'm going to go after you. This is the intention of the mysteries.

Meaningful letters.
[...]

An example of the ninth.
The devoted faithful of religion, the saviour of Jesus, who most gently calls upon all, receive the weak, deliver the lowly ones, indulge those who pray for their crimes, and give glory to those who are in trouble. Give peace to those who are faithfully devoted for salvation, we seek the Lord of true humility. You are worthy to be present to those who seek the eternal determination of the blessed. You are worthy to be present to those who seek it, the faith of those who begged for Catholic liberty to be cleared away, and to turn away the sinful traps of the Christians. The giver of light and holy judgment, put on the belt of innocence, and bind the holy Christian laziness to the begging Christians. Redeem the faithfulness which I took, seeing you like Christ be humble. In the year 1500. Kalen. March, Johannes Trithemius, Abbot of Spanheim.

Mode X
The tenth mode makes use of each indicator, and the last letter is transferred to the last one.

The tenth method of this chapter, after the manner of the previous ones, is used in concealing the mystery by means of individual sayings, when no empty space is more prominently mixed in. Just as it would be difficult to conceal the intention without the similarity of the sentence through each sentence, you will be able, both in this and in the others, to use different options, twos, threes, fours, and many more. Now all the letters which are significant like those before them, in this way are moved over in anticipation of the tenth preceding letter, so that for a, n, because in the order of the alphabet the scrolls are attached to the demonstration 10, before it for b, let o be taken for c, p for d, q, and so on throughout the whole alphabet, as he can by looking at the measure of the circumference.

The alphabet is flat.

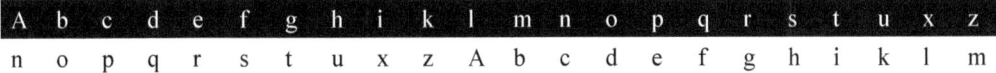

A	b	c	d	e	f	g	h	i	k	l	m	n	o	p	q	r	s	t	u	x	z
n	o	p	q	r	s	t	u	x	z	A	b	c	d	e	f	g	h	i	k	l	m

The intended message of the mysteries.
We keep these books secretly. This is the intention.
Literally significant.
[…]

The tenth example.
Everyone chooses to keep the rule of humility and govern his life with Catholic faithfulness, and he must embrace the religious norm of truth. Every Christian who truly seeks the glory of Christ loves the goodness of Christ and is a righteous Christian. Goodbye Johannes Trithemius, abbot of Spanheim. In 1400. 7. Cal. April.

Mode XI

The eleventh mode as the preceding one uses each indicator, and the letters in 11 are anticipated.

The eleventh mode proceeds, after the manner of the previous ones, with each significant saying in concealing a mystery, to which no laziness should be mixed. Furthermore, all the letters are immediately converted into the previous eleventh, as is clear from looking clearly at the alphabet on the table.

The end

Imprint of Darmbstad at Balthasar Hofmann, Anno 1606.

Bibliography

Abusch, T. "Ishtar," In *Dictionary of Deities and Demons in the Bible*, edited by Karel van der Toorn, Bob Becking, and Pieter W. van der Horst, pp. 452–455. Leiden, Netherlands: Brill, 1999.

Aune, D. E. "PGM V. 96–172." In *The Greek Magical Papyri in Translation Including the Demotic Spells*, edited by Hans Deiter Betz, p. 103. Chicago, Illinois: The University of Chicago Press, 1986.

Author Unknown. *Grimorium Verum: The True Grimoire*, edited by Tarl Warwick. Vermont: Tarl Warwick, 2018. Kindle Edition.

Author Unknown. "Jake Stratton-Kent." *Scarlet Imprint Publishing*. Accessed August 15, 2024. https://scarletimprint.com/jake-stratton-kent.

Barstad, H. M. "Sheol." In *Dictionary of Deities and Demons in the Bible*, edited by Karel van der Toorn, Bob Becking, and Pieter W. van der Horst, pp. 768–796. Leiden, Netherlands: Brill, 1999.

Beale, G. K. *Handbook on the New Testament Use of the Old Testament: Exegesis and Interpretation*. Grand Rapids, Michigan: Baker Academic, 2012.

Belanger, Michelle. *Dictionary of Demons: Names of the Damned*. Woodbury, Minnesota: Llewellyn Publications, 2017.

Betz, Hans Deiter. *The Greek Magical Papyri in Translation Including the Demotic Spells*. Chicago, Illinois: The University of Chicago Press, 1986.

Bevere, John. *The Fear of the Lord: Discover the Key to Ultimately Knowing God*. Lake Mary, Florida: Charisma House, 2006.

Block, Daniel Isaac. *Judges, Ruth, volume 6, The New American Commentary*. Nashville, Tennessee: Broadman & Holman Publishers, 1999.

Borchert, Gerald L. *John 1–11, volume 25A, The New American Commentary*. Nashville, Tennessee: Broadman & Holman Publishers, 1996.

Brand, Chad, et al., editors. "Necromancy." In *Holman Illustrated Bible Dictionary*, p. 1181. Nashville, Tennessee: Holman Bible Publishers, 2003.

Bratrud, Tom. "Chapter 9 Spiritual War: Anointing Ahamb Island." In *Pentecostalism and Witchcraft: Spiritual Warfare in Africa and Melanesia*, edited by Knut Rio, Michelle MacCarthy, and Ruy Blanes, pp. 217–239. Ingersoll, Ontario: Devoted Publishing, 2023.

Brooks, James A. *Mark, volume 23, The New American Commentary*. Nashville, Tennessee: Broadman & Holman Publishers, 1991.

Brown, Francis, Samuel Rolles Driver, and Charles Augustus Briggs. *Enhanced Brown-Driver-Briggs Hebrew and English Lexicon*. Oxford: Clarendon Press, 1977.

Bruce, F. F. *The Epistle to the Hebrews, Rev. ed., The New International Commentary on the New Testament*. Grand Rapids, Michigan: Wm. B. Eerdmans Publishing Co., 1990.

Burkert, Walter. *Greek Religion*. Malden, Massachusetts: Blackwell Publishing, 1985.

Calvin, John and Charles William Bingham. *Commentaries on the Four Last Books of Moses Arranged in the Form of a Harmony, volume 1*. Bellingham, Washington: Logos Bible Software, 2010.

Carsten, Janet. *Blood Work: Life and Laboratories in Penang*. Durham, North Carolina: Duke University Press, 2019.

Chajes, J. H. *Between Worlds: Dybbuks, Exorcists, and Early Modern Judaism*. Philadelphia, Pennsylvania: University of Pennsylvania Press, 2003.

Cole, R. Alan. *Mark: An Introduction and Commentary, volume 2, Tyndale New Testament Commentaries*. Downers Grove, Illinois: InterVarsity Press, 1989.

Conway, David. *Magic: An Occult Primer*. Newport, Rhode Island: The Witches Almanac LTD, 2017.

Davidson, Gustav. *A Dictionary of Angels including the fallen angels*. New York, New York: The Free Press, 1971.

Davila, James R. *Hekhalot Literature in Translation: Major Texts of Merkavah Mysticism*. Leiden, Netherlands: Brill, 2013.

de Laurence, L. W. *Sixth and Seventh Books of Moses: The Mystery of All Mysteries*. Chicago, Illinois: de Laurence, Scott & Co., 1910.

Durham, John I. *Exodus, volume 3, Word Biblical Commentary* (Dallas, Texas: Word, Incorporated, 1987.

Elwell, Walter A. and Barry J. Beitzel. "Necromancer, Necromancy." In *Baker Encyclopedia of the Bible*, p. 1535. Grand Rapids, Michigan: Baker Book House, 1988.

Eckhardt, John. *Deliverance and Spiritual Warfare Manua*l. Lake Mary, Florida: Charisma House, 2014.

Estes, Daniel J. *Psalms 73–150 volume 13, New American Commentary*. Edited by E. Ray. Clendenen. Nashville, Tennessee: B&H Publishing Group, 2019.

Ford, Michael W. *The Bible of the Adversary: 10th Anniversary Edition*. Houston, Texas: Succubus Productions, 2017. Kindle Edition.

France, R. T. *The Gospel of Matthew, The New International Commentary on the New Testament*. Grand Rapids, Michigan: Wm. B. Eerdmans Publication Co., 2007.

Garcia, Zen. *The Collected Works of Enoch The Prophet*. Atlanta, Georgia: Sacred Word Publishing, 2017.

———. *Lucifer – Father of Cain*. Atlanta, Georgia: Sacred Word Publishing, 2011.

Goll, James W. *Angelic Encounters: Engaging Help from Heaven*. Lake Mary, Florida: Charisma House, 2013. Logos Edition.

Green, Joel B. *The Gospel of Luke, The New International Commentary on the New Testament*. Grand Rapids, Michigan: Wm. B. Eerdmans Publishing Co., 1997.

Greenwood, Susan. *Magic, Witchcraft and the Otherworld*. New York, New York: Berg, 2000.

Grese, W. C. "PGM V. 1–53." In *The Greek Magical Papyri in Translation Including the Demotic Spells*, edited by Hans Deiter Betz, pp. 101–102. Chicago, Illinois: The University of Chicago Press, 1986.

———. "PGM VII. 348–58." In *The Greek Magical Papyri in Translation Including the Demotic Spells*, edited by Hans Deiter Betz, p. 127. Chicago, Illinois: The University of Chicago Press, 1986.

Guiley, Rosemary Ellen, Ph.D. *The Encyclopedia of Angels: Second Edition*. New York, New York: Checkmark Books, 2004.

———. The Encyclopedia of Demons & Demonology. New York, New York: Checkmark Books, 2009.

Gyūichi, Ōta. *The Chronicle of Lord Nobunaga*. Edited and translated by J.S.A Elisonas and J.P. Lamers. Leiden, Netherlands: Brill, 2011. [Footnote 9].

Hagee, John. *The Four Blood Moons: Something Is About To Change*. Brentwood, Tennessee: Worthy Publishing, 2013.

Hardy, Elle. *Beyond Belief: How Pentecostal Christianity Is Taking Over the World*. London, England: C. Hurst & Company, 2021. Kindle Edition.

———. "The Evangelicals Calling for War on Poor People." *The New Republic*. Accessed October 23, 2024. https://newrepublic.com/article/176117/prosperity-gospel-christian-war-poor.

Heiser, Michael S. *Demons: What the Bible Really Says about the Powers of Darkness*. Bellingham, Washington: Lexham Press, 2020.

———. *Reversing Hermon: Enoch, The Watchers & The Forgotten Mission of Jesus Christ*. Bellingham, Washington: Lexham Press, 2017.

———. *The Unseen Realm: Recovering the Supernatural Worldview of the Bible, First Edition*. Bellingham, Washington: Lexham Press, 2015.

Hendriksen, William, and Simon J. Kistemaker. *Exposition of Paul's Epistle to the Romans, volume 12–13, New Testament Commentary*. Grand Rapids, Michigan: Baker Book House.

Hermes. *The Emerald Tablet of Hermes*. Location of publication unknown: IAP, 2009. Kindle Edition.

Hoheisel, Karl. "Esotericism." In *The Encyclopedia of Christianity*, edited by Karl Hoheisel et. al., p. 132, volume 2. Leiden, Netherlands: Brill, 1999–2003.

Holladay, Carl H. *Theios Aner in Hellenistic Judaism: A Critique of the Use of This Category in New Testament Christology*. Missoula, Montana: Scholars Press, 1977.

Homer, "The Odyssey with an English Translation by A.T. Murray, PH.D. in Two Volumes." Cambridge, Massachusetts, Harvard University Press; London, William Heinemann, Ltd., 1919.

Houston, Bobbie. *Heaven is in this House. Castle Hill*, New South Wales Australia: Leadership Ministries Inc., 2001.

James, Montague Rhodes. *The Apocryphal New Testament: being the Apocryphal Gospels, Acts, Epistles, and Apocalypses*. Oxford, England: Clarendon Press, 1924.

Johnson, Bill and Heidi Baker. *Hosting the Presence: Unveiling Heaven's Agenda*. Shippensburg, Pennsylvania: Destiny Image, 2012. Logos Edition.

Johnson, Bill and Mike Seth, *When Heaven Invades Earth for Teens: Your Guide to God's Supernatural Power*. Shippensburg, Pennsylvania: Destiny Image, 2014. Logos Edition.

Johnston, Philip S. Johnston. *Shades of Sheol: Death and the Afterlife in the Old Testament*. Downers Grove, Illinois: Intervarsity Press, 2002.

Klaassen, Frank and Sharon Hubbs Wright, *The Magic of Rogues: Necromancers in Early Tudor England*. University Park, Pennsylvania: The Pennsylvania State University Press, 2021.

Klein, Ralph W. *1 Samuel, volume 10, Word Biblical Commentary*. Dallas, Texas: Word, Incorporated, 1983.

Kruse, Colin G. *John: An Introduction and Commentary, Second edition, volume 4, Tyndale New Testament Commentaries*, edited by Eckhard J. Schnabel. London: Inter-Varsity Press, 2017.

Larson, Bob. Jezebel: *Defeating Your #1 Spiritual Enemy*. Shippensburg, Pennsylvania: Destiny Image, 2015. Logos Edition.

Levi, Eliphas. *The History of Magic*. London, United Kingdom: William Rider & Son Limited, 1922.

Lewis, Charlton T. *An Elementary Latin Dictionary*. Medford, Massachusetts: American Book Company, 1890.

Liddell, Henry George, et al. *A Greek-English Lexicon*. Oxford: Clarendon Press, 1996.

Louw, Johannes P., and Eugene Albert Nida. *Greek-English Lexicon of the New Testament: Based on Semantic Domains*. New York, New York: United Bible Societies, 1996.

Merrill, Eugene H. *Deuteronomy, volume 4, The New American Commentary*. Nashville, Tennessee: Broadman & Holman Publishers, 1994.

Michaels, J. Ramsey. *The Gospel of John: The New International Commentary on the New Testament*. Grand Rapids, Michigan: William B. Eerdmans Publishing Company, 2010.

Miller, Stephen R. *Daniel, volume 18, The New American Commentary*. Nashville, Tennessee: Broadman & Holman Publishers, 1994.

Morris, Leon. *1 Corinthians: An Introduction and Commentary, volume 7, Tyndale New Testament Commentaries*. Downers Grove, Illinois: InterVarsity Press, 1985.

———. *Luke: An Introduction and Commentary, volume 3, Tyndale New Testament Commentaries*. Downers Grove, Illinois: InterVarsity Press, 1988.

Motyer, J. Alec. *Isaiah: An Introduction and Commentary, volume 20, Tyndale Old Testament Commentaries*. Downers Grove, Illinois: InterVarsity Press, 1999.

Nagel, Peter. "Gnosis." In *The Encyclopedia of Christianity*, edited by Erwin Fahlbusch et. al. Leiden, pp. 417–420, volume 2. Netherlands: Brill, 1999–2003. Logos Edition.

Noegel, Scott B., and Brannon M. Wheeler. *The A to Z of prophets in Islam and Judaism*. Plymouth, United Kingdom: The Scarecrow Press, Inc., 2010.

Ogden, Daniel. Greek and Roman Necromancy. Princeton, New Jersey: Princeton University Press, 2001.

O'Neil, E. N. "PGM I, 42–195". In *The Greek Magical Papyri in Translation Including the Demotic Spells*, edited by Hans Deiter Betz, pp. 4–8. Chicago, Illinois: The University of Chicago Press, 1986.

Ostberg, René. "witching hour." *Britannica*. Last accessed October 6, 2024. https://www.britannica.com/topic/witching-hour.

Péter-Contesse, René and John Ellington, *A Handbook on the Book of Daniel, UBS Handbook Series*. New York, New York: United Bible Societies, 1994.

Polhill, John B. *Acts, volume 26, The New American Commentary*. Nashville, Tennessee: Broadman & Holman Publishers, 1992.

Revealing Truth. "Kenneth Copeland Takes Creepy to a Whole New Level." *YouTube*. Last accessed November 4, 2024. https://www.youtube.com/watch?v=-At56s393Ko.

Scholem, Gershom. *Origins of the Kabbalah*. Princeton, New Jersey: Princeton University Press, 2018.

Shaked, Shaul, James Nathan Ford, and Siam Bhayro, *Aramaic Bowl Spells*. Leiden, Netherlands: Brill, 2013.

Shirbini, Ranya. "Aqiqah FAQs – Rules and Fiqh of Aqiqah." *Muslim Hands*. Last accessed October 28, 2024. https://muslimhands.org.uk/latest/2021/09/rules-and-fiqh-of-aqiqah-for-new-born.

Smith, Gary V. *Isaiah 1–39*, edited by E. Ray Clendenen, *The New American Commentary*. Nashville, Tennessee: B & H Publishing Group, 2007.

Stein, Robert H. *Luke, volume 24, The New American Commentary*. Nashville, Tennessee: Broadman & Holman Publishers, 1992.

Stratton-Kent, Jake. *Geosophia volume I*. London, United Kingdon: Scarlet Imprint, 2010.

Stuart, Douglas K. *Exodus, volume 2, The New American Commentary*. Nashville, Tennessee: Broadman & Holman Publishers, 2006.

Swete, Henry Barclay Swete. *The Old Testament in Greek: According to the Septuagint*. Cambridge, UK: Cambridge University Press, 1909.

Tate, Marvin E. *Psalms 51–100, volume 20, Word Biblical Commentary*. Dallas, Texas: Word, Incorporated, 1998.

Taylor, Mark. *1 Corinthians*, edited by E. Ray Clendenen, *volume 28, The New American Commentary*. Nashville, Tennessee: B&H Publishing Group, 2014.

Tomlin, Chris, and Darren Whitehead, *Holy Roar: 7 Words That Will Change The Way You Worship*. Nashville, Tennessee: Thomas Nelson, 2017. Kindle Edition.

Torigano, Pablo A. *Solomon the Esoteric King: From King to Magus, Development of a Tradition*. Leiden, Netherlands: Brill, 2002.

Uyl, Anthony. *Biblical Demonology: Their Origins and Unwilling Role in Sanctification*. Ingersoll, Ontario, Canada: Devoted Publishing, 2022.

———. *The Emergence of the Neo-Satanist Church: The Reality of the Prosperity, Hillsong, Word-of-Faith, and New Apostolic Reformation Death Cult*. Ingersoll, Ontario, Canada: Devoted Publishing, 2023.

Maro, P. Vergilius (Virgil). "Bucolics, Aeneid, and Georgics Of Vergil." Editor J. B. Greenough (Ginn & Co., 1900).

Wagner, C. Peter. *Spiritual Warfare Strategy: Confronting Spiritual Powers*. Shippensburg, Pennsylvania: Destiny Image, 2011), p. 216.

———. *Your Church Can Grow: Seven Vital Signs of a Healthy Church.* Eugene, Oregon; Wipf & Stock Publishers, 1998.

Weller, Philip T. *Roman Ritual II: Christian Burial, Exorcism, Reserved Blessings, etc.* Jeffersonville, Indiana: Caritas Publishing, 2017.

Wise, Michael O., Martin G. Abegg Jr., and Edward M. Cook. *The Dead Sea Scrolls: A New Translation.* New York, New York: HarperOne, 2005.

Wyatt, N. "Asherah." In *Dictionary of Deities and Demons in the Bible*, edited by Karel van der Toorn, Bob Becking, and Pieter W. van der Horst, pp. 99–104 (Leiden, Netherlands: Brill, 1999).

Zschech, Darlene and Brian Houston. *Extravagant Worship: Holy, Holy, Holy Is the Lord God Almighty Who Was and Is, and Is to Come…* Grand Rapids, Michigan: Bethany House, 2004. Logos Edition.

Other Books by Anthony Uyl MTS

Biblical Demonology: Their Origins and Unwilling Role in Sanctification

Many Christians are searching for answers when it comes to the spiritual and demonic. Unfortunately with the plethora of material out there, most of it is not any good theologically. This book attempts to correct that by offering a biblical argument for where the demonic not only comes from by how and why they are allowed to oppress believing Christians.

Four biblical texts are observed to see that it is by God's will alone that covenant community members can be tormented by the demonic. As well, an appendix on the biblical method for dealing with demonic issues such as oppression is offered.

ISBN: 978-1-77356-437-1

The Emergence of the Neo-Satanist Church: A Comparison with the Theology of the Prosperity, Hillsong, Word-of-Faith, and New Apostolic Reformation Movements (Revised Title, same book)

With all the podcasts, papers, and other reports about the heretical teaching of Hillsong, Prosperity, Word-of-Faith, and New Apostolic Reformation churches, has the final line been drawn about what these "churches" really believe? It does not appear that it has.

In doing an academic study on what these churches believe, not by relying solely on other Christian writers about what these churches believe or how they compare to heretical teaching or the occult, Anthony Uyl has researched the very occult texts themselves to make a comparison. In doing this academic research, a much more dangerous reality has been found when it comes to these churches and their "seven-mountain mandate". In looking at the comparisons, a much more devious Left-Hand Path Satanist group fits the mold much more accurately about what these churches really believe and are teaching.

In this no-holds barred reveal about how the teaching from these movements, and just how far they are ready to go to push their seven-mountain beliefs, Uyl has shown a much more frightening reality that makes believing "biblical" churches to start having making a much more serious decision about whether these Hillsong, Prosperity, Word-of-Faith, and New Apostolic Reformation church's music and their products should continue to be being used in Sunday morning worship and teaching.

The Neo-Satanist church is here, and the mask is more deceiving than you could even imagine. How far supposedly "biblical" churches are in defending the use of these evil churches music and other products is what is most disturbing.

ISBN: 978-1-77356-527-9

Jezebel's Invasion of Evangelicalism: An Examination of the Evidence and Intentions of the "Jezebel Spirit"

Evangelical Christianity in recent years has been writing books and teaching a lot about the "Jezebel" spirit. The origin of this "spirit" comes from Revelation 2:19–29. The question is, however, does such a spirit really exist? By looking at all the biblical evidence that has been given for the existence of such a spirit/demon, and also extra-biblical evidence that is used to support the existence of such a spirit, Uyl asks the question of whether this spirit is real or not. If such a spirit is in fact real, the question needs to be asked, what effect has this "Jezebel" spirit had on evangelical Christianity, as well as other groups of Christians as a whole? Is this "Jezebel" spirit really what it appears to be? If not, what is really going on with this "Jezebel" spirit that many are trying to hide and use this spirit as a false flag?

Going into biblical texts and many other first century and middle ages texts, Uyl seeks to answer the questions about the "Jezebel" spirit's legitimacy and the effect the spirit/demon has had on Christianity as a whole.

ISBN: 978-1-77356-565-1

www.ingramcontent.com/pod-product-compliance
Lightning Source LLC
Chambersburg PA
CBHW060500240426
43661CB00006B/863
* 9 7 8 1 7 7 3 5 6 5 6 6 8 *